The Desert Will Bloom

Society of Biblical Literature

Ancient Israel and Its Literature

Steven L. McKenzie, General Editor

Editorial Board

Suzanne Boorer
Victor H. Matthews
Thomas C. Römer
Benjamin D. Sommer
Nili Wazana

Number 04
The Desert Will Bloom: Poetic Visions in Isaiah
edited by A. Joseph Everson and Hyun Chul Paul Kim

THE DESERT WILL BLOOM:
POETIC VISIONS IN ISAIAH

edited by

A. Joseph Everson and Hyun Chul Paul Kim

Society of Biblical Literature
Atlanta

THE DESERT WILL BLOOM:
POETIC VISIONS IN ISAIAH

Copyright © 2009 by the Society of Biblical Literature

All rights reserved. No part of this work may be reproduced or transmitted in any form or by any means, electronic or mechanical, including photocopying and recording, or by means of any information storage or retrieval system, except as may be expressly permitted by the 1976 Copyright Act or in writing from the publisher. Requests for permission should be addressed in writing to the Rights and Permissions Office, Society of Biblical Literature, 825 Houston Mill Road, Atlanta, GA 30329 USA.

Library of Congress Cataloging-in-Publication Data

The desert will bloom : poetic visions in Isaiah / edited by A. Joseph Everson and Hyun Chul Paul Kim.
    p. cm. — (Society of Biblical Literature ancient Israel and its literature ; 4)
  Includes bibliographical references and index.
  ISBN 978-1-58983-425-5 (paper binding : alk. paper)
  1. Bible. O.T. Isaiah—Criticism, interpretation, etc.—Congresses. 2. Bible. O.T. Isaiah—Language, style—Congresses. I. Everson, A. Joseph, 1937- II. Kim, Hyun Chul Paul, 1965-
  BS1515.52.D48 2009
  224'.1066—dc22
                                                            2009011552

Printed in the United States of America on acid-free, recycled paper
conforming to ANSI/NISO Z39.48-1992 (R1997) and ISO 9706:1994
standards for paper permanence.

In memory of Roy F. Melugin, 1937–2008

Contents

Abbreviations — ix

Introduction — 1

Poetic Imagination, Intertextuality, and Life in a Symbolic World
  Roy F. Melugin — 7

Persistent Vegetative States: People as Plants and Plants as People in Isaiah
  Patricia K. Tull — 17

"Like a Mother I Have Comforted You": The Function of Figurative Language in Isaiah 1:7–26 and 66:7–14
  Chris A. Franke — 35

A Bitter Memory: Isaiah's Commission in Isaiah 6:1–13
  A. Joseph Everson — 57

Poetic Vision in Isaiah 7:18–25
  H. G. M. Williamson — 77

Yhwh's Sovereign Rule and His Adoration on Mount Zion: A Comparison of Poetic Visions in Isaiah 24–27, 52, and 66
  Willem A. M. Beuken — 91

The Legacy of Josiah in Isaiah 40–55
  Marvin A. Sweeney — 109

Spectrality in the Prologue to Deutero-Isaiah
  Francis Landy — 131

The Spider-Poet: Signs and Symbols in Isaiah 41
    Hyun Chul Paul Kim   159

Consider the Source: A Reading of the Servant's Identity and Task
in Isaiah 42:1–9
    James M. Kennedy   181

"They All Gather, They Come to You": History, Utopia, and the
Reading of Isaiah 49:18–26 and 60:4–16
    Roy D. Wells   197

From Desolation to Delight: The Transformative Vision of Isaiah
60–62
    Carol J. Dempsey   217

The Nations' Journey to Zion: Pilgrimage and Tribute as Metaphor
in the Book of Isaiah
    Gary Stansell   233

Contributors   257

Bibliography   259

Index of Scripture References   277

Index of Authors   295

Abbreviations

AB	Anchor Bible
ABD	*Anchor Bible Dictionary*. Edited by D. N. Freedman. 6 vols.
ABR	*Australian Biblical Review*
AcT	*Acta theologica*
AnBib	Analecta biblica
ANEP	*The Ancient Near East in Pictures Relating to the Old Testament*. Edited by J. B. Pritchard. Princeton, 1954
ANET	*Ancient Near Eastern Texts Relating to the Old Testament*. Edited by J. B. Pritchard. 3rd ed. Princeton, 1969.
AOAT	Alter Orient und Altes Testament
ApcIs	Apocalypse of Isaiah
ArBib	The Aramaic Bible
ATA	Alttestamentliche Abhandlungen
BETL	Bibliotheca ephemeridum theologicarum lovaniensium
BEvT	Beiträge zur evangelischen Theologie
BHK	*Biblia Hebraica*. Edited by R. Kittel. Stuttgart, 1905–1906. 1925^2, 1937^3, 1951^4, 1973^{16}
BHS	*Biblia Hebraica Stuttgartensia*. Edited by K. Elliger and W. Rudolph. Stuttgart: Deutsche Bibelgesellschaft, 1983.
BHT	Beiträge zur historischen Theologie
BI	book of Isaiah
Bib	*Biblica*
BibInt	*Biblical Interpretation*
BibInt	Biblical Interpretation
BK	*Bibel und Kirche*
BKAT	Biblischer Kommentar, Altes Testament
BN	*Biblische Notizen*
BSac	*Bibliotheca sacra*

BTB	*Biblical Theological Bulletin*
BWANT	Beiträge zur Wissenschaft vom Alten und Neuen Testament
BZ	*Biblische Zeitschrift*
BZAW	Beihefte zur Zeitschrift für die alttestamentliche Wissenschaft
CBQ	Catholic Biblical Quarterly
CC	Continental Commentaries
CR:BS	*Currents in Research: Biblical Studies*
DCH	Dictionary of Classical Hebrew. Edited by D. J. A. Clines. Sheffield, 1993-
DI	Deutero-Isaiah
EB	Echter Bibel
EBib	*Etudes bibliques*
EHAT	Exegetisches Handbuch zum Alten Testament
EstBib	*Estudios bíblicos*
ETL	Ephemerides theologicae lovanienses
EvT	Evangelische Theologie
FAT	Forschungen Zum Alten Testament
FB	Forschung zur Bibel
FOTL	Forms of Old Testament Literature
FRLANT	Forschungen zur Religion und Literatur des Alten und Neuen Testaments
FS	Festschrift
Gesenius[18]	*Hebräisches und Aramäisches Handwörterbuch über das Alte Testament*. 18. Aufl. Hg. von U. Rüterswörden, R. Meyer, H. Donner. Berlin 1987–
HB	Hebrew Bible
HBC	*Harper's Bible Commentary*. Edited by J. L. Mays et al. San Francisco, 1988.
HCOT	Historical Commentary on the Old Testament
HKAT	Handkommentar zum Alten Testament
HSM	Harvard Semitic Monographs
HTR	*Harvard Theological Review*
HTKAT	Herders Theologischer Kommentar zum Alten Testament
IB	Interpreter's Bible. Edited by G. A. Buttrick et al. 12 vols. New York, 1951–57.
IBC	Interpretation: A Bible Commentary for Teaching and Preaching

IBT	Interpreting Biblical Texts
ICC	International Critical Commentary
Int	*Interpretation*
ISBE	International Standard Bible Encyclopedia. Edited by G. W. Bromiley. 4 vols. Grand Rapids, 1979-88.
JBL	*Journal of Biblical Literature*
JJS	*Journal of Jewish Studies*
JQR	Jewish Quarterly Review
JR	*Journal of Religion*
JSOT	*Journal for the Study of the Old Testament*
JSOTSup	Journal for the Study of the Old Testament: Supplement Series
JTS	*Journal of Theological Studies*
KAT	Kommentar zum Alten Testament
KBL	Köhler Baumgartner Lexicon = HALOT (Hebrew and Aramaic Lexicon of the Old Testament)
KHAT	Kurzgefaßtes exegetisches Handbuch zum Alten Testament
LHBOTS	Library of Hebrew Bible/Old Testament Studies
LS	Louvain Studies
LXX	Septuagint
MT	Masoretic Text (of the Hebrew Bible)
MT	*Modern Theology*
NCB	New Century Bible
NIB	*The New Interpreter's Bible*. 13 vols. Nashville: Abingdon: 1994-2004.
NIBC	New International Biblical Commentary
NICOT	New International Commentary of the Old Testament
NJPS	*Tanakh: The Holy Scriptures: The New JPS Translation according to the Traditional Hebrew Text*
NRSV	New Revised Standard Version
OBO	Orbis biblicus et orientalis
OBT	Overtures to Biblical Theology
OTL	Old Testament Library
OTS	Old Testament Studies
OtSt	*Oudtestamentische Studiën*
PI	Proto-Isaiah
POut	De Prediking van het Oude Testament
RB	*Revue biblique*
RevistB	*Revista bíblica*

RevQ	*Revue de Qumran*
SAALT	State Archives of Assyria Literary Texts
SANE	Sources from the ancient Near East
SBL	Society of Biblical Literature
SBLAcBib	Society of Biblical Literature Academia Biblica
SBLDS	Society of Biblical Literature Dissertation Series
SBLSP	*Society of Biblical Literature Seminar Papers*
SBLSymS	Society of Biblical Literature Symposium Series
SBS	Stuttgarter Bibelstudien
SC	Sources crétiennes. Paris: Cerf, 1943–.
SSN	Studia semitica neerlandica
SubBi	*Subsidia biblica*
ST	*Studia theologica*
STDJ	*Studies on the Texts of the Desert of Judah*
TB	Theologische Bücherei: Neudrucke und Berichte aus dem 20. Jahrhundert.
TDOT	*Theological Dictionary of the Old Testament.* Edited by G. J. Botterweck and H. Ringgren. Translated by J. T. Willis, G. W. Bromiley, and D. E. Green. 8 vols. Grand Rapids, 1974–
TI	Trito-Isaiah
TZ	*Theologische Zeitschrift*
UUA	Uppsala Universitetsårsskrift
VT	*Vetus Testamentum*
VTSup	Supplements to Vetus Testamentum
WBC	Word Biblical Commentary
WMANT	Wissenschaftliche Monographien zum Alten und Neuen Testament
WTJ	*Westminster Theological Journal*
WW	*Word and World*
ZABR	*Zeitschrift für altorientalische und biblische Rechtsgeschichte*
ZAW	*Zeitschrift für die alttestamentliche Wissenschaft*
ZBK	Zürcher Bibelkommentare
ZTK	*Zeitschrift für Theologie und Kirche*

INTRODUCTION

> The wilderness and the dry land shall be glad,
> The desert shall rejoice and blossom,
> Like the crocus it shall blossom abundantly,
> And rejoice with joy and singing.
> (Isa 35:1–2)

Each year in the desert regions north of Los Angeles, a miracle happens. For much of the year, the sloping hills of this high desert region lie brown and barren, parched and dry from the east winds and the hot sun. Occasionally one sees only a few cattle or a small flock of sheep, for the ground produces very limited grass and vegetation. But each year in the springtime a miracle takes place. In springtime the desert blooms! For as far as the eye can see, fields turn bright with colors. Hills come alive with the rich golden hues of California poppies and yellow fiddlenecks. Other fields are brilliant with purple lupine, or white with evening primrose, desert pincushion, ghost flowers, and rock daisies. The world seems renewed with life and beauty.

The vision set forth in the Isaiah scroll is similar. It includes both desert-like descriptions of the horrors of war and at the same time Eden-like portraits of the future based on the conviction that new generations of people are capable of renewing all things on the earth. Isaiah's vision of the future is nothing less than that: a portrait of shalom, involving peace, wholeness, and well-being both for the human community and the earth. Throughout the scroll, imagery drawn from nature affirms that renewal of life, like the renewal of the earth, is a possibility for the human family. The essays in this volume explore the poetic artistry and symbolic imagery in the Isaiah scroll.

This volume is another product of the collective dialogues from the Formation of the Book of Isaiah Group of the Society of Biblical Literature. Previously, in *New Visions of Isaiah*,[1] contributors explored interpretive ques-

---

1. Roy F. Melugin and Marvin A. Sweeney, eds., *New Visions of Isaiah* (JSOTSup 214;

tions such as whether the meaning of a text is located in the author or in the reader. Addressing significant issues related to the overall unity of the book of Isaiah, that publication generated groundbreaking contributions to Isaiah scholarship in terms of both diachronic and synchronic reading strategies. The subsequent publication, *"As Those Who Are Taught": The Interpretation of Isaiah from the LXX to the SBL*, picked up the theme of the dynamic interactions between the text and the reader. It produced an admirably rich collection of investigations on the history of interpretation, ranging from the LXX all the way down to the present Isaianic guild at the SBL, via the broad spectrums of scribal locations such as Qumran, New Testament, Patristic, Rabbinic, Reformation, modern Romanticism, and Postmodernism.[2] Indeed, the vision projected by the first generation of the SBL's Isaiah Seminar that "the new visions contained herein will lead to still more new visions," has generated flowering and pluriform offspring.[3] Thus, the current project is like a new bloom and fruit, inspired by the visions of Isaiah scholars of the previous generation. It intends to carry forward the legacy and passion for this beloved prophet to ensuing generations, with special attention to the synchronic dimensions of the text, figurative language, specific imagery, metaphors, and matters of intertextuality.

With these essays, we remember our colleague Roy Melugin in a special way. We have chosen to include his presentation to the Formation of Isaiah Group meeting in Toronto in 2002, "Poetic Imagination, Intertextuality, and Life in a Symbolic World," as an opening essay. Roy was a strong advocate for looking beyond traditional historical-critical analysis to consider the power of figurative language present in the poetic imagery of the Isaiah scroll and the power of that imagery to shape future generations. He argues that the commissioning images in Isa 6 and 40 have had lasting influence upon people, not only through the symbolic imagery dominated by judgment, but just as much by the marvelous images that promise deliverance.

Patricia K. Tull, "Persistent Vegetative States: People as Plants and Plants as People in Isaiah," calls our attention to the abundant imagery in Isaiah that focuses on the world of agriculture: vineyards, cucumber fields, plowshares, pruning hooks, and threshing sledges. What does the author know about beat-

---

Sheffield: Sheffield Academic Press, 1996); repr., Atlanta: Society of Biblical Literature, 2006.

2. Claire Mathews McGinnis and Patricia K. Tull, eds., *"As Those Who Are Taught": The Interpretation of Isaiah from the LXX to the SBL* (SBLSymS 27; Atlanta: Society of Biblical Literature, 2006).

3. Melugin and Sweeney, eds., *New Visions of Isaiah*, 28.

ing an olive tree with sticks or running carts over grain? From the worlds of farming and botony, the poets employs imagery to offer words both of judgment and hope concerning the welfare of the human community. Tull hears in the poetry of the scroll a powerful word for our time that we "belong to the ground beneath us, and we cannot afford to let ourselves be cut off from its sustaining power."

Chris A. Franke, "Like a Mother I Have Comforted You: The Function of Figurative Language in Isaiah 1:7–26 and 66:7–14," probes the questions of figurative language in Isa 1:7–26, in which Zion/Jerusalem is first seen in a state of desolation and then as a restored and faithful city. She explores in particular the relationship of that text with 66:7–14, where Zion/Jerusalem is portrayed as a pregnant woman writhing in labor, bearing a child, and in the process of delivering a child. Then in 66:13, God is compared to Zion and is described as a nursing mother, who supports, nourishes and protects the child. Franke discusses poetic passages in the scroll that describe God's relationship to Zion/Jerusalem and devotes particular attention to the ways in which imagery from these particular texts have been used or misused.

A. Joseph Everson, "A Bitter Memory: Isaiah's Commission in Isaiah 6:1–13," is convinced that to understand the poetic imagery in Isaiah's call vision in ch. 6, we need to hear the text as a "bitter memory" preserved from a time in the postexilic era, from a time after the prophet's sad word of judgment had come to pass. It is in retrospect that people from an earlier era of history are understood to have been deaf, blind, and insensitive. From the postexilic perspective, the text preserves a memory of the difficult but faithful witness of the prophet. The text is preserved as a warning but it is to be heard in conjunction with later texts that also speak of deafness and hearing, blindness and sight, fatness of heart (insensitivity) and compassion, namely, Isa 29:18; 35:5, and portraits that reverse the sad memories of Isa 6, promising hope for humanity, such as 42:18–21 and 43:8–9. These words echo the early summons of Isa 2:4: "Come, let us walk in the light of the Lord!"

Hugh G. M. Williamson, "Poetic Vision in Isaiah 7:18–25," analyzes a lesser known passage that nonetheless displays rich rhetorical and poetic forces. In the text, Yhwh "whistles for the fly" and "shaves with a razor," Williamson explores certain unifying threads, which he contends mark an intentional connection with the song of the vineyard in 5:1–7. Phraseological citations or allusions also point to a close relationship with chs. 6 and 7. The passage speaks "of the possibility of some invasion in the future that will be more cataclysmic even than those already experienced at the hands of the Assyrians and the Babylonians." The imagery remains on the "dark side of the path" (judgment and its consequences) so that wherever we site Isa 40–55 geographically, "it is clear that the first part of the book is far more concerned with judgment and its consequences within the land." Williamson believes that this passage may be part of a final step in the trajectory before the start of the new Persian age. He contends that the text "makes its contribution by way of a foil to the announcement of deliverance that would follow soon after."

Willem A. M. Beuken, "Yhwh's Sovereign Rule and His Adoration on Mount Zion: A Comparison of Poetic Visions in Isaiah 24–27, 52, and 66," sets out a bold thesis about the trajectory evident in poetic visions in Isa 24–27, the "Isaiah Apocalypse," continued in Isa 52 and 66, focusing around the themes of the universal kingship of Yhwh on Mount Zion and Yhwh's worship there by the gathered exiles. Rather than viewing Isa 24–27 as a separate "lonely mountain" of poetry, Beuken contends that an extensive web of semantic connections provides evidence that this poetry constitutes the background for later chapters that describe how the city will once again become the royal seat of Yhwh's dwelling.

Marvin A. Sweeney, "The Legacy of Josiah in Isaiah 40–55," proposes a new insight into the question, "Why does Second Isaiah choose to portray the interplay between the male servant figure Jacob or Israel (Isa 40–48) and the female figure of Bat Zion (Isa 49–55)?" Reading key allusions implicit in the story of Jacob, Sweeney interprets the interplay of the male Jacob (representative of the northern kingdom of Israel) and the female Bat Zion (Jerusalem and southern Judah) in Isa 40–55 in light of the symbolic ideals of the reform proposals from the era of King Josiah, reforms that called for the reunification of Israel and Judah. Sweeney then examines similar symbolic references to key ancestral figures in Jeremiah, Ezekiel, Hosea, and Zephaniah, which all lead to a common result, namely, that every one of the texts that employs the motif of reunion is tied in one way or another to the Josianic reform as a thematic template. Second Isaiah's construction of the images of Jacob and Bat Zion presupposes reflection on the earlier traditions concerning Jacob and Israel or Bat Zion as the bride of YHWH. Sweeney contends that "the Isaiah tradition developed extensively in relation to Josiah's reform" even when the prophet had to rethink the tradition in relation to Cyrus of Persia and the new prospects for restoration.

Francis Landy, "Spectrality in the Prologue to Deutero-Isaiah," includes a preface wherein he rejects the idea that he is a reader response critic but then expresses passionate concern for the manner in which a reader hears a biblical text. He focuses on the function of Isa 40:1–11 as a prologue to Deutero-Isaiah and how we should understand the spectral (ghostly) voices that are present in the text. How are we to understand: "A voice cries out" and "A voice says, "Cry out!" in Isa 40:3 and 40:6? Is it the same voice or are there different "disembodied" voices here? The charges lead to the herald-like command to Zion and Jerusalem to declare the advent of God. In his analysis, Landy sees a progression from the female or maternal word of comfort in 40:1–2, to the declaration of God's theophany in 40:3–5, then to the "pathos of transience" in 40:6–8, and finally to the "deferred resolution" in 40:9–11.

Hyun Chul Paul Kim, "The Spider-Poet: Signs and Symbols in Isaiah 41," analyzes some of the key features of the poetic artistry in the book of Isaiah that resemble the web of threads in a tapestry. To do so, Kim examines the concatenated Stichwörter (catch words), with special focus on Isa 41 which, together with ch. 40, exhibits key words and motifs in parallel with chs. 34–35. These correlations of similar signs in Isa 34–35 and 40–41 then build a pillar-like structure around Isa 36–39 which shares comparable phrases and thereby forms a thematic apex of these chapters and possibly of the entire book of Isaiah. These concatenated signs thus signify essential messages of the book of Isaiah, such as the contrast between the nullification of the idols and the affirmation of Yhwh's restoration, the key motif "to strengthen" (חזק) associated with the model of trust of King Hezekiah, and the limitations of human beings, whether kings Hezekiah and Cyrus or the whole people in their vital need to see, hear, know, and trust in Yhwh.

James M. Kennedy, "Consider the Source: A Reading of the Servant's Identity and Task in Isaiah 42:1–9," contends that Isaiah's presentation of Yhwh's servant should be heard, at least in part, as a challenge to the established function of the cult statue, which was understood as an instrument of mediation between the divine and the human. Texts in Isaiah contend that the cult statue purveys ignorance and supports social policies that has catastrophic and exploitive consequences. Isaiah 42:1–9 is a pivotal text in the book's development of the servant of Yhwh as the paradigmatic replacement for cult statues, not only in Israel, but among all humankind. The book of Isaiah configures the human community of Israel as the agent through which divine teaching flows. Israel is not to turn to cult statues but must rather adopt a communal attitude that exhibits an awareness of being God's servant.

Roy D. Wells, "'They All Gather, They Come to You': History, Utopia, and the Reading of Isaiah 49:18–26 and 60:4–16," probes the questions of "diachronic" and "synchronic" reading as he focuses on the interrelationships between two quite distinct apostrophes, or textual digressions, in which Zion is personified as a woman (Isa 49) and Jerusalem is personified as the city of Zion (Isa 60). He suggests that the texts are interrelated by an intricate pattern of verbal connections, ranging from echoes of words and sounds to replication of specific and unusual phrases. In Isa 60, he contends that something radically new is present in the text. A utopian vision of the future is set out, suggesting that the entire cosmos—including the wealth, the people, the flora, and fauna of the world—is drawn toward its true center in such a way that even foreigners may enter the sacred space.

Carol J. Dempsey, "From Desolation to Delight: The Transformative Vision of Isaiah 60–62," explores the imagery of Isa 60–62, contending that it is distinct from Isa 40–55 and yet dominated by echoes from themes set forth in Isa 1–39. Most of all, she wants to suggest that the imagery of Jerusalem is at the center of the unfolding vision of hope expressed with imagery of a new heaven and new earth for all people and all of creation.

Gary Stansell, "The Nations' Journey to Zion: Pilgrimage and Tribute as Metaphor in the Book of Isaiah," focuses on the metaphors of "pilgrimage" and "bringing tribute," especially when those passages speak of the "wealth of nations." Do the nations come freely or are these references to be understood as dramatic reversal of the current situation of captivity and oppression? Will the oppressor nations come at a future time as servants and servants in a restored Jerusalem or will they come freely to bring tribute or hear Torah? Working backward in the scroll, he focuses first on the poetic references in Isa 60 and 61, then considers Isa 55, 49, and 45, then references in Isa 35 and 23 and finally the famous poem in Isa 2:2–4, suggesting that this dramatic imagery helps to establish a certain literary unity for the book and contributes to the "symbolic world" which, in Roy Melugin's words, "constitutes the richness of the poetic vision in the book."

The essays in this volume are only a small portion of the fruit that has resulted from the planting and pruning efforts of the Isaiah Seminar at the SBL. In some ways, the articles included in this volume are as diverse and multifaceted as a bountiful basket of acacias, grapes, pomegranates, grains, and olives. In other ways, they describe the wealth of poetic artistry evident within the scroll and speak to the transforming possibilities of Isaiah's vision for communities of faith. Our hope is that these works will prompt new reflections and insights for analyzing and appreciating the rich imagery found in the tapestry of the Isaiah scroll.

Roy F. Melugin, an exceptionally gifted master of exegesis, was always fond of such engagement with the texts of Isaiah. With these essays, we remember his inspiring passion for the book of Isaiah. We will miss dearly his contagiously gentle and pastoral smile and his words of encouragement. Current and future generations involved with Isaiah scholarship will continue to carry the torch of his leadership and vision, just as the disciples of the servant of Yhwh and the offspring of Daughter Zion preserved and proclaimed the poetic visions of Isaiah.

Joe Everson and Paul Kim

Poetic Imagination, Intertextuality, and Life in a Symbolic World

Roy F. Melugin

The book of Isaiah was and is a dynamic and powerful piece of literature. It has been able to capture the imagination of individuals and communities over many centuries, and it still seems to be a powerful voice with its vision of social justice, its visions of the relationships between suffering, healing, and liberation, its visions regarding Jerusalem and the nations. How can we as Isaiah scholars go beyond what has been done up to now to capture even more profoundly what this book has to offer?

Beginning next year, the Formation of the Book of Isaiah Group has been granted six more years of life. We proposed to the SBL Program Committee that one of the things we would do is to explore more carefully than before the potential power of Isaianic *figurative language* in the shaping of a vision (or multiple visions) concerning the relation of humans to God and humans to humans. Poetic vision can become a vehicle through which individuals and communities can come to dwell in symbolic worlds that can work powerfully to shape identity, both in antiquity and even in the present. We've not focused intently thus far in the life of the Isaiah Seminar or the Isaiah Group on *how* the figurative language in the book of Isaiah might function in shaping symbolic worlds in which Yhwh-worshippers could/can dwell and be shaped and transformed in their individual and communal existence. In the next several years, with the aid of Ricoeur and others, such questions might well become a significant part of our inquiry together.

Because Isaiah is a complex book and is most probably a redactional composition, we might profitably address more extensively than before how intertextuality (or intratextuality) contributes to the richness of the poetic vision of the book. We might also profitably ask who determines how we decide what imagery in the text is most important or how we can most fruitfully interpret the imagery that we consider important. Who determines the nature of the symbolic world that the text is said to articulate? To what extent is it the text itself, or to what extent it is it the interpreter? And for *what particular* communities are given interpretations developed? For communities at the time in which the texts originated, or for later communities, up to and including the present? Reader response theory and use-theory from the philosophy of language, along with approaches that are perhaps more familiar to many of us, could possibly be useful in our reflections together.

As is surely obvious, there may well be a distinct new emphasis on poetics and hermeneutics in our next few years together. Yet, as we laid plans last year, it wasn't our intent to focus on hermeneutics abstractly, but rather to center primarily on the interpretation of particular Isaianic *texts*. As we focus intently on particular texts and their interpretation, we may well focus on these texts from the vantage point of asking how poetry shapes life and identity, how language shapes symbolic worlds in which human life is transformed, and how use-theory can help us better understand how language can be appropriated by its users.

I

A. The book of Isaiah opens, for all practical purposes, with the language of poetic imagination. Immediately following a superscription (1:1), heaven and earth are summoned to hear an accusation against Yhwh's stupid and rebellious children—children who, unlike ox and ass, don't know their owner or where their food comes from (vv. 2–3). The composition continues in vv. 4–9 to portray Yhwh's children as rebellious and stupid, although Yhwh is no longer the speaker but the one spoken about: "Woe sinful nation, people heavy with iniquity, seed of evildoers, destroying children; they have forsaken Yhwh, spurned the Holy One of Israel...." (v. 4). Indeed, these children are so stupid that they don't know not to keep inciting more beatings: "Why will you still be smitten, again rebel? The whole head is sick, the whole heart faint; from the bottom of the foot to the top of the head there's no healing...." (v. 5). Moreover, "your land is a waste, your cities burned with fire...." (v. 7). And strangers eat their land—the land of the stupid and rebellious children who don't know who gives them food! And then, says an unidentified voice: "Had not Yhwh of hosts left us a few survivors, we would have been like Sodom and become like Gomorrah" (v. 9). Were these rebellious children perhaps also too stupid to see the significance of Yhwh's gracious activity in leaving them a few survivors?

Then follows torah from Yhwh to these "rulers of Sodom, people of Gomorrah" (vv. 10–17). "What do I care about the multitude of your sacrifices?" (v. 11). Yhwh doesn't want them. Indeed these sacrificial "meals" brought to Yhwh are too much; Yhwh is "sated" with them—"full up to here," so to speak. (Notice how the imagery of food and eating holds this composition together.) Moreover, God won't listen to their prayers. God wants instead justice: "seek justice, correct oppression, judge the orphan, plead the case of the widow" (vv. 16–17).

Next comes an initiation of legal dispute: "Come, let's argue it out" (v. 18). Can scarlet sins become white as snow? Can these crimson sins become like wool? No! There are but two choices: "If you are willing and obedient, you will eat the good of the land, but if you refuse and rebel, you will be eaten by the sword…." (vv. 19–20). Once again the imagery of eating shapes this poetic composition!

Then the text moves into the genre of lamentation: "How the faithful city has become a harlot, she that was filled with justice, and righteousness lodged in her" (1:21). Her silver has become dross and her wine mixed with water (v. 22), and her princes have gone after bribes rather than judging the orphan or pleading the widow's case (v. 23). Then follows an announcement of judgment: "therefore says the Lord Yhwh of hosts, the mighty one of Israel, *hôy*, I will get comfort from my foes and vengeance from my enemies, and I will turn my hand against you" (1:24–25). But then the punishment turns into an act of purification: removal of dross and return of ruling officials. And the city once again becomes righteous city, faithful city (v. 26). Then the future is depicted in still more detail: Zion will be redeemed in justice and "her returners" in righteousness, but sinners will be destroyed and those who forsake Yhwh will perish (v. 27). And in vv. 29–31 further judgment is pronounced upon the wicked. This poetic vision is a vision about politics, about the restoration of justice in the social and political order as Yhwh's most sacred intent!

Isaiah 1 may well be a redactional composition. But it's also a poetic vision that its audience can live in and by which its self-understanding may be shaped. A reading audience might indeed imagine itself as summoned to trial as Yhwh's stubborn and rebellious children who, unlike ox and ass, do not know who feeds them. They might recognize themselves as learning nothing from the stripes that have produced sores from head to foot with the result that they keep returning for additional blows. Moreover, their land is "eaten" by aliens so that they can perhaps see themselves as left alone like a booth in a vineyard—as opposed to a once-vibrant full community upon which aliens had nibbled until little remained. The audience also could see itself as a pious group whose sacrificial meals and prayers Yhwh hates because it did not turn its attention to its legal and economic responsibilities toward widow and orphan. Furthermore, the figurative language of Isa 1 might enable an audience to envision itself as once-faithful bride now turned harlot—as a community in which justice once dwelt but now murderers, that is, the injustice of forsaking responsibilities for widow and orphan—with the result of the community's seeing itself as purified and restored figuratively as faithful bride in a renewed political order that will once again be just.

Such figurative speech does far more than explain how the poet saw the world. Indeed, it proposes a symbolic world by means of which a faith community could develop a particular identity and relationship with God and fellow humans. No Ricoeurian scholarly interpretation would limit itself to explanation of how the poet saw the world, nor would philosophers trained in use-theory focus primarily on the poet's explanatory intent. Both would center on how the language of this poetic text could be used—used to shape its readers' way of being in the world.

B. Isaiah is a big book, and its poetic language is rich and diverse. Therefore, the use of the book in its entirety for the purpose of symbolic world construction can profit immensely from intertextual (or intratextual) interpretation. For example, messianic texts in Isa 9, 11, and 32 share with Isa 1 the theme of just governance of the social and political order; but the imagery of each of the texts is somewhat different, so that exploration of inter/intratextual relationships can make possible the creation of a very richly textured symbolic world that can be used to unfold for the community's self-understanding of a portrayal of itself as both judged and renewed by God. Furthermore, inter/intratextual comparison of the poetic vision of nations' flowing to Zion and and beating their swords into plowshares as a consequence of having learned Yhwh's torah can enrich even more the social and political vision available for a faith-group's re-imagination of its own communal identity. Let us add still more inter/intratextual comparison by means of texts that portray in figurative terms military-political hegemony on the part of Assyria (e.g., Isa 8:5–8; 10:5–19), and the possibilities of an even more profound symbolic world are expanded greatly.

If we add into our emerging inter/intratextual world of poetic imagination the narrative of Isaiah's commissioning in ch. 6, an even richer communal self-understanding becomes possible. In the critical year of the death of a king, we are told, the prophet receives a terrifying vision of Yhwh—whose holiness is attested by the liturgical chants of nothing less than heavenly beings, and the foundation of the thresholds shake and the house is filled with smoke. And the prophet can only say, "Woe is me, for I am a person of unclean lips, and I live in the midst of a people of unclean lips, for my eyes have seen the king, Yhwh of hosts."

No sooner than Isaiah's lips were purified, he heard Yhwh's voice calling, "Whom shall I send, and who will go for us?" And Isaiah said, "Here am I. Send me." And then came the commission to harden the people's hearts lest they see and hear and understand, and repent and be healed. When the prophet asks, "How long?," he is told: "Until cities lie waste without inhabitant and houses without people and the land is completely desolate." Even if a remnant remains, like a stump after the felling of a tree, it will be burned again. Yet the stump represents a "holy seed" (v. 13).

I cannot here spell out in any detail the relationships between Isa 6 and other Isaianic texts, especially regarding the condition of blindness and deafness—both in the first part of the book and in Isa 40ff. Suffice it to say that they are numerous and that they can play an immense role in the audience's construction of a symbolic world based on a careful reading of the book of Isaiah as a whole. The task to which I now turn is an exploration of relationships between Isa 6 and Isa 40.

II

At the beginning of Isa 40 we find what appears to be a commissioning scene that has some affinities with the commissioning of Isaiah in ch. 6. As Isaiah once heard the "voice" of Yhwh "speaking" (אמר) ... קול; Isa 6:8), Isa 40:3 says that a "voice is calling" (קול קורא). And in 40:6–8 a "voice speaks" (קול אמר). Yet here what the "voice speaks" is not, as in Isa 6, a question introduced by מי ("Whom shall I send?"), but rather a command to "cry" (40:6). Not only do the plural imperatives ("comfort ye my people"; "prepare ye the way of the Lord") support a supposition that we have to do with language associated with a context of the heavenly council, but so does language in Zech 1:7–17: In a scene involving heavenly messengers, an angel says "Cry!" (Zech 1:14, 17). Furthermore, the angel commands that in "crying out" the message there is to be a message of "comfort" (Zech 1:17; cf. Isa 40:1). Even in the angel's question, "Yhwh of hosts, how long will you not pity Jerusalem and the cities of Judah...?" (Zech 1:12; see the "how long?" question also in Isa 6:11), we have an additional indicator that many of the linguistic features shared in common by Isa 6, Isa 40:1–8, and Zech 1:7–17 represent typicalities of speech commonly connected with visions of activities in the heavenly council.

A. What might an inter/intratextual reading of Isa 6 and Isa 40:1–8 lead to in the shaping of a symbolic world that could emerge by reading the book of Isaiah holistically? Certain things are immediately obvious: (1) Isa 6 is a narrative in which an individual receives a commission. Isaiah 40:1–8, by contrast, is not a narrative, and it is questionable whether it involves a prophetic commissioning. (2) It is clear that, while Isa 6 seems to emphasize a commissioning regarding a time of judgment and 40:1–8 appears to focus on a time of forgiveness and deliverance, both texts point forward and backward. Thus it is productive to ask how sharply the two texts represent a dividing line between a symbolic world dominated by judgment and a symbolic world characterized by deliverance.

Let us turn to the first question. It is unambiguously clear that Isa 6 is a narrative in which the prophet Isaiah, in a vision involving members of the heavenly council, is commissioned to prevent the people's seeing and hearing and to harden their hearts lest they turn and be healed. Isaiah 40:1–8 also, as I argued above, seems to presuppose speech that takes place in the context of the heavenly council. But it isn't clearly a narrative about an individual prophet. The plural imperatives in vv. 1–2 seem to address a group rather than an individual: "Comfort ye, comfort ye my people"; "speak ye upon the heart of Jerusalem and call ye to her that her time of service is ended, that her iniquity is pardoned...." And so also in vv. 3–5: "In the wilderness prepare ye the way of Yʜᴡʜ, make ye straight in the desert a highway for our God." Even in vv. 6–8, where the imperative is masculine singular ("a voice says 'Cry'..."), it is by no means certain that the imperative is addressed to a prophet. Immediately following the singular imperative "Cry!" comes a report "and he said (ᴍᴛ)"—or perhaps to be translated "and someone said." If the text read, "and I said" (ʟxx), it might make sense to think of it as a prophet's objection to the commission to "cry" ("and I said, 'all flesh is grass....'"). But if the speaker is someone among the members of the heavenly council, then we should not see here the commissioning of a new prophet who is connected with a new "prophetic book," that is, "Deutero-Isaiah," but perhaps rather a new episode in Isa 1–66.

Furthermore, we may ask how sharply Isa 40:1–8 represents a dividing line between a symbolic world dominated by judgment and a symbolic world characterized by deliverance. To be sure, Isa 6 has a strong emphasis on judgment, and Isa 40:1–8 speaks of a time of comfort and hope. But Isa 6 also speaks of a "holy seed" (6:13), and thus seems to point to something beyond judgment. And Isaiah's own "iniquity" (עון) that is removed when the seraph touches his lips (6:7), if one reads the book of Isaiah sequentially, has already (Isa 1:4) been used to describe to the people ("Woe sinful nation, people heavy with iniquity"), and later in Isa 22:14 ("Surely this iniquity will not be forgiven you until you die"), in Isa 30:13 ("Therefore this iniquity will become for you like a broken, bulging wall"), in Isa 40:2 ("speak upon the heart of Jerusalem and cry to her that her time of service is filled, that her iniquity is pardoned"), in Isa 53:7 ("Yhwh has laid upon him the iniquity of us all"). Also נחמ ("Comfort, comfort my people"; Isa 40:1) appears both earlier and later in prominent places in the book: 12:1 ("I will give thanks to you O Yhwh; you were angry with me; but let your anger be turned away, that you may comfort me"), 51:12 ("I, I am the one who comforts you"), 66:13 ("As one whom his mother comforts, thus will I comfort you"). The theme of the glory of Yhwh is not only present in Isa 6 and 40 (6:3: "Holy, holy, holy is Yhwh of hosts; all the earth is filled with his glory"; 40:5: "The glory of Yhwh shall be revealed and all flesh shall see it together"), but it is present also in 59:19 ("They shall fear the name of Yhwh from the west, and in the east his glory"), 60:1–2 ("Arise, shine, for your light comes, and the glory of Yhwh rises upon you"; "Yhwh arises upon you and his glory appears upon you"), and 66:18 (Yhwh will bring together "all nations and all tongues, and they shall come and see my glory").

B. Even though Isa 40:1–8 does not appear to represent the commissioning of a prophet and is not presented as an introduction to an independent body of prophetic literature, it does play an important role in the present book's synchronic shift from talk about Assyria in God's plan to language regarding Yhwh's plans for a future beyond the Babylonian exile. Chapters 36–39 move us from Sennacherib's threat (36:1ff.) to Assyria's defeat (37:36–38) all the way down to prophecy of exile to Babylon (ch. 39). But the book itself does not narrate the events of the crushing of Jerusalem by Babylon, nor does this book focus on happenings throughout the period of exile. Instead, immediately following the narration of the prophecy of an exile to Babylon (39:5–8), Isa 40–55, from its very beginning in 40:1–8(11) all the way to the end of ch. 55, focuses upon visionary depictions of return of the exiles and the restoration of Israel at Zion and the bringing of torah, salvation, and light to the nations. And in so doing, certain creative literary patterns emerge through which a community of readers can imagine itself in relationship with God.

Isaiah's commissioning in the heavenly council to harden hearts has run its course. Now members of the heavenly council are told to comfort Jerusalem (40:1–2). Although language about the comforting of God's people appears earlier (Isa 12:1), now it becomes an important theme in chs. 40ff. (see 51:12; 66:13). Furthermore, in 40:3–5 Isaiah's earlier commission associated with making the land completely desolate (Isa 6:11–12) is replaced with the heavenly council's instruction to prepare a highway in the wilderness. Exodus-wilderness traditions are indeed remolded here to portray the return home through the wilderness as unimpeded by the necessity of climbing mountains and having to descend into valleys. How indeed this new exodus transcends the limitations of the first exodus! Moreover, the glory of Yhwh, earlier revealed to Isaiah alone by the heavenly beings, is now to be seen by all flesh. And the command to someone to "cry" (masc. sg.; 40:6) elicits an objection ("all flesh is grass...."; cf. "woe is me ... for I am a person of unclean lips" [Isa 6:5]). In Isa 40:6 the objection is countered by contrasting human weakness with the power of God: "The grass withers, the flower fades, but the word of our God will stand forever" (40:8).

The intertextual interplays between Isa 6 and 40 function intratextually to stimulate a dramatic imaginative picture of God's intricate purposes. What began with a divine plan to make the people blind, with the consequence of destroying the land and everything in it, now encompasses a new exodus/new creation that all flesh will see. And the new exodus/new creation will surpass that of the days of old. Furthermore, the image, "proud crown of the drunkards of Ephraim" that became "faded flowers" (Isa 28:1, 4), is used intertextually to create an intratextual comparison between prideful-yet-unreliable humans and the reliability of God's word—a word that will stand forever (Isa 40:8).

III

Where could we as a Group go from here in looking at the book of Isaiah holistically from the perspective of the potential of figurative language in shaping a community's symbolic world? We might, for example, think about how the depiction of the servant's task to bring משפט and תורה to the nations in 42:1–9 might be understood in relationship to the place of torah in the instruction of the nations in Isa 2:2–4 in the building of an Isaianic symbolic world, or how the servant's task of bringing light to the nations might interrelate with figurative speech about light and darkness in the book of Isaiah as a whole. Or it might perhaps be useful to inquire about the relationships of the "fear not" oracles in so-called Second Isaiah to "fear not" passages throughout the entire book. Or it might be profitable to consider whether the trial speeches in Isa 41, 43, 45, and 48 have any relationships with Yhwh's word which "stands forever" (Isa 40:6–8), or even to human words/plans that "will not stand" (e.g., Isa 7:7; 8:10). At this time I'm only thinking out loud rather than trying to promote a particular plan for the Group to follow.

I suspect that as we discuss the use of figurative language for the shaping of identity in relationship with God and humanity in communities of faith, we as a Group will find ourselves running into questions about the relative importance of synchronic as opposed to diachronic approaches to the task. I myself believe that the guild of biblical scholars has greatly overemphasized diachronic questions and has not paid sufficient attention to the richness of synchronic interrelationships of texts to one another. Indeed, I myself am inclined to explore poetic imagination and the study of inter/intratextual relationships with synchronic approaches more in the forefront than diachronic methods. This is partly the result of Ricoeurian influence, and also influences from Hans Frei, George Lindbeck, and Brevard Childs, from performative language theory, and from reader response criticism. But it is not my intention to encourage this group to become a carbon copy of me or anyone else. While I will undoubtedly continue to articulate my views with some vigor, I look forward to discussions, both today and in the future, in which different points of view can be argued freely. I very much want this Group to shape its directions on the basis of collective leadership. Right now I would be satisfied if this paper might have stirred up enough snakes that we can, at this very moment, have a useful, if not rip-roaring, discussion.

Persistent Vegetative States: People as Plants and Plants as People in Isaiah

Patricia K. Tull

A large city park designed by Frederick Olmsted stands next to Louisville Seminary.[1] The campus itself is filled with splendid trees. One afternoon last May, a colleague who teaches Christian Education and I set out with our field guides to identify some of the less obvious ones, so we could stop calling them "trees" and start seeing them more particularly as black gums, basswoods, and bald cypresses. After he managed to work our experience into a course on multiple intelligences, one of his students called me, a young Malawian named Fletcher, and asked if I would teach him the American trees.

I walked around humbly but proudly imparting wisdom I had learned in amateur gardening and naturalist classes—compound versus simple leaves, alternate versus opposite branches, different bark patterns, seeds and fruits. First he looked simply bewildered. Finally he said, "In Malawi we don't talk about categories like these. We just know our trees. Don't Americans know their trees?" He spoke as if we were getting acquainted with human friends by cataloging the shapes of their chins or ears. I study my landscape like an adult learning a foreign language, substituting grammatical terminology for childhood immersion. Fletcher knows the trees of Malawi like a native tongue.

---

1. Many thanks to the Lilly Theological Research Grants Program for the sabbatical time that enabled me to write this essay, which is offered in fond remembrance of Dr. Roy Melugin, a fellow Texas Presbyterian and mentor who kindly welcomed me to the Isaiah Seminar many years ago and generously made me his colleague, friend, and co-chair. Roy continually encouraged us to hear the prophet as both poet and theologian. I am sorry he is not here to greet this volume and check whether we actually listened to him. Still, it is easy to picture him relishing these essays as he relished all the work of the Isaiah group.

Americans are increasingly being told we neglect the natural world to our peril. Cavalier ignorance was illustrated recently by Bill McKibben, who quoted a Yale economist saying we should not worry much about global climate change, since "most economic activity in industrialized countries depends very little on the climate," and damage from global warming will be confined to farming and forestry.[2] McKibben responded, "If global warming only damages agriculture, the rest may not matter much."

His is one of thousands of voices being raised in alarm. In May 2008 over 1,700 American scientists and economists, including six Nobel laureates and more than a hundred members of the worldwide Intergovernmental Panel on Climate Change (IPCC), signed a letter once again urging the U.S. toward swift and deep cuts in greenhouse gas emissions, saying, "The most risky thing we can do is nothing."[3] The IPCC itself has published extensive reports developed by international research teams on the science of climate change, its probable impacts, and possible mitigations.[4] Warnings permeate the news. Papers, books, and documentaries bear witness for all who will hear and heed. Yet like Isaiah, who accused his contemporaries of massive denial ("Tell us smooth things; envision deceptions," Isa 30:10[5]), environmental prophets "see things most prefer not to see, and say things many wish went unsaid"[6] in a generation characterized by ignorance of both the natural world and our effect on it.[7]

Writing the Isaiah commentary for Smyth & Helwys while thinking about these things has drawn me to notice the imagery Isaiah consistently finds in the plant world, a world much more immediate to the prophet and his ancient audience, as to Fletcher, than to dwellers of urban America. I have found unexpected pleasure in puzzling out the prophet's agricultural references. These examples drawn from daily life were originally meant to help elucidate hidden aspects of human experience. They were not meant to be

---

2. Bill McKibben, *Deep Economy: The Wealth of Communities and the Durable Future* (New York: Holt, 2007), 26.

3. http://www.ucsusa.org/assets/documents/global_warming/Scientist_Economists_Call_to_Action_fnl.pdf.

4. http://www.ipcc.ch/.

5. Biblical translations in this chapter are my own.

6. David W. Orr, "The Uses of Prophecy," in *The Essential Agrarian Reader* (ed. Norman Wirzba; Washington, D.C.: Shoemaker & Hoard, 2003), 177.

7. In a chapter entitled "Culture as the Denial of Creation," in his *The Paradise of God: Renewing Religion in an Ecological Age* (Oxford: Oxford University Press, 2003), 61–92, Norman Wirzba chronicles the philosophical and finally practical loss of human awareness of the natural environment in the modern world.

puzzlers in and of themselves, as they appear to modern readers, including myself. Why a shelter in a field of cucumbers, or melons? What is tow? How can a well-planned vineyard go bad? What exactly are plowshares, pruning hooks, threshing sledges? Why beat an olive tree with sticks, and why run cart wheels over grain? Even the familiar shoot from the stump of Jesse became much more real when I saw a three-foot sapling growing from what was left of an ash tree that had fallen down a year before.

Twenty years ago, Kirsten Nielsen explored the use of plant metaphors in several key texts in Isaiah.[8] She highlighted these as expressions receptive to reuse over the course of time. Many of the metaphors involving trees and vineyards in Isaiah are, in fact, commonly understood as having undergone textual expansion and reinterpretation. The classic example is Isa 5:1–7, the song that describes God's careful planting of Israel as a choice vineyard that yielded fetid, diseased grapes.[9] Even if we doubt the claim of some that redactional expansion can be seen within the parable, interpretation is clearly present in the placement, immediately following it, of woe oracles involving fields and vineyards and eating and drinking, as we will see below. Interpretation of this parable is also evident in the new song in ch. 27 that finds God standing in a different relationship to the vineyard, a relationship of ongoing solicitous protection.

Clearly Isaiah and the prophets in his tradition were onto something vibrant and vital when they invited their hearers to consider and reconsider themselves in terms of botany.[10] Such ideas were deeply rooted in the religious and literary traditions that preceded Isaiah and other eighth-century prophets. These poets in turn employed the full rhetorical toolbox available to them to convey the historic and necessary connections between the Israelite commu-

---

8. Kirsten Nielsen, *There Is Hope for a Tree: The Tree as Metaphor in Isaiah* (JSOTSup 65; Sheffield: JSOT Press, 1989).

9. For the translation "fetid" or "stinking," see Carey Walsh (*The Fruit of the Vine: Viticulture in Ancient Israel* [Winona Lake, Ind.: Eisenbrauns, 2000], 88–89), who points out that the root used here means "stink" in other contexts (Exod 7:21; 16:20). Oded Borowski (*Agriculture in Iron Age Israel* [Boston: ASOR, 2002], 161), citing C. Westcott (*Plant Disease Handbook* [New York: Van Nostrand, 1950], 297), suggests that the grapes are diseased with black rot, which begins when the fruit is half grown and causes it to become a "black wrinkled mummy." These bad fruits must be destroyed to prevent spread of the disease. Weed control and pruning can keep conditions unsuitable for the development of black rot (see Isa 27:3–4).

10. Ellen Davis, who analyzes Amos's and Hosea's advocacy for just use of land in ancient Israel, calls Isaiah "the first urban agrarian" (*Scripture, Culture, and Agriculture: An Agrarian Reading of the Bible* [Cambridge: Cambridge University Press, 2009], 121).

nity and their agricultural lands, the injustices accompanying the monarchic social order, and the fruitful future that a restoration of economic balance could engender. Like the plants themselves, the metaphors grew under the prophets' care, offering new insight into what it meant to be God's pleasant planting.

Clearly Nielsen too was onto something when she noted the fruitfulness of such imagery as the prophecies were revisited over time.[11] Though she more recently criticized the certainty with which she reconstructed Isaiah's redactional development, she continues to affirm the importance of the metaphors themselves and their relevance to biblical theology.[12] What I hope to do in this paper is first to argue for expanding the scope of the texts in Isaiah that utilize agricultural images as signs of human conditions. Second, I will survey the uses of plant imagery in Isaiah according to this expanded definition. Third, I will consider what the prophet's interest in the plant domain can mean in our generation as a vehicle for pondering human life, its challenges, and its potentials.

The first creation story in Genesis juxtaposes, nearly back to back, two orders of relationship between humans and plants. This same juxtaposition is found frequently in Isaiah, as well as in contemporary discourse. First, humans are posed as analogous to plants, sharing a common origin in divine decree. On the third day of creation God says, "Let the earth sprout vegetation" (Gen 1:11), and on the sixth day, "let us make humankind in our image" (1:26). This parallel origin in divine imagination and command suggests that it is quite reasonable to compare people to plants, to draw lessons about humanity by observing the life cycles of grass, trees, vineyards, and fields of grain, as Isaiah did. Biologist Colin Tudge similarly outlines the family tree through which we humans and the oaks and cedars around us evolved as cousins, sharing DNA, cell structure, and common history.[13] Such observations reiterate scientifically what ancient writers knew by experience, back when analogies between people and the rest of creation were not argued but assumed, when no one would have thought to suggest that a threat to fields and forests was peripheral to human existence, when humans were not a separate category, culture

---

11. In this regard see especially her concluding discussion (Nielsen, *There Is Hope for a Tree*, 232–39).

12. Nielsen, "'From Oracles to Canon'—and the Role of Metaphor," *SJOT* 17 (2003): 26. See also her "Metaphors and Biblical Theology," in *Metaphor in the Hebrew Bible* (ed. Pierre van Hecke; Leuven; Leuven University Press, 2005), 263–73.

13. Colin Tudge, *The Tree: A Natural History of What Trees Are, How They Live, and Why They Matter* (New York: Crown, 2006).

as opposed to nature, but inescapably and gloriously rooted in the created world—back when, as Tikva Frymer-Kensky has pointed out, realization of where we come from was intrinsic to the language itself, in which the same word זרע meant both seed and semen, where פרי meant both offspring and fruit, and יונק, both sapling and nursling.[14]

The second way the creation narrative relates humans to the plant world—and this is where I wish to expand the discussion—is by drawing attention to our direct and literal dependence: "See, I have given you every seed-bearing plant that is on the face of all the earth, and every tree that has seed-bearing fruit; they will be your food" (Gen 1:29). This more prosaic reality is likewise reflected throughout Isaiah, where human security and insecurity are frequently represented through the food supply. Chapters 15–16, for instance, describe the failure of water and the withering of vegetation, so that desperate Moabites are forced to flee their homeland carrying their stored grain. "Joy and gladness have been gleaned from the farmland; and in the vineyards no one sings, no one cheers" (16:10). Such nonmetaphorical yet poetically expressed snapshots capture the human predicament when vegetation suffers. If agriculture is damaged, Isaiah seems to say, the rest may not matter very much.

Over and over the book of Isaiah draws attention to the dual significance of plants that was highlighted by Gen 1: as metaphors for human life and as necessities upon which we quite literally depend.[15] Only part of the power of plant imagery in Isaiah resides in the metaphors. The other part resides in the literal, in humans' absolute dependence upon plants, in the recognition

---

14. Tikva Simone Frymer-Kensky, "The Planting of Man: A Study in Biblical Imagery," in *Love and Death in the Ancient Near East: Essays in Honor of Marvin H. Pope* (ed. John H. Marks and Robert M. Good; Guilford, Conn.: Four Quarters, 1987), 131. Wirzba likewise notes, "Our perception of the 'being' of the world ... has, in the modern period, taken a turn that is clearly at odds with scriptural views. If it was central to scripture that the whole of reality (ourselves included) exists as the expression of God's good pleasure and that reality is therefore a reflection of a divine intention and goal, it is clear today, especially given naturalist, materialist, and consumer assumptions, that the world has little purpose other than the instrumental purposes humans ascribe to it" (*Paradise of God*, 62).

15. It is interesting that, according to Davis (*Scripture, Culture, and Agriculture*, 120–38), Amos's discussions of Israel's improper land use remain primarily on the literal level, while Hosea constructs an elaborate metaphor presenting the wealthy's unjust land use as prostitution. I am suggesting that Isaiah combines the two rhetorical strategies of metaphorical and literal relationship to plants. The extent to which Isaiah's discussion echoes those of Amos and Hosea is an interesting question that I will set aside for the moment.

common to the prophet's time and to almost every generation since that, as the plant world goes, so goes the human world.

If humans' literal dependence on plants has not stood out to recent Western readers of Isaiah as much as the metaphors, perhaps it is because this reality seems so utterly prosaic. At one time it could simply have been assumed that prophecies about disrupted harvests would strike fear in any hearer's heart. They continue to resonate in regions of the world where food remains scarce. But the peril of famine no longer appears compelling or even particularly relevant in American locales where grocery shelves mysteriously refill every night and health is compromised more often by too much food than too little.

Yet such abundance is as fragile in its own way as were the levees and barrier islands that were presumed to protect New Orleans. In September 2008, when Hurricane Ike devastated Galveston and then raced a thousand miles northward to fell trees in apocalyptic proportions and knock out power to much of Louisville's metro area, freezers, refrigeration, and cooking were lost; grocery stores and restaurants closed down; neighbors were forced to share; and electric companies imported workers from across the eastern U.S. to restore power over the course of nearly two weeks.[16] Though it was ultimately time and patience that suffered most, this unprecedented hurricane in the heartland exposed the fragility of systems we presume upon for our survival. Ironically, the least-disrupted food chains were those unprotected from the elements. While other foods spoiled in warm refrigerators, the humble urban gardens and truck farms prevailed, growing, ripening, joyfully proffering their goods as if nothing had happened.

A vast field of variegated agricultural images, filling the book from one end to the other, is rooted in these two tropes, people as plants and people needing plants, both together shaping the imaginative landscape Isaiah invites audiences to inhabit. In many cases, in fact, the two usages merge, and no clear division between them can be drawn. Early in the book, for example, the prophet accuses the leading class, the elders and princes, saying, "You have yourselves devoured the vineyard; the plunder of the poor is in your houses" (3:14). Readers versed in biblical parallelism readily note the chiastic structure in which three repetitions of the masculine plural "you"

---

16. Ironically, or perhaps portentously, this extraordinary windstorm was overlooked in national news not because of Ike's far greater impact on Galveston, but because of the extraordinary windstorm on Wall Street the same weekend, which blew down Lehman Brothers, AIG, Merrill Lynch, and the economic house of cards on which worldwide stock markets and banking institutions relied.

surround the victimized topics "vineyard," "plunder," and "poor." But to what does the devoured vineyard of the first line correspond: to the stolen plunder, or to the poor themselves? It can be taken either way, or both ways.[17] On the one hand, the leaders are accused of literally gobbling up the produce of vineyards, contrary to law and custom, leaving nothing for the poor to glean. This is sin enough. But the vineyard can also be read as a metaphor, as it often is, for God's people themselves, those whom God planted on God's own mountain (Exod 15:17), the vine that God brought out of Egypt (Ps 80:8 [Heb 80:9]), the vineyard that Isaiah himself identifies with the people of Israel and Judah (5:7).[18] The polyvalent possibilities—vineyard as the poor's food supply and vineyard as the poor of Israel themselves—suggest a both/and that strengthens the rhetoric: when leaders appointed to defend the poor hoard the vineyard's fruit for themselves, they consume—they cannibalize—their own nation, fencerow to fencerow.

Isaiah's metaphorical and literal agricultural language frequently cross-pollinate in this way. Two chapters earlier, two alternative futures are imagined: those who "agree and obey" will "eat the good of the land," enjoying a quite literal bounty. But those who "refuse and rebel" will themselves become food, food for the sword (1:19–20). Similarly, those accused of venerating trees, the prophet says, will themselves become like trees, desiccated ones with withered leaves (1:30; see also 57:5; 66:17). They will also become like tow, the weak and tangled flammable fiber that is removed when a stalk of flax is combed for spinning linen thread (1:31).

In ch. 5, the metaphorical and the literal are planted side by side. At the conclusion of the parable of the vineyard, the prophet identifies the people of Israel and Judah as God's vineyard, from whom the fruits of justice and righteousness were expected, but in whom only the fetid grapes of bloodshed and outcry are found (5:7). In a sudden shift to literal accusations, the wealthy are then accused of joining house to house and field to field until there is no room left for anyone else in the land (v. 8). Their consumption leads to crop failure: "for ten acres of vineyard will yield one bath, and a homer of seed will yield an ephah," a tenth of what was sown (v. 10). In quick succession, hearers are positioned both as the vineyard itself and as the foolish managers of a precious food supply.

---

17. See especially the discussion of this passage in Thomas L. Leclerc, *Yhwh Is Exalted in Justice: Solidarity and Conflict in Isaiah* (Minneapolis: Fortress, 2001), 53–55.

18. In fact, two verses earlier in Isa 3:12, where the Hebrew text says, "children are their oppressors, and women rule over them," LXX says something very different that pointedly relates to the vineyards: "your debt collectors glean you, and extortioners rule over you."

Thus the plant world serves both as a metaphor for the people Isaiah addresses and as a powerful signifier of their fate through the fate of their vegetation. Such images occur so frequently in Isaiah that other instances can only be surveyed.

Several of the passages seen above exemplify the use of agricultural imagery in accusations. Other accusations of engaging in illicit rituals involving vegetation follow, often intertwined with hints or declarations of judgment. Those who "set out alien slips," apparently as a ritual for the prematurely dying god Adon, will see their harvest disappear (17:10–11).[19] Garlands of flowers adorning the heads of drunken revelers will be trampled underfoot when the divine tempest hurls them down (28:1–4).[20] These flowers, beginning as literal emblems of honor, fade into metaphors for the washed-up glory of their wearers. Plants also insinuate themselves into unexpected settings: feebleness of resolve is pictured as the king's and people's hearts shaking like trees of the forest before the wind (7:2), while defiance against God is encapsulated as the intent to replace with cedars the sycamores that had been cut down (9:10).

Even more persistently than accusations, judgments employ vegetation imagery. The book opens, as noted above, with judgment already underway, the landscape already resembling a decimated field, the people already warned that they may be sword fodder. The two images at the end of ch. 1, drought and fire, signal the most pervasive means of destruction found in Isaiah. Fire represents both evil itself and judgment upon that evil. Those who disdain God's commands by depriving the innocent of their rights will become stubble devoured by fire, dry grass sinking into the flame (5:24). The desolate land

---

19. The description has been linked to a cult practice known through Greek and Roman writers, which may have appeared in Aram as well. Greek writers as far back as Plato describe the ritual planting by women of "gardens of Adonis," small dishes in which seeds of fennel, lettuce, wheat, or barley were sprouted in midsummer and then died off within days to commemorate the short life and violent death of the handsome god the Phoenicians knew as Adon, later adopted into Greek mythology as Adonis (Plato, *Phaedrus* 276–77; see Marcel Detienne, *The Gardens of Adonis: Spices in Greek Mythology* [trans. J. Lloyd; Princeton: Princeton University Press, 1994]). Like the prophet, Plato highlights the ephemeral nature of the life produced. He contrasts this with the farmer's sensible planting of seeds in the earth in their appropriate season. See also Hans Wildberger, *Isaiah 13–27* (trans. Thomas H. Trapp; CC; Minneapolis: Fortress, 1997), 180–86.

20. For suggestions about the connection between Isaiah's description and the Ugaritic festival called *marzeah* (see Amos 6:7), which was celebrated by the affluent and characterized by flowers, perfume, oil, rich food, and plenty of wine, see especially Bernhard A. Asen, "The Garlands of Ephraim: Isaiah 28:1–6 and the *Marzeah*," *JSOT* 71 (1996): 73–87; and Theodore J. Lewis, *Cults of the Dead in Ancient Israel and Ugarit* (HSM 39; Atlanta: Scholars Press, 1989), 80–94.

resulting from hearers' intransigence is compared to the burned stump of a felled tree (6:13). Evil burns like a fire "consuming thorns and thistles" and kindling the forest thickets (9:18 [Heb 9:17]). People likewise become like fuel for the fire, no one sparing another (v. 19 [Heb v. 18]). The people are told, "You conceive straw, give birth to stubble; your breath is a fire that devours you. And the peoples will be burned to ash, thorns cut up and set ablaze" (33:11–12). Proud Assyria, imagined as a forest, is burned in the divine fire (10:16–19). The fortified city dries up and what is left of it is grazed by calves and burned by women (27:10–11). The day of God's vengeance will turn the land of Edom into a burning pitch where thorns, nettles, and thistles grow up, and only the most marginal of nondomesticated animals can reside (34:9–15).

Related to fire is drought, a constant threat where, without the benefit of rivers, farmers count on timely rainfall for the growth of grain and vegetables.[21] The earth dries up and withers because of its inhabitants, and the wine dries up, causing the mirth of celebrators to cease (24:4–9). Even the Nile dries up, leaving bare places along the parched river and despairing those who fish and weave flax (19:5–10). The vintage and fruit harvest fail, causing carefree women to shudder, tremble, and beat their breasts in mourning for fields and vines, for soil that grows into thorns and thistles (32:9–13). Sennacherib is commissioned by God to make fortified cities crash into heaps of ruins and their inhabitants become like blighted grass on the housetops (37:26–27). "The grass withers, the flower fades" when God's breath blows upon it (40:7). Princes and rulers wither and are carried off like stubble (40:23–24, cf. 41:2).

While drought and fire are nonhuman destroyers, a further image is that of God as a human destroyer of vegetation. God is the vineyard owner who removes its protective hedge and wall, allowing it to be trampled down, and neglects its maintenance, so that it is overgrown with thorns and thistles (5:5–6). God lops the boughs and hacks down the thickets of the forest (10:33–34); God cuts off shoots of grapes in the vineyard (18:4–6). God is the harvester, gathering grain and olives so that only gleanings are left (17:4–6; 24:13), or treading the human winepress in divine anger (63:3, 6). The people are described as threshed and winnowed (21:10), and in a much more drawn-out allegory they are compared with both a field being plowed and grain and other crops being threshed by the farmer (28:23–29).

---

21. For a comprehensive discussion of the geological landscape and the resultant dependence of agriculture on gentle, well-timed rain, and of the imprint of such concerns in scripture, see Daniel Hillel, *The Natural History of the Bible: An Environmental Exploration of the Hebrew Scriptures* (New York: Columbia University Press, 2006), 140–62.

In short, just as accusations are couched in terms of plant metaphors, so also divine decrees are imagined as the destruction of trees, vineyards, and fields by fire, drought, cutting, or harvest. But that is not all, and this is where the persistence in vegetative growth comes in. Embedded in the nature of plant life, and therefore in the imagery relating people to plants, is the potential for regeneration. Even in the devastating metaphor at the end of Isaiah's commissioning scene in ch. 6, where the empty land is compared to a repeatedly ravaged tree stump, a three-word upturn concludes: "the holy seed is its stump" (6:13).

Job said that there was hope for a tree, if it was cut down, that it would resprout, and that its shoots would not cease. He contrasted this quality with that of mortals who lie down, never to rise again (Job 14:7–12). But Isaiah's tradition sees even in the midst of doom a tree-like hope for the human family, if not for individuals. The stump of the fallen tree of Judah still holds the marvelous capacity to grow once again (Isa 6:13). The image of the shoot from Jesse's stump, the branch growing out of his roots (11:1), likewise cites the potential of trees to regenerate vegetatively from their roots even when everything else has died or been cut down. Similarly, the reprise of the parable of the vineyard in ch. 27 concludes with the vibrant image of Israel once more taking root, blossoming, growing shoots, and filling the whole world with fruit (v. 6).

The regeneration of plant life serves not only as a metaphor but also as a concrete sign of human regeneration. When nations come to the holy mountain to learn from God, the tools they will find most useful will no longer be instruments of death, but instruments of life: plowshares to cultivate the fields and pruning hooks to tend the vines (2:2–4). God not only teaches prudent farmers (28:23–29), but participates directly to awaken the soil for the nourishment of people and animals, setting the not-quite-closed loop of agricultural productivity into motion:

> God will give rain for the seed with which you sow the ground, and the food that comes from the ground will be lush and abundant. On that day your livestock will graze in large pastures, and the cattle and donkeys that are working the ground will eat savory feed that has been winnowed with shovel and fork. (30:23–24)

Similarly, the wilderness turns into a fruitful field (32:15), and the desert blossoms and rejoices as waters break forth, the haunt of jackals becomes a swamp, and reeds and rushes abound (35:1–7). "The survivors of the house of Judah who are left will again take root downward and bear fruit upward" (37:31).

Such imagery dominates the final half of the book, where it is often impossible to distinguish the metaphorical from the literal. The wilderness becomes a pool of water where cedars, acacias, myrtles, olives, and evergreen trees grow (41:18–19). Water is poured on thirsty land, and spirit is poured on the hearer's own seed and offspring, who will spring up like tamarisks and willows (44:3–4). The skies rain down righteousness so that salvation springs up (45:8). Zion's deserts become like Eden, like the garden of God (51:3). Those who practice justice and satisfy the needs of the afflicted will become like a watered garden (58:11). They are called oaks of righteousness, God's own planting (61:3). They will build houses and inhabit them; they will plant vineyards and eat their fruit (65:21); and their bodies themselves will be like grass (66:14)—not, finally, in their perishing but in their flourishing. Like human decimation, human regeneration is envisioned in vegetative terms.

Thus Isaiah directly and pervasively employs plant imagery to tie human spiritual and societal health to environmental well-being. Perhaps the prophet would not go as far as Deuteronomy in positing human virtue as the vital condition for agricultural prosperity. But the interconnections between spiritual and physical wasteland and between societal and agricultural replenishment are quite insistent, and seem to signal the insight that what happens in the fields is inseparable from what happens in cities and towns.[22]

Isaiah maintains, in fact, that responsibility for both ecological and economic health lies not simply with the people as a whole but most urgently with their leaders, the very aristocracy accused of devouring the vineyard. Having inherited the traditional idea that it was God who sponsored Judah's king, Isaiah proceeds to assert that it is the king who, in turn, is charged with sponsoring justice and righteousness, conditions that lead to a future of endless peace (9:7 [Heb 9:6]) in which poor and meek, lambs, kids, and children alike live safe from predation (11:4, 6), where folly no longer passes for nobility, nor villainy for honor (32:5), a world where even the poorest enjoy food

---

22. Ellen Davis tells of a group of farmers with whom she studied Gen 3. Though theologically untrained, they noted what any ordinary Israelite would have seen but she and her urbanized students had missed: "when humans are disconnected from God, the soil will be the first to suffer." Throughout the Hebrew Scriptures, she continues, "land degradation is a sure sign that humans have turned away from God. Conversely, the flourishing of the land (e.g., Lev 26:3–6, 10; Deut 28:2–5, 11–12; Isa 35; Pss 65; 72) marks a return to God. In short, the Old Testament represents the condition of the land as the single best index of human responsiveness to God" ("Becoming Human: Biblical Interpretation and Ecological Responsibility" [cited Apr. 25, 2009]. Online: https://www.vts.edu/ftpimages/95/misc/misc_53462.pdf).

and water security (32:6).²³ In Isaiah, social and environmental health do not compete with each other for scarce public resources, as is often claimed today. Rather, they inhabit the same framework:

> Then justice will reside in wild lands,
> and righteousness will abide in farmlands,
> and the fruit of righteousness will be peace
> and the outgrowth of righteousness, calm and security forever.
> My people will abide in a peaceful habitat,
> in secure homes, in carefree resting places. (32:16–18)

Ties between social and ecological spheres are further reinforced by the imputing not only of plant characteristics to people but of human characteristics to plants. In ch. 33 the verdant places that are drying up also grieve: "The land mourns, it wastes away; Lebanon is ashamed, it withers; Sharon has become like the desert, and Bashan and Carmel shake off their leaves" (v. 9).²⁴ Yet trees that lament defeat can celebrate victory as well, taunting a fallen tyrant: "Since you were laid low, no logger comes up against us" (14:8). Trees sing and shout for joy at redemption (44:23). They clap their hands with glee at the procession of exiles returning home (55:12–13). Attribution of human characteristics to plants, like the attribution of plant characteristics to people, affirms the critical ties binding humans to the landscape they depend upon, and evokes respect for the rights and dignity of nonhuman creation.²⁵

---

23. On Isaiah's insistence on the royal responsibility for justice, see, e.g., Hugh Williamson, "The Messianic Texts in Isaiah 1–39," in *King and Messiah in Israel and the Ancient Near East* (ed. John Day; JSOTSup 270; Sheffield: Sheffield Academic Press, 1998), 238–70.

24. The imagery of the land in mourning because of the sins of its inhabitants is also found in Isa 24:4, though the same words ארץ and אבל are there rendered not "the land mourns" but "the earth dries up" in the NRSV and other translations. The motif of the land in mourning is shared widely in the prophets, found also in Jer 4:28; 12:4, 11; 23:10; Hos 4:3; Joel 1:10; and Amos 1:2. See Katherine M. Hayes, *"The Earth Mourns": Prophetic Metaphor and Oral Aesthetic* (SBLAcBib 8; Atlanta: Society of Biblical Literature, 2002) for a full discussion of these passages; for a discussion of the problem of translating the verb אבל, see pp. 12–18.

25. In an extended exercise in relating human characteristics to plants, Michael Pollan (*The Botany of Desire: A Plant's Eye View of the World* [New York: Random House, 2002]) explores the ways in which plants may be viewed as exercising intent, inviting humans and other species to further their vegetative interests. His essays gently critique anthropocentrism, raise questions around the idea of agency, and inspire respect for the complexity and sophistication of apples and other species.

Thus plants convey the state of humans and human nations in Isaiah: the connections between the death of civilization and that of vegetation, and the thriving of plants and that of people, are closely and repeatedly drawn. Long before the disastrous effects of human activity on creation could be imagined, millennia before fossil fuels first ignited both the industrial revolution and its complications, the moral and often literal ties between human behavior and the natural world's future were set forth by a prophet who saw colossal military disasters in his own lifetime, and by a tradition following him that endured the destruction and, less often, the regeneration, of many nations both great and small: the Northern Israelite kingdom, Syria, Moab, Edom, the Philistines, Assyria, Babylon, and Judah itself all suffered catastrophe during Isaiah's development. Vegetation signals the fall and rise of nations: empires dry into wastelands; deserts transform themselves into divine gardens; life springs anew from dying stock and thirsty land.

Unfortunately for many if not most us, though, something is lost in translation. Metaphors communicate effectively by employing vehicles that are more familiar to their audience than the tenors they seek to elucidate, so that insight into the better-known topic can lend understanding to the obscure or elusive one. But vast societal changes have made peering into many of the Bible's root metaphors difficult. If interpretive problems arise because monarchy and slavery no longer convey the divine–human relationship as meaningfully as they once did, there may be cause to celebrate. By contrast, metaphors from the natural world fade into inaccessibility not when plants themselves become archaic but when human awareness lapses. And ironically, according to the reports of economists, conservation biologists, and human and animal rights observers, widespread contemporary lapses in our ties to agriculture have facilitated not only environmental degradation and danger— with up to a third of all greenhouse gases attributable to production and distribution of food, especially meat[26]—but enslavement to new empires, this time in the form of deregulated yet deeply subsidized corporations that have dramatically transformed food systems, bestowing on consumers, on terms

---

26. Estimates of contributions to greenhouse gas emissions by the industrial production and distribution of food range from 20 to 33 percent of all emissions. See, e.g., Tara Garnett, "The World on a Plate: Food and Its Contribution to Climate Changing Emissions" (December 2007) [cited Apr. 26, 2009]. Online: http://www.climateactionprogramme.org/features/article/the_world_on_a_plate_food_and_its_contribution_to_climate_changing_emission/. See also Johns Hopkins School of Public Healther Agricultural and Public Health Gateway [cited Apr. 26, 2009]. Online: http://aphg.jhsph.edu/?event=browse.subject&subjectID=18. According to the EPA, one-third of all methane and nearly three-fourths of all nitrous oxide emitted by the U.S. comes directly from agriculture.

of their own making, the daily bread our ancestors used to receive from the ground itself. These terms include, among other things, widespread deforestation,[27] pollution and erosion of farmland,[28] genetic modification and patented control of seeds,[29] and killing of rivers and oceans with run-off fertilizer and animal waste.[30] Not so long ago freed from monarchic rule, we now see—or, more typically, fail to see—land-owning farmers in the U.S. and elsewhere transformed once again into serfs, wage-earning workers turned into indentured servants performing inhumanely unsafe work at substandard wages, subject to deportation here and to the loss of family farming land abroad, and domestic animals reduced to food factories bereft of dignity, living space, and basic comfort from birth to slaughter.[31] While such practices spring from cor-

---

27. Documentation on this and the following abuses of agribusiness is widespread and readily available. On deforestation, see for instance Andrew Downie, "The Amazon Gets Less and Less Green," in *Time* (Jan 25, 2008) [cited Apr. 26, 2009]. Online: http://www.time.com/time/health/article/0,8599,1707121,00.html.

28. David Pimentel, "Environmental and Economic Costs of Pesticide Use," *Environment, Development and Sustainability* 7 (2005): 229–52; idem, "Environmental and Economic Costs of Soil Erosion and Conservation Benefits," *Science* 267 (1995): 1117–23. Sean McDonagh, "The Transition from Agriculture to Agribusiness" [cited Apr. 26, 2009]. Online: http://www.columban.com/stateofplanet2.htm#_edn20.

29. Margaret Mellon and Jane Rissler, "Environmental Effects of Genetically Modified Food Crops—Recent Experiences" (paper presented at conference entitled "Genetically Modified Foods—The American Experience," sponsored by the Royal Veterinary and Agricultural University, Copenhagen, Denmark, June 12–13, 2003) [cited Apr. 26, 2009]. Online: http://www.ucsusa.org/food_and_agriculture/science_and_impacts/impacts_genetic_engineering/environmental-effects-of.html; Vandana Shiva, "Force-Feeding GMOs to the Poor" [cited Apr. 26, 2009]. Online: www.organicconsumers.org/ge/poor.cfm; Debi Barker, "Globalization and Industrial Agriculture," in *Fatal Harvest: The Tragedy of Industrial Agriculture* (ed. Andrew Kimbrell; Washington, D.C.: Island Press, 2002), 313–19; Vandana Shiva, *Stolen Harvest: The Hijacking of the Global Food Supply* (Cambridge, Mass.: South End Press, 2000), 79–94.

30. Union of Concerned Scientists, "Hidden Costs of Industrial Agriculture" [cited Apr. 26, 2009]. Online: http://www.ucsusa.org/food_and_agriculture/science_and_impacts/impacts_industrial_agriculture/costs-and-benefits-of.html; "Clean Water and Factory Farms" [cited Apr. 26, 2009]. Online: http://www.sierraclub.org/factoryfarms/factsheets/water.asp; Doug Gurian-Sherman, "CAFOs Uncovered: The Untold Costs of Confined Animal Feeding Operations." Union of Concerned Scientists, April 2008 [cited Apr. 26, 2009]. Online: http://www.ucsusa.org/assets/documents/food_and_agriculture/cafos-uncovered.pdf.

31. For farming issues, see Carole Morison, "Organizing for Justice: DelMarVa Poultry Justice Alliance," Johns Hopkins Bloomberg School of Public Health, 2007 [cited Apr. 26, 2009]. Online: http://ocw.jhsph.edu/courses/nutritionalhealthfoodproductionandenvironment/PDFs/Lecture8.pdf. For issues of human safety and wages, see for example Eric Schlosser, *Fast Food Nation: The Dark Side of the All-American Meal* (Boston: Houghton Mifflin Harcourt,

porate greed, they could not have taken root in a society aware of the sources of its food, a society attentive to the moral and social costs of agricultural larceny, discerning enough to resist the tempting fruit of low, low prices,[32] wise enough to name and refuse iniquitous decrees and oppressive statutes (Isa 10:1–2). When ancient, time-tested values are lost in cultural translation, sometimes a great deal more is lost.

We all recall the national controversy in 2005 surrounding the coma from which Terry Schiavo, a victim of brain damage, never recovered. The term used to describe her degenerating condition, "persistent vegetative state," was coined in 1972 by a spinal surgeon and a neurologist. It is more than notable that this phrase partakes of a botanical metaphor that is completely foreign both to the Bible and to biology, the same metaphor employed when people casually speak of vegging out or being couch potatoes. This is the idea that a vegetative state is one of unconsciousness, passivity, and even deterioration. Quite apart from what we do or do not know about what constitutes consciousness when one is a plant, it does not take a botany degree to know that vegetables do not vegetate much. Instead they respire, photosynthesize, and grow, sometimes with almost visible rapidity. They track the sun and tuck leaves and blooms away at night. They make seeds, bear fruit, and turn water not only into wine but tomatoes, corn, eggplant, apples, potatoes, flowers, timber, forests. They entice birds, bees, beasts, and humans to further their interests. They expand their domain, sending out suckers and shoots in "vegetative growth"—a term that is really not an oxymoron. Even in winter, roots continue to grow, and buds of leaves and flowers develop under cover of bark,

---

2001), 169–91; Charles Dillard Thompson and Melinda Wiggins, *The Human Cost of Food: Farm Workers' Lives, Labor, and Advocacy* (Austin, Tex.: University of Texas Press, 2002); and Desiree Evans, "Bearing the Fruits of Their Labors," *Facing South*, Dec. 5, 2008 [cited Apr. 26, 2009]. Online: http://www.southernstudies.org/2008/12/bearing-the-fruits-of-their-labor.html. For concerns of foreign workers in the U.S. and abroad see Lucky Severson, "Kosher Ethics," *Religion and Ethics Newsweekly* (Oct. 3, 2008) [cited Apr. 24, 2009]. Online http://www.pbs.org/wnet/religionandethics/week1205/cover.html); Katherine Ainger, "The New Peasant Revolt," *The New Internationalist*, January/February 2003 [cited Apr. 24, 2009]. Online: http://www.thirdworldtraveler.com/Food/New_Peasants_Revolt.html. For discussion of animal abuse, see, for instance, Michael Pollan, *The Omnivore's Dilemma: A History of Four Meals* (New York: Penguin, 2007), 65–84.

32. For a discussion of grocery stores and consumer options, see, e.g., Elanor Starmer, "Power Buyers, Power Sellers: How Supermarkets Impact Farmers, Workers, and Consumers—And How We Can Build a Fairer Food System," in *Leveling the Field—Issue Brief #3* [cited Apr. 24, 2009]. Online: http://www.ase.tufts.edu/gdae/Pubs/rp/AAI_Issue_Brief_3.pdf).

preparing for the burst of spring growth that surprises and delights us every year.[33] Perhaps our viewing vegetation as comatose says less about plants and more about our own awareness. This is a mistake neither Job nor Isaiah could have made. In fact, I imagine it is a mistake not many would have made before our generation. Insulation from the biological realm has altered our moral and aesthetic ordering of reality: "We see, feel, taste, smell, think, plan, and engage the world in ways that would be unrecognizable to the more traditionally minded and to the scriptural authors who first articulated creation's character and meaning."[34]

Much is lost when the natural world becomes foreign to us. With such awareness goes our connection to our own roots, the knowledge of what we are as a species that withers or potentially flourishes like grass, is felled or potentially bears fruit like trees, or like vineyards yields fruit that may be diseased or potentially sweet and sustaining, a species that can flourish again even when it appears all has been lost. Especially in times like these, we need such hope in the generativity of living species and of our own species.[35]

But more than that, what is lost is knowledge of how this foreign land we call nature goes about providing for our needs—cooling and replenishing our air, recycling our waste, feeding us every single thing we eat—and of what it needs from us in order to continue doing so. The ecological destructions Isaiah witnessed now read as eerie and local foreshadowings of the worldwide devastation envisioned by today's scientific prophets of doom. The devouring of earth's vineyard by the wealthy minority is indeed leading to general destruction; neglect of our kinship to the world does indeed cause the land to

---

33. The remarkable capability of plants to do what they evolved to do renders the transformation of agri-*culture* into agri-*business* superfluous. Numerous case studies have shown that "small farms almost always produce far more agricultural output per unit area than larger farms," both in the U.S. and around the world (Peter Rosset, "Small Is Bountiful," *Ecologist* 29 [1999]: 452–56).

34. Wirzba, *Paradise of God*, 64.

35. The need is not simply aesthetic or emotional. Failure to recognize the prophets' this-worldly hopes and failure to see the natural marvels that surround us every day have contributed to widespread yearning to witness divine transformation in the form of the world's violent decreation according to apocalyptic end-times theologies, theologies that are no longer content simply to wait for Armageddon and have become determined to bring it on. On Christian apocalypticism, see, e.g., Timothy P. Weber, *On the Road to Armageddon: How Evangelicals Became Israel's Best Friend* (Grand Rapids: Baker, 2004). On violent apocalypticism in Judaism and Islam as well as Christianity, see Gershom Gorenberg, *The End of Days: Fundamentalism and the Struggle for the Temple Mount* (Oxford: Oxford University Press, 2000).

mourn and languish. The earth does indeed lie polluted under its inhabitants, who have transgressed natural laws, violated ancient statutes, and "broken the everlasting covenant" (24:5).[36] Those of us who deal in Hebrew poetry know the power of this ancient language to evoke and provoke, to awaken the imaginations of hearers and to posit worlds both as they are and as they can be. Reading scripture in the contemporary world may compel us to hear more than ever before the reminder to take seriously what hundreds of generations before us took for granted, that we are indeed both related to the plant world and completely dependent upon its health for our survival.

Branches of our society do indeed seem to be waking up once again to our plant cousins as more than color-coordinated yard art, and trying to retrieve what has been lost and to redeem what could yet be lost. Neither ancient prophets nor contemporary biblical scholars can do what scientists are equipped to do to educate the public to the environmental threats we face. But, especially in circles where the Bible carries more weight than science, the prophets speak a language that still has currency, and their voices can and must be amplified.[37]

According to Gen 3, sin entered the world as an eating disorder, when the fruit perceived as making wise led the first couple instead to alienation from God, the land, and each other. Today it is this alienation itself that has facilitated the belief that we can act without limits, eat without limits, and perform an end-run around our original vocation to till and keep the soil.[38] University of Louisville biologist Margaret Carreiro employs a forest metaphor to communicate her hopes for humanity's ecological coming of age. Forested areas show discernible growth patterns, stages of succession in which the first pioneering species of trees to dominate are those that grow rapidly and do not have to compete with each other for relatively abundant resources of light and nutrients. As these species change their own environment over time and find fewer resources to aid their growth and reproduction, slower-growing species that use resources more efficiently come to dominate. Carreiro voices the

---

36. See Davis, *Scripture, Culture, and Agriculture*, 17–20.

37. The need to amplify prophetic voices that highlight care for the earth, deplore environmental and human destruction, and envision the bright future as continuous with present life is particularly crucial in evangelical circles where selective biblical interpretation supports an eschatology of longing for or even attempting to hasten the world's demise; see above, note 35.

38. On the political and religious responsibility to be "earthkeepers," see especially W. Eugene March, *God's Land on Loan: Israel, Palestine, and the World* (Louisville, Ky.: Westminster John Knox, 2007), 111–13.

hope that humanity is a forest undergoing succession into a species that can live tolerantly within the resource boundaries offered by the natural world.[39]

The rough divine justice by which ancient Judah gradually learned what the prophets were trying to teach is summarized in Isaiah's parable of the farmer who, instructed by God, plowed the ground and threshed the grain not to destroy them but to prepare them for the next stage in their vegetative cycle (28:23–29). The rough justice American society seems as yet unprepared to help forestall will involve much suffering that is likely to fall hardest on the poor, who contribute least to the crisis. Its only redemptive feature, should we survive, could be a renewed affiliation with the rest of creation. Many are saying that it will take every tool in the collective human toolbox to divert us from today's vector and restore us to health. This toolbox certainly includes the powerful language of Isaiah and other biblical poets, who remind us that we belong to the ground beneath us, and we cannot afford to let ourselves be cut off from its sustaining power. Deep into exile, a sobered Judean audience heard the message of their restoration in this way:

> For as the rain and snow come down from heaven
> > and do not return there without watering the earth,
> causing it to give birth and sprout,
> > and give seed to the sower and food to the eater,
> so is my word that comes out of my mouth:
> > it does not return to me empty,
> without doing what I wish,
> > and accomplishing what I intend.
> Yes, in joy you will come out
> > and in peace you will be brought back.
> Even the mountains and hills will burst into song before you,
> > and all the trees of the field will clap their hands.
> In place of the thorn, the cypress will grow.
> > And in place of the nettle the myrtle will grow,
> And this will endure for Yhwh's renown,
> > an everlasting sign that will not be cut down. (55:10–13)

---

39. Margaret S. Carrerio, "Helping Louisville Become Ecologically Sustainable," Mending the Earth Teach-In, September 4–5, 2007, Louisville Presbyterian Seminary.

"Like a Mother I Have Comforted You": The Function of Figurative Language in Isaiah 1:7–26 and 66:7–14

Chris A. Franke

Roy Melugin was a founding member of the Formation of Isaiah Group of the Society of Biblical Literature, and his influence on Isaiah scholarship is obvious from the ways this Group has developed over the years.[1] We originally asked questions mostly related to the way the book as a whole was edited and shaped by various redactors/redactions during the long period of its formation. Roy's scholarship over the years reflected his desire to find additional ways of reading texts. He explored a wide variety of different disciplines and waded into uncharted territory thereby expanding the possibilities of new and creative Isaiah scholarship.

In 2002, Roy proposed that the Group work on the potential power of Isaianic figurative language in shaping multiple visions concerning the divine-human relationship.[2] The focus was on reading and interpreting particular texts to get at larger questions relating to the shape of the Book of Isaiah. He asked how figurative language functions to shape "symbolic worlds in which Yhwh-worshippers could/can dwell and be shaped and transformed in their individual and communal existence." Who decides what imagery is most important? How can we most fruitfully interpret the images that we hold as

---

1. Thank you to my student assistants, Claire Hagen-Fleck and Christine Anderson for their work in making this document possible. Thanks also to the College of St. Catherine for grant support for these student workers.

2. Roy F. Melugin, "Poetic Imagination, Intertextuality, and Life in a Symbolic World," 7 (see the opening chapter of this volume).

important? Who decides the nature of the symbolic world that the text articulates—the text or the interpreter? For which communities in particular are interpretations developed—earliest or latest? How does poetry shape life and identity? How does language shape symbolic worlds in which human life is transformed? How can reader-response theory and use-theory from the philosophy of language be helpful? His own publications reflect the vitality of his interests in these areas.[3]

My interest in how a poet uses images, or figurative language, and what such language does to a variety of audiences was spurred by Roy's interests and encouragement with respect to how language could be used for transformation of an audience; this included contemporary as well as ancient audiences. He saw the need of understanding how ancient Israel might interpret certain images, and how later communities would view these images, given the characteristic nature of metaphors to be "open to more than one interpretation."[4] Others who have influenced my thinking on how images function include Luis Alonso Schökel, Rémi Lack, Cynthia Chapman, and Red Auerbach.[5]

---

3. Roy F. Melugin, "The Book of Isaiah and the Construction of Meaning," in *Writing and Reading the Scroll of Isaiah: Studies of an Interpretive Tradition* (ed. Craig C. Broyles and Craig A. Evans; VTSup 70.1; Leiden: Brill, 1997), 39–55; idem, "Texts to Transform Life: Reading Isaiah as Christians," *WW* 19 (1999): 109–16; idem, "Poetic Imagination, Intertextuality, and Life in a Symbolic World"; idem, "Recent Form Criticism Revisited in an Age of Reader Response," in *The Changing Face of Form Criticism* (ed. Marvin A. Sweeney and Ehud Ben Zvi; Grand Rapids: Eerdmans, 2003), 46–64; idem, "Figurative Speech and the Reading of Isaiah 1 as Scripture," in *New Visions of Isaiah* (ed. Roy F. Melugin and Marvin A. Sweeney; JSOTSup 214; Sheffield: Sheffield Academic Press, 1996), 282–305.

4. Roy F. Melugin, "Figurative Speech and the Reading of Isaiah 1 as Scripture," 284.

5. Luis Alonso Schökel, *A Manual of Hebrew Poetics* (SubBi 11; Rome: Pontifical Biblical Institute, 1988). In chs. 8 and 9 on images and figures of speech, pp. 95–168, Schökel frequently speaks to the same concerns as does Melugin. E.g., cataloguing and studying images may help one to reconstruct the world of the biblical writer (121); the "originality and strangeness" of anthropomorphic language may provoke a reader to make mental adjustments in thinking (135); the analysis and study of images and symbols "within the work to which they belong" may be the most important work of all (140); R. Lack, *La symbolique de livre d'Isaïe: Essaie sur l'image littéraire comme élément de structuration* (AnBib 59; Rome: Pontifical Biblical Institute, 1973); Cynthia R. Chapman, *Gendered Language of Warfare in the Israelite-Assyrian Encounter* (HSM 62; Winona Lake, Ind.: Eisenbrauns, 2004).

Not Erich Auerbach, author of the classic *Mimesis: The Representation of Reality in Western Literature* (W. R. Trask; Princeton: Princeton University Press, 1953), but Red Auerbach, former coach of the Boston Celtics. When asked how he managed to inspire his team to great heights he said, "It's not *what* you say but *how* you say it!"

Terry Eagleton in his book *How to Read a Poem*, especially in the second chapter, "What is Poetry?", describes poems and the function of poetry.[6] His observations about poetry relate to Melugin's publications and his questions for further work on the book of Isaiah. Eagleton views poems as "moral statements ... because they deal in human values, meanings and purposes."[7] Poems "shed light on human feelings and relationships...."[8] Any poem is "a statement released into the public world for us to make of it what we may.... [it] could by definition never have just one meaning."[9] Eagleton's comments about the very look of a poem on a printed page and how it affects readers is instructive for those of us who are interested in the stichometric arrangements of biblical texts. The author, says Eagleton, decides where lines of poems should end.[10] While biblical scholars do not have access to the ancient authors' arrangement of lines, the importance of how poems are arranged in our own translations is important to questions of interpretation and meaning.[11] Eagleton's observations can be very helpful to future work on how biblical poetry and images function.

In 2003, the Group began its new focus with a panel consisting of Peter D. Miscall and myself, with respondents Francis Landy, and Roy Melugin. Our charge was to discuss the question of how images function, and in addition to identify whether we read synchronically or diachronically.[12] I am thankful for the presentations and comments of the panelists as well as the observations of the audience members. Their helpful observations are reflected in this paper.

I will first discuss several similes and metaphors in Isa 1:7–27, and in 66:7–14.[13] Then, I will compare various images of Zion/Jerusalem as well as images that describe the nature of God's relationship to Zion/Jerusalem. Finally, I will explore how these poetic images might shape life and identity and transform ancient and modern audiences, as well as noting how they have malfunctioned.

---

6. Terry Eagleton, *How to Read a Poem* (Malden, Mass.: Blackwell, 2007).
7. Ibid., 29.
8. Ibid., 31.
9. Ibid., 32. He also cautions that while poems are fraught with ambiguity, they are not occasions for "verbal free-for-all."
10. Ibid., 25.
11. See, e.g., Isa 66:12 on how the stichometric arrangement of lines can influence a translation.
12. Johannes C. de Moor, ed., *Synchronic or Diachronic? A Debate on Method in Old Testament Exegesis* (OTS 34; Leiden: Brill, 1995).
13. My translations of portions of these sections are found in Appendix I.

The first chapter of Isaiah can be read as a sort of table of contents to the entire book of Isaiah and serve as an introduction of the main ideas in the rest of the book. The last chapter can be read as a summary of the previous chapters.[14] This final chapter also shows a development with respect to the image of Zion/Jerusalem from what is presented in the first chapter of the book of Isaiah.[15]

I. Figurative Language in Isa 1:7–26

The superscription in 1:1 sets the vision of Isaiah in the eighth century during the reigns of four Judean kings. The remaining verses in 1:2–31 include a series of condemnations and indictments of God's people, punishments that have been meted out to the country for their evil deeds, as well as the promise of transformation, redemption, and restoration for Zion. The condemnations move from general to more specific. People rebel against God, don't know the Lord, are laden with iniquity, deal corruptly, and despise the Lord. Specific examples include accusations of ritual activities being odious performances, oppression instead of protection of the vulnerable, rulers consorting with thieves, rampant bribery, and a corrupt court system which serves not the poor but the interests of the judges.

Numerous images of Zion are included in this chapter. Daughter Zion (1:8) is compared to a hut in a field, a besieged city. In 1:21, the once "faithful city" Zion is called a "whore." Finally, after a fiery transformative purification, the city will be restored to her previous status (1:26) and be called "city of righteousness" and "faithful city."

A. The Condition of Zion (1:7–9)

1:7: The land is in a state of desolation: cities are burned, aliens have overthrown the country. The sorry result of the enemy attack is made more

---

14. Lack, *La symbolique de livre d'Isaïe*. Lack reads chs. 1 and 65–66 as an inclusio for the entire book (p. 35). Key words and themes of ch. 1 are repeated and elaborated in chs. 65–66 (see pp. 139–40). Of special interest in his stylistic analyses (pp. 149–230) are the poems of Zion presented as a maternal archetype.

15. For the development of Zion within the book of Isaiah, see Ulrich Berges, "Personifications and Prophetic Voices of Zion in Isaiah and Beyond," in *The Elusive Prophet* (OTS; ed. J. de Moor; Leiden: Brill, 2001), 54–82. His work is of special interest for this paper in that he shows how, when reading the book of Isaiah from beginning to end, Zion more and more resembles a female servant figure.

palpable by the images. The soil is "devoured." The image of "consuming" or "eating" the land recalls what the marauding enemy does as it storms through the attacked country, stripping the fields of produce, seizing food wherever it can be found. It also recalls the image of a devouring sword (1:20) that slaughters. Reading in light of 1:8, the agricultural context of the similes of Zion like a "booth in a vineyard" or "shelter in a cucumber field" can call up an even more concrete feature, that of locusts literally consuming the land as in Joel 1. The figure of consuming takes on different features, one from the agricultural setting, another from the language of warfare, both of which would be well understood by the eighth century audience of the southern kingdom.

"Desolation" (שממה occurs twice in 1:7) for some commentators is seen as an image of hostile military action.[16] Others consider it a reference to an earthquake.[17] In the context of the eighth century B.C.E., it certainly could refer to more than one event in Judah's past.[18] But read as describing the state of Daughter Zion, it is a figure of the city as a desolate woman, abandoned by her husband.[19] NJPS translates "your land is a waste," and "a wasteland as overthrown by strangers" which may have echoes of other realities, perhaps with eschatological overtones.

"Like an alien takeover": The construct noun "takeover" (מהפכה) appears elsewhere in the Bible always as a simile for the destruction of Sodom and Gomorrah (e.g., Isa 13:19, "God's *overthrow* of Sodom and Gomorrah"; see also Deut 29:22; Jer 49:18; 50:40; Amos 4:11). Only here in Isaiah is an alien action against the country described in the same way as God's action against Sodom and Gomorrah. This is a hint of what is to come in the more direct comparison in 1:9.

1:8: Daughter Zion is in a pathetic state. The first two similes describe situations familiar in a rural setting: a booth in a vineyard, a hut in a cucumber

---

16. Joseph Blenkinsopp, *Isaiah 1–39* (AB 19; New York: Doubleday, 2000), 183.
17. John H. Hayes and Stuart A. Irvine, eds, *Isaiah, the Eighth Century Prophet: His Times and His Preaching* (Nashville: Abingdon, 1987), 69–73.
18. Blenkinsopp, *Isaiah 1–39*, 183.
19. See L. Zalcman, "Ambiguity and Assonance at Zephaniah II 4," *VT* 36 (1986): 367. In his discussion of the destruction of four Philistine cities, Zalcman provides an example of an elaborate sequence of puns in which cities are personified as women who suffer the worst fates endured by women: abandonment (העזב), spinsterhood or abandonment by a husband-to-be (שממה), divorce (כריתות), and barrenness (עקרה). The passive participle עזובה occurs five times in the HB, three in Isa 54:6; 60:15; 62:4. In Isa 54:6 the reference is to an abandoned wife, in 60:15 and 62:4 Zion is the referent. In 62:4 עזובה and שממה are parallel terms, both describing the state of Zion. In Isa 1:7 שממה is an image of Zion as an unmarried or spurned woman.

field. Blenkinsopp translates "lean-to" and "shack" emphasizing the precarious nature of impermanent structures.[20] A city once capital of a nation and residence of an anointed king has been reduced to a ramshackle structure in a vegetable patch. These concrete images can bring to mind the contrast of what a once secure city had been to its current pitiful and very reduced circumstances.

The third simile "like a city under siege" (or "under guard") uses language of military confrontation. While scholars generally relate this reference to Sennacherib's siege of Jerusalem during Hezekiah's kingship, others see it referring to any period during an enemy attack on a city.[21] Like the generalized language of many of the Psalms, such an image can function in a wide variety of situations.

1:9: The reference to Sodom and Gomorrah compares the total destruction of these cities to the almost total destruction of Zion. The similes "we would have been like Sodom, we would resemble Gomorrah" can function fully only in a community familiar with the account in Gen 19. God rains down on Sodom and Gomorrah a sulfurous fire from heaven and destroys the cities, their inhabitants, and all the vegetation of the "soil." They are annihilated; they are burned as if in a kiln. Nothing remains.

Daughter Zion's fate is almost but not quite as bad. At least God left "a little remnant." Zion, though besieged, still stands. However, cities have been burned, the soil has been consumed. The similes in 1:9 compare total destruction of Sodom and Gomorrah to almost total destruction of Daughter Zion. Here alien invaders are almost but not quite as powerful as God.

The Sodom and Gomorrah motif also hints at another feature of comparison: the serious nature of the sins of those who have rejected the Lord (1:4). Such a comparison is so shocking that it may have been missed by the listeners who perhaps did not imagine themselves quite as unregenerate as those evil cities. But the word of the Lord identifies the sinful nation with "rulers of Sodom, and people of Gomorrah" and in the next section (1:10–15) accuses them of specific ritual offenses. God's reaction to these offenses makes it clear that they are serious.

---

20. Blenkinsopp, *Isaiah 1–39*, 184.
21. Roy F. Melugin, "Figurative Speech and the Reading of Isaiah 1 as Scripture," 284.

B. God's Reactions to the Once-Faithful City (1:12–26)

God's reaction to ritual offenses in 1:14 illustrates another feature of figurative language.

The usual translation of שנאה נפשי is "my soul hates." Luis Alonso Schökel cautions against a "hasty *spiritualization* of what is perceived by the senses" when translating images.[22] The word נפש is all too often and too quickly translated "soul" when it can refer to something more concrete. When it can be understood as "neck" or "throat" it should be translated that way. Isaiah 1:14 could be translated "I feel nausea" as in the reaction of the throat to a distasteful thing. Other renderings could be "your feasts and festivals stick in my throat" or "make me sick," or the more colloquial "I've had it up to here!"

Likewise, relatively benign translations of ritual festivals as a "burden," or of God saying "I am weary of carrying" do not adequately describe the effect these odious behaviors have on God. Reading the *nip'al* of לאה as being impatient or incapable or tired of something communicates more effectively the strong response of God: for example, "I have no patience with this dead weight," or "I'm sick of dragging around this load."

Vivid descriptions of the relationship between God and the people who committed vile offenses in ritual and toward the underprivileged in eighth century Judah (1:10–20) need further explication. References to body parts in the Bible are sometimes in danger of becoming dead metaphors especially when interpreters read or translate them as if all generally understand what the metaphor "means." Isaiah 1:12 describes people coming to God in ritual: תבאו לראות פני. The notion of people coming to God in ritual situations is often translated by the phrase "when you come to appear before me" as in 1:12 (e.g., NRSV and NJPS when "you come to appear before me," or AB "you come to appear in my presence"). Watts explains his translation "come to appear before me" and avoids speaking of actually seeing God because "the OT teaches that one may not see the face of God and live."[23] In a paper presented at the annual meeting of the SBL in 2008, Ziony Zevit commented on translations of Isa 1:12.[24] His reading of Isa 1:12 ("when you come to see my

---

22. Schökel, *A Manual of Hebrew Poetics*, 102. A lexicalized image is one which "due to excessive use has lost its reference to the sense object." Part of the problem with certain images is the "lack of imagination and perception" on the part of some exegetes. However, a lexicalized image "may regain its sense quality when used by a skilled writer."

23. John D. W. Watts, *Isaiah 1–33* (WBC; Waco, Tex.: Word, 1985), 21.

24. Ziony Zevit, "Seeing God in All the Right Places" (paper presented at the annual

face" rather than "when you come to appear before me") presents the reader with a more concrete image for what it means to bring offerings to God. Zevit's discussion is convincing. A literal reading of Isa 1:12 allows the image to function by challenging readers to come to terms with the reality that the Bible asserts two different views regarding seeing the face of God. Neither of these theologies should be allowed to supersede or deny the opposing view.

Descriptions and references to various body parts of God and humans abound in 1:11–25. God's face (as above in 1:12), God's neck or throat (1:14), God's eyes (1:15), and God's mouth (1:20) are involved with those who are present at the offensive ritual actions. The human hands (1:12) contain unwanted offerings, are stretched out to God in prayer and filled with blood (1:15). God refuses to take offerings from such hands, refuses to look at the offerings, refuses to listen to many prayers. God demands of these people that they "remove your evil doings from before my eyes" (מנגד עיני). While the image of the hand of God usually is associated with military might and strength, in Isa 1:25 it is the hand of a smelter stoking a furnace to remove the impurities from the waste products of precious metals. The latter image calls up a powerful craftsman creating and perfecting a work of art rather than a warrior using strength in the destructive activities of battle.

The reference in 1:20 to the mouth of the Lord is an unusual oracular phrase found three times in the book of Isaiah and only in Isaiah.[25] The phrase כי פי יהוה דבר "for the mouth of the Lord has spoken" occurs in Isa 1:20; 40:5; 58:14 (Mic 4:4 uses this phrase with an addition, כי־פי יהוה צבאות דבר). In Isa 1:21 God promises that those who listen will eat the good of the land, and those who rebel will be eaten by the sword. In Isa 58 God rejects fasting as a way to gain God's attention, and promises that those who care for the poor and hungry in their midst will feed on the inheritance of Jacob. In both Isa 1:21 and Isa 58:14 the mouth of God warns against false piety in worship.[26] Translations that present a more concrete image of God's presence could indeed be more threatening to people whose behaviors lacked

---

meeting of the SBL, Boston, Mass., Nov. 24, 2008). The expression as found in Exod 34:23–24, Deut 31:11, and Isa 1:12 means literally "to see the face of God," *not* "to come before" God. NRSV notes a variant translation of Isa 1:12 "appear before me" as "see my face."

25. Michael Fishbane, *Biblical Interpretation in Ancient Israel* (Oxford: Clarendon, 1985).

26. Perhaps this rare phrase has some larger significance in the book of Isaiah since it is found only three times in the Hebrew Bible, once each in the usual tripartite divisions of the book.

righteousness when it meant seeing God's face, and hearing words from God's mouth rather than "appearing before God."

In this opening chapter of the book of Isaiah, Zion's destruction is not complete annihilation. God leaves a "bit of a remnant." The only difference between the devastation of Zion and that of Sodom and Gomorrah is that there is a little bit left of Zion. The rulers of Sodom disgust and repel God by their proliferation of offerings and multiplication of ritual activities.[27] The images used to describe the relationship of God to humans in this chapter are dynamic because of their vividness, their concrete sensory features. Translations which highlight the tangibility of images and avoid "hasty spiritualization" allow readers to use more fully their imaginations in an experience of a relationship with God.

II. Figurative Language in Isaiah 66:7–14

The introductory chapter of Isaiah describes the Daughter Zion first as a besieged city (1:8), then a faithless city and a whore (1:21–23), and finally restored as "a city of righteousness, the faithful city" (1:26–27). Relationships with God are possible for those who survive the purificatory actions of God and are part of the restored faithful city. The concluding chapter in the book of Isaiah (in particular 66:7–14) presents an extended metaphor for this restoration, and a dramatically different view of the divine/human relationship.

I have selected this passage for several reasons. First, during a seminar on the book of Isaiah at the College of St. Catherine, my students were fascinated by the wildly differing translations and interpretations of the images of Zion/Jerusalem and God in these as well as other sections of Isaiah. Students represent one of the communities that decide which images are important, and who therefore help to develop and transmit interpretations to a wider community.[28] Second, this section coming in the last chapter of the book offers a hopeful vision of the future of Zion/Jerusalem to which the first chapter alludes.[29] Third, Last Isaiah presents an image of the relationship between

---

27. I will return later to this text to touch on how these verses have been misappropriated in a contemporary setting.

28. Melugin's questions about who decides what imagery is important and in which communities interpretations are developed are relevant here. As teachers we hope that students' lives may be transformed by their classroom experiences and that they will become transmitters of knowledge.

29. The vision in Isa 66 is not an entirely rosy one. The last line of the poem in 66:7–14 ends with God's rage against the enemies, and the conclusion of the book in 66:24 is so

God and Zion and an interaction between the two that is dramatically different from other divine/human relationships elsewhere in Isaiah, and is perhaps unique in the prophetic corpus.

Numerous poetic techniques add to the drama of this poem, but I will deal primarily with the metaphor of motherhood. Extending throughout Isa 66:7-14, various figures describe the process of birth, the nursing of the young baby, and the enjoyment of the baby in the mother's care. The metaphor is enhanced by mention of key body parts, a technique also evident in Isa 1. The concrete language appeals directly to the senses. It is lavish, almost excessive.

A. Zion/Jerusalem as Mother (66:7-12)

66:7: The first lines of the poem begin *in medias res*, describing an unidentified woman in the process of an unusual birth. The lines are heavily weighted (readers of Isa 40-66 are familiar with the technique of piling up words in lines) with words for the birth process: "writhing in labor" (חיל), "bearing a child" (ילד), "birth pains" (חבל), "delivering" (מלט). What makes these common experiences uncommon is the order of the events. Birth comes before labor, delivery before birth pains. The result of the seemingly impossible order of things is the delivery of a "male" (זכר). The subject undergoing this amazing experience has yet to be identified.

66:8: Astonishment and amazement are registered in the next four lines of 66:8 in the form of interrogatives. Who has heard of or seen such things? "Can it be…?" Two verbs from 66:7 are repeated: חיל and ילד in different binyanim. The subject gives birth and delivers the country and people. That the birth is almost instantaneous since it happens "in one day," "at once," is another unusual, unbelievable aspect of the birth process. The subject of the verbs is finally identified specifically as Zion: she is the one who writhes in labor, has birth pains, and gives birth to her children. The anonymous male of 66:7 is now identified as the offspring of Zion, "her children."

66:9: God asserts involvement in Zion's miraculous birth in the form of rhetorical questions. Images used to describe the process include breaking ("the membrane" Watts' translation),[30] and delivering. God assists at the birth acting as the midwife (המוליד).[31] The rhetorical questions "would I break and

---

grim that Jewish practice repeats the more positive 66:23 after 66:24.

30. John D. W. Watts, *Isaiah 34-66* (WBC; Waco, Tex.: Word, 1987; rev. ed. 2005), 358.
31. Since the noun is masculine, should one read "midhusband"?

not deliver? be a midwife and not deliver?" emphasize God's active involvement in seeing the birth come to fruition. As midwife God would surely not shut up the womb.

66:10–11: Jerusalem and all her inhabitants are called to rejoice. After the child is born it will nurse. The child will "nurse" (ינק), "suck" or "slurp" (*mss*),[32] and be sated, comforted. Effusive language highlights the deep satisfaction and exquisite delight (התענג) that the child experiences at the comforting breast (משד תנחמיה), and from the "generous" (NJB) or "glorious" (NRSV) "nipple" (מזיז כבודה).[33] The mother's body furnishes comforting and lavish sustenance.

66:12: This verse moves from the image of the glorious nipple that filled the child to that of the glory or wealth (כבוד) of nations.[34] Similes for prosperity and wealth of nations, that is, the flowing of a river and the gushing torrent of a wadi, echo the description in 66:11 of sustaining and overflowing liquids. In both 66:11 and 12 generous quantities and effusive delivery portray an embarrassment of riches.

"And you will nurse": MT reads וינקתם as the end of 66:12a, but *BHS* and many translations (e.g., AB) read with Qumran "your infants" (literally, "your suckers") and consider it the beginning of the next line. The NJPS translation "and you shall drink of it" highlights the motif of nursing from 66:11 and ties it to the gushing waters image in 66:12. Perhaps the phrase acts as a hinge between the two sections, since the following (66:12b and 13) return to the mother image.

The child is carried at the side (on the hip), and dandled or played with on the knees. Thus far the images of giving birth, nursing, and caring for the child are actions of the mother. This is not meant to be a claim that fathers do not carry or play lovingly with children. In these verses, however, the image is of a mother.

---

32. Joseph Blenkinsopp, *Isaiah 56–66* (AB 19B; New York: Doubleday, 2003), 303 note f.

33. Blenkinsopp, *Isaiah 56–66*, 303 note g. Based on "an Arabic cognate the meaning is probably 'teat, nipple.'" Blenkinsopp further notes that "the versions are paraphrastic."

34. See the article by Gary Stansell in this volume, which speaks to the economic elements in Last Isaiah.

B. God as Zion/Jerusalem's Mother (66:13)

Up to this point, Zion has been portrayed as the mother by virtue of references to her male child (66:7) and her children (66:8). The word "mother" appears only once in ch. 66, in a simile that pairs the word "mother" (אם) with God. In God's own words, "like a man whose mother comforts him, I will comfort you." All of this mothering activity is described by the root of נחם in a tricolon;[35] it occurs with three different subjects: as a mother comforts, I, God will comfort, and Jerusalem will be the place of comfort.[36]

The twofold נחמו נחמו in 40:1 is an important motif indicating a change in the divine-human relationship wherein God commands that Jerusalem be comforted and announces that her time of service is over. God's comforting care is described in a variety of images throughout Isa 40–66. Several images in Last Isaiah describe God providing the thirsty with water and/or milk (e.g., 41:17–18; 43:20; 48:21; 49:9–10; 55:1). Whereas in the previous chapters, the sources of the liquids are rivers, fountains, pools, springs, and rock (recalling Exod 17:1–7), in 66:11–13 it is God as mother who is the source of the nourishing milk. This dramatic image forms an inclusio with Isa 40:1. The images identify God as the source and underline the relationship of God's relationship with Zion as mother to child.

C. People will Flourish like Grass (66:14)

Another change or reversal of imagery occurs in the simile comparing the sprouting of grass to the flourishing of the bones or body of the people. In Isa 40:6–7 the ephemeral nature of people is likened to that of grass and flowers which wither and fade when God's breath blows on it. The simile is meant as a contrast to the permanence of the word of God. However, in 66:14 grass is depicted as a flourishing plant that sends out shoots. The image of bones sprouting like a plant is striking, almost bizarre.[37] Grass, an image of

---

35. Recalling the comforting breast in 66:11.
36. Christl M. Maier, *Gender, Space, and the Sacred in Ancient Israel* (Minneapolis: Fortress, 2008), 203–4. Maier reads a double meaning in 66:13b. In addition to the meaning "in Jerusalem" the preposition can also be translated "by" or "through" understanding Jerusalem as the "mediator of divine blessing and salvation."
37. Others read "bodies" (NRSV) or "limbs" (NJPS). Joseph Blenkinsopp, *Isaiah 40–55* (AB 19A; New York: Doubleday, 2002), 307 reads "bones" and cites the figure used in individual psalms and laments as a "deeply internalized" expression of emotion of joy or terror that is felt in the bones. The graphic figure of bones sprouting like plants in 66:14 can

a withered dried up plant, is likened to people in 40:6. The contrast between the images in 40:6–7 and 66:14 is extreme. The latter is awash with images of abundant fertility most associated with life-giving liquids of milk and water. The people will see these marvelous results, and the heart of the people will rejoice.

D. Images of Women in Isaiah 66:7–14 and in Ancient Near Eastern Texts

It is not a new thing for scholars to comment on depictions of God as mother.[38] Darr rightly sees Jerusalem as "a central concern of the book [of Isaiah] from beginning to end."[39] Jerusalem is personified as "bride, mother, wayward wife, childless widow"; these are the usual commonplaces associated with women. Darr also notes that the metaphor for woman connotes the usual negative aspects attributed to women, including "ignorance, inexperience, and naiveté," as in Isa 3:12. A common use of the images of writhing in birth pains (חיל, ילד) are as figures of fear and anguish before a threatening enemy. (See also Isa 13:6–8; 23:5; 26:17–18 for images of cowering in fear.)

Cynthia Chapman[40] compares images of women in Assyrian inscriptions and in preexilic prophets (e.g., Nahum), in Jeremiah and Ezekiel, and in Second Isaiah, and asserts that all have negative connotations.[41] Assyrian inscriptions and biblical prophets "shared a common ancient Near Eastern literary tradition concerning the recording of warfare wherein the same gendered metaphors were used to associate victory with perfected masculinity

---

also be seen as a contrast to the equally graphic image of the exposed corpses of people who have rebelled against God in 66:24.

38. M. E. Gruber, "The Motherhood of God in Second Isaiah," *RB* 90 (1983): 351–59; J. J. Schmitt, "Motherhood of God and Zion as Mother," *RB* 92 (1985): 557–69; Katheryn Pfisterer Darr, "Two Unifying Female Images in the Book of Isaiah," in *Uncovering Ancient Stones: Essays in Memory of H. Neil Richardson* (ed. Lewis M. Hopfe; Winona Lake, Ind.: Eisenbrauns, 1994), 17–30; Julie A. Foster, "The Motherhood of God: The Use of *Hyl* as God-Language in the Hebrew Scriptures," in *Uncovering Ancient Stones: Essays in Memory of H. Neil Richardson* (ed. Lewis M. Hopfe; Winona Lake, Ind.: Eisenbrauns, 1994), 93–102; Sarah J. Dille, *Mixing Metaphors: God as Mother and Father in Deutero-Isaiah* (JSOTSup 398; London: T&T Clark, 2004).

39. Darr, "Two Unifying Female Images," 23.

40. Chapman, *Gendered Language of Warfare*. See chs. 3 and 4.

41. See also Gale Yee, *Poor Banished Children of Eve: Woman as Evil in the Hebrew Bible* (Minneapolis: Fortress, 2003) for discussions of similar portrayals of women in prophetic texts.

and defeat with the feminization of men."[42] Assyrian materials focused on the masculinity of the king as demonstrated by success in battle, and contrasted this with the failed masculinity, that is, feminization of the conquered. Biblical authors portrayed their God in much the same way as Assyrians did their king, so that prophets viewed Yhwh as a perfect example of incomparable masculinity, and described the defeat of Israel/Judah and its soldiers who failed to defend their land with the feminine images of fallen Jerusalem.

Some examples of appropriate gender roles for women are "weaving, childbearing, marriage, fear of battle, need for protection."[43] For soldiers appropriate features include the following: going out to battle, living in the camp, and preparing for siege, as well as the use of uniforms and weapons. When two areas or "domains," that is, woman and soldier, are brought together, they overlap, but only in certain ways. Features that "woman" and "defeated soldier" have in common, for example, are weakness, fear, submission. Defeated soldiers are characterized by weakness in battle, fear of fighting, inability to manipulate weaponry. Other points of comparison that affect both the image of woman and of the defeated soldier yield the following: femininity is equated with failed masculinity; with defeat, weakness/docility, being blameworthy, vulnerability, being in need of protection, being emotional and fearful, lacking in ability, and nakedness. The model of failed masculinity also is described as inability to produce heirs, failure to provide for and protect family, losing land, being controlled or possessed, having low social/sexual status, being the object of aggression rather than the aggressor.

The metaphors in Isa 66:7–14 depart from the above conventions with respect to images of women as weak, vulnerable, and lacking in ability, and they also do not conform to the view of God as the model of "perfectly realized masculinity." The image of mother defies the conventional commonplaces associated with women. In Isa 66 this image has no negative connotations. The stereotypical way of describing people's response to the threat of attack in the figure of a woman in the throes of labor pains, anguish, and fear (e.g., Isa 13:6–8; 23:5; 26:17–18 and elsewhere in the prophets) has been replaced by heretofore unheard of images: speedy birth, surprise at the unexpected, rejoicing and celebration, and enjoyment of nourishment and comfort.

More than any other texts in Isaiah, and perhaps in the prophetic corpus, the metaphor in which God is compared to a woman transforms the conventional biblical and ancient Near Eastern cultural models of masculinity and

---

42. Chapman, *Gendered Language of Warfare*, 142.
43. Ibid., 13.

femininity. Chapman's thesis is that gender metaphors of preexilic prophets were used by later biblical prophets, and that these later prophets transformed the metaphors for their own use.[44] Isaiah 66:7–14 does more than transform the image; it defies and overturns the model. While Zion is usually the figure of people either righteous and just or rebellious and sinful (e.g., Isa 1:21, 26–27), in 66:13 God is now compared to Zion. God is described as a woman, a nursing mother. The mention of specific body parts, for example, breast and nipple, makes the image more concrete, and feminizes God. The commonplaces usually associated with an ideal husband and ideal king, that is, able to provide for and protect family, are now associated with a mother, who provides for children.

While God-language in the Bible often uses masculine images, Isa 66:7–14 uses images that are undoubtedly feminine.[45] God is like the mother who supports, nourishes, and protects the child. The commonplaces associated with God interact with the commonplaces associated with mother, woman: they overlap; both God and mother/woman are understood differently. The figure of the mother provides a different way of imagining and relating to God. The figure of God as mother also presents a new way to relate to and imagine mothers and women. Here as nowhere else in the prophets the transformed feminine commonplaces are elevated by association with the God of Israel. The conventional negative features of the domain of woman are replaced by positive, nonconventional features.

How would the images in 66:7–14 be understood by the prophets' audiences? How would such images function in the ancient Near Eastern world of cultural commonplaces? Chapman's work on gendered language is extremely helpful for understanding the symbolic world out of which the book of Isaiah arose. Since, as Chapman demonstrates, the prophets typically portrayed God as the model of perfectly realized masculinity and women as weak, vulnerable, docile, and in need of protection, the image of God as a woman, a

---

44. Ibid., 169. Chapman deals only with texts in Isa 40–55. She does not cite Isa 66 in her book.

45. Other texts in Isaiah that use feminine imagery for God include 42:13–14 and 49:14, and perhaps 46:3–4. Hanne Løland (*Silent or Salient Gender?: The Interpretation of Gendered God-Language in the Hebrew Bible, Exemplified in Isaiah 42, 46 and 49* [Tübingen: Mohr Siebeck, 2008]) reads בטן in 46:3 as God's womb in which God carried the child from conception, rather than from the moment of birth. I am not convinced that this is a clear example of God having a womb or that it is a reference to carrying a child through pregnancy. The repetition of the archaic preposition מני and the parallels between בטן and רחם allow a variety of interpretations. Loland's extended discussion of terminology in 46:3–4 demonstrates that her translation is one of many possible legitimate readings.

pregnant woman, a nursing woman, must have evoked a response from the audience. It can easily be seen how the unlikely features of the image of God as mother in Isa 66:7–14 could catch the attention of the first audiences to the message. Bringing to mind all the concrete images of a woman writhing in labor and giving birth, and then putting these images together with God as the subject could be startling to an audience more used to imagining God as a majestic and powerful king. Moving to the portrayal of God as a mother nursing a child who slurps with delight from her glorious nipple might easily cause an audience used to a quite different kind of glory to stop and listen to this astounding description. Surely the reaction would be mixed. Perhaps the description would arouse the listeners to react negatively to a new and unconventional way of thinking about God. Perhaps it would arouse discussion. However these images function, they did so well enough to be included in the canon.

III. Contemporary Interpretations and Uses of Texts

Melugin asked various questions about the function of figurative language (see above). He focused frequently on questions of how language can work to transform human life in both the ancient world and communities in our own time. He also asked how poetry can shape life and identity.

I chose the particular images from ch. 1 not only to reflect on the concreteness of the language, but also because in recent times this part of the Bible Isa 1:9 has taken on a "life" of its own. It is an excellent example of how figurative language, in this case a simile, has been misappropriated.

On several occasions students have brought their questions to class after hearing references to Isaiah on the nightly news, or seeing it in print on the front pages of local newspapers or in magazines. One student reported an incident that happened during the funeral of Matthew Shepherd, a Colorado man who was pistol whipped and killed because he was a homosexual. People claiming to be a Christian group stood outside the church and held up a poster which read "God hates fags Isaiah 1:9." They were protesting his identity as a gay man at his funeral. It was their claim that Isa 1:9 proved that God hated gay people. The same group has appeared with the same citation from Isaiah at protests against gay marriage in various states, and even at funerals of soldiers, not because they were gay, but because the group claimed that the war is a curse of God on rampant homosexuality in our country.

I included this example of a contemporary misreading of Isa 1:9 at our session of the Society of Biblical Literature in 2003. One of my colleagues spoke to me afterwards asking why I spoke of this at a gathering of professional Bible scholars. In his view it was unnecessary to include this example because he said that all of us in the audience could understand that this was not the meaning of Isa 1:9. While that might have been the case, nonetheless it is an example of how certain communities claiming to be based on the Bible continue in our own day to misappropriate texts.

How can texts such as Isa 1:7–26 function to transform people today? As teachers as well as scholars, we can help our students and other communities to read the text. A careful reading of Isa 1:9 does not say what the poster claims it does. Reading this verse in its larger context does show what God hates—the feasts and festivals, the trappings of religiosity without the observance of covenant injunctions. What God desires is "seeking justice, rescuing the oppressed, defending the orphan, pleading for the widow." As teachers and scholars we can help our students and others to learn how to read what a text says, and then explore the meaning behind the words and images.

The striking images in Isa 66:7–14 also have the power to shape and transform today's audiences. They have the power to prompt strong reactions both negative and positive in contemporary communities. The audience of students at the College of St. Catherine were taken aback by the failure or the timidity of some scholars to pay sufficient attention to Isa 66:7–14. They disagreed strongly with John Oswalt who asserted that in 66:13 there is a "careful distancing of God from the nursing motif ... for the same reason that God is never said to impregnate or to give birth."[46] Nor did they take to his idea that the Bible must "protect the truth of the transcendence of God." They applauded Claus Westermann's assertion that "the witness borne to [Yhwh] breaks through the reserve which elsewhere it observes so strictly, and associates feminine predications with him," while at the same time noting Westermann's use of the masculine pronoun.[47] They lamented that in general the feminine images were underplayed, not given enough attention, or went unnoticed.

It is an unhappy fact that the insights of Last Isaiah with respect to motherhood/women as well as startling language about God have not yet made it in a widespread way into the twenty-first century, especially in the larger religious/cultural experience. This includes official church statements, such as the example from the Catechism of the Catholic Church on the revelation

---

46. John N. Oswalt, *The Book of Isaiah: Chapters 40–66* (NICOT; Grand Rapids: Eerdmans, 1998), 678.

47. Claus Westermann, *Isaiah 40–66: A Commentary* (trans. David M. G. Stalker; OTL; Philadelphia: Westminster, 1969), 420.

of God as Trinity. This document asserts that God is neither man nor woman while continuing to refer to God as "he" (see Appendix II).

It is all too clear that in many metaphors, similes, and other language referring to women, the associated commonplaces for women are negative in the extreme. Comparing bad football players to "girls in petticoats" is meant to be an insult to the football players; it is surely an insult to girls. Arnold Schwarzenegger's infamous "girly men" taunt does nothing to enhance the image of women. The author of Isa 66:7–14 had it right. This author's insight about the full humanity of women still remains to be understood by many contemporary audiences.

The renewed Isaiah Group took on the goal of exploring the potential power of Isaianic figurative language in the shaping of a vision or multiple visions concerning the interrelationship between God and humans.[48] In this article I have attended to the nature of certain images and to how their very concreteness helps an attentive reader to go beyond the world of the senses to discover something more.

Describing the divine–human relationship as a face-to-face encounter with God can provoke a listener to reflect on the ramifications of such a profound interaction. Comparing a city or country once beloved by God to an abandoned desolate woman has the possibility of evoking a number of different reactions, depending upon the person or community hearing the message. Someone abandoned by a beloved protector might ask how the beloved could do such a thing. Another might ask what the woman/city has done to deserve such treatment.

Who decides what imagery is most important? Experience is a key feature in recognizing and highlighting certain images. A group of students at a women's college may have reactions to images in ways that others in a different time or place have not. Being captivated by the description of God as a nursing mother is an example of how a response to figurative language is influenced by experience.

Information about the ancient Near Eastern world can help modern day readers of the Bible come to a better understanding of these ancient texts. Cynthia Chapman's work on the connections between Assyrian and biblical images shed light on how images functioned in the prophetic texts and for the prophets' audiences.

How can poetry shape life and identity? An essential feature of poetry is how words are used and arranged. The Boston Celtics were shaped and

---

48. Melugin, this volume, pp. 7 and 14–15.

empowered to great heights by their coach Red Auerbach who was aware of the importance of *how* he spoke to his team. This is not to say that Red Auerbach was a poet, but he knew the importance of words. Terry Eagleton explains that poetry and poetic imagery is "not what shuts us off from reality, but what yields us the deepest access to it."[49]

Roy Melugin's goal for the renewed Isaiah Group of the SBL was to go beyond what Isaiah scholars have done up to the present to "capture even more profoundly" what the book has to offer.[50] His interests have always spanned scholarly, academic, and pastoral concerns, and he has striven to combine these interests so that scholars, teachers, and worshiping communities could learn and be transformed by one another.

He has helped us as scholars to talk to one another, encouraged us by his own actions to be open to new and different ways of seeing texts. I have been influenced by Roy throughout my career about reading Isaiah. At first, I knew him through the ideas in his book *The Formation of Isaiah 40–55*;[51] it was an important and enduring part of my education in Isaiah scholarship. When I first met Roy and was invited to be part of the Formation of the Book of Isaiah group, it was a privilege to work with him through this new connection.

Roy has always been a model of moving forward into new uncharted territory to see what more he might learn and bring to his understanding of the biblical text. He was never afraid to admit that he had something more to learn. He invited the Isaiah group to move from a strictly diachronic approach to include synchronic readings as well, having already explored this perspective by his forays into philosophy of language, comparative literature, performative language theory, and new areas of literary criticism.

Roy was not afraid of a good argument and looked forward to discussions in which "different points of view could be freely argued."[52] One of the things he looked forward to with the formation of the renewed group was that his paper "might have stirred up enough snakes" so that we would have a "useful, and perhaps even a rip-roaring discussion." This we have done, and will continue to do with Roy in memory.

---

49. Eagleton, *How to Read a Poem*, 69.
50. Melugin, this volume, p. 7.
51. Roy F. Melugin, *The Formation of Isaiah 40–55* (BZAW 141; Berlin: de Gruyter, 1976).
52. Melugin, this volume, p. 15.

Appendix I

Translations

Isaiah 1:7-9, 14

7   Your country: a desolation,
    your cities: burned by fire.
    Your soil: right before your eyes
    aliens devour it,
    Desolation like an alien takeover.
8   Daughter Zion is left
    like a booth in a vineyard,
    like a hut in a cucumber field,
    like a city under siege.
9   If the Lord of hosts
    had not left us a little remnant
    We would be like Sodom,
    we would resemble Gomorrah....
14 Your new moons and your appointed feasts
    I hate.
    They have become to me a dead weight
    I am tired of lugging around.

Isaiah 66:7-14

7   Before she was in labor she brought forth,
    before birth pains came to her
    she delivered a male.
8   Who has heard a thing like this?
    Who saw things like these?
    Can a country be born in one day
    and a people be delivered at once?
    Yet Zion was in labor
    and brought forth her children.
9   Shall I break (the membrane)
    yet not deliver? says the Lord.
    Shall I assist at the birth (be a mid-wife/husband)
    yet shut up the womb? says your God.
10 Be glad with Jerusalem
    and rejoice with her, all you who love her,
    Exult with her in exultation,
    all you who mourn over her,

11 so that you may nurse and be satisfied
    from her comforting breast,
    so that you may drink deeply and with exquisite delight
    from her glorious nipple.
12 For thus says the Lord:
    Look, I am spreading out before her
    like a river: prosperity,
    and like an overflowing torrent:
    the wealth of nations; and you will nurse.
    At (her) side you will be carried,
    and on (her) knees you will be dandled.
13 Like a man whom his mother comforts
    So I will comfort you
    and you will be comforted in Jerusalem.
14 You will see and your heart will exult,
    and your bones like grass will sprout,
    and the hand of the Lord will be revealed to his servants,
    but rage to his enemies.

Appendix II

From *Catechism of the Catholic Church*, on the Revelation of the Trinity, # 239:

> By calling God "Father," the language of faith indicates two main things: that God is the first origin of everything and transcendent authority; and that he is at the same time goodness and loving care for all his children. God's parental tenderness can also be expressed by the image of motherhood, (fn 62, cf. Isa 66:13; Ps 131:2) which emphasizes God's immanence, the intimacy between Creator and creature. The language of faith thus draws on the human experience of parents, who are in a way the first representatives of God for man. But this experience also tells us that human parents are fallible and can disfigure the face of fatherhood and motherhood. We ought therefore to recall that God transcends the human distinction between the sexes. He is neither man nor woman; he is God. He also transcends human fatherhood and motherhood, although he is their origin and standard: (fn 63, cf. Ps 27:10; Eph 3:14; Isa 49:15) no one is father as God is Father.

A Bitter Memory: Isaiah's Commission in Isaiah 6:1–13

A. Joseph Everson

> Go and tell this people: hear but do not understand!
> see but do not perceive!
> Make the heart of this people fat!
> Make their ears heavy!
> Shut their eyes!
> lest seeing with their eyes and hearing with their ears and understanding with their heart, they return and be healed! (Isa 6:9–10)

The Isaiah scroll presents us with a richly woven fabric of themes, images, and motifs that appear and then reappear in later texts. Among them are images relating to deafness and hearing, blindness and sight, fatness of heart (insensitivity), and compassion. Probably no text in the scroll of Isaiah has presented a more puzzling dilemma for the interpreter than the images set before us in the text of Isa 6:1–13. We want to ask, Did Isaiah really have such a frightening commission? Can we trust our own abilities to hear, see, or understand his message?[1]

Brevard Childs has written concerning this text: "Needless to say, the subject of divine hardening is one of the most difficult topics in the Bible. It appears to run in the face of God's very nature. Does not the God of Israel will only good for his people? Was not the purpose of divine election to bestow life, not death?"[2]

In this essay I contend that the text is most properly understood from the perspective of the post-exilic era, possibly as early as the time of Ezra and Nehemiah, at a time when the scroll was approaching its present sixty

---

1. This essay originally appeared in the *Gurukul Journal of Theological Studies* 17 (January 2006): 118–34. Reprinted by permission.
2. Brevard S. Childs, *Isaiah* (OTL; Louisville, Ky.: Westminster John Knox, 2001), 56.

six chapter form. From that vantage point, Isa 6:1–13 preserves a memory of the faithful witness of the prophet Isaiah for whom this scroll is named. The text is part of a larger portrait that is preserved throughout the entire Isaiah scroll and needs to be heard together with later texts.[3] It is one in a collection of "bitter memories" concerning Judah and Jerusalem gathered in chs. 1–12, followed by "bitter memories" about Judah among the nations preserved in chs. 13–35.[4] Each of these sections, chs. 2–12 and chs. 13–35, has been edited and shaped in light of the destruction of Jerusalem in 587 B.C.E. and the fall of Babylon following the death of Nebuchadnezzar in 562 B.C.E. Those were events that changed the world for people in Judah. In the post-exilic era, a new generation of people clearly understood that Isaiah's announcements of impending judgment in the opening sections of the scroll had come to pass.[5] Jerusalem and Judah had been reduced to rubble. Babylon and other nations had also known the horrors of war.[6] In a very real sense, therefore, the two opening sections of the scroll (chs. 2–12 and 13–35) constitute theological commentary on past events in Judah and the surrounding world. It is against the backdrop of that earlier history that dramatic contrasts are set forth in the central message of the scroll in chs. 40–66. The text in Isa 6:1–13 preserves a memory against which later texts will speak of the importance of hearing (שמע), seeing (ראה) and knowing (ידע) in texts such as Isa 29:18; 35:5; 40:1–11; 42:18–25; and 43:8–13.

I. Approaches to Isaiah 6:1–13

In 1927, Theodore H. Robinson summarized the development of prophetic literature in terms of three stages: First, there were small independent oracles that were collected and preserved by disciples of a prophet. Later, disciples gathered the individual oracles into collections, adding new material and

---

3. On the emergence of the "final form" of the canonical text and so-called "canonical theology," see further, Barry A. Jones, "Canon of the Old Testament," in *Eerdmans Dictionary of the Bible* (Grand Rapids: Eerdmans, 2000), 215–17; Brevard S. Childs, *Introduction to the Old Testament as Scripture* (Philadelphia: Fortress, 1979); James A. Sanders, *From Sacred Story to Sacred Text* (Philadelphia: Fortress, 1987).

4. When I speak of "bitter memories," I am thinking specifically of the imagery of באשים "wild or bitter grapes" in Isa 5:4 and the use of מר "bitter" in Isa 5:20.

5. The classic test of the "true prophet" is set forth in Deut 18:20–22: "If a prophet speaks in the name of the Lord but the thing does not take place or prove true, it is a word that the Lord has not spoken" (v. 22).

6. Chris Hedges, *War is a Force that Gives Us Meaning* (New York: Random House, 2002) is a compelling contemporary study of the horrors of war in every age.

arranging the oracles into new thematic arrangements. Still later, these collections were reorganized and expanded into what today is the final form of the text. An entire generation of twentieth-century scholars tended to follow Robinson's analysis, drawing also from the form-critical analysis of Hugo Gressmann and the concerns for genre analysis of Hermann Gunkel. It is interesting that still today, many scholars still focus on Robinson's first stage, the attempt to discover the actual words of the original prophet. This approach inevitably involves critical judgments about what is "authentic" and what is "later redaction" in a text.[7]

In recent years, however, a growing number of scholars have recognized that the attempt to discern earlier stages in the formation of the scroll is a highly subjective task.

Canonical criticism provides a focus for looking at biblical texts in a more comprehensive manner. Rather than searching for "authentic words" from an original author, the focus is on discerning the theological meaning of a text as it is found in the redacted form of the scroll, while still acknowledging that there are earlier written and oral sources behind the present text. In any study of Isa 6:1–13, the question of perspective is critical. Where do you stand to hear the text? Against what historical background should the text be interpreted? How is the text related to other passages within the scroll? Because the themes in Isa 6 reappear in later poetry in the scroll, the text of Isa 6:1–13 needs also to be interpreted primarily as a memory from the post-exilic perspective. The attempt to do otherwise, that is, to interpret this text from an earlier historical setting runs the repeated risk of distorting both the literary and the kerygmatic intentions of those who preserved the memory within the Isaiah scroll.

---

7. See essays in Roy F. Melugin and Marvin A. Sweeney, eds., *New Visions of Isaiah* (JSOTSup 214; Sheffield: Sheffield Academic Press, 1996); Craig C. Broyles and Craig A. Evans, eds., *Writing and Reading the Scroll of Isaiah: Studies of an Interpretive Tradition* (VTSup 70.1; Leiden: Brill, 1997). Marvin A. Sweeney, *Isaiah 1–39 with an Introduction to Prophetic Literature* (FOTL 16; Grand Rapids: Eerdmans, 1996) combines both synchronic and diachronic analysis and uses a fourfold redactional approach, working back from the completed scroll in the time of Ezra and Nehemiah, to a sixth-century redaction at the end of the Exile, to a collection dating from the time of Josiah, and to a collection dating from the end of Isaiah's lifetime.

II. The Poetic Imagery in Isaiah 6

Isaiah 6:1–13 can be analyzed in three parts: the vision account (vv. 1–4), the account of cleansing and forgiveness (vv. 5–8) and the actual commission (vv. 9–13).

A. The Appearance before the Divine Council (vv. 1–4)

In the first section (vv. 1–4), the report is set out concerning Isaiah's appearance before the heavenly court.[8] In first person singular speech, the prophet shares the report:

> Holy, holy holy is the Lord of hosts;
>   the whole earth is full of his glory.
> The pivots on the threshholds shook at the voices of those who called,
>   and the house filled with smoke. (6:3-4)

The vision report emphasizes a sense of holiness; the prophet feels a sense of awe and wonder at the experience of being in the presence of God. It is not clear if this report is the account of an inaugural call experience that resulted in Isaiah becoming a prophet, or if it is a later commissioning experience for a particular task.[9] There are parallels with other reported call visions: Moses in Exod 3:1–17, Micaiah ben Imlah in 1 Kgs 22:19–22, Jeremiah in Jer 1:4–10, and Ezekiel in Ezek 1–3.[10] In each of those texts, the common theme is the response of the prophet: awe, humility, and feelings of inadequacy at the experience of standing in the presence of God.

B. Divine Purification, Cleansing, and Forgiveness (vv. 5–8)

Regardless of how Isaiah's vision is understood, either as an initial call vision or as a later commissioning experience, the second section (vv. 5–8) clarifies that after being purified and cleansed, the prophet volunteered for a very dif-

---

8. See H. Wheeler Robinson, "The Council of Yahweh," *JTS* 45 (1944): 151–57. On call narratives, see also Norman Habel, "The Form and Significance of the Call Narratives," *ZAW* 77 (1965): 297–323.

9. For a summary of the debate, see Childs, *Isaiah*, 51–53.

10. See further, Gene M. Tucker, "The Book of Isaiah 1–39" (*NIB* 6; Nashville: Abingdon, 2001), 101–5.

ficult assignment.[11] In this section of the text, the striking contrasts between the divine and the human realms are emphasized:

> And I said:
> "Woe is me! I am lost, for I am a man of unclean lips,
> and I live among a people of unclean lips;
> yet my eyes have seen the King, the Lord of hosts!"
> Then one of the seraphs flew to me, holding a live coal that had
> been taken from the altar with a pair of tongs. The seraph touched
> my mouth with it and said:
> "Now that this has touched your lips, your guilt has departed
> and your sin is blotted out."
> Then I heard the voice of the Lord saying,
> "Whom shall I send, and who will go for us?"
> And I said,
> "Here am I; send me!" (6:5–8)

Isaiah is painfully aware that he is a human being of "unclean lips living among people of unclean lips" (6:5). It is only after he declares his unworthiness that one of the seraphim touches his mouth with a live coal and declares to him that his guilt has departed and that his sin has been blotted out (6:7).

It is interesting that the themes of divine cleansing and forgiveness have in some ways become the focal points for understanding this text, especially within Christian worship traditions. In an essay in 1991, Donald Gowan contrasted the New Testament usage of Isa 6 with the ways in which this text appears in the Roman Catholic and Protestant Revised Common Lectionary.[12] In the New Testament, Isa 6 is cited five times (Matt 13:14–15; Mark 4:12; Luke 8:10; John 12:40; and Acts 28:26–27). In the four gospel texts, Isa 6 is remembered primarily in conjunction with the inability of people to perceive, understand, or embrace the proclamation of the Christian gospel. Typical is the passage in Mark 4; the evangelist reports Jesus' telling of the parable of the sower and the seed and concludes with the words, "Let anyone

---

11. Moses does not volunteer; he is given a command at Horeb in the "burning bush" narrative and he is a very reluctant volunteer; see Exod 3–4); Micaiah's vision report is similar to the report in Isa 6 but it is a spirit that volunteers in response to the divine request, "Who will entice Ahab"; Micaiah simply reports what he has heard in the heavenly court (I Kgs 22:19–23). Jeremiah also does not volunteer but is commissioned "to pluck up and pull down, to destroy and to overthrow, to build and to plant" (Jer 1:10); Ezekiel is literally overpowered by his call vision that concludes with the words: "let those who will hear, hear; and let those who refuse to hear, refuse; for they are a rebellious house" (Ezek 3:27).

12. Donald E. Gowan, "Isaiah 6:1–8," *Int* 45 (1991): 172–76.

with ears to hear listen!" In the narrative that follows, Jesus quotes Isa 6 as he explains to the disciples:

> To you has been given the secret of the kingdom of God,
>   but for those outside, everything comes in parables; in order that
> "they may indeed look, but not perceive,
> and may indeed listen, but not understand;
> so that they may not turn again and be forgiven." (Mark 4:11–12)

In a similar way in the text from Acts, Paul uses Isa 6 to explain the inability of people to hear his message. He is remembered as saying:

> The Holy Spirit was right in saying to your ancestors
> through the prophet Isaiah,
> Go to this people and say,
> You will indeed listen, but never understand,
> you will indeed look, but never perceive.
> For this people's heart has grown dull,
> and their ears are hard of hearing,
> and they shut their eyes;
> so that they might look with their eyes,
> and listen with their ears,
> and understand with their heart and turn—
> and I would heal them. (Acts 28:26–27)

While the New Testament texts focus on the inability of people to hear, the contemporary Roman Catholic and protestant Revised Common Lectionary appears to use the text primarily to focus on discipleship and God's divine forgiveness. As the lesson for Holy Trinity Sunday, the First Sunday after Pentecost in Series B, Isa 6:1–8 is set together with Rom 8:12–17; Ps 29, and John 3:1–17 (the encounter with Nicodemus). As the appointed lesson for the fifth Sunday after the Epiphany in Series C, Isa 6:1–8 (9–13) is to be read together with Ps 138; 1 Cor 15:1–11; and Luke 5:1–11 (the calling of Peter, James, and John). In Series B, only vv. 1–8 are listed as the text; in Series C, vv. 9–13 are bracketed as optional reading. It is also interesting to note the epistle and gospel texts selected for each of those Sundays. In those texts, primary attention is focused on God's holiness, calling, and forgiveness for all people.

Isaiah 6:1–8 is also a text frequently used at ordination services for those entering professional Christian ministry but one wonders how often vv. 9–13 are included in such services. Although Isa 6 is in many ways appropriate for an ordination service, there is something troubling about the use of this text when the decision is made to stop at v. 8 with the words:

Then I head the voice of the Lord saying, "Whom shall I send, and who will go for us?" And I said, "Here am I; send me!"

The text can then convey a heroic or even a romantic message, but when that happens, the scandal of this text is lost. The scandal is that this text goes on to describe a time and a situation when there was no forgiveness!

C. Isaiah's Painful Commission (vv. 9–13)

The words here are unambiguous. Isaiah is remembered as having been told by God to do a strange work. People were to listen and not comprehend; they were to look but not understand; the prophet was to make their minds dull, to stop their ears and shut their eyes so that they would not see, hear, or comprehend!:

> And he said, Go and say to this people:
> "Keep listening, but do not comprehend;
> keep looking, but do not understand"
> (שמעו שמוע ואל־תבינו וראו ראו ואל־תדעו)
> Make the mind of this people dull (השמן לב־העם הזה),
> and stop their ears,
> and shut their eyes (ואזניו הכבד ועיניו השע),
> so that they may not look with their eyes (פן־יראה בעיניו)
> and listen with their ears (ובאזניו ישמע)
> and comprehend with their minds (ולבבו יבין)
> and turn and be healed (ושב ורפא לו). (Isa 6:9–10)

In the rhetoric of the Isaiah scroll, the verbs clustered here in vv. 9 and 10 contribute in very powerful ways to the larger canonical portrait: "to hear" (שמע), "to understand" (בין), "to see" (ראה), "to know" (ידע), "to make fat" (שמן), "to make heavy" (כבד), "to shut" (שעע), "to return, to repent" (שוב), and "to be healed" (רפא). Then, Isaiah's commission is made even stronger as the prophet is remembered asking the lament question:

> How long, O Lord?
> And the answer comes:
> Until cities lie waste without inhabitant
> and houses without people,
> and the land is utterly desolate (שממה);
> until the Lord sends everyone far away,
> and vast is the emptiness in the midst of the land.

> Even if a tenth part remain in it,
> it will be burned again,
> like a terebinth or an oak
> whose stump remains standing when it is felled.
> The holy seed is its stump! (Isa 6:9–13)[13]

Only the final line holds out the possibility of some hope. A "holy seed" still bears the potential for new life. Otherwise, the text declares that there is no hope and that the end will be destruction. By his words, the prophet is to actively prevent repentance.

III. Isaiah's Commission in the Context of Prophetic Theology

So how is the memory to be understood? In the first place, it is important to note that the words of this particular text and, indeed, the words of the Isaiah scroll, were not heard in isolation. They were heard within the broader perspective of Israel's Torah and wisdom traditions, together with other prophetic writings and the psalms, all anchored in the memories of Moses. Israel's prophetic tradition takes specific shape with the memories of Nathan, Elijah, Elisha, Micaiah ben Imlah, and other earlier prophets. The tradition expands with the writings attributed to the so-called classical prophets. Like other prophets, Isaiah is remembered for his bold words concerning righteousness and justice. He is remembered speaking both words of judgment and words of hope. And the themes of hope are not just found in later parts of the scroll; they are also heard in a number of places within chs. 1–12. Already in the first chapter of Isaiah, a dominant theme of prophetic theology is sounded: "Wash yourselves; make yourselves clean; remove the evil of your doings from before my eyes; cease to do evil, learn to do good; seek justice, rescue the oppressed, defend the orphan, plead for the widow" (1:16–17). In 2:1–5, the vision of future peace for Zion is set forth as a promise both for people of Jerusalem and all peoples. The conclusion of that text may be the central invitation of the entire scroll: "O house of Jacob, come, let us walk in the light of the Lord!" (2:5). In 4:2–6, in what may be an inclusio with 2:1–5, a word

---

13. The final half line is missing in LXX. Based on the reference to "holy seed" in Ezra 9:2, some scholars have argued that the final line is a "late addition." Such suggestions relegate the final line as being of lesser importance. I suggest rather that the reference provides helpful insight for understanding the message of the Isaiah scroll in the era of Ezra. See a summary of the debate in Childs, *Isaiah*, 58.

of hope is set forth concerning a day when Jerusalem will once again "be a shade by day from the heat, and a refuge and a shelter from the storm and rain!" (4:6). In ch. 7, Isaiah addresses Ahaz, apparently with the hope that he can still change his already stubborn mind: "Take heed, be quiet, do not fear, and do you let your heart be faint because of these two smoldering stumps of firebrands, because of the fierce anger of Rezin and Aram and the son of Remaliah" (7:3–4).[14] This passage presupposes that Ahaz had the freedom and the possibility of taking actions other than calling for Assyrian intervention.[15] In Isa 9:1–7, people are invited to take hope in the birth of a child who will be a future ideal king. Likewise, in Isa 11:1–9, people are invited to find a basis for hope by envisioning the wisdom and ideal leadership qualities of that future king. And finally, Isa 12:1–6 concludes the opening section with a doxology, offering not judgment but rather words of praise and thanksgiving. In each of these texts, the reader is offered encouragement even as the "bitter memories" of past judgment are recalled. Isaiah's words, both those spoken as announcements of judgment or as summons to hope, have the fundamental

---

14. Sweeney attempts to discern the "original intent" of the commission in ch. 6 against an eighth-century setting and he acknowledges a dilemma. Does the commission to "make blind, deaf and harden hearts" represent the prophet's actual purpose? Is the text "his self-understanding at the time of his commission ... or is it a reflection on his task after failing to persuade Ahaz to avoid reliance on the Assyrian Empire during the Syro-Ephraimite War? If the commission represents his actual self-understanding, then how do we understand his warning to Ahaz or his warnings to the people as though he was attempting to help them avoid punishment. On the other hand, if the commission declaration comes at a time after a time when the prophet experienced utter failure and lack of response from the people, then the veracity of Isaiah's commission is undermined" (Sweeney, *Isaiah 1–39*, 140). Ultimately I suggest that the canonical text of Isaiah does not allow us to know what the "historical Isaiah" actually thought. What we have is the memory; a narrator tells us that at a certain point in his life, Isaiah concluded that God must have decided to "harden the hearts" of particular people. In the Exodus narrative, the "hardness of heart" motifs declare the power of YHWH over all created humans, including the Pharaoh. But it is interesting to note how the poetry alternates: "God hardened Pharaoh's heart" (Exod 7:3, 14, 22; 9:12; 10:1, 20, 27; 11:10; 14:4, 8, 17) and on occasion: "Pharaoh hardened his (own) heart" (Exod 8:15, 19, 32; 9:7, 34, 35). William Stringfellow, in his work *A Public and Private Faith* (Grand Rapids: Eerdmans, 1962), offers a compelling definition of "hardness of heart"; it is a disease peculiar to humans that involves "paralyzed conscience."

15. The text of 2 Kgs 16:1–20 suggests that Assyrian intervention was a concern of Isaiah; we may sympathize with Ahaz as he sought all possible military assistance to secure his country against invasion from northern Israel and Syria. In broader terms, the critique in Isaiah focused on Ahaz' syncretistic practices, such as Baal worship and child sacrifice (one child according to 2 Kgs 16:3; two or more according to 2 Chr 28:3).

purpose of calling the reader or the hearer to a new commitment to justice and righteousness in faithfulness to Torah traditions.[16]

IV. Isaiah 6:1–13 within the Rhetoric of the Isaiah Scroll

Within the canonical portrait, Isa 6:1–13 can be examined in four particular literary contexts, first as part of chs. 6–11, then from the perspective of ch. 1, and chs. 2–12, next as a prophetic word heard in conjunction with texts in chs. 13–35 and finally as one text within the full sixty-six-chapter canonical portrait.

A. Chapter 6 within Isaiah 6:1–11:16

First of all, the vision in Isa 6 seems particularly related to the chapters that directly follow it. Together, they seem to recall and reflect the frustrations that Isaiah experienced during the reign of King Ahaz of Judah (735–715 B.C.E.).[17] The poetic units in the following chapters (7:1–9, 10–17, 18–19, 20, 21, 23–25; 8:1–4, 5–8, 9–10, 11–22) all seem to relate to the difficulties experienced by the prophet at a time when his words were not heeded. The only response we hear from Ahaz are his pious words:

> I will not ask, and I will not put the Lord to the test! (7:12)

Chapters 7 and 8 culminate with the declarations of 8:11–15, which echo the frustrations heard in Isaiah's call vision:

---

16. Isaiah's life as a social critic is further confirmed by his walking naked in Jerusalem as a warning of impending doom (20:1–6) and his pleading with people to change (e.g., 28:12; 30:15).

17. Sweeney is certainly correct when he writes: "Insofar as ch. 6 is related to the time of the death of King Uzziah (742) and insofar as 7:1–25 relates to the Syro-Ephraimite war some ten years later (735–732), it is clear that ch. 6 was not composed in relation to ch. 7, but was associated with it only some time after the initial composition. This means that the original intent of ch. 6 must be defined apart from its relationship to ch. 7 and the 'memoir' as a whole" (*Isaiah 1–39*, 141). It is certainly clear that narratives and poetic units have been collected and arranged in a particular way within chs. 2–12; Sweeney suggests that 6:1–11 originally was an expression of condemnation for northern Israel and that vv. 12–13 paved the way for introducing the narratives in chs. 7–8, which illustrate the punishment for the remaining "tenth" part (v. 13), namely, Judah. This is an intriguing suggestion but it directly contradicts the stated focus that this material is all part of the "word which Isaiah saw concerning Judah and Jerusalem" (2:1).

> For the Lord spoke thus to me while his hand was strong upon me, and warned me not to walk in the way of this people, saying:
> Do not call conspiracy all that this people calls conspiracy, and do not fear what it fears, or be in dread.
> But the Lord of hosts, him you shall regard as holy; let him be your fear, and let him be your dread....
> Bind up the testimony, seal the teaching among my disciples. I will wait for the Lord, who is hiding his face (המסתיר פניו) from the house of Jacob, and I will hope in him. (8:11–14, 16–17)

God is "hiding his face"; the rhetoric complements the "hardening" motif in Isa 6. A gulf separates Isaiah's world of thought and that of Ahaz. Ahaz is deemed to be one whose heart was so hardened that he is beyond redemption. Isaiah's task was to announce to him and to those connected with him the verdict of the divine court:

> If you do not stand firm in faith,
> you shall not stand at all. (7:9b)

B. Chapter 6 within Isaiah 1, 2–12

In a larger sense, Isa 6:1–13 is remembered as a central text among the "bitter memories" that are preserved in both the introductory ch. 1 and throughout chs. 2–12.[18] The opening words of the scroll set the dominant theme:

> Hear (שמע), O heavens, and listen (והאזיני), O earth;
> for the Lord has spoken.
> I reared children and brought them up,
> but they have rebelled against me.
> The ox knows (ידע) its master, and the donkey its master's crib;
> but Israel does not know (לא ידע),
> my people do not understand (לא התבונן). (1:2–3)

Similar bitter memories appear throughout chs. 2–12, now gathered under the superscription in 2:1: "The word that Isaiah son of Amoz saw concerning

---

18. There is widespread agreement that ch. 1 is an introduction to the entire scroll. Chapters 2–12 incorporate both words of hope and words of judgment. It is significant that hopeful words both open and close the section: Isa 2:1–5 sets out a "vision of peace for Zion" and 12:1–6 concludes the section with words of praise and thanksgiving.

Judah and Jerusalem." In the lengthy "day of the Lord" poem in 2:6–22, Isaiah's primary message announcing judgment is sounded. The prophet boldly declares that arrogant and haughty conduct will bring its own inevitable consequences:

> The haughtiness of people shall be humbled, and the pride of everyone shall be brought low; and the Lord alone will be exalted on that day. (1:17)

In 3:13–15, with lawsuit language, the charge against the leaders is bluntly stated:

> It is you who have devoured the vineyard; the spoil of the poor is in your houses. What do you mean by crushing my people, by grinding the face of the poor? says the Lord God of hosts. (3:14–15)

With even greater clarity, the judgment theme is spelled out in the parable of the vineyard poem in 5:1–7.[19] Pre-exilic Judah is remembered as a maze of grapevines bearing only bitter grapes. Despite every possible effort by their creator, Judah had become like useless vines and bitter grapes so that the reader must understand that the logical action is to uproot and destroy:

> When I expected it to yield grapes, why did it yield wild grapes?
> And now I will tell you what I will do to my vineyard.
> I will remove its hedge, and it shall be devoured;
> I will break down its wall, and it shall be trampled down.
> I will make it a waste; it shall not be pruned or hoed,
> and it shall be overgrown with briers and thorns;
> I will also command the clouds that they rain no rain upon it. (5:4b–5)

In 10:5–19 and again in 10:27b–34, Assyria is identified as the instrument of Yhwh by which the vineyard will be destroyed. The fact that Assyria understands the world in quite a different way has no bearing. The prophet declares that Yhwh is using Assyria to carry out an act of punishment for Judah.

---

19. Childs contends that a turning point in God's history with Israel can be discerned with the "destruction of the vineyard" imagery in ch. 5 and then the "commission" imagery in Isaiah, ch. 6 (*Isaiah*, 56–57); I suggest rather that in the literary portrait set forth in Isaiah, the real turning point comes with the memories of the destruction of Jerusalem, the fall of Babylon, and the rise of Cyrus.

C. Chapter 6 and Isaiah 13–35

Isaiah 6:1–13 also has echoes within the poetry preserved in Isa 13–35. In this second major section (chs. 13–35), Judah is remembered among the nations of her world. The new section is marked by the superscription in 13:1, the first in a series of oracles that focus both on Judah and on surrounding nations: "The oracle concerning Babylon that Isaiah ben Amoz saw."[20] In this chapter and in the oracles that follow, it is interesting to note the themes that relate to "hearing" or "not hearing," "seeing," and "not seeing."[21] People from the eras both before and after the fall of Jerusalem are remembered as those who brought disaster on themselves by their reckless and selfish conduct.[22] Babylon is included in the poetry of the opening ch. 13! And yet, certain texts declare that people in a future era will still have the capacity to hear, to see and to understand as a remnant community. Those who hear this text are to understand! Two particular texts in chs. 13–35 illustrate the contrasts set out between the past and the envisioned future. In 29:18, the prophet envisions a future time when changes will occur:

> On that day the deaf shall hear (ושמעו) the words of the scroll,
> and out of their gloom and darkenss
>   the eyes of the blind shall see (תראינה).
>   The meek shall obtain fresh joy in the Lord,
> and the neediest people shall exalt in the Holy One of Israel! (29:18)

And in ch. 35, the poet again dreams of a future era as he declares:

> Then the eyes of the blind shall be opened (תפקהנה עיני עורים),
>   and the ear of the deaf unstopped (ואזני חרשים תפתחנה);

---

20. I no longer feel that it is helpful or appropriate to use the traditional distinctions concerning "first Isaiah," "second Isaiah, or "third Isaiah." As much as they may have helped us to a better understanding of the historical development of the canonical work, they also can keep us from hearing the text. In a similar way, I no longer think it is valid to speak of Isa 13–23 as "oracles addressed to the nations." Isaiah 22 is clearly addressed to a community in Judah that has survived a disastrous military attack but has failed to learn or discern anything from that experience; it seems much more accurate to see chs. 13–35 as poetry addressed to "Judah among the nations." See further, A. Joseph Everson, "Isaiah," in *Eerdmans Dictionary of the Bible* (Grand Rapids: Eerdmans, 2000), 648–52.

21. See Robert P. Carroll, "Blindness and the Vision Thing: Blindness and Insight in the Book of Isaiah," in Broyles and Evans, *Writing and Reading the Scroll of Isaiah*, 79–93.

22. One striking example in Isa 22:15–19 is Shebna, an official in the era of Hezekiah. We may also think of later kings, Manasseh, Jehoiakim, and Zedekiah.

>   and the lame shall leap like a deer
>   and the tongue of the speechless sings for joy! (35:5)

The judgments announced for various nations and for Judah in chs. 13–23 and the mythic reflections in chs. 24–27 all speak to the horrors of war. Those who were alive in post-exilic Jerusalem knew of the devastations that had happened in the eras of Assyria and Babylon. Through the tumult of war, both empires and small countries learned painfully that they are not gods!

D. Chapter 6 within the Canonical Text of Isaiah 1–66

Within the sixty-six chapter context of the scroll, Isa 6:1–13 should be understood as one very important scene in the larger portrait that is preserved. The memory of Isaiah's commission provides a backdrop for the words of hope and encouragement that are so prevalent throughout chs. 40–66.[23] The prophet is remembered as a courageous prophetic figure from an earlier era of history. Sadly, his words of warning were not heeded; divine judgment came. Judah and Jerusalem were brought low! Isaiah's word was to continue "until cities lie waste without inhabitant, and houses without people, and the land is utterly desolate; until the Lord sends everyone far away, and vast is the emptiness in the midst of the land" (6:11–12). Those who heard the prophetic word in the late exilic and post-exilic eras could not escape understanding that these words had come to pass with the destruction of Jerusalem and the experience of exile that followed. In the same way, people who heard the concluding words of the text, "The holy seed is its stump," must have pondered

---

23. I am indebted to Rolf Rendtorff, "Isaiah 6 in the Framework of the Composition of the Book," in *Canon and Theology: Overtures to an Old Testament Theology* (trans. and ed. Margaret Kohl; Minneapolis: Fortress, 1993), 170–80 for his helpful study of the rhetoric of Isa 6 as it appears in later texts. Regarding Isa 6 and 40, he writes: "... the two texts mark two corresponding fundamental aspects of the book of Isaiah: the climax of the announcement of judgment, whose inescapability is expressed in the statements about the hardening of the people's hearts in Is 6:8ff., and the beginning of the announcement of salvation, in which it is explicitly stated that now sin has been canceled (40:2). The two aspects are therefore related. It is obvious that without the preceding judgment the announcement of salvation has no function" (179). I differ from Rendtorff only when he discusses ch. 6 as a text that "points forward," where "the gaze travels into the future ... to the time after the judgment has been executed, in which the salvation that is imminent is announced and with it the end of the time when God hides his face" (174). I no longer think that we can stand with Isaiah in the eighth century; we can only stand with the late-exilic or post-exilic community that incorporates these texts as memories from a "bitter" past era.

what it might mean to be that "holy seed." With that concluding word, the text of Isa 6 is primarily an admonition concerning faith and obedience to Torah.

In Isa 40–66, a new era begins. Isaiah 6 was remembered specifically "in the year that Uzziah died" (6:1); now the new era is marked with references to Cyrus of Persia (44:28; 45:1; 45:13). Assyria and Babylon were remembered as instruments of judgment; now Cyrus and Persia are understood as instruments for salvation and liberation from bondage.

In Isa 40:1–5, a heavenly voice speaks with a message quite different from Isa 6: "Comfort, o comfort my people!" concluding with the declaration that "the glory of *See,* the Lord shall be revealed and all people shall see it together" (וראו כל־בשר יחדו).[24] Throughout ch. 40, further imperatives to "see" are set forth: "the Lord comes with might" (40:10), "see, he takes up the isles like fine dust" (40:15b), and "Lift up your eyes on high and see" (40:26). In 40:12–31, Yhwh is affirmed as the mysterious source of all life, a source that cannot be controlled or manipulated, the one who gives power to the faint and strength to the powerless (40:29–30). In 41:17–20, the new era for Judah is heralded as God transforms the desert into fruitful lands precisely "so that all may see and know" (למען יראו ידעו). In direct contrast with Isa 6, Isa 42:18–21 declares:

> Listen, you that are deaf (החרשים שמעו);
> and you that are blind, look up and see (והעורים הביטו לראות)!
> Who is blind but my servant,
> or deaf like my messenger whom I send?
> Who is blind like my dedicated one,
> or blind like the servant of the Lord?
> He sees many things, but does not observe them (ראית רבות ולא תשמר);
> his ears are open, but he does not hear (פקוח אזנים ולא ישמע).
> The Lord was pleased for the sake of his righteousness,
> to magnify his teaching and make it glorious. (42:18–21)

The striking aspect of this text is that the servant, identified as Israel/Jacob in 41:5, is still spoken of as being blind and deaf. Yhwh "gave up Jacob to the spoiler, and Israel to the robbers" because they refused to obey the Torah and to walk in an upright way (42:24). But now the servant is no longer to be

---

24. Of particular interest is the dramatic contrast between 1:4 and 40:2. In 1:4, we hear of a sinful people (גוי חטא) and a people "laden with iniquity" (כבד עון); in 40:2, we hear of Jerusalem "that her sins" (חטאתיה) are forgiven and "her iniquity is pardoned" (נרצה עונה).

bound by the "former things." The servant is to see and hear the "new things" that are now being declared (42:9).

At the beginning of the scroll, Isaiah declared that even "the ox knows his owner" (ידע שור קנהו) but Israel "does not know" (לא ידע). The theme of "not knowing" was also present in 6:9 when people are told to "see but do not comprehend or perceive" (וראו ראו ואל־תדעו). But throughout Isa 40–66, the word is now set forth that people are to comprehend and understand. Typical are the rhetorical questions posed in 40:21 and repeated in 40:28 in second person plural forms: "Have you not known?" (הלוא תדעו). "Have you not heard?" (הלוא תשמעו).[25] In the poetry of 43:8–13, the reversal is dramatically presented:

> Bring forth the people who are blind, yet have eyes (עם־עור ועינים יש),
> who are deaf, yet have ears (וחרשים ואזנים למו)!
> Let all the nations gather together,
> and let the peoples assemble.
> Who among them declared this,
> and foretold to us the former things. (43:8–9)

The author claims that the events of history should now allow people to hear, see and understand. It is in this context that the declaration concerning "knowing" is made in 43:10:

> You are my witnesses, says the Lord,
> and my servant whom I have chosen,
> so that you may know and believe me (למען תדעו ותאמינו לי)
> and understand that I am he (ותבינו כי־אני הוא).
> Before me no god was formed, nor shall there be any after me.

In 43:18–19, those who constitute the servant community are told again:

> Do not remember the former things,
> or consider the things of old.
> I am about to do a new thing;
> now it springs forth, do you not perceive (know) it (הלוא תדעוה)?
> I will make a way in the wilderness, and rivers in the desert.

Commands to see and to hear continue for the servant:

---

25. See further on "knowing," Isa 41:20, 22, 23, 26; 42:16; 43:10, 19; 44:9, 28; 45:3, 4, 6, 8; 49:23, 26; 51:7; 52:6; 59:12; 60:16.

"But now hear, O Jacob my servant...." (44:1); "Hear this, O house of Jacob...." (48:1) and "Listen to me, O Jacob...." (48:12); "Listen, your sentinels lift up their voices...." (52:8); and "all the ends of the earth shall see the salvation of our God." (52:10)[26]

The understanding of past history here is that Yhwh had previously attempted to speak to a stubborn people through various tribulations and finally, through the language of the war. Judah should have heard Yhwh's voice in the destruction that came for Samaria, the northern kingdom. Already in Isa 9:8–12, Isaiah had declared "the Lord sent a word against Jacob and it fell on Israel and all the people knew it." So also people in Judah should have learned from a close call with tragedy such as the invasion of Sennacherib in "the fourteenth year of Hezekiah" (Isa 36:1, probably 701 B.C.E.). Isaiah 22:1–14 appears to have been written in the aftermath of such a near tragedy; the real disaster is that people failed to hear or learn from their close call with disaster, as is expressed in the final line of the poem:

> The Lord of hosts has revealed himself in my ears;
> surely this iniquity will not be forgiven you until you die,
> says the Lord of hosts. (22:14)[27]

In Isa 30:30, the prophet speaks of war as the most frightening voice of God in the world. Amid the devastating sounds of battle, a people (in this text, Assyria) should hear the sound of God's divine judgment:

> And the Lord will cause his majestic voice to be heard and the descending blow of his arm to be seen, in furious anger and a flame of devouring fire, with a cloudburst and tempest and hailstones. The Assyrians will be terror-stricken at the voice of the Lord, when he strikes with his rod. (30:30)

---

26. Rendtorff points to a number of other contrasts, including the pardoning of sin (see 6:7; 33:24; 44:22–23; 53:5) and the rebuilding and repopulating of Jerusalem in ch. 49ff. as the reversal of the devastation (שממה) of 6:11.

27. The "valley of vision" poem in 22:1–14 clearly is a reflection on a past event; all four strophes describe past action; therefore, the reference to a "day of tumult, trampling, and confusion" in 22:5 should also be translated in a preterite or past tense manner: "For the Lord God of hosts has had a day of tumult and trampling and confusion in the valley of vision." The near catastrophe of 701 B.C.E. is remembered in 2 Kgs 18:13–27 and in Isa 36:1 as "the fourteenth year of King Hezekiah"; from the postexilic era, that earlier event may have been remembered. But certainly, the text of 22:1–14 would also have been remembered in conjunction with the fall of Judah in 587 B.C.E.

Concluding Observations

In Isa 63:17, we hear a further reference to "hardness of heart" as a perennial danger for human people:

> Why, O Lord, do you make us stray from your ways?
> and harden our hearts (תקשיח לבנו)
> so that we do not fear you?

What seems apparent from this passage is that the motif of the Lord "hardening" hearts was quite synonymous with "straying from the way" and "not fearing the Lord." The text is a reminder that "hardness of the heart" is a constant danger for people in any age. The Isaiah scroll provides a wealth of rhetoric, seeking to affirm the sovereignty of God over all of life, even as that follows from God's intentions and the actions of human individuals.[28] People are called to understand that humility, compassion, and justice are appropriate activities for the human family. Isaiah 6:1–13 describes a past era when people refused that path with the resulting outcomes of blindness, deafness, and lack of discernment. In Israel's prophetic tradition, as well as in the broader world of Hebrew thought, it was possible simply to declare that this is what God must have caused. This mode of interpretation was one option available for explaining divine activity in the world.[29] We may choose to interpret divine activity in other ways. But when we do, we must guard against "softening" the message of a biblical text. In Isa 30:9–10, there is a warning about those who would soften or simply disregard the frightening message of a text such as Isaiah's commission. The prophet is remembered giving this instruction:

---

28. See further, the declarations "God hardened Pharaoh's heart" in Exod 7:3, 14, 22; 9:12; 10:1, 20, 27; 11:10; 14:4, 8, 17 and the statements "the heart of Pharaoh was hardened" in 8:15, 19, 32 or "he sinned and hardened his heart" in 9:34, 35.

29. There is an interesting parallel in the rhetoric of Isa 6 with the interpretation of history offered by the author of the Joseph saga in Gen 37–50. We hear of the evils committed by the brothers as they sold Joseph into slavery in Egypt. The brothers are clearly portrayed as being responsible for their actions. But at the end of the saga, we hear the interpretation given in the words of Joseph: "God sent me before you to preserve for you a remnant on earth, and to keep alive for you many survivors. So it was not you who sent me here, but God; he has made me a father to Pharaoh, and Lord of all his house and ruler over all the land of Egypt" (45:7–8); and later, "Even though you intended to do harm to me, God intended it for good, in order to preserve a numerous people, as he is doing today!" (Gen 50:20). It was in retrospect that people discerned God's presence in all things.

> Go now, write it before them on a tablet,
> and inscribe it in a book,
> so that it may be for the time to come
> as a witness forever.
> for they are a rebellious people, faithless children,
> children who will not hear the instruction of the Lord;
> who say to the seers, "Do not see";
> and to the prophets, "Do not prophesy to us what is right;
> speak to us smooth things, prophesy illusions,
> leave the way, turn aside from the path,
> let us hear no more about the Holy One of Israel."

The text of Isa 6:1–13 is not a "smooth thing." But it provides a profound perspective and a sense of urgency about the words of invitation: "Come, let us walk in the light of the Lord!" (2:4) and "Incline your ear, and come to me; listen, so that you may live (55:3). Isaiah 6 is a reminder that the human abilities to see, to hear, and to respond to life with compassion and mercy are precious gifts.

Poetic Vision in Isaiah 7:18-25

H. G. M. Williamson

Isaiah 7:18-25 is a somewhat neglected passage within an otherwise much studied context.[1] Its poetic value is apparently not very high. It is made up of four short sections, each beginning with "in that day" or "it will come to pass in that day." It includes a number of so-called prose particles, such as את and אשר. Although there are elements of parallelism and similar poetic devices, they are not employed consistently. The lines are of uneven length, so that it is difficult to analyze its rhythmic structure, and it is certainly not justifiable to propose emendations on that basis.[2] It uses a mixture of different imagery, one element of which does not seem to relate particularly to another except in the sense that they all refer to military disaster and its aftermath. There is a good deal of inelegant repetition, especially towards the end of the passage, so that it does not read particularly fluently.

---

1. The case for defining the passage as 7:18-25 is strong. That a new section of some sort begins with v. 18 is evident from the change from second-person address in the preceding material to third-person here (contrast, for instance, Karl Budde, *Jesaja's Erleben: Eine Gemeinverständliche Auslegung der Denkschrift des Propheten (Kap. 6,1-9,6)* [Gotha: Leopold Klotz, 1928], 58-59, who thinks that the section begins with 7:17 and who ascribes it wholly to Isaiah himself). The repeated use of the introductory clause "it shall come to pass on that day," though not decisive in this regard, is also indicative of a break. Nevertheless, the use of the conjunction at the start of 7:18 suggests that the material has been deliberately joined to what precedes. In its present setting, the passage amplifies and develops the evident threat of 7:17, underlining the typical elements of invasion, decline of population and loss of cultivated land. Its movement away from the previous specific focus on Ahaz and the house of David towards the land and its people in general serves also as a useful bridge into Isa 8 immediately following.

2. *Contra*, for instance, Otto Procksch, *Jesaia I* (KAT 9.1; Leipzig: Deichert, 1930), 126.

Given this gloomy catalogue, there seems no point in trying to make out that the passage is more superior than it is. In their enthusiasm, biblical scholars sometimes advance larger claims for parts of their material than are warranted, but the result is only to detract from the value of the material that is genuinely high. As is well known, all the major parts of the book of Isaiah include some of the finest poetry as known to us from the Hebrew Bible. That claim would only be devalued if we were to include 7:18–25 in the same category.

This does not mean, of course, that the passage is therefore devoid of interest. As I shall try to show, it includes a higher than usual proportion of allusions to or even citations from earlier material within the book, and this gives us the necessary key to unravel some of its exegetical puzzles and to understand better what it is attempting to achieve. It is this significant complex of intertextual allusions which justifies a study of this passage within the present volume, and it is something which it is hoped would have been of particular interest to Roy Melugin, whose memory we honor jointly by this collective enterprise.

For the convenience of the reader in following the subsequent discussion, I here include a translation of the passage in somewhat traditional style:

> [18]And it shall come to pass on that day,
>   the Lord will whistle for the fly
>   which is at the end of the streams of Egypt,
>   and for the bee which is in the land of Assyria,
>   [19]and all of them will come and settle
>   in the ravines of the precipices and in the clefts of the rocks
>   and on all the thorn-bushes and on all the pasture-lands.
>   [20]On that day the Lord will shave
>   with a razor hired in the regions beyond the river, even the king of Assyria,
>   the head and the hair of the feet,
>   and it will also sweep away the beard.
> [21]And it shall come to pass on that day,
>   a man will keep alive
>   a cow's heifer and a couple of sheep,
>   [22]and because of the quantity of milk produced
>   he will eat butter,
>   indeed, everyone who remains in the midst of the land
>   will eat butter and honey.
> [23]And it shall come to pass on that day,

every place where there are found
> a thousand vines worth a thousand pieces of silver
>> will become briers and thorns.
²⁴One will (only) go there with arrows and a bow,
> because all the land will be briers and thorns;
²⁵And all the mountains which used to be hoed with a hoe,
> you will not go there for fear of briers and thorns;
>> but it will become a place where cattle are let loose and
>> sheep trample.

It will be simplest to start with the last section of the passage, 7:23–25, because elements of the case to be made there are already well known and uncontroversial. The section begins by affirming that every place in which valuable vineyards[3] used to grow will in this coming day be turned into שמיר ושית "briers and thorns."[4] This is clearly a reference to the Song of the Vineyard in 5:1–7, where the vineyard suffers the same fate according to 5:6. The phrase was obviously one that made an impression on later contributors to the book, for it is repeated in other later or redactional passages (10:17; 27:4), while at 9:17 it is probably mentioned again by Isaiah himself. Consciousness of the verbal reprise is thus unmistakable.[5] In language characteristic of the book, we are told that the fertile land will revert to an uncultivated wilderness as an element of God's judgment.

---

3. Although it is possible to speculate about the price of vines in antiquity, it is probable that the rhetorical emphasis here, "a thousand vines worth a thousand pieces of silver," is simply to exaggerate both the extent and the high value of the vineyard (alluded to by the use of "every place"). The traditional interpretation of Lev 5:15 has been that it values a ram at two shekels, though this is not clearly stated, while Cant 8:11 appears to tell that in Solomon's vineyard a vine would yield a thousand pieces of silver, though again there are uncertainties as to whether this is precisely what the verse is saying. It seems better, therefore, just to conclude that the repetition of "a thousand" is meant to indicate highest quantity and quality, the opposite of the picture in 5:10.

4. It is probable that the phrase was coined more for its alliterative effect (as in English, "thorns and thistles") than out of any particular botanical concern. For a survey of suggestions regarding the latter, see Hans Wildberger, *Jesaja 1–12* (vol. 1 of *Jesaja*; 2nd ed.; BKAT 10.1; Neukirchen-Vluyn: Neukirchener, 1980), 171 = *Isaiah 1–12* (trans. Thomas H. Trapp; CC; Minneapolis: Fortress, 1991), 183–84.

5. See Kirsten Nielsen, *There Is Hope for a Tree: The Tree as Metaphor in Isaiah* (JSOTSup 65; Sheffield: JSOT Press, 1989), 104–6, though her conclusion that "a political code lies behind the use in all cases" is questionable; Donald C. Polaski, *Authorizing an End: The Isaiah Apocalypse and Intertextuality* (BibInt 50; Leiden: Brill, 2001), 341–47.

In the following verse, the result of this reversal (rather pedantically spelled out again by way of a repetition of "briers and thorns" in the second half) is that the formerly cultivated land will become an area fit only for hunting—an activity that normally took place in the uncultivated but, for obvious reasons, not totally barren land between the desert and the sown. Hunting was practiced sparsely in ancient Israel, if the infrequent occurrence of references in the texts is anything to go by, but there are also a significant number of references to the need to hunt and kill dangerous wild animals in order to protect both people and domesticated animals. This too may be in mind in our passage.

The reference to "arrows and a bow" seems to be intended to say more than simply that one will go there armed because of the fear of danger.[6] Although we hear more often of the use of nets, traps, and snares in regular hunting in ancient Israel,[7] the use of bows and arrows is also well attested from Assyrian iconography, even if there it is predominantly as an elite sport, as well as more locally in such cases as those of Ishmael (Gen 21:10) and of Esau (Gen 27:3); see too Job 41:26–29. It is likely, therefore that, as in the previous verse, the language has been chosen primarily for its rhetorical impact: to draw a sharp contrast between previous and present circumstances.

In 7:25 immediately following, our phrase recurs yet a third time. Added to the loss of vineyards (or alternatively, in further development of the same image, since vineyards could be planted on hillsides; see 5:1), the formerly cultivated hillsides will become areas fit only for grazing (and that with use of vocabulary that has negative overtones in Isa 5). The middle line of the three, "you will not go there for fear of briers and thorns," interrupts the intended connection between the first and the third, and it is also obviously somewhat repetitious of the previous verse. It cannot be an alternative reading, because its לא־תבוא שמה, "you will not go there," would not fit as a replacement for the יבוא שמה, "one will (only) go there," of 7:24. It must, therefore, have been

---

6. There is some evidence, we may note in passing, for an understanding in antiquity which referred the image to warfare, perhaps in part because of the preceding sections, but there is no supporting contextual evidence for this. 1QIsa^a has plural, ובקשתות; similarly LXX and Targum; Vulgate follows MT. While either is possible, and a scribal error either way is readily conceivable in the Hebrew by dittography or haplography, it is just possible that the plural for both nouns reflects what I regard as the less plausible understanding of the verse as referring to armies rather than a hunter. This judgment follows in particular from the fact that in the following verse 1QIsa^a adds a supralineal ברזל, "iron," between שמיר and יראת, which is doubtless another indication of a military line of interpretation for this passage but which can hardly be original.

7. For references, see Adrianus van Selms, "Hunting," *ISBE* 2:782–84.

some sort of marginal explanatory comment that has been incorporated into the main text in the early course of transmission. While the original, 7:24, appears to state that the area of former vineyards will become fit only for hunting, the commentator has sought to add to the pessimism by adding that in fact one will even fear to go there in the first place.

If this threefold use of שמיר ושית (or at least its repeated use, if the occurrence in 7:25 is indeed secondary) makes clear that the writer had the Song of the Vineyard in mind, two other striking allusions in 7:25 indicate the extent to which reflection on that passage influenced his composition. First, the once-fertile mountainsides, it is said, "used to be hoed with a hoe" (במעדר יעדרון). The same verb was used at 5:6, where it was stated that the vineyard would no longer be pruned or hoed. As these are the only two places in the Hebrew Bible where the word occurs, this seems certainly to be due once again to influence from the earlier passage.

Secondly, the same will be true of the wording of "sheep trample"; מרמס occurs in 5:5, "I shall break down its wall so that it will be trampled down." Admittedly, the allusion there is to animals in general, but in the present verse they are specified by the use of a standard pair for large and small domestic animals, "cattle" and "sheep," so that the outcome is much the same. The emphasis in the final line, then, is not so much the advantage of having good pasture for the herds and flocks as the destructive effects of their being able to roam freely over formerly productive agricultural land.

On the basis of this material in 7:23–25, then, we may be confident that our author was especially influenced by reflection on 5:1–7. This enables us next to find a further probable allusion earlier in our passage, though in this case the evidence is not quite so clear-cut. In 7:18–19 we are told that God is going to summon hostile nations which, depicted as a fly and a bee, will come and settle in various parts of the land. The language used to describe where they will settle is sometimes rare and so not entirely clear, as a survey of the renderings in the ancient versions could demonstrate. It seems, however, that the list of places is divided into two pairs, the second of which refers to their feeding places: "on all the thorn-bushes and on all the pasture-lands."[8] The

---

8. As a common noun, נהללים is a true *hapax legomenon*. I have followed the derivation that has become traditional since it was proposed by Wilhelm Gesenius, *Philologisch-kritischer und historischer Commentar über den Jesaia* (2 vols; Leipzig: Vogel, 1821), 1:318, who suggested that it comes from the familiar נהל (*pi'el*), "lead, guide (to a watering place etc.)." The formation might be by analogy with נאצוצים just before, though the *holem* is odd; just this element seems to have been unstable, however; this is evident in connection with the place name of a village in Zebulun, both in MT and in its Greek renderings (see

first pair, by contrast, speaks of the remote places where they would settle, perhaps to indicate that there will be no hiding place in such traditional refuges as remote caves in the rocky hillsides. The second pair, נקיקי הסלעים, is clear enough; the same phrase occurs at Jer 16:16, and the singular, again in the construct before סלע, at Jer 13:4, and it means "clefts of the rocks." The first phrase in this pair is less certain, however: נחלי הבתות. The vocalization of בַּתּוֹת suggests that it derives from the root בתת, which on the basis of Arabic means "cut off." In our verse, therefore, it may mean "cut-off places," that is, "precipices." In a discussion elsewhere of the occurrence of בתה in 5:6, I arrived at the negative conclusion "that association with בתת faces fewest difficulties," and that in that verse it had the meaning "something cut off," that is, "end, destruction."[9] In view of the extreme rarity of the word and the fact that Rashi and Ibn Ezra already linked both passages by way of an association of sense in each case with שממה, I conclude that the choice of vocabulary in our passage is again best explained by an allusion to 5:6.

Still within this first section of our passage, there is another indication that the author was familiar with what we call ch. 5 of Isaiah in his reuse of the concept of God "whistling" for his agents of judgment on Judah. At 5:26 this referred, as would have been appropriate in the eighth century, to the summoning of the Assyrians, and given that the only other use of the verb with this particular sense is at the much later Zech 10:8, it seems very probable that our passage is a direct allusion to Isa 5. Indeed, this finds further support in the continuation, where in 5:26 God whistles for one to come "from the end of the earth" (מקצה הארץ), whereas in 7:18 this may be reflected in the more specific "at the end of the streams of Egypt" (בקצה יארי מצרים).

The language derives from the world of bee control (they were not yet domesticated at that time, but still needed to be attracted away from the comb

---

Judg 1:30 and with different vocalization at Josh 19:15 and 21:35; see Barnabas Lindars, *Judges 1–5: A New Translation and Commentary* [Edinburgh: T&T Clark, 1995], 64 and 86), and in addition 1QIsa[a] here has נהלילים with, apparently, a *waw* written above the first *yod*, presumably to correct the spelling to reflect the same as what we now have in MT; see E. Yechezkel Kutscher, *The Language and Linguistic Background of the Isaiah Scroll (1QIsa[a])* (STDJ 6; Leiden: Brill, 1974), 379. Thus the present vowel may not be original. Others, however, prefer to find a nearer parallel to נעצוצים and so suggest that this is another type of thorn bush (e.g., Gustaf Dalman, *Der Ackerbau* [vol. 2 of *Arbeit und Sitte in Palästina*; Gütersloh: Bertelsmann, 1932], 323), but I am not aware of any linguistic support for this otherwise attractive proposal.

9. Hugh G. M. Williamson, *A Critical and Exegetical Commentary on Isaiah 1–27* (vol. 1 of *Commentary on Isaiah*; ICC; London: T&T Clark, 2006), 322–23.

in order to access the wild honey).[10] In the present verse, that is suitable for the application to the "bee which is in the land of Assyria" in the final line, but it has been further applied, strictly erroneously, so far as we know, to "the fly which is at the end of the streams of Egypt." Such a reapplication of imagery under literary pressure, even if not making much sense in terms of natural history, is understandable.

Furthermore, the suggestion that 7:18–19 is dependent on Isa 5 (and on the earlier part of Isa 7, as will be maintained below) suggests that those scholars who have wanted to omit parts of the verse as later glosses because they are deemed to be historically inappropriate are themselves misguided. Quite a few commentators have argued that the phrases "which is at the end of the streams of Egypt" and "which is in the land of Assyria" are later additions to the verse; originally, they suggest, there was reference only to the fly and the bee, both referring to the Assyrian. Historically, it would not have been appropriate to refer to the involvement of Egypt as early as the Syro-Ephraimite crisis.[11] In my opinion, however, this argument begins from a misunderstanding of the composition history of the passage. These scholars tend to assume that 7:18–19 as well as 7:20 are original to Isaiah and so are anxious to eliminate the reference to Egypt. If, however, 7:18–19 are rightly seen as later, then the linkage of Assyria and Egypt in a somewhat less historically bound prophecy ceases to be a problem (see 11:11 and 15–16, and much later 19:23–25; Jer 2:36; Hos 9:3; 11:5, 11); Oswalt rightly explains: "It is more likely that Isaiah is speaking generally, demonstrating Judah's vulnerability to powerful enemies on either hand apart from God's protection."[12]

Moving on from instances of dependence on Isa 5, I turn next to two echoes of phraseology from the previous part of Isa 7 itself. The second is clear beyond any shadow of doubt, so that it helps reinforce the case for the first, which is not quite so strong when considered in isolation. I start with the

---

10. For references, see Williamson, *Commentary on Isaiah 1–27*, 406; and Wildberger, *Jesaja 1–12*, 304 = *Isaiah 1–12*, 322–23.

11. E.g., Bernhard Duhm, *Das Buch Jesaia. Übersetzt und erklärt* (4th ed.; HKAT 3.1; Göttingen: Vandenhoeck & Ruprecht, 1922), 76–77; Karl Marti, *Das Buch Jesaja* (KHAT 10; Tübingen: Mohr Siebeck, 1900), 79–80; George B. Gray, *A Critical and Exegetical Commentary on the Book of Isaiah I–XXVII* (ICC; Edinburgh: T&T Clark, 1912), 138; Edward J. Kissane, *The Book of Isaiah, Translated from a Critically Revised Hebrew Text with Commentary* (2 vols.; Dublin: Browne & Nolan, 1941), 1:93; Ronald E. Clements, *Isaiah 1–39* (NCB; Grand Rapids: Eerdmans, 1980), 90.

12. John N. Oswalt, *The Book of Isaiah: Chapters 1–39* (NICOT; Grand Rapids: Eerdmans, 1986), 216.

less certain example, however, because, like the previous cases just discussed, it comes in the first section of our passage, 7:18–19.

In describing the arrival of the "insects" that represent Egypt and Assyria, we are told that they will come and "settle" (ונחו) in the rocks and so on. This is an unusual use of the verb נוח, which normally has the meaning "to rest." It is true that it is used once, in Exod 10:14, with regard to real locusts, but its application in the present verse to the threatening arrival of foreign troops is almost unprecedented. There is one other possible example, however, in 7:2, where it is used with reference to Aram. Admittedly, some commentators have difficulty believing that this can be the same verb in 7:2, precisely because of its unusual meaning, so they seek alternative explanations. However, it seems entirely reasonable to claim that our author in 7:19 understood it in the way I have indicated and so applied it again, though on a wider canvass, to his anticipation of the possibility of a future invasion.

The second example of dependence on the earlier part of Isa 7 comes in the third section of our passage, 7:21–22. While the general fact of dependence is widely agreed, these verses pose difficulties for interpretation of a different kind, so our discussion here will necessarily be slightly longer and more wide-ranging. At stake are both the integrity of the text as we have it and the question whether this passage too is negative in tone, as the other three sections certainly are, or whether it is exceptional in bearing a more positive message.

There is undoubtedly an ambiguous element in the saying. On the one hand, it clearly speaks of survival after the invasion, even if for a much-reduced population, and of the fact that there will be sustaining nourishment for them. Wagner, for instance, therefore takes the section in a wholly positive sense.[13] On the other, there is a marked contrast with other prophetic passages that speak of natural fertility as a mark of eschatological well-being; see, for instance, Joel 4:18; Amos 9:13–15, as well as the promise of blessing for obedience to the divine command in Lev 26:3–5 and Deut 28:1–14. In addition, "a cow's heifer and a couple of sheep" contrasts in its limitation with the usual expression of abundant flocks and herds as a symbol of divine blessing (e.g., Gen 12:16; 13:1–6; 20:14; 24:35; 30:43; 32:14–15; Job 1:3; 42:12), while there is no reference whatever to the fertility of the soil, crops, and so on. The verb "keep alive" (*pi'el* of חיה) is used in two main ways, "to restore to life, revive," which is clearly not appropriate here, and "to preserve alive." The

---

13. Thomas Wagner, *Gottes Herrschaft: Eine Analyse der Denkschrift (Jes 6,1–9,6)* (VTSup 108; Leiden: Brill, 2006), 263–65.

latter often appears in contexts where there is reference to a threat from which preservation is acknowledged, such as Josh 9:15; Jer 49:11; Ezek 18:27,[14] while of a number of uses in the Psalms Ringgren observes that "in such contexts there is often a reference to the grave, the pit, or the realm of the dead."[15] The choice of verb thus suggests as much the aspect of escape from danger as of positive blessing.

Beyond the fact of survival, the interpretation that the verse is meant to be wholly positive probably depends on two particular factors in 7:22, namely, the reference to "the quantity (רב, abundance) of milk produced" and the repetition of "butter and honey" from 7:15. The latter point, of course, immediately raises the question of how our later writer will have understood the allusion (and we may note here that the allusion also encompasses "will eat": the clause חמאה ודבש יאכל is identical in both verses). It is generally considered that there are both positive and negative possibilities in 7:15, so that we cannot be sure which interpretation the later editor would have favored.[16] But beyond that, the more important observation is that the language is here once again determined by this reuse of earlier terminology and that this form of citation (if that is not too strong an expression) probably means that in the present context we should not be too concerned to draw out the possible implications of the words as an indication of whether he considered the fare to be sparse or abundant.

Moving back from that conclusion, it may be suggested that the already given reference to "butter" would have led him to speak of "the quantity of milk produced," since this would simply have been a precondition of what he was already committed to mentioning.[17] The suggestion of Luther, Calvin, and others that the point is to underline the small size of the population (so also justifying a negative interpretation) seems to outstrip what is stated.

I thus conclude that, although these verses certainly envisage a small population surviving the disaster of the previous verses, there is no impli-

---

14. See Willem A. M. Beuken, *Jesaja 1–12* (HTKAT; Freiburg; Herder, 2003), 208–9.
15. Helmer Ringgren, "חָיָה; חַי; חַיִּים; חַיָּה; מִחְיָה," *TDOT* 4:334.
16. Wolfgang Werner, *Eschatologische Texte in Jesaja 1–39: Messias, Heiliger Rest, Völker* (FB 46; Würzburg: Echter, 1982), 133–38, studies the usage of these words elsewhere and concludes that on their own they cannot settle the question. Against his otherwise satisfactory argument that this is primarily a *Gerichtswort* but that 7:22a should be deleted as a later salvation gloss, see below.
17. According to William McKane, "The Interpretation of Isaiah vii 14–25," *VT* 17 (1967): 217, two and a half gallons of full-cream milk from an Ayrshire cow are needed for each pound of butter. I should add that, as will be readily apparent, I am unable to share McKane's generally very positive interpretation of this passage.

cation that they should expect to be entering some new age of blessing and plenty; rather, it seems they will survive with a minimum of livestock and with a diet that results from the milk of the animals together with naturally produced honey.[18] (I cannot see how the livestock mentioned lend any support to the notion that there is a description to a return to the nomadic way of life.) While the choice of terminology in 7:15 should probably be taken to have wider significance, its reuse here empties it of that particular force.

The recognition of the pressure exerted by the editor's habit of citing from preexisting material suggests that we should not seek to avoid the difficulties of the passage by proposing that part of it has been added secondarily. There is no support for such a move from the attested textual history of the passage.[19] The citation in 7:22b has to be original, on this understanding, but as it stands it does not flow naturally from 7:21. Verse 22a is therefore required in order to make the move from the reference to animals to the eating of

---

18. This conclusion would stand even if there were included an allusion to the description of the promised land as "flowing with milk and honey," as correctly stated by Etan Levine, "The Land of Milk and Honey," *JSOT* 87 (2000): 52.

19. The LXX offers no rendering of the words יאכל חמאה כי. This cannot be explained as an omission of everything "from the first to the second 'shall eat' of the original" (Richard R. Ottley, *The Book of Isaiah according to the Septuagint (Codex Alexandrinus)* [2 vols; Cambridge: Cambridge University Press, 1906], 2:146), because the words חמאה ודבש, which also come between the two identical verbs, are translated. Joseph Ziegler, *Untersuchungen zur Septuaginta des Buches Isaias* (ATA 12.3; Münster: Aschendorff, 1934), 48, is undecided whether this is the explanation or whether the words represent a later gloss in the Hebrew text. Gray, *A Critical and Exegetical Commentary on the Book of Isaiah I–XXVII*, 140, strongly affirms the latter possibility, because, following his understanding of v. 21, he thinks that the shorter text can imply depopulation: "two or three cattle will yield more than enough for the handful of survivors." It may be questioned, however, whether this approach does justice to the opening words of the verse, which seem already to imply an unexpected abundance, and moreover, as an explanation of MT—that it represents the incorporation of a variant text in which יאכל preceded rather than followed ודבש—חמאה—it does not account for the word כי. The element of repetition in the Hebrew probably simply led to an error by the translator. MT is supported by 1QIsaᵃ, Vulgate, and Targum; Peshitta agrees so far as the words omitted by LXX are concerned, though it does not then include a rendering of חמאה ודבש. As indicated above, some have certainly argued that these verses reveal evidence of secondary expansion, but textual criticism cannot be adduced in support of that conclusion.

butter. Proposals to omit 22a[20] or "he will eat butter because"[21] therefore seem unnecessary.

After these two allusions to the earlier part of Isa 7, it is worth drawing attention to one further possible example of borrowing, again in this third section, but this time from Isa 6. Although the parallel is not precise, nor the vocabulary especially rare, "everyone who remains in the midst of the land" (כל־הנותר בקרב הארץ) in 7:22 sounds very like an echo of 6:12, "that which is left in the midst of the land" (העזובה בקרב הארץ). It implies that "everyone who remains" is still thought of primarily as a reference to those who have literally escaped from the preceding destruction and that they are not yet thought of in the more theologically technical sense of the remnant.[22] For that, with use of the same word (הנותר), we might compare the (later) 4:3, where the reference to Zion and Jerusalem, together with the wider context, suggests a rather narrower definition: "whoever is left in Zion and remains in Jerusalem."

After this survey of the main examples of dependence by the author(s) of Isa 7:18–25 on earlier material within the same book, it is time to draw some broader consequences, both diachronic and synchronic. First, it is striking to observe that we have found several examples within each of three of the four sections in this passage but none whatsoever in the second section, 7:20. This verse also has some other distinguishing features, however:[23] (1) it starts with ביום ההוא, that is to say without a conjunction and without the והיה that precedes the phrase at the start of each of the other sections; (2) it refers to Assyria alone as the threat to Judah, which suits the eighth century satisfactorily; (3) it makes use of a colorful image that is not paralleled elsewhere in Isaiah, a feature that might incline us to favor the view that this is an original saying by the prophet; and (4) it uses the divine title אדני, "Lord," in contrast with the commoner יהוה in 7:18; this was characteristic of Isaiah's language in Isa 6. There is thus much to be said for concluding that 7:20 could represent an original Isaianic saying which was added to 7:1–17 at an early stage,

---

20. See, for instance, Marti, *Das Buch Jesaja*, 80–81; Franz Feldmann, *Das Buch Isaias* (EHAT 14; 2 vols.; Münster: Aschendorff, 1925–1926), 1:97; Procksch, *Jesaia I*, 127; Georg Fohrer, *Das Buch Jesaja* (3 vols.; Zürcher Bibelkommentare; 3rd ed.; Zurich: Theologischer Verlag, 1991), 1:120.

21. Gray, *A Critical and Exegetical Commentary on the Book of Isaiah I–XXVII*, 139–40.

22. See Werner, *Eschatologische Texte in Jesaja 1–39*, 136; and Jutta Hausmann, *Israels Rest: Studien zum Selbstverständnis der nachexilischen Gemeinde* (BWANT 124; Stuttgart: Kohlhammer, 1987), 147–49.

23. See too Marvin A. Sweeney, *Isaiah 1–39 with an Introduction to Prophetic Literature* (FOTL 16; Grand Rapids: Eerdmans, 1996), 154–55.

perhaps when that passage was edited and added into its present location; the inclusion of the gloss במלך אשור, "even the king of Assyria," might come from the same hand, comparable with את מלך אשור, "namely, the king of Assyria," in 7:17. Where the saying would have been preserved in the early Isaianic corpus cannot now be known. It could well have been pronounced in connection with Isaiah's opposition to Hezekiah's policy in the years running up to 701 B.C.E.

So far as the origins and dating of the remainder are concerned, while many recognize that the third and fourth sections (7:21–25) are likely to be later than Isaiah, they also seek to maintain that the first section, 7:18–19, is from the eighth-century prophet. On that basis, as we have already seen, they then go on to eliminate some of the material so as to make it fit its supposed historical setting better; this applies especially to the phrases "which is at the end of the streams of Egypt" and "which is in the land of Assyria." We have already questioned this conclusion above, but in fact there is more to be said about the matter. We have noted that this section (as well as 7:21–22) includes an allusion to the first part of Isa 7. For some decades, many scholars have worked on the assumption that this part of the chapter is an integral part of the so-called Isaiah Memoir, comprising the bulk of 6:1–8:18 (or 9:6). In line with one or two other more recent studies, however, I have argued at length elsewhere that this is a mistake.[24] It is difficult to see how the third-person narrative of 7:1–17 can be of a single literary piece with the first-person Isa 6 and 8. In addition, the chapter has many close parallels and contrasts with Isa 36–39, suggesting that they must have been composed as part of a single work, presumably, therefore, originally separate from our book of Isaiah. (It is likely that Isa 20 will also have come from this same source.) The Deuteronomic features of the Hebrew style are also apparent, so that it seems probable that 7:1–17 will not have been incorporated into the book until or shortly after the time when the Deuteronomic History took something approaching its final shape. The first and third sections of our passage must, then, be later than that. Thus on this matter I disagree with Sweeney (with whose analysis I am otherwise in considerable agreement). He ascribes the whole passage to the time of the Josianic redactor, because it was during Josiah's reign that Egypt became a significant threat to Judah.[25] However, that would be too early from my perspective, and in any case the exegesis in 7:18–19 has shown that the writer may not have had any specific historical threat in mind. All

---

24. Hugh G. M. Williamson, *Variations on a Theme: King, Messiah and Servant in the Book of Isaiah* (Carlisle: Paternoster, 1998), 73–112.

25. Sweeney, *Isaiah 1–39*, 155–59.

the more are suggested earlier dates ruled out.[26] Without any great certainty, the possibility that the passage reflects on the experience of the fall of the nation to the Babylonians and the conditions in the land which followed that disaster seems to me least open to objection, making a later exilic date most plausible.

However in detail the passage came to be compiled, it clearly speaks to the reader of the possibility of some invasion in the future that will be more cataclysmic even than those already experienced at the hands of the Assyrians and the Babylonians. The first two sections portray that in terms of graphic imagery, and the third and fourth go on to tell of the consequent severe decline in population and the loss of previously well-cultivated land. As yet there is no hint of the knowledge of another prophet in the same tradition who would come to announce that the long-delayed day of salvation had arrived and that the community could anticipate a miraculous restoration. The imagery remains on the dark side of the path within the book of Isaiah from judgment to salvation—still, therefore, within the sphere of those who sought to justify the ways of God in allowing the nation to be defeated and to paint a picture of its possible repetition in ways which were no doubt intended to evoke the kind of response that would avert it. Furthermore, the perspective is very much on the land, not the community in exile. Wherever we site Isa 40–55 geographically, it is clear that the first part of the book is far more concerned with judgment and its consequences within the land, and our passage takes its place as perhaps the final step in that trajectory before the start of the new Persian age. In terms of conventional poetic technique, the passage may not have much to be said for it, as indicated at the start of this paper. But in terms of its own form of poetic vision, it seeks to carry forward the message of the prophet Isaiah himself by reapplying his words to the author's own dark days. As such, it makes its contribution by way of a foil to the announcement of deliverance that would follow soon after.

---

26. E.g., Friedrich Huber, *Jahwe, Juda und die anderen Völker beim Propheten Jesaja* (BZAW 137; Berlin: de Gruyter, 1976), 161–62; and Stuart A. Irvine, *Isaiah, Ahaz, and the Syro-Ephraimitic Crisis* (SBLDS 123; Atlanta: Scholars Press, 1990), 171–76: 734–732 B.C.E.; Wildberger, *Jesaja 1–12*, 305 = *Isaiah 1–12*, 323: 726–725 B.C.E.; Walter Dietrich, *Jesaja und die Politik* (BEvT 74; Munich: Kaiser, 1976), 121–22: 713–711 B.C.E.; Jacques Vermeylen, *Du prophète Isaïe à l'apocalyptique: Isaïe, I–XXXV, miroir d'un demi-millénaire d'expérience religieuse en Israël* (EB; 2 vols.; Paris: Gabalda, 1978), 222; and Jörg Barthel, *Prophetenwort und Geschichte: Die Jesajaüberlieferung in Jes 6–8 und 28–31* (FAT 19; Tübingen: Mohr Siebeck, 1997), 182–83: around 701 B.C.E.

Yhwh's Sovereign Rule and His Adoration on Mount Zion: A Comparison of Poetic Visions in Isaiah 24–27, 52, and 66

Willem A. M. Beuken

The understanding of the overall structure of the book of Isaiah (henceforth BI) has entered a new avenue since the so-called Apocalypse of Isaiah (chs. 24–27) is no longer looked upon as an erratic block but rather as an integral part of it (we keep the name "Apocalypse of Isaiah" [henceforth ApcIs] without attributing a so-called apocalyptic character to these chapters). While it remains disputed in which epoch the ApcIs was drawn up, it has become clear, however, that these chapters are closely connected to the preceding collection of the so-called oracles against the nations (chs. 13–23). These pave the way for chs. 24–27. The ApcIs itself brings to completion lines of thought that are developed in chs. 1–12 and elaborated in chs. 13–23 to completion. This completion regards the exercise of power by Yhwh as king of the universe (24:23) and his inauguration by the returning exiles (27:13).[1]

This contrapuntal climax raises the question whether the rest of the BI from ch. 28 on starts all over again and delineates the course of history by means of other theological metaphors. Yet, whether and how the subsequent text elaborates the principal bipartite event just mentioned, is a better way of putting the problem. This regards, in the redaction-historical arrangement of this prophetic book, chs. 28–39, the whole of Deutero-Isaiah (DI) and of Trito-Isaiah (TI; we keep using these terms as referring to the second and third part of the BI, not to their "authors").

---

1. W. A. M. Beuken, *Jesaja 13-27* (HTKAT; Freiburg: Herder, 2007), 310–14.

With regard to the first part of chs. 28–39, the collection of five woe cries in chs. 28–32, applies the judgment on the earth as it has been announced in chs. 24–27, to the concrete situation of God's own people. It addresses those, mainly in Judah and Zion, who do not comply with Yhwh's kingship on Zion (28:16). In principle, they fall under the verdict passed on the world in the ApcIs: the arrogant Ephraim (28:1–4), the reckless rulers of Jerusalem (28:14), the blinded people in Ariel (ch. 29), "the rebellious children" (30:1) and "those who go down to Egypt for help" (31:1).

Chapter 33 does not give the impression to have been designed in connection with the ApcIs but strong semantic agreements suggest that it has redactionally been adapted as a supplement to chs. 24–27 and chs. 28–32. The former chapters have soberly announced Yhwh's rule on Mt. Zion and his adoration by the gathered deportees, the latter have depicted the strong resistence in Zion against government and politics that reckon with Yhwh, and therefore they have announced the appropriate punishment. Consequently, ch. 33 brings various aspects of life in the purified and saved Zion into vision. The confessions there and here clearly show that the same group of people is at stake (cf. 25:9; 26:1–9 with 33:22).

Chapters 34–35 and chs. 36–39 nowadays count for links between PI and DI. The first couple continues the theme of Yhwh's universal rule from Zion (chs. 24–27): ch. 34 proclaims the judgment on the nations now to begin in an exemplary way on Edom (cf. 26:21), ch. 35 announces the effective return of the exiles to Zion (cf. 27:13). Chapters 36–39 enjoy a great amount of literary and theological independence, yet chs. 36–37 continue the dominant question of the ApcIs: who is entitled to rule over the whole earth, Yhwh or "the great king" of Assyria? The theme of Zion's security is the other side of this question. Furthermore, it is a distinct problem whether and how ch. 38, the story of king Hezekiah's recovery, continues the main topic but ch. 39, the story of Hezekiah's naive confidence in the embassy of the king of Babylon, focuses again on the theme whether reliance on another sovereign than Yhwh will help the royal house of Judah.

The distribution of the term "king," from chs. 24–27 forward into DI, is a suitable point of departure to compare Yhwh's rule in the ApcIs with that in the second half of the prophetic book. The twofold perspective of the former, that is, the beginning of Yhwh's kingship and his veneration on Mt. Zion by the deportees, has indeed a counterpart in other composite passages that also serve as a conclusion on the level of redactional composition. These are: (1) the restoration of Zion as Yhwh's holy city in 51:17–52:6; (2) the return of Yhwh King to Zion in 52:7–10, both at the end of the literary drama which unfolds in DI; (3) the going up of "all flesh," the survivors of Israel and the nations, to worship in the house of Yhwh in ch. 66, the conclusion of the whole book. It seems to be that the diptych of Yhwh's kingship and his worship on Mt. Zion in the ApcIs is unfolded in these three passages, each with a distinctive aspect.

This selection of texts may surprise in as far as (1) 40:1–11, as opposed to 52:7–10, will not specifically be included; (2) a term for Yhwh's kingship does not occur in 66:15–24. As for the former objection, 40:1–11 is indeed closely connected to 52:7–10 in literary and semantic regard.[2] The passage will come up in the discussion of 52:7–10, for though it misses the term "king / to reign" (מלך), it does say "his arm rules for him" (40:10: משל). As for the latter objection, it is true that the closure of the BI does not use the term "king / to reign" (מלך) but it is specifically connected to the end of ApcIs by means of the topic of Yhwh's adoration on the holy mountain in Jerusalem (27:13; 66:20–23: השתחוו).

The comparison will be carried out on the level of the semantic field. It is the configuration of Hebrew terms and metaphors that constitutes the differences of poetic vision within the overall development of BI. Therefore, the article will prescind from literary-historical questions and focus on continuous reading as a process that registers the full development of Isaiah's vision.

I. The Restoration of Zion as Yhwh's Holy City (51:17–52:6)

The proper inauguration of Yhwh (52:7–10) is preceded by a diptych: the end of Jerusalem's oppression, parallel to Zion's solemn presentation (51:17–23; 52:1–6). The three acts are inseperably connected, for Yhwh cannot return to his city as long as it finds itself in humiliated state.[3]

Two calls to Zion define the diptych: "Rouse yourself (התעוררי), rouse yourself, stand up, O Jerusalem" (51:17) and "Awake (עורי), awake, put on your strength, O Zion" (52:1). Other parallels between these scenes strengthen their connection. The most conspicuous is the reversal of fortune: the cup

---

2. Christina Ehring, *Die Rückkehr JHWHs: Traditions- und religionsgeschichtliche Untersuchungen zu Jesaja 40,1–11, Jesaja 52,7–10 und verwandten Texten* (WMANT 116; Neukirchen-Vluyn: Neukirchener, 2007), 50–95, 156–62.

3. The delimitation of the three passages agrees with that of Marjo C. A. Korpel and Johannes C. de Moor (*The Structure of Classical Hebrew Poetry: Isaiah 40–55* [OTS 61; Leiden: Brill, 1998], 490–544). They take 51:9–52:12 as one canto and define 51:9–16 as canticle A, 51:17–23 as canticle B, 52:1–6 as canticle C.i–ii and 52:7–10 as canticle C.iii. In this study, the passage 52:11–12 (C.iv) is not taken into consideration because it does not bear on the topic at stake.

of wrath passes from Jerusalem to her tormentors (51:22-23); Jerusalem was sold "for nothing," her liberation will come about "without money" (52:3).

1. 51:17-23: The End of Jerusalem's Suppression

The first one of these parallels, the threefold "wrath of Yhwh" (51:17, 20, 22: חמת יהוה), refers to the ApcIs. In his personal song on his "vineyard of fine wine" (27:2), Yhwh has resolved the perplexing misfortune of Zion by the simple statement that he is not enraged against Israel: "I guard it night and day. I have no wrath (חמה אין לי). If it gives me thorns and weeds, I will wage war against it" (27:3-4).[4] This contention is supposed to evoke objection that is replied by the prophet in advance in 27:7. This can be interpreted in this way: "Has he (Yhwh) smitten him (Israel) as he (Yhwh) smote him who smote him (Israel)? Or has he (Israel) been killed as his (Israel's) killers (1QIsa[a]) have been killed?"[5] Starting with ch. 40, the discussion between Yhwh or the prophet and the people regards the question how they can explain Israel's tribulations if it would be true that God does not harbor a groundless grudge against Israel: "Who gave Jacob up to the spoiler, and Israel to the robbers? Was it not Yhwh, against whom we have sinned...? So he poured on him the heat (חמה) of his anger and the might of battle" (42:23-25). The metaphor that Yhwh has thrusted "the cup of his wrath" first into the hands of Jerusalem but now passes it to her enemies (*translatio poculi pro translatione criminis*) helps to modify the allegation about Yhwh's action in 27:4.

The metaphor "the cup of wrath / the bowl of staggering" (51:17; with inversion of nouns in v. 22) contains a poetical incongruency as compared to reality. It is also found in the ApcIs (without any chance to prove that a quotation or allusion is involved). Older commentaries on ch. 51 have pointed to this parallel. Although Jerusalem drinks the cup "to the dregs" (51:17), Yhwh passes it to her enemies without filling it again (v. 23).[6] A similar incongruency occurs in the sketch of "the city of chaos" in ch. 24. The description

---

4. Translation of v. 4b according to Blenkinsopp, *Isaiah 1-39*, 373; cf. Joseph A. Alexander, *Commentary on the Prophecies of Isaiah* (2 vols.; New York: Scribner, 1874; repr. Grand Rapids: Zondervan, 1976), 437-38.

5. Henk Leene, "Isaiah 27:7-9 as a Bridge between Vineyard and City," in *Studies in Isaiah 24-27: The Isaiah Workshop - De Jesaja Werkplaats* (ed. Hendrik J. Bosman et al.; OTS 43; Leiden: Brill, 2000), 200-203.

6. *Pace* Franz Delitzsch, *Commentar über das Buch Jesaia* (Biblischer Commentar über das Alte Testament 3.1; Leipzig: Dörffling & Franke, 1889), 505: "den neugefüllten Becher."

"The wine mourns / the vine languishes" (24:7) mixes imagery with reality. In the same way the verse lines: "No more do they drink wine with singing / strong drink is bitter to those who drink it" (24:9) and "There is an outcry in the streets for wine" (24:11) contradict each other in reality but together they aptly express the overall destruction by means of a product of the earth that by itself symbolizes happiness and prosperity. This shared poetic incongruency, of course, cannot serve as an argument for the hypothesis that YHWH's return to Zion in 51:17–52:12 would elaborate his enthronement in 24:23 in such a way that "the inhabitants of the earth" in the latter context (24:1, 5–6) are identified with Zion's oppressors in the former passage (51:22–23). Yet this much is for sure: the imagery of disturbed drinking wine is used in both passages in order to depict the situation which precedes YHWH's access to kingship.

2. 52:1–6: ZION'S RESTORATION TO HONOR

Several elements allow comparing this passage with the ApcIs. First of all, the investiture of Zion (52:1: "Put on your strength / put on your beautiful garments") is described as something that she is entitled to ("your") since YHWH is to exercise his kingship from her midst. The term "strength" (עז) links the verse to the song that is heard in Judah after the effective establishment of YHWH's rule in ch. 25: "We have a strong city; he sets up salvation as walls and bulwarks" (26:1). The term parallel to "strength" in this text, that is, "salvation," returns later in the proclamation of the messenger of good tidings: "who brings good tidings of good, who publishes salvation" (52:7: משמיע ישועה).

Next, the agreement of 52:1 with 35:8, 10 comes close to an allusion:

- 52:1 Put on your beautiful garments, O holy city (עיר הקדש). For there shall no more come (בוא) into you the uncircumcised and the unclean (טמא).
- 35:8 And a highway shall be there, and it shall be called "the holy way" (דרך הקדש). The unclean (טמא) shall not pass over (עבר) it, and fools shall not err therein.... 10 The ransomed of YHWH shall return, and come (בוא) to Zion with singing.

There is a difference of perspective: the latter text draws much attention to the way: only in v. 10 Zion itself comes into sight but it is clear that "the holy way" leads to "the holy city." "The unclean" are banned in both texts. On the way to Zion, only "redeemed (גאולים) / ransomed of YHWH" go (35:9–10), as opposed to the highways that lie waste under the broken covenant (33:8).[7] The concept that Yhwh has "ransomed" his people, returns in the valuation of Zion's inhabitants: "You were sold at no cost, and you shall be redeemed (תגאלו) without money" (52:3; cf. 52:9: "Yhwh has redeemed Jerusalem"). The assumption that 52:1–6 allude to 35:8–10 is strenghtened by the fact that 51:10–11 corresponds to 35:9–10, in part even literally.

This parallel gains weight if we take into account the verses following 35:10. The prophecy of the coming of Yhwh's ransomed to Zion is continued by the story that the Assyrian king Sennacherib marches against Judah and sends his Rabshakeh with a mighty army to Jerusalem (36:1–2). This story ends with Yhwh's promise: "He shall not come into this city, or shoot an arrow there, or come before it with a shield, or cast up a siege mound against it. By the way that he came, by the same shall he return, and he shall not come into this city. For I will defend this city and save it, for my own sake and for the sake of my servant David" (37:33–35; cf. 37:29). The outcome of this story agrees: "Then Sennacherib king of Assyria departed and went home" (v. 37). In this way, chs. 36–37 serve as an illustration of 35:8–9 and seem to be referred to in 52:1: unclean people and even rulers do not succesfully set foot on the way to Zion.

In line with this, the issue at stake in the story of the Assyrian army before Jerusalem modifies also the background of Yhwh's return as king to Zion in 52:8–10. That issue runs as follows: "O our God, save us from his hands, that all the kingdoms of the earth may know that you alone are Yhwh" (37:20). Yhwh transcends all the kings of the earth. It is in this role that he returns to Zion (52:7–8), not as the king of one nation or one city. This is heard in the song that the prophet puts in the mouth of Jerusalem: "Yhwh has bared his holy arm before the eyes of all the nations" (52:10). In connection to this, we notice the following. "The daughter of Zion," who in 37:22–35 has defended the honor of "the Holy One of Israel" vis-à-vis the king of Assyria, does not make appearance prior to her restoration in dignity in 52:2: "Loose the bonds from your neck, O captive daughter of Zion" (after the fall of "the daughter of Babylon" in 47:1, 5).

The continuing effect of Sennacherib's unsuccessful campaign against Jerusalem is intensified by the mention of Assyria and its being put on one line with Egypt in the divine oracle: "My people went down at the first into Egypt to sojourn there and the Assyrian oppressed him for nothing" (52:4).[8]

---

7. Øystein Lund, *Way Metaphors and Way Topics in Isaiah 40-55* (FAT 28; Tübingen: Mohr Siebeck, 2007), 84.

8. The adjunct (באפס) is usually explained in connection with 52:3 (חנם / בכסף

Possibly, in the last sentence Israel is envisioned as the aggrieved party but more probably it is Yhwh himself in view of his ensuing question: "Now therefore what have I here, says Yhwh, seeing that my people have been taken away at no cost? Their rulers mock,[9] says Yhwh, and continually all the day my name is despised (מנאץ)" (52:5). As for Assyria, this complaint will refer to the grandiloquence and blasphemy of the Assyrian general and his king in 36:13–20 and 37:23–25, characterized by king Hezekiah in the following way: "This day is a day of distress, of rebuke and of disgrace (נאצה)" (37:3). The term "their rulers" (משלו) refers in this context to foreign oppressors while the very use of the Hebrew term משל prepares the contrast with "your God reigns" (מלך אלהיך) in 52:7 (cf. 40:10: "His arm rules for him [משלה לו]").

Finally, "the name of Yhwh" is worth mentioning as a topic that relates 52:1–6 to the ApcIs. The change-over from the ordeal on the whole earth (24:1–13) to the inauguration of Yhwh's rule on Mt. Zion (24:21–23) makes a start at the hymn on "the name of Yhwh, the God of Israel" from the four corners of the world (24:14). The prophet agrees with this song (25:1), and those in Judah who are willing to enter Yhwh's city (26:1–2) confess this name as their unique authority: "O Yhwh our God, other lords besides you have ruled over us, but your name alone we acknowledge" (26:13). The great story of the failing Assyrian campaign does not explicitly use the term "the name of Yhwh" but its content is at stake in the boasting of the great king and the defense of Yhwh's honor by Hezekiah, the prophet, and the daughter of Zion (36:20; 37:4, 10–13, 16–20, 23–24). The conclusion of the divine oracle in 52:1–6 links up to this by God promising: "Therefore my people shall know my name; therefore in that day (they shall know) that it is I who speak; here am I" (52:6).

לא, "at no cost / without money") as "for nothing, without recompense." Some scholars interpret it as "at the end," parallel to "at the first" (cf. DCH, I, 359). A third group considers it to mean "without reason" (*Gesenius*[18], 89: "grundlos") or "in vain," in reference to the unsuccessful Assyrian campaign against Zion (Klaus Baltzer, *Deutero-Jesaja* [KAT 10.2; Gütersloh: Gütersloher, 1999], 469: "vergebens").

9. According to Charles C. Torrey (*The Second Isaiah: A New Interpretation* [Edinburgh: Scribner's, 1928], 251, 407), the verb יהילילו should be read as יהללו, the *pi'el* of הלל (cf. Targum, Aquila). It would be "an intentional alteration, brought about by the fact that the *pi'el* הלל is used in the O.T. almost exclusively of praising God."

II. The Return of Yhwh King to Zion (52:7–10)

The preceding discussion has shown that the topic of Yhwh's universal kingship, proclaimed in the ApcIs (24:23), continues to make itself felt all the way into DI, namely in connection with the topic of God's royal seat, Zion: her moral decay and restoration, the holy way leading to her (chs. 28–35) and her security at a time of oppression and blasphemy of Israel's God (chs. 36–37). Now it remains to check how this topic takes shape in the proclamation of Yhwh's return as king to Zion in 52:7–10.

Within this overarching theme, the messenger who proclaims Yhwh's kingship (52:7: מבשר) appears in contrast to the king of Assyria who literally praises himself to the heavens at the expense of Yhwh (37:24–25). This contrast is strenghtened by the qualification of the messenger's feet: instead of the usual translation "how beautiful" the term "how timely" seems to be more appropriate. The verb concerned, נאה, basically means that something is fitting and that it corresponds to what reasonably can be expected:[10] "(It) is much more coherent if we understand this verse as intimating that the help appears at the very juncture when it is most needed, than if we take it as a mere expression of delight."[11] In the situation in which tyrants slander the name of Yhwh (52:5), it is convenient that his people be told what his name really involves: presence and intervention (52:6).

The verbs "to speak" and "to hear" connect the grandiloquence of the Assyrians, the Rabshakeh and the great king, with the appearance of the messenger of good tidings (אמר: 36:4, 14, 16; 37:10, 24; 52:7; שמע: 36:13, 16; 37:1, 6, 11; 52:7). The latter announces "peace, good tidings, and salvation." These three words are lacking in the boasting of the oppressors, the term "to save" (הושיע) occurs only in the mouth of Hezekiah and Yhwh (37:20, 35). As opposed to the messenger, the Assyrian proclaims his overlordship, manifest in provocations like: "Should Yhwh deliver (יציל) Jerusalem out of my hand?" (36:20) and "You have heard what the kings of Assyria have done to all lands, destroying them utterly, and shall you be delivered?" (37:11). Other elements serve the fundamental contrast between the Assyrian and the messenger of good tidings:

- In rivalry with Yhwh, the great king prides himself on the following: "I have gone up the heights of the mountains, to the far recesses of Lebanon; I felled its tallest cedars" (37:24), the messenger of good

---

10. DCH, V, 578: "fitting"; Gesenius[18], 768: "geziemend"; Baltzer (Deutero-Jesaja, 477–78) sees a wordplay with the roots נאה, "to be fitting," and אוה, "to be desirable."
11. Alexander, Commentary on the Prophecies of Isaiah, II, 278.

tidings, on the contrary, is arriving "upon the mountains" without any ostentation of power, only "publishing peace" (52:7). To explain the latter adjunct of place, scholars often refer to the geographical location of Jerusalem, yet the "literary situation," too, plays a role. For the mountains in the BI can represent the position of rulers (2:2–3, 14; 14:13) and in the ApcIs, Mt. Zion acquires the meaning of an unassailable stronghold of authority and power (24:23; 25:6–7, 10; 27:13).

- The proclamation of the messenger culminates in the term "salvation" and this is echoed in the song to which Jerusalem is invited (52:7a, 10: ישועה). It is this concept that in the story of Jerusalem's deliverance connects the prayer of king Hezekiah and Yhwh's promise of security (37:20, 35). In the ApcIs, the same term stands central in the prayer of those whom Yhwh gathers on his mountain at his access to kingship: "Lo, this is our God. We have waited for him, that he might save us. This is Yhwh. We have waited for him. Let us be glad and rejoice in his salvation" (25:9; cf. 26:1) and furthermore in the call to enter the holy way to Zion: "Behold, your God will come with vengeance, with the recompense of our God. He will come and save you" (35:4). It appears that in the BI Yhwh's sovereign rule is closely connected to a group that looks for salvation.

The core of the message of good tidings in ch. 52 consists of the clause: "Your God reigns" (52:7: מלך אלהיך). The progress of the topic of Yhwh's kingship, from the ApcIs unto ch. 52, is the subject matter of this essay. The distribution of the title "king" in chs. 33–39, the series of "bridges" between chs. 28–32 and ch. 40, illustrates that progress. After the emphatic occurrence of this title for Yhwh in the confession of those who are saved in Jerusalem in 33:22 and before its use by the prophet in 41:21, the title embodies the absurd claim of Assyria's ruler on absolute power (chs. 36–37 *passim*; 38:6; of Babylon's ruler: 39:1, 7) vis-à-vis the true king of Jerusalem (36:2, 21; 37:1, 5, 10; 38:9; 39:3). In ch. 40 Jerusalem is appointed as herald of the following good tiding: "Behold your God! Behold, the Lord Yhwh comes with might and his arm rules (משלה) for him" (v. 10). From this text on, only earthly "kings" (מלכים) are mentioned: in the plural and mostly parallel with "nations" (41:2; 45:1; 49:7, 23; 52:15; 60:3, 10–11, 16; 62:2).[12] Without individuality and in rivalry among themselves, these leaders are nothing more than exchangeable figures.

---

12. Konrad Schmid, "Herrschererwartungen und –aussagen im Jesajabuch," in *Prophetische Heils- und Herrschererwartungen* (ed. K. Schmid; SBS 194; Stuttgart: Katholisches Bibelwerk, 2005), 47; Ulrich Berges, *Jesaja 40–48* (HTKAT; Freiburg: Herder, 2008), 327.

From ch. 40 on, Yhwh goes for the one who is entitled to sovereignty under his own name (41:21: "the King of Jacob"; 43:15: "Your Holy One, the Creator of Israel, your King"; 44:6: "the King of Israel and his Redeemer"; 52:7: "Your God reigns as King"). In this way, it becomes reality what king Hezekiah has confessed: "You are God, you alone, of all the kingdoms of the earth" (37:16, 20), becomes reality, contrasting with Sennacherib's boast in 37:13: "Where is the king of…?" (cf. 60:12).

When comparing the proclamation of Yhwh's kingship in ch. 52 with that in the ApcIs, it becomes clear that, first of all, the difference lies in the divine titles: "Yhwh of hosts reigns" (24:23) and "Your God reigns" (52:7). The former, "Yhwh of hosts," is fitting in the dethronement of "the host of heaven and the kings of the earth," the latter, "your God" (feminine pronominal suffix), alludes, after the emphatic "my people" pronounced by God (52:4-6), to the covenant formula: under Yhwh's sovereignty Zion is the new partner of the covenant (cf. 51:16). Herewith the problematic nature of Zion as the seat of Yhwh's rule, announced in 24:23; 27:13 but brought under discussion in chs. 28–39, comes to a solution and the restoration of Zion in chs. 40–51 (esp. 41:27; 46:13; 49:14; 51:3) arrives at its completion.

The strikingly new element in the proclamation of 52:7–10 is the fact that Yhwh King "returns (שוב) to Zion" and that the city in the person of the watchmen observes him arriving (52:8). In this way, a specific question of DI, Yhwh's absence or presence in the city, shows up well. The part of the BI that comes after the ApcIs has raised the issue of Zion's relationship to Yhwh (chs. 28–39) but it has not been said therein that Yhwh has withdrawn from the city, only that the "redeemed / ransomed of Yhwh" will return to Zion along the holy way (35:9-10). This theme will return in 51:11. Yet in the opening scene of DI, Zion itself is summoned to announce that Yhwh "comes" (בוא), without any adjunct of place from where he would come but evidently in the interest of herself and the cities of Judah (40:10). The theophany is here open to further geographic precision. Chapter 52 provides this precision in a new role of Zion: the city welcomes Yhwh King and his people for they return to the city to which they on principle belong.

At this point it is suitable to set up a closer comparison of 52:7–10 with 40:1–11, the passages that open and close the "drama" of DI and may have come into being or have received their final wording in connection to each other.[13] Next to their affinity in visual and auditive constellation, they display strong semantic analogies: "to comfort" (40:1; 52:9); "the messenger of good

---

13. For all this, see Ehring, *Die Rückkehr JHWHs*, 67–95.

tidings" (40:9; 52:7); Yhwh "comes" / "returns" (40:10; 52:8); "his arm rules for him" / "Yhwh has bared his holy arm" (40:5; 52:10); "all flesh shall see it" / "all the ends of the earth see" (40:5; 52:10); "the glory of Yhwh" / "the salvation of our God" (40:5; 52:10). At the same time there exists a clear difference. Yhwh's coming in 40:1–11 has the character of the triumphant entry of a military commander with his booty; 52:1–10 sketches the return of a king to his rightful royal seat, with all the reactions and salvific consequences thereof for that location. In this connection, the peculiar Hebrew formulation of the sentence "They see the return of Yhwh to Zion" (יראו בשוב יהוה ציון) does not only involve a local sense but it also forms "Ausdruck der inneren Wiederzuwendung Yhwhs zu Zion" (cf. Zech 1:3; 8:3; Ps 6:5).[14]

The scene of Yhwh's return in 52:10 is made more realistic by the call to Zion to listen to her watchmen (52:8: צפיך). These have lifted up their voice since they see Yhwh returning. The event has a counterpart in the earlier vision of the watchman who interprets the approaching cavalry in this way: "Fallen, fallen is Babylon! And all the images of her gods he has shattered to the ground" (21:9). The fall of this hostile city by itself is no cause for rejoicing (21:10), it is only at the return of Yhwh that the watchmen "cry for joy" and "the waste places of Jerusalem" are summoned to do so (52:8–9: רנן). This event brings the book spanning theme of Isaiah's call to Zion "to shout and sing for joy" in 12:6 to completion (cf. the joyful singing at the reversal of the judgment in 24:14, at the opening of the holy way in 35:2, 6 and the summons to heaven and earth in 44:23 and 49:13).

While the first half of the scene, 52:7–9a, shows semantic connections to PI, the second half, 52:9b–10, refers more to the preceding text of DI ("the arm [זרוע] of Yhwh": 30:30; 33:2; 40:10–12; 48:14; 51:5, 9; "to comfort" [נחם]: 12:1; 40:1; 49:13; 51:3, 12, 19; "to redeem" [גאל]: 35:9; 41:14; 43:1, 14; 44:6, 22–24; 47:4; 48:17, 20; 49:7, 26; 51:10; 52:3, 9; 54:5, 8). The term "salvation" brings the perspective of PI back (cf. above).

The last element to be compared is the position of the nations under Yhwh's rule. It is in the whole BI a theme of primary importance. Its development in chs. 1–39 has been explained elsewhere.[15] If we restrict the present inquiry to texts in which the terms of 52:10, that is, "nations / ends of the earth" (אפסי־ארץ / גוים), occur in relation to Yhwh's rule and his acknowl-

---

14. With regard to the addition of 1QIsaᵃ to the end of 52:8: ברחמים, "with compassion," see Ehring, *Die Rückkehr JHWHs*, 84–86.

15. W. A. M. Beuken, "Woe to Powers in Israel that Vie to Replace Yhwh's Rule on Mt. Zion! Isaiah Chs. 28–31 from the Perspective of Isaiah Chs. 24–27" in FS A. van der Kooij (Leiden: Brill, forthcoming).

edgment by people, the following picture arises. After the establishment of his kingship on Mt. Zion (24:13), Yhwh lays on a banquet "for all people" on the same mountain (25:7) where these concur with Israel's song of gratitude: "We have waited for him, that he might save us.... Let us be glad and rejoice in his salvation" (25:9). Subsequently, the king of Assyria boasts about the fact that the gods were not able to deliver their nations out of his grasp (36:18; 37:12: יציל), yet king Hezekiah confesses Yhwh's sovereignty over "all the kingdoms of the earth" (37:16, 20).

The opening chapter of DI maintains this perspective (40:12–31). Jacob/Israel is here the addressee, the subject matter is the distressful situation of the people. This does not result from lack of confidence in Yhwh at the side of the leaders (as was the case before the exile, cf. chs. 28–33), but it is due to the fact that the people are handed over to the power politics of foreign nations and their rulers (vv. 15, 21–26). Against this, the transitoriness of the latter is expatiated upon. Yhwh's "spirit / counsel" and "justice" in the government of the cosmos cannot be measured (vv. 12–14); unimpededly he extends his authority over all the nations (vv. 15–26) and therefore it is improper that Jacob/Israel blames his God for lack of interest in his fate and of support for his "way / justice" (vv. 27–31). In the corpus of DI, Yhwh's controversy with Israel before the nations figures largely (chs. 41–51). It culminates in the invitation by Yhwh himself: "Turn to me and be saved, all the ends of the earth" (45:22). It is under discussion to which extent the world outside Israel takes part in Yhwh's salvation here. Against the background of chs. 40–55 as a whole, however, two extremes are to be ruled out: neither do the nations receive equal rights on salvation with Israel nor are they simply ashamed witnesses of their own wrong. The passage prepares the prophecy concerning the return of Yhwh King to Zion: "All the ends of the earth shall see the salvation of our God" (52:10). Here the same question puts itself forward and it should receive the same answer.

III. The Gathering of All Nations on the Mountain of Jerusalem to Worship Yhwh (66:15–24)

The finale of the BI assembles many isotopes from the preceding prophecies and visions. Since the change of paradigm in the exegesis of this prophetic book, a large number of studies have been published that investigate and describe the connection of ch. 66 with the overture of the whole book (chs. 1–2) and with the opening of DI (ch. 40) and TI (56:1–8). The following conclusion seems suitable to describe the current state of affairs:

Die eschatologische Konzeption in Jes 56,1–7.8 und Jes 65/66 bildet die Summe jesajanischer Theologie am Buchschluss, indem sie anhand der drei großen jesajanischen Themen von Recht/Gerechtigkeit, Schöpfung und Tempel die endzeitliche Herrschaft Jhwhs über Himmel und Erde umfassend beschreibt. Die Vorstellungen von Tempel, Schöpfung und Recht/Gerechtigkeit werden miteinander verbunden und zugleich in die Vertikale und Horizontale entgrenzt. Es geht nicht mehr um die Schöpfung von Himmel und Erde, sondern um die Neuschöpfung (Jes 65). Es geht nicht mehr um das Thronen Jhwhs im Tempel oder im Himmel, sondern der Himmel selbst wird zum Thron (66,1f). Und schließlich geht es nicht mehr um den Gottesberg, auf den sich Völkerzug und Völkerhuldigung richten. Stattdessen werden die Völker in die kultischen Vorgänge auf dem Gottesberg integriert (66,18ff/56,6f) und der Völkerzug auf alles Fleisch, d.h. nach Jes 66,23 auf die Frommen aus allem Fleisch ausgeweitet.[16]

Henceforth the question arises whether it be possible to read the finale of the BI in line with the contrapuntal end of the ApcIs (24:23; 27:13). In any case, the ApcIS with its reticence (*aposiopesis*) concerning the conditions of Yhwh's kingship and his adoration on Mt. Zion asks for an in-depth account. As indicated above, the conclusion of the "drama" of DI has given a first explanation in the scene of Zion's restoration to public dignity and Yhwh's subsequent return as king to the city (51:17–52:6 and 52:7–10). Chapter 66 brings another and final elaboration. It is self-evident that this chapter is determined by the immediate literary and theological context of chs. 56–66. This context mirrors the situation of the temple community in postexilic Yehud. Although scholars regularly situate the ApcIs in the same era, the precise contemporaneous situation of this community finds less expression in these chapters (somehow in ch. 26 and 27:9–11). This difference, however, does not keep from reading ch. 66 in the perspective of chs. 24–27: both compositions are simultaneously oriented towards Yhwh's cosmic dominion and his adoration on the concrete site of Jerusalem.

At first glance, agreements and differences between 27:12–13 and 66:18–23 present themselves. The former text announces the coming (בוא) of "the gathered people of Israel," specified as "those who were lost in Assyria / driven out to Egypt," in order "to worship (השתחוו) Yhwh on the holy mountain at Jerusalem" (27:12–13). The latter text announces the coming (בא) of "all flesh to worship (השתחות) before me (Yhwh)" (66:23) on the place called

---

16. Judith Gärtner, *Jesaja 66 und Sacharja 14 als Summe der Prophetie: Eine traditions- und redaktionsgeschichtliche Untersuchung zum Abschluss des Jesaja- und des Zwölfprophetenbuches* (WMANT 114; Neukirchen-Vluyn: Neukirchener, 2006), 63.

earlier "my holy mountain Jerusalem" (66:20). Chapter 66, however, begins with the question whether a "house" built by human beings can be "a place of rest" for Yhwh (v. 1). The ApcIs does not speak of the temple, chs. 33–35 in which the theme Zion dominates mention only that "Yhwh dwells on high" (33:5), chs. 36–39 speak twice of "the house (בית) of Yhwh", that is, "the temple" (היכל) as the place of Hezekiah's prayer (37:1, 14 and 38:20), and chs. 40–55 link the rebuilding of the "temple" to that of Jerusalem (44:28; cf. 6:1). Only from 56:1–8 on, "the house of Yhwh" is explicit subject matter (ch. 60; 62:9; 64:10). Chapter 66 now extends Yhwh's presence in his "house" to the cosmic space (vv. 1–2), yet it presents Yhwh's action against his challengers as starting from "the temple" (vv. 5–6). In this way, the universal perspective of the ApcIs shows up well (24:23) and it is completed in respect to the place where it all happens.

A different term for Yhwh's presence that connects ch. 66 with 24:23 is the challenge of his adversaries in 66:5: "Let Yhwh be glorious" (יכבד). The basic text for the theologoumenon of Yhwh's "glory" (כבוד) in the BI is the theophany granted to the prophet at the beginning of his mission (6:3). Yet the wording of 24:23 is remarkably detached: "Yhwh of hosts reigns on Mount Zion and in Jerusalem, and before his elders: glory." The fact that the noun "glory" is not determined here has given rise to a variety of interpretations but the explanation that the verse may refer to the appearance of Yhwh's glory on Mount Sinai (Exod 24:16) is based on good grounds. It is told there that Moses and Aaron, with the elders of Israel, went up to the mountain "to worship afar off" (Exod 24:1) and that "they beheld God, and ate and drank" (Exod 24:11). The ApcIs continues Yhwh's enthronement (Isa 24:23) with the banquet that he prepares for all the nations on his mountain (25:6). The wording of 24:23 apparently keeps off from mentioning Yhwh's presence in Jerusalem in its full weight at this place of the ongoing text where his kingship only takes a beginning (cf. Isa 4:5).[17] The unlimited acknowledgment of Yhwh's glory is heard later on in the song of those who enter his city: "You have increased the nation, you are glorified" (26:15: נכבדת). In the following chapters, the term "glory" for Yhwh's presence in Zion is continued (35:2; 40:5; 42:8; 43:7; 48:11; 58:8; 59:19; 60:1–2).

The theme offers full scope in the conclusion of the chapter, also the conclusion of the book: "I am coming to gather all nations and tongues; and they shall come and shall see my glory, and I will set a sign among them. And

---

17. Hans Wildberger, *Jesaja 28–39* (vol. 3 of *Jesaja*; BKAT 10.3; Neukirchen-Vluyn: Neukircher, 1982), 949; Beuken, *Jesaja 13–27*, 337.

from them I will send survivors to the nations ... to the coastlands afar off, that have not heard my fame or seen my glory; and they shall declare my glory among the nations" (66:18–19). At first sight, the identity of the various groups mentioned is problematic, nevertheless, Yhwh's judgment clearly distinguishes between "his servants" and "his enemies," not between Israel and the nations (66:16), and therefore it comes "upon all flesh" (66:17). The ultimate purpose of the judgment is "to gather all nations and tongues; and they shall come and shall see my glory" (66:18). To that end, Yhwh sets a sign among them, that is, he makes his action (mentioned in 66:16) public by sending survivors from the judgment to the lands far off (66:19) in order that they declare his glory among the nations (66:20). The context of the chapter and the allusions to 37:31–32 (survivors from Judah and Jerusalem) and to 45:20 (survivors from the nations) allow to conclude that these survivors do not come from either Israel alone or the nations alone, for Yhwh's judgment distinguishes only between his servants and his enemies (66:16).[18] Subsequently, the nations on their turn bring in "all your brethren" ("your" refers to those addressed as people "who tremble at his [God's] word" in 66:5), in other words the exiles who live among the nations, as an offering for Yhwh back to Jerusalem (66:20–21).[19]

The strongest aspect of 66:15–24 in contrast with 27:12–13 regards the fact that Yhwh's action against the godless is announced to the nations and that these recognize the God of Israel, moreover that the nations undertake to return the exiles as an offering for Yhwh so that some of them are incorporated as priests and Levites into the temple service on the holy mountain in Jerusalem (66:21). This new development does not mean that the distinction between Israel and the nations is abolished nor that Zion loses its special status. For the creation of the new heavens and the new earth implies first of all that "your descendants and your name shall stand before me" (66:22b). In preceding texts, both words refer to Israel ("descendants," זרע: 41:8; 44:3, 5: 45:19, 25; 48:18–19; 53:10; 59:21; 61:9; 65:9, 23; "name," שם: 43:1; 44:5; 45:3–4; 48:1, 19), on the understanding that Yhwh will open his house to foreigners and will give "a monument and a name" to eunuchs who keep his covenant (56:3–5). Whereas the wicked will leave their name for a curse, Yhwh will call his servants by a different name (65:15). Consequently, 66:22b seems to be directed to loyal Israel. This people, the addressees and their descendants, will stand at Yhwh's service just like the new heavens and the new earth will

---

18. A. E. Gardner, "The Nature of the New Heavens and New Earth in Isaiah 66:22," *ABR* 50 (2002): 16–17.

19. Ibid., 18–27.

do.²⁰ As such they will enjoy a different status than the nations out of whom Yhwh will take only some as his qualified ministers (66:21).

Taken together, 66:21-22 imply: "All flesh shall come to worship (להשתחות) before me" (66:23). This worship is as comprehensive as the judgment "upon all flesh" (66:16). It constitutes a climax as compared to Yhwh's adoration by "the lost and driven out" after they are gathered on "the holy mountain at Jerusalem" (27:13: והשתחוו), and the reverse of the worship of the idols which, from the opening of the book, has provoked intensive loathing (2:20; 37:38; 44:15, 17; 46:6). In this way, the sovereignty of Yhwh finally becomes manifest in the service rendered by Israel (66:22) and also in the worship of all humankind (66:23):

> Although it is tenuous to suggest that this verse [66:23] envisions worldwide conversion, this oracle does foresee the universal recognition and *worship* of Yhwh. The distinction between Israel and the nations may remain, but the worshipping of God together in Jerusalem by all eclipses any subservience on the part of the nations to Israel.²¹

In retrospective, from 66:18-24 back to the ApcIs, the lapidary wording of 24:23 gains significance as an announcement in advance of an unexpected, yet necessary consequence of the fact that Yhwh has established his rule over the cosmos on Mt. Zion.

The description of the judgment employs several terms that strengthen the connection with the ApcIs. First of all, "the sword (חרב) of Yhwh" (66:16) calls to mind that Yhwh will slay Leviathan, the chaos monster of the beginning and the mythical representation of the iniquity of the earth (27:1). The topic of Yhwh's "sword" has played a prominent role in the announcement of the judgment on the nations and Edom in particular (34:5-6), and again in that on "those who forsake and forget my holy mountain" (65:11). The announcement that "Yhwh will execute judgment" (66:16: נשפט) is precisely what the prayerful in Yhwh's city have asked for (26:8-9; cf. 40:14, 27). In addition, the terms "anger" (חמה: 27:4; 34:2; 42:25; 51:17, 20, 22; 63:3, 5-6; 66:15) and "fire" (אש: 26:11; 66:15-16, 24) reinforce the overall reference to the ApcIs. Finally, it is remarkable that the ApcIs never speaks of "heavens and earth" (השמים והארץ), rather of "heavens and height," in the course of

---

20. For "to stand before" (עמדים לפני) in the sense of "to be at the service of," see Willem A. M. Beuken, *Jesaja. Deel IIIB* (POut; Nijkerk: G. F. Callenbach, 1989), 144-45.

21. Joel S. Kaminsky and A. Stuart, "God of All the World: Universalism and Developing Monotheism in Isaiah 40-66," *HTR* 99 (2006): 161.

which "height" connotes haughtiness and judgment (מרום: 24:4, 18, 21; cf. 26:5). The couplet "heavens and earth" carries Yhwh's creative government with it and suits his adoration by all flesh on Mt. Zion (1:2; 37:16; *passim* in chs. 40–55; 65:17; 66:1, 22).

Conclusion

The ApcIs has a contrapuntal end: the universal kingship of Yhwh on Mt. Zion (24:23) and his worship there by the gathered exiles (27:13). Both verses are formulated in a most succinct way and the rupture between this composition (chs. 24–27) and the next one (chs. 28–33) is so rigid that one is tempted to consider the former as a lonely mountain that sticks out against the landscape while the ways do not lead to it but pass by it. It would seem that after the ApcIs, the argument of the prophet commences again in order to arrive, by means of a different trajectory, at another announcement of Yhwh's rule on Mt. Zion, which unfolds the various aspects thereof.

This study leads to a different insight. In the sequel to the ApcIs, various compositions of different origin and tendency describe what is lacking in the actual Zion and how Yhwh proceeds in making the city into his royal seat, according to his claim on it. An extensive web of semantic connections affirm the ApcIs as the background of many subsequent prophecies and visionary events while some of these mark the development as milestones. Two conspicuous ones are the return of Yhwh King to Zion in 52:7–10 and his universal worship, by Israel and "all flesh," on Mt. Zion in 66:22–23. These passages hold good for counterparts of 24:23 and 27:13, but they do not stand alone. The former passage (52:7–10) is closely connected to the preceding restoration of Zion to her fundamental position of honor (51:17–52:6) and is in line with two other episodes: (1) the challenge of Yhwh's sovereignty by Sennacherib, king of Assyria, and the confession of his universal rule by Hezekiah, king of Jerusalem (chs. 36–37); (2) Yhwh's coming as a conquerer to Jerusalem and Judah (40:10–11). The latter passage (66:15–24) extends Yhwh's presence from the temple to the cosmos (66:1–2). In this way, the difference between Israel and the nations becomes subservient to that between the righteous and the godless that ensues, after all, from the announcement that foreigners have access to Yhwh's house (56:1–8).

I dedicate this study to the memory of Roy F. Melugin. By his perceptive investigation into the inner coherence of the book of Isaiah and his participant interest in like-minded research of colleagues junior and senior he has helped the summons of the prophet to be obeyed: "Come, let us walk in the light of Yhwh" (2:5).

The Legacy of Josiah in Isaiah 40–55

Marvin A. Sweeney

I

Interpreters of the book of Isaiah—and of Isa 40–55 in particular—have long noted a fundamental distinction between Isa 40–48 and Isa 49–55. Isaiah 40–48 focus especially on the figure of Jacob as a representation of the exiled nation of Israel as a whole. Isaiah 40–48 also emphasize the role of King Cyrus of Persia as the divinely appointed monarch who inaugurates a new age for the exiled Israelites by allowing them to return to their homeland in Jerusalem. Isaiah 49–55 focus especially on the Bat Zion or Daughter Zion figure to represent the humiliated city of Jerusalem who now looks forward to the coming restoration as her husband Yhwh and her exiled children return to her. Blenkinsopp explains the interrelationship between these two textual blocks by maintaining that Isa 40–48 take up the contemporary political situation of the exiled nation Israel and that Isa 49–55 take up the internal situation of the community.[1] Goldingay and Payne maintain that Isa 49–55 also emphasize the servant of Yhwh as an individual whereas Isa 40–48 emphasize the corporate aspects of the servant.[2] Insofar as the commission to leave Babylon in Isa 48:20–21 so clearly marks the conclusion of a major subunit in the work of Second Isaiah, interpreters have posited that Isa 40–48 marks a first stage

---

[1]. Joseph Blenkinsopp, *A History of Prophecy in Israel* (Louisville, Ky.: Westminster John Knox, 1996), 186.

[2]. John Goldingay and David Payne, *Isaiah 40-55*. Vol. 1 (ICC; London: T&T Clark, 2006), 19.

in the prophet's career,[3] the conclusion of the work of Second Isaiah,[4] or the first stages in the history of Second Isaiah's composition.[5]

With the rising influence of structural form criticism, rhetorical criticism, and intertextuality in biblical exegesis,[6] more and more interpreters have come to recognize that the distinctions between Isa 40–48 and Isa 49–55 represent different stages or foci in the prophet's argumentation.[7] Patricia Tull Willey's study of intertextuality in Second Isaiah is particularly insightful in this regard as she examines the interrelationships between the male Servant of Yhwh (Israel and Jacob) and the female figure Bat Zion (Jerusalem) both within the work of Second Isaiah and in relation to the various intertextual references, such as Jeremiah and Lamentations, apparent in the text.[8] She notes the interplay of masculine plural, masculine singular, and feminine singular address forms employed throughout Isa 40–55 to indicate that both figures appear in parallel movement throughout the work of Second Isaiah as figures who have suffered at the hands of their enemies and of Yhwh and who are promised by Yhwh a joyful return of exiles from distant lands. Both figures clearly give voice to the theological concerns, questions, and aspirations of the exiled Jewish community at the outset of Cyrus's reign and the beginning of the restoration of Zion.

Yet a key question remains open, namely, why does Second Isaiah choose to portray the interplay between the male servant figure Jacob or Israel and the female figure of Bat Zion? It is well known that Second Isaiah draws heavily on various traditions, such as the creation traditions that depict Yhwh's sovereignty over the natural world; the ancestral traditions concerning Abra-

---

3. E.g., Menahem Haran, "The Literary Structure and Chronological Framework of the Prophecies in Is. xl–xlviii," in *Congress Volume: Bonn 1962* (VTSup 9; Leiden: Brill, 1963), 127–55.

4. E.g., Julian Morgenstern, "The Message of Deutero-Isaiah in Its Sequential Unfolding," *HUCA* 29 (1958): 1–67; *HUCA* 30 (1959): 1–102.

5. E.g., Rosario Pius Merendino, *Der Erste und der Letzte: Eine Untersuchung von Jes 40–48* (VTSup 31; Leiden: Brill, 1981).

6. See Marvin A. Sweeney, "Form Criticism," in *To Each Its Own Meaning: An Introduction to Biblical Criticisms and their Applications* (ed. S. L. McKenzie and S. R. Haynes; Louisville, Ky.: Westminster John Knox, 1999), 58–89; Patricia K. Tull, "Rhetorical Criticism and Intertextuality," in McKenzie and Haynes, *To Each Its Own Meaning*, 156–80.

7. E.g., Marvin A. Sweeney, *Isaiah 1–4 and the Post-Exilic Understanding of the Isaianic Tradition* (BZAW 171; Berlin: de Gruyter, 1988), 65–95.

8. Patricia Tull Willey, *Remember the Former Things: The Recollection of Previous Texts in Second Isaiah* (SBLDS 161; Atlanta: Scholars Press, 1997); cf. Benjamin D. Sommer, *A Prophet Reads Scripture: Allusion in Isaiah 40–66* (Stanford: Stanford University Press, 1998).

ham, Sarah, Jacob, and others to portray Yʜᴡʜ's covenant or relationship with Israel; the Exodus and Wilderness traditions employed here to portray a new exodus from Babylon; and the royal Davidic tradition employed here to justify the role of Cyrus as Yʜᴡʜ's messiah and Temple builder and Israel as the recipient of Yʜᴡʜ's eternal promise to David at the conclusion of the Babylonian exile. It is also well known that the figures of Israel/Jacob and Bat Zion/Jerusalem are key figures in the marriage traditions of ancient Israel that are employed to address questions of exile and return. Jacob leaves his homeland for Aram, and serves twenty years in exile before returning to his homeland in Israel with his wives Rachel and Leah, their handmaidens, and their children only to lose his beloved Rachel as she gives birth to their second son Benjamin. Whereas Jacob/Israel serves as the groom in the ancestral traditions, he serves as the wayward bride in the prophetic representations of the covenant between Yʜᴡʜ and Israel as a failed marriage in clear need of restoration between Yʜᴡʜ the groom and Israel in Hos 1–3 and Jer 2. A similar metaphor of failed marriage in need of restoration is employed for the portrayal of the relationship between Yʜᴡʜ and Jerusalem in Ezek 16. Zephaniah 3:14–20, however, emphasizes a time of restoration insofar as it portrays Jerusalem as the abandoned Bat Zion whose husband Yʜᴡʜ and exiled children are now returning to her.

Indeed, the marriage traditions of ancient Israel, whether they are between Jacob and Rachel and Leah; Yʜᴡʜ and Israel; or Yʜᴡʜ and Jerusalem, are clearly constitutive elements in Second Isaiah's portrayal of Israel's and Zion's exile and restoration. And yet interpreters must note another dimension of these figures, viz., the degree to which the figure of Jacob/Israel is identified with northern Israel in both the ancestral and the prophetic traditions and the degree to which Bat Zion/Jerusalem is identified with southern Judah in the prophets. Indeed, the interplay between the northern figures Israel, Jacob, or Rachel and the southern figure Bat Zion or Jerusalem is often a characteristic feature of Judean texts from the time of Josiah and other settings that envision the restoration of a unified Israel as the exiled or afflicted north returns to the south. In an effort to determine why Second Isaiah employs the Jacob and Bat Zion figures to address the questions of exile and restoration at the end of the Babylonian exile and the outset of the Persian period restoration, this paper analyzes Second Isaiah's use of both figures in relation to the traditions from which they are drawn, including the ancestral traditions concerning Jacob, Rachel, and Leah in Gen 25–35; the traditions of Yʜᴡʜ's marriage with Israel in the northern prophets Hosea and Jeremiah, and the traditions of Yʜᴡʜ's marriage with Jerusalem/Bat Zion in the southern prophets Zephaniah and Ezekiel. Insofar as these traditions appear to give expression to King Josiah's failed efforts to reunite northern Israel with southern Judah in the late seventh-century B.C.E.,[9] this paper maintains that Second Isaiah's use of the Jacob and Bat Zion figures draws upon the earlier Josian paradigm for the restoration and reunification of northern Israel and southern Judah.

II

Second Isaiah's use of the Jacob/Israel figure in Isa 40–48 emphasizes an interplay between the portrayal of Yhwh's role as creator and king of Israel and the exodus tradition that takes up Jacob's exile and return.[10] Although the prolog in Isa 40:1–11 focuses on Jerusalem/Zion, subsequent material addresses Jacob/Israel, asking if Jacob/Israel knows Yhwh's role as creator and redeemer from old (Isa 40:27–28). Isaiah 41:8–9 identified Jacob as Yhwh's servant and the seed of Abraham whom Yhwh has chosen and whom Yhwh will help and redeem in a scenario in which all creation participates in the projected scenario of Jacob's redemption (Isa 41:5–20). The first servant song in Isa 42:18–25 identifies Jacob and Israel as Yhwh's blind and deaf servant given over to despoilment and plunder, and Isa 43:1–8 again promises that Yhwh is Jacob/Israel's creator who will see to the return of the people from the ends of the earth. Isaiah 43:22–28 charges Jacob/Israel with failing to worship Yhwh, but Isa 44:1–8 identifies Yhwh as Jacob/Israel's king and creator, who reassures the servant Jacob of blessing and redemption. Isaiah 44:21–22 exhorts Jacob/Israel to remember Yhwh's past actions on behalf of the nation and promises to wipe away the nation's sins in an effort to call for their return to Yhwh and to Jerusalem as Cyrus restores Jerusalem and rebuilds the Temple. Isaiah 45:1–8 emphasizes that Yhwh the creator and G-d of the servant Jacob has chosen Cyrus for the sake of Yhwh's people. Isaiah 46:3–4 calls upon Jacob/Israel to recognize that Yhwh has brought down Babylon, personified in Isa 47:1–5 as the humiliated maiden Babylon. The final appeal to Jacob in Isa 48:1–22 reiterates the promises to the ancestors of numerous offspring

---

9. For discussion of Josiah's reform and its impact on biblical literature, see Marvin A. Sweeney, *King Josiah of Judah: The Lost Messiah of Israel* (Oxford: Oxford University Press, 2001).

10. For commentaries and studies on Second Isaiah, see esp. the above-noted works by Westermann, Goldingay and Payne, Tull, and Sommer. In addition, see Joseph Blenkinsopp, *Isaiah 40–55*; Brevard S. Childs, *Isaiah* (Louisville, Ky.: Westminster John Knox, 2001); Roy F. Melugin, *The Formation of Isaiah 40–55*; Klaus Kiesow, *Exodustexte im Jesajabuch. Literarkritische und motivegeschichtlichen Analysen* (OBO 24; Fribourg: Editions Universitaires; Göttingen: Vandenhoeck & Ruprecht, 1979).

(Isa 48:19) and calls upon the servant Jacob to leave Babylon for a journey through the wilderness that will bring the nation home (Isa 48:20–22).

Although Isa 40–48 employs the creation and exodus/wilderness traditions to construct its portrayal of Yhwh as sovereign of creation and redeemer of Israel, the choice of Jacob/Israel as the means to portray the exiled nation is an apt one, particularly in relation to the role that the ancestor Jacob plays in Israelite tradition. Jacob is the key ancestral figure who is exiled from his land to Aram to find a bride and returns to the land of Israel after twenty years service when he has finally found his brides and fathered his sons. Indeed, the association of Jacob with exile is a powerful insofar as goes into exile a second time to Egypt to escape famine in his homeland and ultimately to find his lost son Joseph.

Interpreters largely see the Jacob traditions in Gen 25:19–35:29 as the product of a combined JE and P tradition that reflects upon Jacob and his wives as foundational figures in the early history of Israel,[11] but it is also important to recognize that the Jacob traditions also give expression to the political and historical realities of much later times.[12]

Indeed, the basic narrative structure of the Jacob traditions, including both Jacob's conflicts with his brother Esau and his relationship with his wives Rachel and Leah and their father Laban appear to have been composed as a reflection on northern Israel's relationships with Edom and Aram during the ninth century B.C.E.[13] The Jacob narrative emphasizes that the key male figures, Jacob, Esau, and Laban, are eponymous ancestors for the nations Israel (Gen 32:28; 35:10); Edom (Gen 25:30); and Aram (Gen 31:47) respectively. Furthermore, the emphasis on puns to illustrate the meanings of the names of the key male figures in the narratives, including Jacob, Esau, and Laban as well as Jacob's twelve sons, highlights the geographical and political concerns underlying this narrative insofar as the puns also identify boundaries between Israel, Edom, and Aram and the twelve tribal and geographical components of the kingdom of Israel.

---

11. For current assessment of the Jacob tradition in Genesis, see Antony F. Campbell and Mark A. O'Brien, *Sources of the Pentateuch: Texts Introductions, Annotations* (Minneapolis: Fortress, 1993).

12. For treatment of the Jacob traditions as a block rather than as the product of sources, see Erhard Blum, *Die Komposition des Vätergeschichte* (WMANT 57; Neukirchen-Vluyn: Neukirchener, 1984), 5–270; cf. Rolf Rendtorff, *The Problem of the Process of Transmission in the Pentateuch* (JSOTSup 89; Sheffield: Sheffield Academic Press, 1990).

13. See Marvin A. Sweeney, "Puns, Politics, and Perushim in the Jacob Cycle: A Case Study in Teaching the English Hebrew Bible," *Shofar* 9 (1991): 103–18.

Thus, the description in Gen 27:11 of Jacob as a "smooth" (Hebrew, *ḥālāq*) man and Esau as a "hairy" (Hebrew, *śāʿîr*) man recalls the place names Mt. Halak and Mt. Seir in Josh 11:17 that mark the boundaries between Israel and Edom. Esau's willingness to trade his birthright to Jacob for some lentils, described in Gen 25:30 in Hebrew as *hāʾādōm*, "red stuff," and his description in Gen 25:25 as a "ruddy" (Hebrew, *ʾadmônî*) and a "hairy" (Hebrew, *kĕʾadderet śēʿār*, lit., "like a hairy mantle") likewise reinforces Esau's identification with Edom (Hebrew, *ʾĕdôm*) and Seir (Hebrew, *śēʿîr*). The name Laban, Hebrew, *lābān*, means "white," which is associated with the Valley of Lebanon (*hallĕbānôn*) that defines the boundaries between Aram, Phoenicia, and Israel in Josh 11:17. Likewise the Hebrew reference *galʿēd*, "heap of witness," in Gen 31:47 to the pillar set up by Jacob and Laban as a boundary marker between their respective territories recalls the location Baal Gad (Hebrew, *baʿal gād*) which also marks the boundary between Israel and Aram in Josh 11:17 and the tribe of Gad that inhabits the region together with the half tribe of Manasseh.

The various puns employed to interpret the names of Jacob's sons highlight the tribal units that constitute ancient Israel. The name of Reuben (*rĕʾûbēn*), first-born son to Jacob and Leah means, "Yhwh has seen (*rāʾâ*) my affliction" and "now my husband will love me (*yeʾĕhābanî*)" according to Gen 29:32; Simeon (*šimʿôn*) is so-named "because Yhwh heard (*šāmaʿ*) that I was unloved" in Gen 29:33; Levi (*lēwî*) is named because "this time my husband will become attached (*yillāweh*) to me" in Gen 29:34; and Judah (*yĕhûdâ*) is named because "this time I will praise (*ʾôdeh*) Yhwh." When Bilhah gives birth to Dan, Rachel states, "G-d has vindicated me (*dānannî*)" in Gen 30:6, and when Naphtali is born, Rachel states, "a divine/fateful contest I waged (*naptûlê ʾĕlōqîm niptaltî*) with my sister" in Gen 30:8. When Zilpah gives birth to Gad (*gād*), Leah states, "What luck (*bāʾ gād*)!" in Gen 30:11, and when Asher (*ʾāšēr*) is born, Leah states, "What fortune (*bĕʾašrî*)!" in Gen 30:12. When Leah gives birth to Issachar (*yiśśāśkār*), she exclaims, "G-d has given me my reward (*śĕkārî*)" in Gen 30:18 (cf. Gen 30:16), and when Zebulun (*zĕbulûn*) is born, Leah states, "G-d has given me a choice gift (*zebed*); this time my husband will exalt me (*yizbĕlēnî*)" in Gen 30:20. No pun is uttered when Leah's daughter Dinah is born in Gen 30:21. When Joseph (*yôsēp*) is born, his mother Rachel states, "G-d has taken away/gathered (*ʾāsap*) my disgrace" and "May Yhwh add (*yōsēp*) another son for me" in Gen 30:23–24. When Rachel dies while giving birth to Benjamin (*binyāmîn*), Jacob names him "son of the right hand (*binyāmîn*)" in Gen 35:18 to indicate his exalted status.

The locations of major events during Jacob's return to Israel from Aram to face his brother Esau also evoke puns, which point to Israel's presence on the east bank of the Jordan River. When Jacob departs from Aram and sees angels of G-d in Gen 32:1-3, he exclaims, "This is G-d's camp (*maḥănēh*)." Jacob divides his family into two camps (*šĕnê maḥănôt*) in Gen 32:8-9, 11 to better protect his family should Esau decide to attack. Both of these puns explain the city name Mahanaim, whose precise location is unknown although it was located along the River Jabbok in the tribal territory of Gad or Manasseh. When Jacob wrestles with the "man of G-d" at Penuel by the River Jabbok, several puns indicate the region. The verb *wayyē'ābēq*, "and he wrestled" in Gen 32:24 indicates the name of the River Jabbok (*yabbōq*). The place name Peniel/Penuel (*pĕnî'ēl/pĕnû'ēl*) is named because of Jacob's statement, "I have seen a divine being (*ĕlōqîm*, lit., "god") face to face (*pānîm 'el pānîm*)" in Gen 32:31-32. The River Jabbok served as the boundary between Gad and Manasseh in the Trans-Jordan, and Penuel served as an important administrative center for the northern kingdom of Israel shortly after its founding by Jeroboam (1 Kgs 12:25). The man of G-d explains Jacob's change of name to Israel (*yiśrā'ēl*) in Gen 32:29 with the statement, "for you have striven (*śārîtā*) with divine and human beings and prevailed." Finally, Jacob journeys to the city of Sukkot (*sukkōt*) to make stalls (*sukkōt*) for his cattle. Sukkot was also situated near the junction of the River Jabbok with the Jordan River in the Trans-Jordan.

Although the puns employed in the Jacob narrative may serve in part as entertainment, their geo-political functions must not be overlooked. The puns ascribed to the twelve sons of Jacob define the twelve tribal units that make up the united people of Israel throughout early Israelite tradition. The puns associated with the Trans-Jordanian region are particularly important because they point to locations associated with the tribes of Gad, Manasseh, and perhaps Reuben early in Israel's history as well. Altogether, the puns point to an ideal twelve tribe structure of Israel that fills the land west and east of the Jordan in accordance with the ideal tribal allotments of Josh 13-23 and Num 34. But the contents of the narrative, particularly the interrelationships between Jacob, Esau, and Laban must also be taken into account. Insofar as these figures serve as eponymous ancestors for Israel, Edom, and Aram, the interrelationships—or more properly conflicts—between these characters must be considered in relation to the interrelationships and conflicts between their corresponding nations must also be considered. Biblical sources in 1 Kgs 16-2 Kgs 14 indicate that Israel was reunited in the ninth century B.C.E. under the reign of the Omride dynasty of northern Israel, which counted Judah and Edom among its vassals.[14] Nevertheless, this was a period of con-

---

14. For treatment of texts in Kings, see Marvin A. Sweeney, *I and II Kings: A Commentary* (OTL; Louisville, Ky.: Westminster John Knox, 2007).

flict in which Israel was attacked by Aram in the Trans-Jordan during the reigns of the Omride monarchs Ahab, Ahaziah, and Jehoram, and conflict with Aram continued during the reigns of the Jehide monarchs Jehu, Joash, and Jehoahaz as well. Ahab was able to strike a treaty with the Aramean King Ben Hadad following an aborted Aramean invasion of Israel at Aphek east of the Sea of Galilee in 1 Kgs 20:26–34. Nevertheless, Ahab was killed in battle with the Arameans at Ramot Gilead, located in the Trans-Jordan. With the death of Ahab, the overthrow of his son Jehoram by his general Jehu while the conflict continued at Ramot Gilead, and finally Jehu containment by the Arameans following his revolt, it appears that Israel lost the Trans-Jordan to the Arameans until it was regained by Jehoahaz. There was also conflict with Edom during this period, which broke away from King Jehoram of Judah, himself a vassal of the Omride King Jehoram at this time, according to 2 Kgs 8:20–24. Although Israelite control of the Trans-Jordan was reestablished by the reign of King Jeroboam of Israel, there is no indication that Edom was ever recovered by either Israel or Judah.

The conflicts between Jacob and Esau and between Jacob and Laban in the Genesis narrative appear to reflect the historical events of the ninth century B.C.E. Israel entered into conflict with Aram in the Trans-Jordan and ultimately settled its boundaries with Aram, first in the time of Ahab and later by the time of Jeroboam. Likewise, Edom began as a vassal of Israel/Judah during this period but ultimately broke away from Israel/Judah, likely due to the reverses that Israel suffered against the Arameans.

These considerations indicate that the Jacob narrative was composed at least in its basic form at some point following the ninth century B.C.E., perhaps in the eighth century B.C.E. when northern Israel had restored its boundaries under Jeroboam and had the opportunity to reflect on its history. But if the basic narrative was composed at such an early date, interpreters must also reflect on the impact it would have had on readers in later periods, particularly following the destruction of the northern kingdom of Israel in 722/1 B.C.E. when the narrative would have been brought south and read by Judeans. The narratives concerning Jacob's/Israel's exiles and reverses on the one hand and his return and restoration to the land of Israel on the other would have played an important role in Judean attempts to reunite Israel and Judah and to restore Davidic authority over the north, either during the reign of Hezekiah whose revolt against Assyria failed so spectacularly or during the reign of Josiah whose efforts to reunite the nation in the aftermath of the collapse of the Assyrian Empire were cut short by his early death at Megiddo at the hands of Pharaoh Necho of Egypt. In the late-monarchic period, the Jacob traditions of Jacob's own exile and return to the land would have given expression to Israel's defeat and exile at the hands of the Assyrians and the prospects for Israel's restoration and reunification with Judah in the aftermath of Assyria's downfall. Such a narrative could well have played a role in motivating attempts by either Hezekiah or Josiah to reunite Israel and Judah and to restore Davidic authority over the north.

III

Interpreters will never be able to know the precise form of the Jacob traditions in the late-monarchic period or even the degree to which they influenced Hezekiah or Josiah, but Jer 30–31, which portray the return of Israel to Zion and the reunification of north and south provides some clues concerning the impact of this tradition in the book of Jeremiah.

The present form of Jer 30–31 clearly presupposes the Babylonian exile insofar as it posits that both Israel and Judah together must be restored in the aftermath of exile and disaster.[15] Such perspectives appear at the outset of the oracular block in Jer 30:3–4, which portray YHWH's promise to restore the fortunes of both Israel and Judah and return them to the land promised by YHWH to their ancestors. They appear in several other subunits of this text as well. Jeremiah 31:27–30 declares that the time to uproot, to pull down, to destroy, and to bring disaster to both Israel and Judah is over and that the time to build and to plant has come. Jeremiah 31:31–34 declares that YHWH will make a new covenant with Israel and Judah—unlike the former covenant with the ancestor that the people broke—in which YHWH will put divine Torah in the hearts of the people so that YHWH will be their G-d once again. Finally, Jer 31:38–40 envisions the restoration of the city of Jerusalem as a result of YHWH's promises never again to uproot or overthrow the people.

It is striking that each of these passages concerned with the restoration and return of both Israel and Judah is introduced by a common formula, *hinnēh yāmîm bā'îm*, "behold the days are coming," whereas the other primary formula throughout the passage is the so-called prophetic messenger formula, *kōh 'āmar yhwh*, "thus says YHWH," which introduces the other prophetic oracular speeches that constitute this unit in Jer 30:1–2; 30:5–11; 30:12–17; 30:18–31:1; 31:2–6; 31:7–14; 31:15; 31:16–22; 31:23–26; 31:35–36; and 31:37. Indeed, if the oracles introduced by the *hinnēh yāmîm bā'îm* for-

---

15. For discussion of Jeremiah 30–31, see esp. Marvin A. Sweeney, "Jeremiah 30–31 and King Josiah's Program of National Restoration and Religious Reform," in his *Form and Intertextuality in Prophetic and Apocalyptic Literature* (FAT 45; Tübingen: Mohr Siebeck, 2005), 109–22.

mula are removed from the passage, the remaining oracles introduced by the *kōh ʾāmar yhwh* formula display a sequence of oracles that are concerned not with the restoration and return from exile of both Israel and Judah but only with the restoration and return of Israel/Jacob to Zion.

Jeremiah 30:1–2 serves as an introduction to the unit insofar as it presents simply Yhwh's command to the prophet to write down the following oracles. Jeremiah 30:5–11 portrays a time of trouble for Jacob, a common designation for northern Israel, and Jacob's anticipated return to its G-d and David, the king that Yhwh will raise for them. The oracle also addresses Jacob as "servant Jacob" in v. 10, a common designation in Second Isaiah. Jeremiah 30:12–17 promises healing from wounds to an addressee who is unclear until after the closing oracular formula of v. 17a. Although Zion emerges as the addressee in v. 17b, its placement after the closing oracular formula suggests later interpretation of a text addressed to another figure. Jeremiah 30:18–31:1 promises the restoration of the fortunes of Jacob's tents and the restoration of the covenant relationship with the classic formula, "You shall be my people, and I will be your G-d," again applied to the clans of Israel in Jer 31:1. Jeremiah 31:2–6 recalls the wilderness traditions when Israel became Yhwh's bride (cf. Hos 2; Jer 2) to address Israel as "maiden Israel" in v. 4. The passage also portrays the planting of the hills of Samaria and the proclamation from the heights of Ephraim that the people should go up to Zion to appear before Yhwh. Jeremiah 31:7–14 employs characteristic language applied to northern Israel, such as the call for Jacob's rejoicing, the return of the remnant of Israel, Ephraim the first born of Yhwh, to portray Yhwh's gathering Israel from the ends of the earth and Yhwh's ransoming of Jacob so that they will rejoice on the heights of Zion. Jeremiah 1:15 portrays Rachel, the avowed bride of Jacob and mother of Joseph and Benjamin, weeping for her lost children. Joseph, of course, is the father of Ephraim and Manasseh, the two key tribes of northern Israel, and Benjamin is the tribe of Saul, the first king of the north. Jeremiah 31:16–22 calls upon Ephraim to cease weeping and for Maiden Israel to return. Jeremiah 31:23–26 envisions the time the actions of the G-d of Israel will be recognized in the land of Judah and its towns; again, an apparent supplement in v. 26 envisions the habitation of Judah's land and towns. Jeremiah 31:35–36 portrays Yhwh's promise to the offspring of Israel that they will always be a nation. Finally, Jer 31:37 reiterates Yhwh's promise to the offspring of Israel in relation to the permanence of heaven and earth.

Altogether, this survey of the oracles introduced by the prophetic messenger formula presents a portrayal of Yhwh's promises of restoration to Israel, Jacob, Maiden Israel, Rachel, and Ephraim, all references to the northern kingdom of Israel, that they will be restored and returned to Yhwh at Zion and to David, the founder of the Judean dynasty. Oracles introduced with the formula, "behold the days are coming," address the restoration of both Israel and Judah, and several instances indicate that an Israelite oracle has been supplemented so that it refers to Jerusalem or Judah. Such a phenomenon indicates that an early cycle of oracles concerned with the restoration of northern Israel to Zion has been reworked so that the edited cycle calls for the restoration of both Israel and Judah. The settings for each of the two stages in the composition of this text are clear; the concern with the restoration of Israel to Zion was a primary concern of the reform of King Josiah who ought to restore Davidic rule over the north in the aftermath of the fall of Assyria in the late seventh century B.C.E., and the concern with the restoration of both Israel and Judah presupposes the Babylonian destruction and exile of Jerusalem and Judah. Insofar as the superscription of the book of Jeremiah maintains that the prophet began his career in the thirteenth year of King Josiah and that it extended to the eleventh year of Zedekiah, that is, the year of Jerusalem's destruction, it appears that the prophet composed the earlier cycle in support of Josiah's efforts to reunite Israel and to restore Davidic rule over the north but later updated the cycle to account for the reverses suffered by Judah, culminating in the Babylonian exile, following the death of Josiah.

But the oracular sequence also demonstrates the degree to which the figure of Jacob, initially as representative of the northern kingdom of Israel and subsequently as representative for both Israel and Judah together, was viewed as a paradigm for Israel's exile and restoration in the book of Jeremiah during the late-monarchic and early-exilic period. It likewise demonstrates the first efforts to associate Jacob with the marriage tradition that identifies Israel as Yhwh's bride in the wilderness (Hos 2; Jer 2), insofar as it employs Rachel, Jacob's favored wife as a symbol for Israel's mourning in Jer 31:15 and immediately shifts to a portrayal of Ephraim's lamenting and Maiden Israel's return to Zion in the following oracle in Jer 31:16–22. Insofar as Jer 30–31 employs some characteristic phraseology and concerns of Second Isaiah, for example, "have no fear, my servant Jacob" (Jer 30:10); "the anger of Yhwh shall not turn back until it has completed His purposes; in the days to come you shall perceive it" (Jer 30:24); "I will bring them in from the northland, gather them from the ends of the earth—the blind and the lame among them (Jer 31:8); "I will lead them to streams of water, by a level road where they will not stumble" (Jer 31:9); "hear the word of Yhwh, O nations, and tell it in the isles afar, say, He who scattered Israel will gather them" (Jer 31:10); "for Yhwh will ransom Jacob, redeem him from one too strong for him" (Jer 31:11); and "thus says Yhwh, who established the sun for light by day, the laws of moon and stars for light by night, who stirs up the sea into roaring waves, who name is Yhwh of Hosts" (Jer 31:35). From these parallels, it appears that Jer 30–31 provided an important basis for the oracles of Second Isaiah to develop the themes of Yhwh's redemption of Israel, Israel's return to Zion, and at least some of basis for the portrayal of Bat Zion as Yhwh's restored bride.

IV

Like the Jacob traditions of Gen 25–35, the portrayal of Israel as the bride of Yhwh in the wilderness has deep roots in northern Israelite tradition, particularly in the work of the prophets, Hosea and Jeremiah.[16] Both have affinities with the north, Hosea because of his concerns with the Jehide dynasty of northern Israel and Jeremiah because he is from Anathoth in the land of Benjamin. Both envision the wilderness period as an ideal period in which Yhwh and Israel were betrothed, much like Jacob and Rachel in Haran, but both portray Israel's subsequent abandonment of Yhwh for other lovers. Such a portrayal differs from the wilderness traditions of the Pentateuch which portray Israel's murmuring against Yhwh from the outset. In both Hosea and Jeremiah, the marriage tradition is employed to critique northern Israel in relation to the concerns of the time in which each book is written and read, Hosea in relation to the last years of northern Israel and again in the time of Josiah, and Jeremiah in the time of Josiah and afterwards.

The book of Hosea presents the work of the prophet Hosea, who lived during the last years of the northern Israelite monarchy.[17] The superscription maintains that he lived during the reigns of the northern Israelite monarch Jeroboam ben Joash (786–746 B.C.E.) and the southern Judean monarchs Uzziah (782–742 B.C.E.), Jotham (742–735 B.C.E.), Ahaz (735–715 B.C.E.), and Hezekiah (715–687/6 B.C.E.). Interpreters explain the discrepancy in the reigns of the king by maintaining that Hosea left northern Israel for the south where his work was edited and published. Reasons for his departure might include his trenchant critique of the Jehide dynasty, particularly while Jereboam ben Joash remained on the throne, or possibly the Assyrian assaults against northern Israel and its ultimate destruction of the kingdom although

---

16. For discussion of the marriage traditions in the prophets, see especially Gerlinde Baumann, *Love and Violence: Marriage as Metaphor for the Relationship between YHWH and Israel in the Prophetic Books* (Collegeville, Minn.: Liturgical, 2003); R. Abma, *Bonds of Love: Methodic Studies of Prophetic Texts with Marriage Imagery (Isaiah 50:1-3 and 54:1-10, Hosea 1-3, and Jeremiah 2-3* (SSN; Assen: Van Gorcum, 1999).

17. For discussion of Hosea, see Marvin A. Sweeney, *The Twelve Prophets* (vol. 1; Berit Olam; Collegeville, Minn.: Liturgical, 2000), 1–144; Sweeney, *King Josiah of Judah*, 256–72.

this process did not begin in earnest until ca. 735 B.C.E. In any case, Hosea's critique of Israel would have served Judean efforts to reestablish Davidic rule over the north during the reigns of Hezekiah and later Josiah.

The basis for Hosea's critique of northern Israel lies in his charges that Israel has abandoned YHWH to pursue other lovers. Although such a contention lends itself easily to a strictly religious understanding in which the people were worshipping other gods, closer examination of the issue indicates that Hosea was especially opposed to the Jehu dynasty's alliance with the Assyrian Empire. King Jehu (842–815 B.C.E.), the founder of the dynasty, is depicted submitting to the Assyrian monarch Shalmaneser III in the Black Obelisk of Shalmaneser III,[18] and King Joash ben Jehahaz (802–786 B.C.E.) is listed among the vassals of Adad Nirari III.[19] The Jehide alliance with Assyria was motivated by the continuing pressure from the Arameans, both during the reign of the Omrides and the early reign of Jehu. Israel's alliance with Assyria meant that Aram would be surrounded and contained, and the period of peace enabled Jeroboam ben Joash to reestablish Israelite control over a kingdom that extended from Lebo-Hamath in northern Aram to the Sea of the Aravah in the south. Hosea's critique emphasized Israel's submission to Assyrian interests to establish a trade route between Egypt and Assyria. Egypt of course was Israel's enemy in the pentateuchal tradition, and Israel's ancestors, including Jacob and his wives Rachel and Leah, had come from Haran in Aram. Although Hosea never calls for the assassination of the king, Jeroboam's son Zechariah was assassinated in 746 B.C.E. A period of instability then followed as pro-Assyrian and pro-Aramean parties vied for the throne and assassinated opposing monarchs until Israel was dragged into war with Assyria by the pro-Aramean monarch Pekah. Although Pekah was eventually killed, pro-Aramean forces continued to push for revolt against Assyria until the kingdom was destroyed in 722–721 B.C.E.

Hosea's own critique of Israel begins with a narrative in Hos 1:2–2:3 in which YHWH instructs him to marry Gomer, described as a woman of harlotry, and bear children with her. Readers will never know whether Gomer was actually a harlot or simply described as one by her accusing husband, but she clearly symbolizes Israel, whom the prophet accuses of harlotry for abandoning YHWH. The children born of the marriage are given names that symbolize the prophet's critique of the Jehide dynasty, that is, the first son is named Jezreel to recall the city where Jehu overthrew the House of Omride;

---

18. *ANEP*, 351–55.
19. S. Page, "A Stele of Adad Nirari III and Nergal-ereš from Tell al Rimnah," *Iraq* 30 (1968): 139–53.

the second child, a daughter, is named Lo Ruhamah, a Hebrew term that means "no mercy" to symbolize Yhwh's lack of mercy for Israel; and the third child, a son, is named Lo Ammi, "not my people," to symbolize Yhwh's break in the relationship with Israel.

The following section in Hos 2:4–3:5 begins with Hosea's reflection on his divorce of Gomer and his accusations against her. As the passage progresses, however, it soon becomes clear that the speaker shifts from Hosea to Yhwh and the wife from Gomer to Israel to demonstrate that Hosea's failed marriage with Gomer is symbolic of Yhwh's failed relationship with Israel. After detailing the accusations against Israel, Yhwh, now the husband in the relationship, decides that he loves his estranged bride Israel and cannot live without her. As a result Yhwh determines to restore the relationship with Israel, and the passage concludes with Yhwh's instructions to Hosea to restore his relationship with a harlot. Although interpreters are not entirely certain that the woman is Gomer, the restored relationship symbolizes Yhwh's intention to restore the relationship with Israel.

One of the most telling features of this passage appears in Hos 3:4–5, which maintains that Israel will go for a long time without king and officials, but will ultimately return to Yhwh and David their king. Although this passage may have envisioned the restoration of a northern king, the present form of the passage clearly envisions restored Davidic kingship over the north. Such a contention clearly serves the efforts to restore Davidic rule over the north at the time of Hezekiah's revolt against Assyria in 705–701 B.C.E., and Josiah's later bid for independence and restored Davidic rule over the north in 640–609 B.C.E. Although Hosea may well have looked for the restoration of a righteous (to him) northern monarchy, the book was later edited and read to support Judean interests, particularly those of King Josiah's program for the reform and restoration of Jerusalem and Judah/Israel, in the aftermath of northern Israel's destruction.

The late-seventh/early-sixth century B.C.E. prophet Jeremiah likewise plays an important role in this scenario. As observed above, Jer 30–31 presupposes the return and restoration of both Israel and Judah in the aftermath of the Babylonian exile, but underlying the present form of the text is an earlier oracle by the prophet that envisioned the return of northern Israel to southern Davidic rule. Such a scenario of course supports Josiah's program of reform and restoration, but the prophet was compelled to change his views following the unexpected death of Josiah at Megiddo in 609 B.C.E. and the subsequent decline of Judah.

Although the marriage metaphor applied to Israel or Judah is not clear in Jer 30–31, it is very clear in Jer 2:1–4:2 in which the prophet depicts Israel as Yhwh's bride in the wilderness.[20] Although Israel initially followed Yhwh in the wilderness, the prophet charges that the people abandoned Yhwh to pursue other gods. The contemporary (for Jeremiah) issue appears in Jer 2:18 in which he claims that the people have gone to Egypt to drink the waters of the Nile and to Assyria to drink the waters of the Euphrates, a charge akin to Hosea's concerns a century earlier. Such a claim recalls Josiah's efforts to free the nation from the control of the Assyrian Empire and its Egyptian vassals in the late latter half of the seventh century B.C.E. as the power of the Assyrian empire waned and Egypt stepped in to replace its former patron in an attempt to fill the gap.

Although much of Jer 2:1–4:2 presupposes images of Israel and Jacob, the passage appears as part of a larger block of material in Jer 2–6, which begins with condemnations of Israel and appeals for its return to Yhwh, but shifts in Jer 3:6–13 and 4:3–6:30 to charge Judah and Jerusalem with abandoning Yhwh and to call for their return to Yhwh as well. Insofar as the oracle displays two very different objects of concern, Israel in the first part of the oracle and Jerusalem and Judah in the second part of the oracle, it appears that Jer 2–6 has undergone a process of redaction and expansion much like that of Jer 30–31, viz., an oracle concerned with the restoration of (northern) Israel to Jerusalem and Judah has been expanded to call for the restoration and return of Judah and Jerusalem as well. Such a scenario fits well with a young prophet Jeremiah who supported Josiah's calls for the return of northern Israel to Davidic rule, but who was forced to rethink his position following Josiah's death in 609 B.C.E. For Jeremiah, Josiah's unexpected death meant that Yhwh was not yet finished bringing judgment to the nation, that is, Judah would also experience judgment like northern Israel before any promised restoration of all Israel could take place.

Judean prophets also take up the marriage motif for portraying the relationship between Yhwh and the nation, but they focus on the metaphorical portrayal of Jerusalem as Bat Zion, "Daughter Zion," rather than on Israel as a whole, as the bride of Yhwh. Although there are hints of sexual characterization for Israel in earlier Judean prophecy (generally charges of harlotry and the like for abandoning Yhwh, e.g., Mic 1:6–7), the full application of the marriage motif does not emerge in Judah and Jerusalem until the reign of Josiah and after in the books of Zephaniah and Ezekiel.

---

20. For discussion of Jer 2–6, see Marvin A. Sweeney, "Structure and Redaction in Jeremiah 2–6," in Sweeney, *Form and Intertextuality*, 94–108.

The superscription of the book of Zephaniah in Zeph 1:1 places the work of the prophet during the reign of King Josiah of Judah (reigned 640–609 B.C.E.).[21] Although many interpreters argue that the book is the product of exilic or post-exilic redaction, my own work argues that the major portion of the book stems from the prophet himself with only light editing in Zeph 1:1 and 3:20. Overall, the book of Zephaniah is written to support Josiah's program of religious reform and national restoration and reunification. It employs charges of apostasy and impending judgment as means to persuade its audience to return to Yhwh and thereby to support Josiah's plans.

The marriage metaphor figures prominently at the end of the book in Zeph 3:14–20. This oracle concludes an oracular sequence in Zeph 3:1–20 which anticipates the restoration of Jerusalem and the return of its exiles once the period of Jerusalem's punishment has been completed. In the context of Josiah's reign, the period of punishment is coming to a close and the time of restoration is at hand.

Zephaniah 3:14–20 begins in vv. 1–15 with exhortations to Bat Zion, also called Israel and Daughter of Jerusalem, that she should rejoice, cry aloud, and be glad because Yhwh has annulled all judgments against her. The following segment in vv. 16–19 portrays the coming day in which Jerusalem/Zion will be reassured that she need fear no further threat as Yhwh her G-d as returned to her. The initial portrayal of Yhwh is as a triumphant warrior, but the imagery immediately shifts to Yhwh's rejoicing over Jerusalem and an enigmatic statement in v. 17, *yaḥăriš bĕ'ahăbātô*, literally, "he shall plow/be silent in his love," followed by "he will rejoice over you in jubilation." The Hebrew verb *ḥrš*, which means both "to plow" and "to be silent," is particularly problematic here as scholars have struggled to ascertain its meaning. Examination of the use of the verb *ḥrš* as "to plow" indicates that can be employed metaphorically to portray sexual relations (e.g., Judg 14:8) and that cognate terms for plowing are employed in the Sumerian Love Songs and the Babylonian Harab myth to describe sexual relations as well.[22] When v. 17 is read in this matter, the portrayal of Yhwh's return to Zion emerges as a portrayal of the return of the groom, Yhwh, to the formerly abandoned

---

21. For discussion of Zephaniah, see Marvin A. Sweeney, *Zephaniah* (Hermeneia; Minneapolis: Fortress, 2003); idem, "Metaphor and Rhetorical Strategy in Zephaniah," in *Relating to the Text: Interdisciplinary and Form-Critical Insights on the Bible* (ed. T. J. Sandoval and C. Mandolfo; JSOTSup 384; London: T&T Clark, 2003), 120–30.

22. Yitzchak Sefati, *Love Songs in Sumerian Literature* (Bar Ilan Studies in Near Eastern Language and Culture; Ramat Gan: Bar Ilan University Press, 1998), 90–92; Thorkild Jacobsen, *The Harab Myth* (SANE 2,101; Malibu: Undena, 1984).

bride, Bat Zion. The remaining elements of the oracle in vv. 18–19 promise that Yhwh will bring to an end the punishment inflicted on Zion's people and the "reproach" suffered by Zion. The term "reproach," Hebrew *ḥerpâ*, is generally employed to describe the humiliation of women who have lost their men in war or otherwise been abandoned by their own men and left to their captors. With the end of this period of humiliation for Bat Zion, Yhwh promises to end the affliction, gather those who have strayed, and exchange disgrace for honor and reputation. Verse 20, perhaps a later editorial addition to the text, clarifies the meaning of v. 19 by stating explicitly that Yhwh will gather Zion's people, bring them home, make them renowned among the peoples of the earth, and restore their fortunes.

In short, the marriage motif appears in Zeph 3:14–20 as a means to describe Yhwh's restoration of Zion as a returning husband who restores his bride. Although this text is written in support of Josiah's reform, it is read as a general portrayal of restoration after the time of Josiah.

Ezekiel likewise employs the marriage metaphor to portray the relationship between Yhwh and Jerusalem in Ezek 16, but his use of the motif focuses especially on judgment rather than on restoration.[23] Such a concern with judgment is hardly surprising since Ezekiel is a Zadokite priest exiled to Babylonia with King Jehoiachin in 597 B.C.E. and he serves as a major interpreter of the fall of Jerusalem and Babylonian exile in 587/6 B.C.E. and following. Ezekiel's work does include oracles of restoration as well, although they do not employ the marriage motif. It is striking that Ezekiel would have been born, raised, and educated in the context of Josiah's reform. His oracle of restoration in Ezek 37:15–28 envisions the reunification of Joseph, that is, northern Israel, and Judah around the Jerusalem Temple and under the rule of a righteous Davidic monarch.[24] Such an oracle indicates Ezekiel's acceptance of the basic Josian perspectives of reunification and restoration of Israel and Judah under Davidic rule, but the experience of the destruction of Jerusalem and Babylonian exile would have compelled him to rethink this paradigm. His vision of the restored Temple in Ezek 40–48 envisions an ideal portrayal of the Twelve

---

23. For discussion of Ezekiel 16, see especially Julie Galambush, *Jerusalem in the Book of Ezekiel: The City as YHWH's Wife* (SBLDS 130; Atlanta: Scholars Press, 1992), esp. 61–63, 64–72, 91–109. For a general orientation to Ezekiel, see Marvin A. Sweeney, *The Prophetic Literature* (IBT; Nashville: Abingdon, 2005), 127–64.

24. See Marvin A. Sweeney, "The Royal Oracle in Ezekiel 37:15–28: Ezekiel's Reflection on Josiah's Reform," in *Israel's Prophets and Israel's Past: Essays on the Relationship of Prophetic Texts and Israelite History in Honor of John H. Hayes* (ed. B. E. Kelle and M. B. Moore; LHBOTS 446; London: T&T Clark, 2006), 239–53.

Tribes of Israel around the Temple and a restored creation, so that at least his visions of the future are still rooted to a degree in the principles of Josiah's reform, but he must account for the realities of judgment in the aftermath of Jerusalem's destruction. As a Zadokite priest, Ezekiel's understanding of Jerusalem's destruction employs a paradigm for purging the city and Temple of its iniquity, much like the scapegoat ritual of Lev 16 symbolizes the purging of the nation at Yom Kippur or the Day of Atonement, and the reconstitution of a purified Temple in place of the Temple that was lost.

Ezekiel 16 portrays the history of Yhwh's early relationship with Jerusalem in relation to the marriage motif. The passage portrays Yhwh's discovery of Jerusalem as an abandoned baby in the wilderness, born to an Amorite father and a Hittite mother. The abandoned baby Jerusalem is described as unwashed from its birth fluids, having an umbilical cord that is not cut, and left lying in the open. Yhwh takes care of the abandoned baby until she grows to adulthood, at which time Yhwh spreads his robe over her and entered into a covenant with her (vv. 7–8). Insofar as Jerusalem had reached the time for love, the spreading of Yhwh's robe signifies a marital relationship with Jerusalem and the covenant signifies a marriage contract, which Yhwh fulfills by providing the now young woman Jerusalem with clothing, jewelry, and food in keeping with the responsibilities of a husband in the ancient world. From v. 15 on, the passage describes Jerusalem's abandonment of Yhwh, described in keeping with the marital metaphor as sexual betrayal and harlotry with the Assyrians, Chaldeans (Babylonians), and anyone else who passed by. Yhwh's response to such action is to gather all of Jerusalem's lovers and strip her bare before them of the clothing, jewelry, and support that Yhwh had formerly given her and to turn her over to the mob. The remainder of the passage focuses on Yhwh's indignation, charges that Jerusalem's behavior is in keeping with sinful behavior of her Amorite and Hittite forebears, and that Jerusalem's behavior was even worse than Sodom's and Samaria's. In the end, Yhwh promises to restore the relationship with Jerusalem, but only after the punishment against her has been carried out.

In sum, the marriage motif has left a deep impression on both Israelite and Judean prophecy, both to portray Yhwh's judgment against Israel or Jerusalem as a means to punish the purportedly wayward bride for abandoning her husband and to portray Yhwh's willingness to restore the relationship once the bride has suffered her punishment. Notably, every one of the texts that employs this motif is tied in one way or another to the Josianic reform.

V

Biblical literature includes major textual traditions concerning Jacob's journey to Aram to find a bride and his return to the land of Israel as well as those concerning the portrayal of Yhwh's relationship with Israel or Jerusalem as a marriage relationship. Both sets of texts are employed to depict Israel's or Jerusalem's exile from the land and realized or potential return once the period of exile is over. Although these texts were composed over the course of various periods, including the mid-ninth through early-eighth centuries B.C.E. for the Genesis traditions concerning Jacob, through the eighth, seventh, and sixth centuries B.C.E. for Hosea, Jeremiah, Zephaniah, and Ezekiel, all are linked in one manner or another to Josiah's reform.

These traditions constitute at least a portion of the material from which Second Isaiah could draw in composing Isa 40–55. Of course, interpreters will never know if there are other materials no longer present in the Bible, but the materials concerning Jacob and the marriage relationship examined here constitute an adequate basis for Second Isaiah's construction of Jacob/Israel and Bat Zion/Jerusalem as the primary Israelite/Judean figures in Isa 40–55. That these texts are all linked to Josiah's reform is crucial for understanding Second Isaiah's construction of Jacob and Bat Zion in relation to the fundamental issues of exile and return. Josiah's reform anticipated a period of return from exile following a long period of Israelite exile and Judean subjugation to the Assyrian Empire. In the case of northern Israel's exile, many Israelites had fled from the Assyrian onslaught, still others were displaced by the Assyrians either to distant countries or to nearby lands, such as Philistia, to serve Assyrian interests, and even others remained in the land. In the case of southern Judah's period of subjugation, again many were killed off or displaced by the Assyrian invasions and displacement, others had fled to safer areas, and still others remained in the land, particularly in the city of Jerusalem. Insofar as Josiah's program envisioned the return of exiles, the return of northern Israel to Davidic rule, and the purification of the Jerusalem Temple at the center of a restored and reunited Israel, Josiah's reform provides the template on which Second Isaiah employed the figures of Jacob and Bat Zion to construct a new scenario of exile and return at the close of the Babylonian exile.

Such a scenario, with its portrayal of Jacob and Bat Zion, was not taken piecemeal from texts related to Josiah's reform, but represents a process of reflection and reinterpretation of these figures as portrayed in earlier texts.

The Jacob traditions emphasize Jacob's exile to Haran, his love for Rachel, and his return to the land of Israel with his beloved bride and family. But Rachel died far too early in life while giving birth to Benjamin, and Leah was never able to take her place in Jacob's heart as indicated by his unqualified love for Rachel's sons, Joseph and Benjamin, in comparison to his other children. Second Isaiah was able to draw extensively on the portrayal of Jacob as a figure for exile to a foreign land and return to the land of Israel throughout Isa 40–48. Perhaps Rachel's initial barrenness plays a role in Second Isaiah's construction of Bat Zion as a barren bride, but Sarah could also serve in this capacity. Furthermore, Rachel was never abandoned by her husband, she did not lose her children, and she was not an exiled figure in Genesis. Second Isaiah may have drawn on the image of Rachel weeping for her lost children in Jer 31:15, but such an image represents further reflection on the Rachel figure in Jeremiah beyond Genesis.

In constructing the image of Bat Zion as the abandoned bride whose husband and children would now return to her, Second Isaiah had to turn to the bridal traditions of the prophets. The portrayal of Israel as Yhwh's bride in Hosea and Jeremiah and Bat Zion or Jerusalem as Yhwh's bride in Zephaniah and Ezekiel is clear. In the cases of Hosea, Jeremiah, and Ezekiel, the bridal traditions posits a disruption of the relationship. The bride, Israel, or Bat Zion/Jerusalem is there accused of abandoning her husband, Yhwh, who purportedly cares for her and provides for her. She is off pursuing other lovers. In each of these cases, the text posits a restoration of the relationship when Yhwh will eventually forgive the wayward bride following a period of punishment. In the case of Zephaniah, Bat Zion's abandonment of Yhwh is presupposed, but this issue is addressed by the exhortations to return to Yhwh and to avoid such apostasy before any punishment is realized. Zephaniah ultimately focuses on the image of Yhwh's return to the bride, Bat Zion, as the scenario of restoration is laid out. Zephaniah presupposes the return of Bat Zion's exiles, which provides some basis for Second Isaiah's depiction of the return of Bat Zion's children. But Jeremiah's depiction of Rachel weeping for her lost children would also have contributed to Second Isaiah's depiction. Zephaniah's depiction of Bat Zion as the restored bride seems to be fundamental to Second Isaiah's portrayal of Bat Zion, but the portrayal of the wayward bride in Hosea, Jeremiah, and Ezekiel must also play a role in constructing Yhwh's earlier abandonment of the bride. In the end, the Bat Zion figure replaces Rachel in relation to Second Isaiah's portrayal of the exiled and returning Jacob.

VI

The influence of the conceptualization of Israel's restoration and reunification around the Jerusalem Temple and the House of David on Second Isaiah's scenario of exile and return in Isa 40–55 should come as no surprise. Josiah's seventh-century reform program addresses the same fundamental issues of exile and restoration taken by Second Isaiah at the end of the Babylonian Exile in the late-sixth century B.C.E. Second Isaiah's construction of the images of Jacob and Bat Zion presupposes reflection on the earlier traditions concerning Jacob and Israel or Bat Zion as the bride of Yhwh and the reconstruction of the images of Jacob and Bat Zion to fit the needs of the time, but such reflection and reconstruction has been witnessed before in biblical tradition. The Isaiah tradition developed extensively in relation to Josiah's reform[25]; Jeremiah was compelled to rethink his early support for Josiah's reform following the king's death as he began to understand that Judah and Jerusalem would suffer judgment prior to restoration much like northern Israel[26]; and Ezekiel was compelled to adjust images of the purification of the Temple and the construction of an ideal twelve tribes of Israel around the Temple in relation to the realities of the Babylonian exile.[27] Second Isaiah was compelled to do the same, although the realities of the time called upon the prophet to rethink the tradition in relation to the rise of Cyrus and the prospects for restoration as the period of the Babylonian exile came to a close.

---

25. See Marvin A. Sweeney, *Isaiah 1–39 with an Introduction to Prophetic Literature* (FOTL 16; Grand Rapids: Eerdmans, 1996), 31–62, esp. 57–59.

26. Marvin A. Sweeney, "The Truth in True and False Prophecy," in Sweeney, *Form and Intertextuality*, 78–93.

27. See Sweeney, "The Royal Oracle in Ezekiel 37:15–28"; idem, "Ezekiel's Debate with Isaiah," *Congress Volume: Ljubljana 2007* (ed. A. Lemaire; VTSup; Leiden: Brill, forthcoming).

Spectrality in the Prologue to Deutero-Isaiah

Francis Landy

In memory of Roy Melugin איש חסד ואמת

Roy Melugin responded to the original draft of this paper at the SBL Meeting of 2004, and identified me as a "reader response" critic. I was rather annoyed by this, and spent my time at the session discussing how I conceived of the reading process and the reader's responsibility. I wish I could pursue this quarrel here, and I am sure that the spirit of Roy will continue to animate our conversations. I wish to preface this reading of Isa 40:1–11 with some comments on reading and writing, as well as the relation between Isa 6 and 40, which was its initial impetus.

In 1999 I published an article entitled "Strategies of Concentration and Diffusion in Isaiah 6,"[1] in which I discussed the rhetorical techniques whereby the text focused attention on the consciousness of the prophet and away from the transgressive vision of God, and proposed that the strange commission to obstruct understanding is among other things a model for reading. I wrote: "The more closely one listens, the less one understands, the more indefatigably one looks, the more complexity and unfathomability one finds."[2] Jean-Pierre Sonnet writes that for the reader the message is that every reading is incom-

---

My paper was originally published as "The Ghostly Prelude to Deutero-Isaiah," *BibInt* 14 (2006): 332–63. It has been substantially revised and updated. Thanks are due to the Social Sciences and Humanities Research Council of Canada for funding that supported this project.

1. *BibInt* 7 (1999): 58–86. Republished in my collection, *Beauty and the Enigma and Other Essays on the Hebrew Bible* (JSOTSup 312; Sheffield: Sheffield Academic Press, 2001), 298–327.

2. "Strategies of Concentration and Diffusion," 81.

plete.³ One may note Gabriel Josipovici's comment on reading the Bible that with books that matter to us, "we are ... drawn to them because they seem to be *other* than us, because they guide us out of ourselves into what we feel to be a truer, more real world."⁴ In my reading of Isa 40, as of Isa 6, I will be concerned with the strangeness of the text, its resistance to interpretation, as well as the possibility of decoding it. Hence a certain tentativeness will accompany the reading, a proliferation of perhapses, to acknowledge that the reader plays with hypotheses, and should hold them open, as much as possible.

In my response to Roy, I spoke of the reader's responsibility to the author, by which I necessarily mean the implied or constructed author, but also the real author. Someone wrote this text out of his most intimate concerns and desires.⁵ Reading the text is listening to a voice that wishes to be heard, despite death; it is a kind of resurrection. There is some continuity between the implied author and the real author, just as there is one between the real reader and the implied one, even if the reading and writing personae represent different parts of the self. Reading and writing are psycho-physical processes in which we necessarily share. I have to imagine the person writing this text, with the full range of his emotional and intellectual resources, out of a life and a body loosely allied to the social body, with its own inherited literary tradition, and finding his own poetic voice in interaction with that tradition, with history, with the violent discovery of a vocation, as is, for instance, allegorically represented by Isa 6. I also have to imagine the quasi-illicit pleasures of poetry, as an autonomous, narcissistic domain of human experience,⁶ an

---

3. "Le Motif de l'endurcissement (Is 6,9–10) et la lecture d'Isaïe," *Biblica* 73 (1992): 234–35.

4. Gabriel Josipovici, *The Book of God: A Response to the Bible* (New Haven: Yale University Press, 1989), 4.

5. Jacques Derrida, "Shibboleth," in *Midrash and Literature* (ed. Geoffrey Hartman and Sanford Budick; New Haven: Yale University Press, 1986), 311. Derrida is commenting on Paul Celan's lecture "Der Meridian," in which Celan says that the poem speaks "in seiner eigenen, allereigensten Sache." The English translation of Celan's prose does not seem to capture the full force of this (Paul Celan, *Collected Prose* [trans. Rosemary Waldrop; Manchester: Carcanet, 1999], 48).

6. See especially Roland Barthes, *The Pleasure of the Text* (trans. Richard Miller; New York: Hill and Wang, 1975). Studies of the relationship of writing and the body are innumerable. Julia Kristeva, *Revolution in Poetic Language* (trans. Margaret Waller; New York: Columbia University Press, 1984) provides a foundational semiotic analysis, from a psychoanalytic perspective. Norman Holland, *The Brain of Robert Frost: A Cognitive Approach to Literature* (New York: Routledge, 1988) examines the feedback loops in literary response, especially emotional ones. There have been rather few studies of pleasure in reading the Bible. See, however, Robert Alter, *The Pleasures of Reading in an Ideological Age* (New York:

incidental perquisite of the ethical mission of the prophet, and correspondingly my own pleasure in reading, and writing about, this poetry.

Biblical criticism, for the most part, has seen its task as the reconstruction of the rhetorical appeal of texts to their immediate audiences; texts, at least according to some critics, are the products of communities and means of social reproduction.[7] Communities write themselves writing themselves. I am more concerned with myself, and ourselves, as readers: why should we find these texts interesting after these millennia? What do they tell us of ourselves and our humanity? This question cannot be separated from that of historical contingency, the text as witness to its own time and place. The separation in time is both the condition of its pathos and its eternity, the word of YHWH that lasts forever, to quote our passage.

Reading the text requires a withdrawal on the part of the reader.[8] The reader's responsibility is to whatever the text has to tell us, without imposing our own desire for coherence, our interests, our conceptualizations—what Levinas calls "thematization."[9] For instance, the question of poetic unity is one that I leave open, in part because I think poetic unity is always problematic, as is the unity of the world. My objection to Roy's characterization of myself as a "reader response critic" was to the implication that this was a license for postmodern subjectivity, in contrast to the alleged objectivity of more traditional scholars.[10] That none of us are free from subjectivity is obvious, just as it is evident that we are all dealing with and trying to interpret an object. Equally, it is clear that Roy did not intend his comments to be a criti-

---

Simon and Schuster, 1989). Fiona C. Black, *The Artifice of Love: Grotesque Bodies and the Song of Songs* (Edinburgh: T&T Clark, 2009) uses Barthes' *The Pleasure of the Text* as a primary critical resource.

7. See, for example, Ehud Ben Zvi, "Introduction: Writing, Speeches, and the Prophetic Books—Setting an Agenda," in *Writings and Speech in Israelite and Ancient Near Eastern Prophecy* (ed. Ehud Ben Zvi and Michael H. Floyd; Atlanta: Society of Biblical Literature, 2000), 1–29, and his commentaries in the FOTL series on *Micah* (FOTL 21B; Grand Rapids: Eerdmans, 2000) and *Hosea* (FOTL 21A; Grand Rapids: Eerdmans, 2005).

8. I have been particularly influenced by Robert Gibbs' discussion of the ethics of reading in his chapter "Why Read?" in *Why Ethics?* (Princeton: Princeton University Press, 2002), 89–113. Gibbs points out that responsible reading, like listening, entails a certain withdrawal on the part of the reader.

9. "Thematization" is characteristic of what Levinas calls "The Said" (*Le Dit*) in contrast to the openness of "Saying" (*Le Dire*) in his magnum opus, *Otherwise than Being or Beyond Essence* (trans. Alphonso Lingis; Pittsburgh: Pennsylvania University Press, 1998).

10. Stanley Fish, *Is There a Text in this Class? The Authority of Interpretive Communities* (Cambridge, Mass.: Harvard University Press, 1980) is the most well-known statement of "reader-response criticism."

cism. However, I would introduce two reservations that would support his characterization of the reader response critic, or any critic.

The first is that every reading is necessarily partial. We read the text in our own way, highlighting some things, ignoring others. The exhaustive reading is a chimera.

The second is that as we read we create difficulties. Reading, rereading, gazing at a text until your eyes hurt is an invitation to cataracts if not blindness. I always like to quote Robert Carroll, who writes: "many questions are raised for me (a blind reader) by this strangest of biblical texts. So is Isaiah a *blinded* text awaiting the *insightful* reader? Or is Isaiah such a blinded text that only a blinded critic can read it?"[11] The task, in other words, is not to paraphrase.[12]

Originally my intention in this paper was to compare Isa 6 to Isa 40:1–11, and in particular to examine the widespread assumption that Isa 40:1–11 was composed as a response to Isa 6. As I continued I became ever less interested in this question, and more preoccupied with the motif of spectrality and doubling in Isa 40:1–11, and in Deutero-Isaiah in general. I do not see much evidence for a particularly close relation between the two chapters, but I do acknowledge that Isa 6 may have been one of the texts in the back of the poet's mind. What interests me is the tentativeness of the call in Isa 40:1–11. If it is an account of a prophetic initiation, and there is little reason to assume it is not, it draws on the tradition of call visions, but maintains a distance from them. It is a prophetic voice in exile.

I

נחמו נחמו עמי יאמר אלהיכם:
דברו על לב ירושלם וקראו אליה כי מלאה צבאה כי נרצה עונה
כי לקחה מיד יהוה כפלים בכל חטאתיה:

(1) Comfort ye, comfort ye my people, says your God. (2) Speak to the heart

---

11. Robert P. Carroll, "Blindsight and the Vision Thing: Blindness and Insight in the Book of Isaiah" in *Writing and Reading the Scroll of Isaiah: Studies of an Interpretive Tradition* (ed. Craig C. Broyles and Craig A. Evans; VTSup 70.1; Leiden: Brill, 1997), 93.

12. For the pervasiveness of paraphrase in biblical interpretation, and its contrast with the relentlessly social task of cultural translation, see Jonathan Z. Smith's essay, "Bible and Religion," in his *Relating Religion: Essays in the Study of Religion* (Chicago: Chicago University Press, 2004), 197–214. The contrast between paraphrase, which he calls "the data writ large," and translation is a perennial theme in Smith's thought. See his autobiographical essay, "When the Chips are Down," *Relating Religion*, 30–31 and references therein.

of Jerusalem and call to her, for she has fulfilled her service, for her punishment/iniquity has been accepted, for she has received from the hand of Yhwh twicefold for all her sins. (40:1–2)

Who speaks? Who comforts? In a sense it is God who comforts, but at one remove. Or it is the prophet who comforts, his voice subsumed in that of God or vice versa, the prophet whose own identity is absorbed into the textual persona of First Isaiah and irreducible to it, not so much or only because of the obvious contextual and stylistic differences, but because of his own struggle to establish a separate textual identity, as is evident most clearly in the so-called servant songs.[13] Is "comfort, comfort my people, says your God" a new beginning or a renewal, a reversion to the old? Does it respond to "the vision of Isaiah" in 1:1, as suggested by Jewish liturgical tradition[14] and much modern commentary?[15] Is it an initiation, equivalent to or paired with Isa 6, and, if so, what is the direction of the relationship? With Williamson, one may think of

---

13. This is irrespective of the question whether there was an historical prophet or whether Deutero-Isaiah is a fictional projection, for instance of a circle of "temple-singers," as proposed by Ulrich Berges, *Das Buch Jesaja: Komposition und Endgestalt* (Herders Biblische Studien 16; Freiburg: Herder, 1998), 38–43.

14. In the Jewish lectionary, Isa 1 is the Haftarah for the Sabbath before the 9th of Av, and Isa 40 for the Sabbath following it.

15. A dialectical relationship between the First and Second Isaiah is posited by many scholars, e.g., Brevard S. Childs, *Isaiah* (Louisville, Ky.: Westminster John Knox, 2001); John Goldingay, *Isaiah* (NIBC; Peabody: Hendrikson, 2001), 80; Walter Brueggemann, "Unity and Dynamic in the Isaiah Tradition," *JSOT* 29 (1984): 89–107, and is inseparable from the question of the unity of the book. A very thorough structural analysis and discussion of the entire book is provided by Marvin A. Sweeney, *Isaiah 1–39 with an Introduction to Prophetic Literature* (FOTL 16; Grand Rapids: Eerdmans, 1996), 39–62. Comparably, Antti Laato, *"About Zion I Will Not Be Silent": The Book of Isaiah as an Ideological Unity* (Stockholm: Almqvist and Wiksell, 1998) treats the book as an ideological unity. See also Edgar W. Conrad, *Reading Isaiah* (OBT; Minneapolis: Fortress, 1991) and Benjamin Sommer's cautionary comments in "Allusions and Illusions: The Unity of the Book of Isaiah in Light of Deutero-Isaiah's Use of Prophetic Tradition," in *New Visions of Isaiah* (ed. Roy F. Melugin and Marvin A. Sweeney; JSOTSup 214; Sheffield: Sheffield Academic Press, 1996), 156–87, and idem, *A Prophet Reads Scripture: Allusion in Isaiah 40–66* (Contraversions; Stanford: Stanford University Press, 1998), as well as those of Patricia Tull Willey, *Remember the Former Things: The Recollection of Previous Texts in Second Isaiah* (SBLDS 161; Atlanta: Scholars Press, 1997), who also provides a valuable review of scholarship (35–43). Both posit a closer relationship with Jeremiah, as does Reinhard G. Kratz, "Der Anfang des Zweiten Jesaja in Jes 40,1f. und das Jeremiabuch," *ZAW* 106 (1994): 243–61. For specific connections between ch. 40, including vv. 12–31, and ch. 6 see John Goldingay, *The Message of Isaiah 40–55* (London: T&T Clark, 2005), 9; Roy F. Melugin, "Poetic Imagination, Intertextuality, and Life in a Symbolic World," 11–14 in this volume.

Deutero-Isaiah as primary, as the author of First Isaiah, the past constructed on the basis of the future. But apart from muddling literary and historical considerations, no bad thing in itself, one cannot avoid the immense caesura between chs. 39 and 40, no matter how much it has been retrojected into the text of First Isaiah. In the space between chs. 39 and 40 is the catastrophe. Chapter 40, and Deutero-Isaiah generally, is a post-catastrophe text. It is thus a work of mourning, and as such spectral. It speaks for the past in the future, the past as having a future, but only as past. The doubleness of the voice of Deutero-Isaiah, suggested by its very name, is compounded by the ambiguity of speaker and addressee. God comforts, but distances himself from comforting. The prophet speaks and comforts, his identity anonymous, diffused, dissembled with and as that of God.

נחמו, "comfort," is ambiguous, in that it refers to a change of mind or mood. To comfort is to induce a change, to leave behind the past, to forget. But God is precisely the one who cannot forget, as Deutero-Isaiah insistently reminds us (40:27; 49:15). It is because God cannot forget that we can forget, traverse the catastrophe, step beyond the abyss. God, however, is notoriously characterized by his changes of mind, denoted by the same verb נחם.[16] God regrets (נחם) his creation of humanity in the Flood Story,[17] with which the catastrophe in Deutero-Isaiah is compared (Isa 54:9). Here the verb signals a transformation in God, from judgment to compassion. But as such it is unstable, since it can always be reversed.

For the moment, though, we are comforted, a comfort doubled by the repetition of נחמו נחמו, "comfort, comfort," as if we can have no end to the comforting.[18] As the initial words, the title, they launch Deutero-Isaiah as the

---

16. John D. W. Watts, *Isaiah 34–66* (WBC 24; Waco, Tex.: Word, 2005), 608, attractively suggests a wordplay linking נחם, "comfort," to נקם, "avenge," and a corresponding transformation of the vengeance predicted in 1:24 and 34:8.

17. Gen 6:6, 7. Another notorious instance is God's retraction of sovereignty from Saul (1 Sam 15:11, 35). The two meanings intersect in Hos 13:14.

18. Joseph Blenkinsopp, *Isaiah 40–55* (AB 19B; New York: Doubleday, 2002), 183, comments on the "emotional weight" of the repetition, and the frequency of the device in Deutero-Isaiah. Similarly, Claus Westermann, *Isaiah 40–66* (trans. David G. M. Stalker; OTL; Louisville, Ky.: Westminster John Knox, 1969), 6, 34, notes Deutero-Isaiah's propensity for piling on "imperative on imperative," as an expression of urgency. Jan Fokkelman, "Stylistic Analysis of Isaiah 40:1–11," *OtSt* 21 (1981): 75, suggests that the doubling of נחמו is the "motor" that shapes the entire poem and is reflected in the doubling of punishment in v. 2. Leo Krinetzki, "Zur Stilistik von Jesaja 40:1–8," *BZ* 16 (1972): 59–60, argues that there is an interchange of double and triple constructions: the former express the divine point of view, the latter the creaturely one.

book or enterprise of consolation,[19] which is either equal to the fissure that precedes it, doubles it, or vastly exceeds it, as 54:8 suggests. Comfort, however, is a maternal function, cross-culturally and within the text of Deutero-Isaiah. As a comforter, God is a super-mother, as Isa 49 claims (49:15).[20] God and prophet evoke between them an encompassing maternity, a womb within which Israel can be reborn. One may note, in passing, the correspondence between נחם and רחם, "compassion/womb," and the euphony of guttural and nasal continuants that redirects our attention from the concept to the sound of consolation. But then why does God eschew, for the moment, the voice of comfort, as if he cannot commit himself to the poetic/prophetic venture?

The voice urges unnamed others to comfort: "Comfort ye, comfort ye, my people." They may be divine beings, comparable to the seraphim of Isa 6, or prophets, or even ordinary people, comforting each other.[21] The indetermi-

---

19. Many authors observe that the initial words introduce the major theme of Deutero-Isaiah, e.g., Karl Elliger, *Deuterojesaja 1: Teilband. Jesaja 40,1–45,7* (BKAT 11/1; Neukirchen-Vluyn: Neukirchener, 1989), 13; Blenkinsopp, *Isaiah 40–55*, 179; Klaus Baltzer, *Deutero-Isaiah: A Commentary on Isaiah 40–55* (trans. Margaret Kohl; Hermeneia; Minneapolis: Fortress), 49, who writes: "This sentence sums up everything that DtIsa has to proclaim." Elliger, *Deuterojesaja I: Teilband*, 10, suggests that an initial קול קורא may have been suppressed to highlight the theme. Hans Barstad, "Isa 40,1–11: Another Reading," in *Congress Volume Basel* (ed. A. Lemaire; VTSup 92; Leiden: Brill, 2001), 225–40, studies the imagistic and thematic correlations between the Prologue and the rest of Deutero-Isaiah in detail, contrary to Rosario Pius Merendino, *Der Erste und der Letzte: Eine Untersuchung von Jes 40–48* (Leiden: Brill, 1981), 13–74, who thinks it has far stronger connections with Trito-Isaiah.

20. An excellent discussion of maternal imagery applied to God in Deutero-Isaiah is Marc Brettler, "Incompatible Metaphors for Yhwh in Isaiah 40–66," *JSOT* 78 (1998): 115–19. Recent studies include Hanne Løland, *Silent or Salient Gender? The Interpretation of Gendered God-Language in the Hebrew Bible, Exemplified in Isaiah 42, 46 and 49* (Tübingen: Mohr Siebeck, 2008) and Sharon Moughtin-Mumby, *Sexual and Marital Metaphors in Hosea, Jeremiah, Isaiah, and Ezekiel* (Oxford: Oxford University Press, 2008), esp. 122–42.

21. Many modern commentators opt for the first possibility, initially proposed by Frank M. Cross, "The Council of Yhwh in Second Isaiah," *JNES* 12 (1953): 275–77, usually without question. Blenkinsopp, *Isaiah 40–55*, 180, however, adopts the second position, that it refers to a plurality of prophets, while Baltzer, *Deutero-Isaiah: A Commentary on Isaiah 40–55*, 51, approvingly cites Duhm's suggestion that it is addressed to "everyone who is able to comfort." Fokkelman, "Stylistic Analysis," 72–73, interestingly considers that the audience, as in 8:16–18, are the prophet's disciples, who are urged to comfort the wider community. Kratz, "Der Anfang des Zweiten Jesaja in Jes 40,1f. und das Jeremiabuch," 260, proposes that it is directed to members of the Golah elite, who are urged to lead the community back from exile. Rainer Albertz, "Darius in Place of Cyrus: The First Edition of Deutero-Isaiah (Isaiah 40.1–52.12) in 521 b.c.e.," *JSOT* 27 (2003): 373 note 7, thinks that Deutero-

nacy introduces the passage as something vague, a gesture outwards inviting and requiring a response, as if only through reciprocity, ultimately from us, can the poetic movement be accomplished. We are then the surrogate authors of the book, or at least responsible for its effectiveness.

"Speak to the heart of Jerusalem, and call to her." The heart of Jerusalem is parallel to "my people" in v. 1, as the object of speech and consolation, but are they the same or different?[22] Is Jerusalem the destroyed city or its surviving inhabitants, wherever they might be? To speak to the heart may be an idiom for sexual seduction or reconciliation, as in Hos 2:16, and anticipate bridal imagery later in the book,[23] but only through or as a result of com-

---

Isaiah is a group composition. Berges, *Das Buch Jesaja*, 381–83, proposes that the objects of the appeal are the watchmen of Jerusalem of 52:8 (and 62:6); the imperative is thus a framing device, deriving from what he identifies as the first Jerusalem redaction. It also corresponds to the "We" group in 1:9 and thereafter (257). See also Jürgen van Oorschot, *Von Babel zum Zion: Eine literarkritische und redaktionsgeschichtliche Untersuchung* (Berlin: de Gruyter, 1993), 115, and Merendino, *Der Erste und der Letzte*, 19–20, for whom the Prologue introduces chs. 40–66, and was composed by an author familiar with at least the core text of Trito-Isaiah. Redaction critics tend to dismiss interpretations of the sequence as a call-vision or a scene in a heavenly council as resulting from secondary additions. The most inclusive view is that of David Noel Freedman, "The Structure of Isaiah 40:1–11," in *Poetry and Orthography* (vol. 2 of *Divine Commitment and Human Obligation: Selected Writings*; ed. David Noel Freedman; Grand Rapids: Eerdmans, 1997), 248–55, who holds that it refers to "all flesh" in v. 5, urged to comfort "my people" and lead them back to their homeland, as in 49:22–23. Likewise, Watts, *Isaiah 34–66*, 606–8, proposes a complex dramaturgy, in which the divine court addresses all peoples, including Israel, urging them to comfort. Klaus Kiesow, *Exodustexte im Jesajabuch: Literarkritische und Motivgeschichtliche Analysen* (Göttingen: Vandenhoeck & Ruprecht, 1979), 26, warns against premature foreclosure of the question. As John Goldingay, *Isaiah 40–55: Volume I* (ICC; London: T&T Clark, 2006), 68, says, the comforters are a "theological/poetic device."

22. Elliger, *Deuterojesaja 1: Teilband*, 15–16, correctly notes the fluidity of the conception of Jerusalem in Deutero-Isaiah, which refers both to the place and its population. For this reason, Kiesow, *Exodustexte im Jesajabuch*, 56, assumes a later redactional context. John Milbank, "'I Will Gasp and I Will Pant': Deutero-Isaiah and the Birth of the Suffering Subject. A Response to Norman Gottwald, "Social Class and Ideology in Isaiah 40–55: An Eagletonian Reading," *Semeia* 59 (1992): 64, interestingly proposes that because of the collapse of Judah, Zion is "nowhere and everywhere." He elaborates that she is nowhere because she is present in the "nothingness, the negativity of suffering," and everywhere since she is identified through "exile and self-exile."

23. Stephen Geller, "A Poetic Analysis of Isaiah 40:1–2," *HTR* 77 (1984): 417, points out "the almost sexual connotation," and suggests that it is reinforced by the feminine suffixes in the rest of the verse. Ulrich Berges, *Jesaja 40–48* (HTKAT; Freiburg: Herder, 2008), 100, however, rejects this connotation, and thinks that the primary reference of the phrase is to the overcoming of intellectual resistance. Goldingay, *The Message of Isaiah 40–*

pleted mourning. Such implications are for the moment displaced, disavowed; the collective indistinct others are adduced, to speak to the heart, the affective center, of the female subject. The imperative, which is also the prophetic imperative, sets the discourse in motion, while not yet impelling the prophet, as if the silence of the catastrophe cannot yet be broken. The voice(s) then address(es) the heart of the prophet, and perhaps of God, as well as of Jerusalem, and, once again, we cannot be sure that these are separate entities.

Before being a lover, Jerusalem is the mother, whose death is the ultimate loss. The maternal ambiance of comfort then consoles one for the death of the mother. Mother Jerusalem and Mother God are opposed, in that God gives life to the dead, or they cannot be distinguished. God maintains his (her) silence, in the wilderness recalled in v. 3, while bidding others to speak on his behalf, and on that of Jerusalem.

The vision of Isaiah, in ch. 1, begins with an address, in the imperative, "Hear, O heavens, and give ear, O earth." Perhaps they may be intimated too by the plural imperative here.[25] There heavens and earth witness human incapacity. Here they evoke creation, and the continuing creative impulse, despite the silence of God and prophet, and anticipate God's rhetorical appeal to his creation of the universe in vv. 12ff.

The voices speak of the end of service (צבא)[26] and punishment or iniquity (עון), or perhaps their message is more general, and the access of comfort coincides with the end of tribulation.[27] The incrementation, from "service,"

55, 13, following Kratz, "Der Anfang des Zweiten Jesaja in Jes 40,1f. und seine literarischen Horizonte," *ZAW* 105 (1993): 400–19, notes the parallel with Joseph speaking "to the heart" of his brothers in Gen 50:21 and suggests a similarity of situation. Merendino, *Der Erste und der Letzte*, 27, adds that in Gen 50:21 and Ruth 2:13, "speaking to the heart" parallels "comfort." For further parallels with Gen 50 and Ruth see Berges (*Jesaja 40–48*, 86–87).

25. Rolf Rendtorff, "Jesaja 6 im Rahmen der Komposition des Jesajabuches," in *The Book of Isaiah/Le Livre d'Isaïe* (ed. Jacques Vermeylen; Leuven: Peeters, 1989), 81 note 28, translated as "Isaiah 6 in the Framework of the Composition of the Book," in *Canon and Theology: Overtures to an Old Testament Theology* (Minneapolis: Fortress, 1993), 79 n. 28, notes the connection.

26. Watts, *Isaiah 34–66*, 609, proposes that צבא does not refer to corvée duty but to Jerusalem's military service, and thus to the end of national independence. Berges, *Jesaja 40–48*, 101, refers to its use in relation to Levitical service in the wilderness, in support of his hypothesis that Deutero-Isaiah was composed by a group of exiled "Temple-singers."

27. Commentators differ whether v. 2b is the content of the call or justifies it. Elliger, *Deuterojesaja 1: Teilband*, 6–7, denies that it can refer to the content, largely on the grounds of a structural parallel with vv. 3–4. See also Freedman, "The Structure of Isaiah 40:1–11," 236–37, and Goldingay, *Isaiah 40–55*, 69. For the alternative view, see Jan L. Koole, *Isaiah: Part 3. Vol. 1: Isaiah 40–48* (trans. Anthony P. Runia; HCOT; Kampen: Kok Pharos, 1997),

through the Janus-parallelism of עון, which may mean both "punishment" and "iniquity," to "all her sins" (כל חטאתיה) recalls the condemnation of Jerusalem in the first part of the book, and is matched by the doubling of the penalty in the last clause.[28] Correspondingly, one may expect the return to divine favour to equal or exceed the retribution. Double the sin = double the compensation. However, the sums are incalculable.[29] What is the appropriate penalty for all her sins? According to First Isaiah, it is death or deportation.[30] What is double that? And what is the reparation that can equal or surpass it?

Chapter 40 is preoccupied with measure, for instance in the description of creation in 40:12–13. But the measure is imposed on that which is immeasurable. Similarly, the verse through the succession of parallel clauses asserts the reestablishment of cosmic order, the order of justice, which is also poetic order, over the incommensurability of the disaster.

The terms עון and חטאת, "sin," may suggest cultic as well as ethical transgression,[31] and indeed the two are interfused in the rhetoric of First Isaiah, especially ch. 1. That Jerusalem's "iniquity" (עון) has been "accepted" (נרצה), in particular, has sacrificial connotations, since elsewhere the verb רצה is used in connection with atonement (cf. Lev 1:4).[32] The iniquity/pun-

---

56. Geller, "A Poetic Analysis of Isaiah 40:1–2," 416, suggests that "the phrase is an artful hinge."

28. Meindert Dijkstra, "Yhwh as Israel's Goʼel," *ZABR* 5 (1999): 240–45, that the double price is not a penalty, but the compensation that Yhwh, as גואל, pays for Israel's redemption. This seems to me to accord ill with the emphasis on Israel's sins.

29. Hans-Joachim Stoebe, "Überlegungen zu Jesaja 40,1–11: Zugleich der Versuch eines Beitrages zur Gottesknechtfrage," *TZ* 40 (1984): 110.

30. Blenkinsopp, *Isaiah 40–55*, 181, and Baltzer, *Deutero-Isaiah: A Commentary on Isaiah 40–55*, 53, suggest a correlation with Jerusalem's double disaster, according to Isa 51:19. Baltzer notes also Babylon's double bereavement in 47:9. Burkhard M. Zapff, *Jesaja 40–55* (Würzburg: Echter, 2001), 229, links it to the doubling of נחמו. Andreas Scherer, "Hyperbolisch oder juridisch? Zu einigen Deutungen von כפלים in Jes 40,2 und zur Semantik der übrigen Belege der Würzel כפל im Alten Testament," *ZAW* 115 (2003), on the basis of an analysis of other uses of KPL, argues that no precise doubling is intended and that it is a hyperbolic expression of the extremity of Jerusalem's suffering. Sommer, *A Prophet Reads Scripture*, 55–56, argues neatly for an allusion to Jer 16:18, in which it is predicted that Israel will suffer twofold for its sins.

31. Elliger, *Deuterojesaja 1: Teilband*, 15, thinks that עון refers consistently in Deutero-Isaiah to moral guilt, conforming to the tradition, especially in Protestant scholarship, to ascribe a primarily ethical and anti-cultic stance to the prophets. However, there are pervasive *metaphorical* transfers between these realms, e.g., 43:24, 53:5–6.

32. See, in particular, Geller, "A Poetic Analysis of Isaiah 40:1–2," 417. Many commentators reject any cultic connotation, identifying the verb as רצה II, "pay, discharge," and citing Lev 26:41, 43. However, it is improbable that the latter lack all ritual or cultic

ishment of Jerusalem conforms to and satisfies God's will, and corresponds to its status as the symbolic capital of the world. If Jerusalem is equivalent to the people, and to the prophet as the representative of the people, never quite distinct from God, then its destruction, and divine self-destruction, succeeds where Lebanon and its wild beasts fail in 40:16, and anticipates the representative suffering of the prophet in ch. 53.[33]

II

קול קורא במדבר פנו דרך יהוה ישרו בערבה מסלה לאלהינו
כל גיא ינשא וכל הר וגבעה ישפלו והיה העקב למישור והרכסים לבקעה:
ונגלה כבוד יהוה וראו כל בשר יחדו כי פי יהוה דבר:

> A voice calling, "In the wilderness open up the way of the Lord; make straight in the desert a paved road for our God. Every valley shall be lifted up, every mountain and hill laid low; the crooked shall be straight, and the rough places a dale. And the glory of the Lord shall be revealed, and all flesh shall see together, for the mouth of the Lord has spoken." (40:3–5)

The voice pauses, resumes, reports another voice, a herald of God. Whether it is one of the voices that is urged to comfort we do not know, and, if so, whether it is a divine or prophetic voice.[34] The voice, at any rate, is detached from the prophet and from God; it is as yet an intimation. The voice, however, identifies with "us"; it displays a certain solidarity, in contrast to the distance implied by "your God," in v. 1. Between the voice, the prophet and people there is community, under the dominion of God, who acknowledges that Israel is his people, עמי, in v. 1. עמי, "my people," recollects the description of Israel as "my people," unaware of its relationship with God, in 1:3, and its repudiation

---

connotations. See also Stoebe, "Überlegungen zu Jesaja 40,1–11," 106, who also assigns a sacred sense to צבא; Zapff, *Jesaja 40–55*, 230; and Berges, *Jesaja 40–48*, 101.

33. For this reason Stoebe, "Überlegungen zu Jesaja 40,1–11," 109, argues that the Prologue in which v. 2 is linked to vv. 9–10, anticipates the "servant songs."

34. Again, opinions differ as to the identity of this voice. Elliger, *Deuterojesaja 1: Teilband*, 7, thinks that it belongs to one of the heavenly beings addressed in vv. 1–2; this accounts for the contrast between "our God" and "your God." Blenkinsopp, *Isaiah 40–55*, 181, considers it to be "a prophetic proclamation," as does Merendino, *Der Erste und der Letzte*, 35. Berges (*Das Buch Jesaja*, 381; *Jesaja 40–48*, 95) thinks that the phrase was secondarily introduced by the composers of Isa 40:6–8, so as to turn the prologue into a dialogue and thus create the rapport with Isa 6. See also Kiesow, *Exodustexte im Jesajabuch*, 30, and van Oorschot, *Von Babel zum Zion*, 114–15.

as "this people" in 6:8 and 8:6.³⁵ Whereas in ch.1 God's paternal claim is unreciprocated by filial consciousness, and the people is "heavy with iniquity" (כבד עון) in v. 4, here the voice crosses the gap through a movement of comfort, of maternal solicitude, irrespective of the children's recognition, and the "iniquity" has been absolved.

A way in the wilderness—to us, especially if we are identified with Jerusalem—but it is also of course our return to ourselves and to our God (אלהינו), even to the acknowledgement of God as our God.³⁶ There is thus a switching and overlapping of roles, since both of us are undertaking this journey, and for both the other is the destination, and for both it is a return from exile, in other words self-estrangement. God is returning to God, Israel to Israel.³⁷

---

35. The relationship between Isa 1 and 40 is noted by several scholars. See Jacques Vermeylen, "L'Unité du Livre d"Isaïe," in Vermeylen, *The Book of Isaiah/Le Livre d'Isaïe*, 45–46; Rendtorff, *Canon and Theology*, 155; idem, "Zur Komposition des Buches Jesaja," *VT* 34 (1984): 302; Roy F. Melugin, *The Formation of Isaiah 40–55* (BZAW 141; Berlin: de Gruyter, 1976), 177–78. Berges, *Das Buch Jesaja*, 382, thinks that Isa 40:1–11 is a conscious inversion of Isa 1, as part of the general composition of the book. See also *Jesaja 40–48*, 84–85.

36. Rudolf Kilian, "'Beut eine Strasse für unseren Gott': Überlegungen zu Jes 40,3–5," in *Studien zu alttestamentlichen Texten und Situationen* (ed. Wolfgang Werner and Juergen Werlitz; Stuttgart: Katholisches Bibelwerk, 1999), 173–82, argues that there is no intimation of a return from exile in these verses, and that it only predicts the advent of Yhwh. Likewise Berges, *Jesaja 40–48*, 103–4, who thinks that the entire prologue is postexilic, denies the Babylonian connection, largely on the basis of the lack of direct reference. However, given the pervasiveness of the motif of the return from Babylon in every part of Deutero-Isaiah, at whatever redactional level, this excision seems excessive. Can one not suppose multivalence? For a study of polysemy and ambiguity in selected passages of Deutero-Isaiah, see Hyun Chul Paul Kim, *Ambiguity, Tension, and Multiplicity in Deutero-Isaiah* (Studies in Biblical Literature 52; New York: Lang, 2003).

37. On the dialectic of distance and proximity as a deep structural element in the passage, see Franco Ettore, "Is 40,1–11: Una Lettura Strutturale," *RevistB* 28 (1980): 295–97.

The voice speaks of or for a way in the wilderness, recalling the Exodus tradition,[38] but also the passage from silence to speech, death to life.[39] We, however, are supposed to clear the path, make straight the highway. Or is it divine beings, or prophets?[40] It suggests, nonetheless, a task to be undertaken by us (or/as divine beings, prophets), a preparation within us.[41] In v. 4 the

---

38. Childs, *Isaiah*, 299; David Carr, "Reaching for Unity in Isaiah," *JSOT* 57 (1993): 66. The importance of the Exodus traditions for Deutero-Isaiah is stressed by many authors and is the subject of Kiesow's monograph *Exodustexte im Jesajabuch*. See especially Watts, *Isaiah 34–66*, 609–10, and Richard J. Clifford, "The Unity of the Book of Isaiah and its Cosmogonic Language," *CBQ* 55 (1993): 3–5; *Fair Spoken and Persuading: An Interpretation of Second Isaiah* (New York: Paulist, 1984), 41–47. Clifford, *Fair Spoken and Persuading*, 21–23, also stresses the cosmogonic aspect of the wilderness, as God's antagonist. Odil Hannes Steck, "Deuterojesaja als theologische Denker," in *Wahrnehmungen Gottes im Alten Testament: Gesammelte Studien* (Munich: Kaiser, 1982), 219, comparably argues that the Exodus is subsumed under the thematic of God as creator. A rather similar argument is made by Horacio Simian-Yofre, "Exodo en Deuteroisaias," *Biblica* 61 (1980): 530–53 and "La teodicea del Deuteroisaias," *Biblica* 62 (1981): 55–72, largely on the grounds of the lack of specific reference to the Exodus. Berges, *Das Buch Jesaja*, 259–60, denies that the primary reference is to the Exodus, but to the recovery of Eden; the desert symbolizes the sinful condition of Jerusalem. Barstad, "Isa 40,1–11: Another Reading," 237–40, esp. 237 note 29, likewise holds that the text does not allude to the Exodus, on the grounds that the way should be understood figuratively and not literally. Surely, however, an allusion is by its very nature figurative rather than literal.

39. Milbank, "I Will Gasp and I Will Pant," 66, suggests that the way in the wilderness aligns the exiles with a nomadic order that systematically undoes the symbols of Babylonian imperialism.

40. Various critics regard vv. 3–5 as addressed to members of the divine council, cf. Elliger, *Deuterojesaja 1: Teilband*, 7; Baltzer, *Deutero-Isaiah: A Commentary on Isaiah 40–55*, 53. There is no real evidence for this, as Blenkinsopp, *Isaiah 40–55*, 179, remarks; see also the form-critical argument of Kiesow, *Exodustexte im Jesajabuch*, 50–51. Fokkelman, "Stylistic Analysis of Isaiah 40:1–11," 77, notes the indeterminacy.

41. Elliger, *Deuterojesaja 1: Teilband*, 19 rejects any allegorical dimension to the way, and provides an abundance of examples of ancient Near Eastern processional routes. However, note Baltzer's stress on the ethical dimension of the passage (*Deutero-Isaiah*, 55), and Berges's insistence that the "way of the Lord" is primarily ethical (*Das Buch Jesaja*, 382–83). On the basis of the parallelism, Kiesow, *Exodustexte im Jesajabuch*, 48, argues that לאלהינו is not dative but genitive. God does not necessarily use this road. See, however, van Oorschot, *Von Babel zum Zion*, 118–20, and Goldingay, *Isaiah 40–55*, 75. As Fokkelman, "Stylistic Analysis of Isaiah 40:1–11," 78, remarks, the question whether the images should be taken literally or symbolically is not productive, and suggests a fundamental misunderstanding of the nature of poetry. David J. A. Clines, "The Parallelism of Greater Precision," in *Directions in Biblical Hebrew Poetry* (ed. Elaine R. Follis; JSOTSup 40; Sheffield: JSOT Press, 1987), 79, argues that מסלה לאלהינו, and hence דרך, "way," is likewise literal; the argument could, however, be reversed.

implications are developed: every vale shall be raised up, every mountain and hill laid low. In ch. 2 it is God who raises and judges mountains, just as he weighs them in v. 12. Mountains are paradigmatic of primary creative elements.[42] It is not clear whether our preliminary task is levelling mountains and filling valleys, but in any case our making straight the highway corresponds to the crooked becoming straight (למישור)[43] and the smoothing of the wrinkles (רכסים)[44] into a plain. In ch. 2, the judgement against the mountains accompanies the day of the Lord, in which God terrifies the earth, and is the obverse of Zion's exaltation and the establishment of universal peace. Here it eases the way of the exiles, and is a sign of reconciliation.

As in v. 2, parallelism suggests poetic and cosmic order, which is at the same time a transformation. The alternation of high and low, rough and smooth, is familiar, simple, and may have political or social implications.[45] It is, however, complicated by the circularity whereby the verse begins and ends with synonyms for valley (גיא ... בקעה), the metathesis of עקב, "crooked," and בקעה, "dale,"[46] and the association of עקב with Jacob, and of מישור, "straight" or perhaps "even," with the poetic term Jeshurun (ישרון) which we find also in Isa 44:2.[47] The verse is enclosed too between compact lines, each with two stresses, round more protracted three stress ones. Between intimations of depth and height, divagation and directness, past and future, expansion and ellipsis, the verse sketches a complete world through which, presumably, the way of the Lord passes, and which is upside down because of it, or in anticipation of it. The fulfilment of ch. 2 leads us to expect an eschatological or perhaps apocalyptic context.[48]

---

42. The motif is all pervasive. See, for example, Ps 90:2; Prov 8:24. Berges, *Jesaja 40–48*, 107) likewise points out connections with ch. 2.

43. The parallelism is often noted cf. Koole, *Isaiah: Part 3. Vol. 1: Isaiah 40–48*, 61.

44. רכסים is a hapax legomenon whose meaning is relatively clear.

45. Sommer, *A Prophet Reads Scripture*, 251 note 4, summarizes the evidence. See also Baltzer, *Deutero-Isaiah: A Commentary on Isaiah 40–55*, 54.

46. On this, see Fokkelman, "Stylistic Analysis of Isaiah 40:1–11," 78, who adds the inversion of מישור in רכסים, which seems much more doubtful to me. See also Wilfred G. E. Watson, *Classical Hebrew Poetry: A Guide to Its Techniques* (JSOTSup 26; Sheffield: JSOT Press, 1984), 240, who thinks עקב "may have been invented for the purpose." Aelred Cody, "A Palindrome in Isaiah 40.4b," *CBQ* 66 (2004): 551–60, proposes emending רכסים to מישור, "peaks," to form a perfect palindrome.

47. Baltzer, *Deutero-Isaiah: A Commentary on Isaiah 40–55*, 55. See also Meira Polliack, "Deutero-Isaiah's Typological Use of Jacob in the Portrayal of Israel's National Renewal," in *Creation in Jewish and Christian Tradition* (ed. Henning Graf Reventlow and Yair Hoffman; JSOTSup 319; Sheffield: Sheffield Academic Press, 2002), 105.

48. Ettore, "Is 40,1–11: Una Lettura Strutturale," 299, in his fine structural analysis,

For what is revealed? The glory of the Lord, in tandem with all flesh seeing, and the mouth of the Lord speaking.⁴⁹ Whether these phrases are equivalent or not is unclear, in particular the syntactic function of *kî* in דבר כי פי יהוה, "for the mouth of Yнwн has spoken." Does all flesh see *that* the mouth of the Lord has spoken, or *because* it has done so, or is the phrase just a formula of divine authentication? The disjointedness of the syntax and the indeterminacy of reference need not be prematurely foreclosed, for example, by combining the first two phrases. Perhaps "all flesh" does see the glory of the Lord revealed, but it is also left inexplicit what exactly they do see, so that between the vision and the revelation there remains a certain difference. What is clear, nonetheless, is that what was formerly concealed has been exposed, that the topographical features of the previous verse, emphasized by the repeated "every," have been collapsed into the totality of "all flesh," sharing a single experience, and that this corresponds to divine speech. "Flesh" (בשר) is frail, as the next verses tell us, yet it is capable of seeing. What effect does the sight have on the flesh? We do not as yet know, but there is nonetheless a transference or transposition between our verse and the previous one. "Seeing" is the crooked being made straight, the mountains diminished, the lowly exalted, and Jacob rectified.

"For the mouth of Yнwн has spoken" obviously corresponds to "a voice calling": the passage, like its central verse, is circular.⁵⁰ The voice concludes by reflecting back on itself, withdrawing into itself, or withdrawing the world it evokes back into itself. In ch. 1, between the initial "for Yнwн has spoken," to which heaven and earth are summoned to listen in v. 2, and "for the mouth of Yнwн has spoken" in v. 20, the world of First Isaiah is introduced in its dereliction, and with its choices between good and evil, survival and disaster. Here the identical phrase, "for the mouth of Yнwн has spoken," summarizes the trajectory of Second Isaiah, from comfort to consolation. It may be a response to First Isaiah, a new word that revokes the old, or a recollection of it: the truth of First Isaiah is vindicated.

---

notes how the cosmic dynamic overcomes the static limits of the topography, and attributes it to the "metonymic imagination" of Deutero-Isaiah.

49. Berges, *Jesaja 40–48*, 95, thinks that this is a later supplement, introduced to make the connection with 1:20. Thereby he tidies the syntax and verse structure, but at the expense of ambiguity.

50. Goldingay, *The Message of Isaiah 40–55*, 22. Merendino, *Der Erste und der Letzte*, 40, points out that it also corresponds to "says your God" in v. 1. He suggests that the parallels with 1:20 and 59:14 impart an ethical connotation.

Brevard Childs has suggested a connection between Isa 40 and 28, for instance through the description of Samaria as being at the top of the גיא שמנים "the valley of fat things" in 28:1.[51] Equally close is the epithet גיא חזיון, "the valley of vision," attributed to Jerusalem in 22:1. There it satirically portrays Jerusalem's failure of vision and impending fall. Here, the word גיא, "valley," may specifically evoke Jerusalem, which is raised above the mountains in 2:1, in its prophetic function.

III

קול אמר קרא ואמר מה אקרא כל הבשר חציר וכל חסדו כציץ השדה:
יבש חציר נבל ציץ כי רוח יהוה נשבה בו אכן חציר העם:
יבש חציר נבל ציץ ודבר אלהינו יקום לעולם:

A voice says: "Cry." And I/one said, "What shall I cry?" All flesh is grass, and all its kindness as the flower of the field. The grass withers, the flower fades, when the wind/spirit of YHWH blows upon it; surely the people is grass. The grass withers, the flower fades, and the word of our God lasts forever! (40:6–8)

קול אמר קרא "A voice says, 'Cry.'" The same voice or different?[52] Would its message be the same as in the previous five verses, or does it look forward to the rest of Deutero-Isaiah, or some other message, or is it entirely open?[53] The imperative seems to be parallel to the injunction to comfort in v. 1 and to open the way in v. 3, as if this were a particular instance of comforting and opening the way. Why does the voice need an interlocutor to cry on its behalf?

---

51. Childs, *Isaiah*, 296, 300. Childs, like Christopher R. Seitz, "The Divine Council: Temporal Transition and New Prophecy in the Book of Isaiah," *JBL* 109 (1990): 242, emphasizes the parallel with נבל ציץ, "the fading flower," but overlooks the additional correspondence with גיא. See also the rather full discussion in Hugh G. M. Williamson, *The Book Called Isaiah: Deutero-Isaiah's Role in Composition and Redaction* (Oxford: Clarendon, 1994), 76–78, who does make this connection; Sommer, *A Prophet Reads Scripture*, 75–76, who sees 40:1–11 as a systematic inversion of 28:1–5; and Berges, *Jesaja 40–48*, 84. Goldingay, *Isaiah 40–55*, 59, notes further connections with ch. 28 throughout ch. 40.

52. Freedman, "The Structure of Isaiah 40:1–11," 244–46, provides an engaging discussion of the possibilities.

53. Some critics attribute vv. 6–8 to a later redactional stratum e.g., Kratz, "Der Anfang des Zweiten Jesaja in Jes 40,1f und seine literarischen Horizonte," 406–7; Antje Labahn, *Wort Gottes und Schuld Israels: Untersuchungen zu Motiven deuteronomistischer Theologie im Deuterojesajabuch mit einem Ausblick auf das Verhältnis von Jes 40–55 zum Deuteronomismus* (Stuttgart: Kohlhammer, 1999), 97–103; van Oorschot, *Von Babel zum Zion*, 114, arguing largely on the basis of the inconsistency of vv. 6–8 with the other sections of the prologue.

And what is the role and responsibility of that interlocutor? Here we come to a central issue of Deutero-Isaiah, as of prophetic literature generally. But we also come to a famous crux, whether we should read, "And I said" with 1QIsa^a etc., or "And one said" with MT, whether the prophet is listening in to disembodied voices, or whether he is summoned on his own account.[54] The first person, "And I said," is simpler and more effective; it also enables a parallel with the opening of the second half of Deutero-Isaiah in 49:1–6. In that case, the prophet speaks on behalf of "all flesh" and its incapacity to speak. The other possibility suggests perhaps a celestial hesitation, or an interplay of voices within the prophet or in God, and the divine as an internal voice of the prophet.

"What should I cry?" may refer to the content of the speech or to the inability to find an appropriate message.[55] Correspondingly, "all flesh is grass" may be the message, culminating in "the word of our God lasts for ever," or it may explicate the problem. At any rate, "What should I cry?" focuses on the speaker on the verge of speech, not knowing what to say or how to say it. The speaker identifies with "all flesh": the prophet, as human, shares its transience. Or, as a divine voice, with the prophet listening in, it perhaps empathizes with human mortality or, on the contrary, feels the insignificance of humans before God and the impossibility of any communication, as, for instance, in 40:15. The "comfort" of v. 1 has apparently met with an inescapable objection. The grief of "my people" and "the heart of Jerusalem" is an example of the general human condition and its inconsolability. The pathos is emphasized by the continuation: וכל חסדו כציץ השדה "and all its *ḥesed* like the flower of the field." *Ḥesed* refers to the affective ties that bind human beings, and hence to the capacity for generosity and loyalty, the opposite of the lack of social solidarity

---

54. Critics are divided on the issue cf. Baltzer, *Deutero-Isaiah: A Commentary on Isaiah 40–55*, 56. It should be noted that Melugin, *The Formation of Isaiah 40–55*, 84, considers the addressee to be also ambiguous. Fokkelman, "Stylistic Analysis of Isaiah 40:1–11," 79 note 26, goes further and insists that it cannot be the prophet, because it does not accord with his "strong faith and glorious optimism." This attributes an uncomplicated personality to the prophet, which I think would be difficult to sustain. A similar assumption, however, underlies redactional approaches.

55. Freedman, "The Structure of Isaiah 40:1–11," 146, for instance, thinks that vv. 6–8 logically precede the other parts of the prologue, and the content of the message is to be found in vv. 3–4. Krinetzki, "Zur Stilistik von Jesaja 40:1–8," 66, considers it to be the message, however. For a good account of the complexities of reading the passage, see Geller, "Were the Prophets Poets?" *Prooftexts* 3 (1983): 215. Berges, *Jesaja 40–48*, 109, holds that it does not refer to the content of the message as to the futility of delivering it and should be translated "How?"

for which Israel was condemned in First Isaiah, and of which v. 2 reminds us. *Ḥesed* exceeds justice; coupled most frequently with אמת, "truth," it points to a truth about human commitment and human potential.[56] *Ḥesed* is strikingly absent from most of First Isaiah,[57] and only here in the book is it used with reference to humanity. That even *ḥesed* is evanescent indicates a despair, not over human evil, but goodness. It is not that it is not good enough, but that it is not durable. The comparison with the flower of the field is one of beauty as well as fragility. Beauty is an ethical quality; "flesh," however, suggests physical desire, dependence, and intimacy. What do we really long for and grieve for? The lament has a long erotic history.[58] With the introduction of *ḥesed*, a complex metaphorical transfer between ethics and aesthetics is intimated, typical of the prophets. The transfer, nonetheless, does not displace the corporeal loss; it focuses on the body as the site from which *ḥesed* arises, as well as beauty, and as that which preeminently dies.

However, "all flesh" sees the glory of the Lord, and/or that the mouth of the Lord has spoken. Will they survive the vision? What will it do to the flesh? Is there a disjunction between the sight and the rest of the body, between present and future? These questions are not easily answerable, but in the gap between v. 5 and v. 6 is invested the hope that "all flesh" may traverse it.[59]

The images of grass and flower are highly conventional, and their iterability is emphasized by the repetition of "the grass withers, the flower fades," in each of the next two verses. The repetition underwrites the truth of human mortality; it is a song that comes back to haunt us. But it is also there for the sake of the sequel:

---

56. Geller, "Were the Prophets Poets?," 216, valuably defines *ḥesed* as "a mixture of love and law beyond any narrow legalism." However, he interprets our phrase negatively as referring to Israel's infirm loyalty, like Hos 6:4. See also Johannes de Moor, "The Integrity of Isaiah 40," in *Mesopotamica, Ugaritica, Biblica* (ed. M. Dietrich and O. Loretz; AOAT 232; Neukirchen-Vluyn: Neukirchener, 1993), 215, who thinks it refers to human unreliability. In the context of human mortality, a positive evaluation of its *ḥesed* would make its passing more grievous. See further Baltzer, *Deutero-Isaiah: A Commentary on Isaiah 40-55*, 57 note 66, on proposals to translate *ḥesed* as "strength" or "beauty."

57. It only occurs in 16:5, in the context of the Oracles Against the Nations. Elsewhere in Deutero-Isaiah the referent is God (54:8, 10; 55:3).

58. The interfusion of death and eros is evident in the laments for Tammuz and in classical Pastoral. Westermann, *Isaiah 40-66*, 24, 41-42 and throughout, rightly stresses the impress of the lament on Deutero-Isaiah.

59. Freedman, "The Structure of Isaiah 40:1-11," 138, regards v. 5 as the centrepiece and climax of the whole poem, and v. 6 as its logical beginning. In contrast, Labahn, *Wort Gottes und Schuld Israels*, 106-7, considers "for the mouth of Yhwh has spoken" a Deuteronomistic supplement.

יבש חציר נבל ציץ כי רוח יהוה נשבה בו
יבש חציר נבל ציץ ודבר אלהינו יקום לעולם

The grass withers, the flower fades/ for the spirit/wind of Yhwh blows upon it;
The grass withers, the flower fades/ and the word of our God lasts forever.

There is an obvious parallelism between the "spirit/wind of Yhwh" and the "word of our God," but are they equivalent or contrasted? The spirit/wind of Yhwh (רוח יהוה) would perhaps be the same as the word, so that the message, anticipating Ecclesiastes, is that only the spirit, the wind, and the word are everlasting. Or, anticipating and reversing Paul, they are opposed, and the spirit kills, while the letter gives life. And this depends on a further, foundational, ambiguity: which word of our God lasts forever? How does it relate to the previous discourse, and all previous discourse, encapsulated in כי פי יהוה דבר "for/that the mouth of Yhwh has spoken" in v. 5? Is this a new word, or the old word in new clothing? How secondary is Deutero-Isaiah?

The "spirit of Yhwh" (רוח יהוה) is associated with creation, for instance in Gen 1:2, as well as in 40:13.[60] The spirit/wind here is responsible for the dessication of the grass and the death it figures. So the God of creation is the God of death, and the despair the prophet enunciates is inherent in the structure of creation. The voices of comfort in v. 1, and that which instigates the opening of the way in v. 3, are linked through repetition to a voice whose message to proclaim is foiled by the absence of any significant message, because of the transitoriness it itself mandates.

The verb נשב, "blow," is a byform of נשף and נשם.[61] Both of these occur in the immediate vicinity in Deutero-Isaiah, in contexts similar to ours and that suggest radical transformation.[62] Both are correlated with terms for the animating spirit: נפש and נשמה. נשבה, "blows," moreover, partially dupli-

---

60. Manfred Görg, "Revision von Schöpfung und Geschichte: Auf dem Wege zu ein Strukturbestimmung von Jes 40,1–8 (11)," in *Ich bewirke das Heil und erschaffe das Unheil (Jesaja 45,7): Studien zur Botschaft der Prophet (Lothar Ruppert Festschrift)* (ed. F. Diedrich and Bernd Willmes; Würzburg: Echter, 1998), 150, argues that 40:1–11 was modelled on the priestly creation narrative, and that the mention of the רוח יהוה, in particular, recalls Gen 1:2. Geller, "Were the Prophets Poets?," 217, interestingly suggests that ambiguity is bestowed on the phrase by its association with prophetic inspiration, and in particular the call vision.

61. KBL ad loc.

62. נשף appears in 40:24, in the context of the uprooting and desiccation of earthly potentates; in 42:14 נשם is part of a series of verbs depicting God's labored respiration, manifest in cosmic drought and a new Exodus.

cates שוב, "turn, return," paradigmatically associated in the prophets with repentance and change. The wind that blows and brings death may become that which gives life. Like עקב and בקע, יבש, "withers," and נשבה, "blows," are linked through metathesis.⁶³ As there, metathesis suggests the possibility of reversal. The wind dries the grass, but it may also be responsible for its revival, for the restoration of נפש and נשמה. This is especially clear in the last verse of the section.

Before that, however, there is a little appendage, אכן חציר העם, "Surely the people is grass," which is conventionally regarded as a gloss. Against this, Görg has argued that it communicates focus, paralleling "all flesh" in v. 6.⁶⁴ The repetition adds plangency. It also recalls "my people" in v. 1.⁶⁵ The people may be grass, evanescent, suffering, like all humanity, but they belong to God, a bond emphasized by the substitution of "our God" for Yhwh in v. 8.⁶⁶ It also recalls the context of comfort. The wind that blows is the wind, spirit and message of consolation; at the very least, we cannot forget that the people who are but grass are the very same to whom the whole address is delivered: "What can I cry?" is answered in the very saying.

In the last verse, the "word of our God" subsists despite the impermanence of everything. Perhaps, however, one can read the Vav of ודבר, "*and* the word," as a conjunction rather than an adversative. The "word of our God" belongs to us, it speaks to us and in us. Then the word of our God is the condition for our permanence; it becomes a metaphor for the grass and flower.

---

63. Krinetzki, "Zur Stilistik von Jesaja 40:1–8," 69, notes the inversion without further comment; Fokkelman, "Stylistic Analysis of Isaiah 40:1–11," 80, also notes the connection formed through alliteration.

64. Görg, "Revision von Schöpfung und Geschichte," 146. See also Freedman, "The Structure of Isaiah 40:1–11," 248, and the sober discussion in Baltzer, *Deutero-Isaiah: A Commentary on Isaiah 40–55*, 57–58. The introduction of the clause by אכן, "Surely," seems to me to be a clear parallel with אכן משפטי את־יהוה, "surely my judgement is with Yhwh," in 49:4, in an autobiographical passage that is widely regarded as corresponding to ours (cf. S. L. Stassen, "The Plot in Isaiah 40–55," *AcT* 17 [1997]: 129). Goldingay, *The Message of Isaiah 40–55*, 29; ibid., 61, argues that it indicates a change of speaker; likewise Merendino, *Der Erste und der Letzte*, 52, regards it as a confirmation by the initial speaker of the addressee's objection. Rudolf Mosis, "Der verlässliche Grund der Verkündigung: Zu Jes 40,6–8," in *Gesammelte Aufsätze zum Alten Testament* (FB 93; Stuttgart: Echter, 1999), 153–71, argues at length that the speaker changes in v. 8, and sees in the phrase evidence that the later glossator recognized this.

65. Freedman, "The Structure of Isaiah 40:1–11," 248.

66. Freedman, ibid., 235–36, notes the parallel with the sequence אלהינו/יהוה in v. 3.

This brings us to the ambiguity of these images. Grass and flower fade, but they may also flourish.[67]

Goldingay, in a beautiful deconstructive reading of Deutero-Isaiah, has pointed out that the word can only survive in writing, that in itself, quoting Stephen Moore, it is the "most ephemeral of substances."[68] I wonder whether the word can be so easily translated, whether, for instance, it is coterminous with our book of Isaiah. The focus on the *mouth* of Yhwh, however we understand it,[69] would suggest a process of cogitation, articulation and expression, which may be physical or psychic, but in any case is not fixed in a book. The word corresponds to the wind[70] and perhaps also to *ḥesed*, as a series of immaterial entities that prove more durable than the solidity of flesh and all it represents. It thus encapsulates a fundamental motif of Deutero-Isaiah, and perhaps of prophetic writings generally, whereby the powerless are vindicated and power is illusory.[71]

In vv. 3–5 the orientation is to the future, when all flesh sees the glory of Yhwh, at the culmination of a way through a violently leveled landscape. Here in vv. 6–8 the repetition evokes the seasons and rhythms of life and death. The repetition recalls that of ונחמו, "comfort," in v. 1, and hence the theme of consolation. There comfort restores maternal care, both of God and the dead, bereaved, or captive heart of Jerusalem; it is both a recovery of the past and a new beginning. Here the rhythm of the seasons transcends and opens a possibility beyond the immediate human disaster. The maternal presence is inferred metonymically from the grass and flower; it is the fecund and inhuming earth, as well as the wind/spirit, which is the only feminine subject, and which is associated with the nurturing of Gen 1:2. Both of these are ethereal, disembodied or implicit; the maternal comfort is entrusted to the wind, or in abeyance, germinating, in the earth.

---

67. Ettore, "Is 40,1–11: Una Lettura Strutturale," 303, comments on the "verticalization" of the image; at the moment of death life can regerminate.

68. Goldingay, "Isaiah 40–55 in the 1990s: Among Other Things Deconstructing, Mystifying, Intertextual, Socio-Critical, Hearer-Involving," *BibInt* 5 (1997): 229. Goldingay is quoting from Stephen D. Moore, *Mark and Luke in Poststructuralist Perspectives* (New Haven: Yale University Press, 1992), 26. Conrad, *Reading Isaiah*, 62–72, suggests translating קרא in v. 6 as "read," with reference to chs. 6–39, which he sees as a book within the book of Isaiah. For Goldingay and myself the "word" is more indeterminate.

69. For a discussion of its place in Deuteronomic traditions, see Labahn, *Wort Gottes und Schuld Israels*, 106. Labahn is rather dismissive of its importance in prophetic writings.

70. Contra Goldingay, *The Message of Isaiah 40–55*, 26.

71. Blenkinsopp, *Isaiah 40–55*, 183.

On the one hand, Deutero-Isaiah asserts tirelessly that redemption is inherent in the structure and narrative of creation; on the other, it is unforeseen and unforeshadowed. There is no apparent way of bridging this contradiction, which it nonetheless attempts to convince us is no contradiction.[72] It is this that accounts for the spectrality, the doubleness of the vision, since that which is revealed, the glory of Y<small>HWH</small>, the word of our God, is primordial and everlasting.

IV

על הר־גבה עלי־לך מבשרת ציון
הרימי בכח קולך מבשרת ירושלם
הרימי אל־תיראי אמרי לערי יהודה הנה אלהיכם
הנה אדני יהוה בחזק יבוא וזרעו משלה לו הנה שכרו אתו ופעלתו לפניו
כרעה עדרו ירעה בזרעו יקבץ טלאים ובחיקו ישא עלות ינהל

> On a high mountain go up, O herald of Zion; lift up your voice in strength, O herald of Jerusalem; lift up, do not be afraid; say to the cities of Judah, behold your God. Behold, my Lord Y<small>HWH</small> comes in power, and his arm rules for him; behold, his reward is with him, his recompense before him. As a shepherd grazes his flock, with his right arm he gathers the lambs, and in his bosom he carries, he leads the nursing ewes. (40:9–11)

So finally we, and he, come back home: that which is spoken to the heart of Jerusalem in v. 2 is completed in the announcement of the herald; the way of Y<small>HWH</small> in v. 3 has reached its destination.[73] One mountain, it seems, escapes the diminution of v. 4, corresponding to the exaltation of Zion above all the mountains in 2:2. The mysterious voices have disappeared, as have the doubts of vv. 6–8;[74] the prophet speaks for himself, and through the posited herald of Zion and Jerusalem.

---

72. On this tension, see especially Willey, *Remember the Former Things*.

73. A number of scholars limit the Prologue to vv. 1–8, e.g., Elliger, *Deuterojesaja 1: Teilband*, 34. Others posit an especially close relationship between vv. 1–2 and 9–11, and hence see the latter as being integral to the prologue. A detailed comparison is provided by Freedman, "The Structure of Isaiah 40:1–11," 234–43 and Fokkelman, "Stylistic Analysis of Isaiah 40:1–11," 83ff. There are a variety of mediating positions, e.g., Melugin, *The Formation of Isaiah 40–55*, 84–85; Carr, "Isaiah 40:1–11 in the Context of the Macrostructure of Second Isaiah," in *Discourse Analysis of Biblical Literature: What It Is and What It Offers* (ed. R. Walter Bodine; Atlanta: Scholars Press, 1995), 62–63; Kratz, "Der Anfang des Zweiten Jesaja in Jes 40,1f und seine literarischen Horizonte," 404–10.

74. Westermann, *Isaiah 40–66*, 43, however, suggests that the voice may be the same as in v. 6. There is no evidence for this; Freedman, "The Structure of Isaiah 40:1–11," 237,

But who is this herald? And why is she feminine (מבשרת)? She is clearly a complement to the male herald (מבשר) in 52:7, and thus cannot be identified in any simple sense with Zion/Jerusalem.[75] But she also cannot be separated from other female figures associated with Zion: the "daughter of Zion" of 1:9, the "inhabitant of Zion" (יושבת ציון) of 12:6 etc., and hence the motif of Zion as the spouse of God.[76] The "herald of Zion" may then be an aspect of Zion that is returning to itself, just as God is in v. 3. But the voice of the prophet is also summoning, or claiming, a female counterpart to itself, as if it cannot speak, at least for the moment, except in this disguise.[77] The prophet is an emissary, perhaps the emissary, from God to Zion, except that his voice is absorbed in that of the multitude of ewes whose ascent, as those who "go up" (עלות), completes the circular structure of vv. 9–11.[78] We began with an anonymous plurality of voices, urged to bring comfort, and so we end, as with the transition from male to female.

The herald of Zion/Jerusalem is presumably human as well as female, in contrast to the ambiguously divine voices in the first part of the passage; at any rate, she is not disembodied. The human quality of the voice is emphasized through the transposition of בשר to מבשרת.[79] That which is flesh will com-

---

argues that here the message initiated in v. 1 finally reaches its destination. See also Ettore "Is 40,1–11: Una Lettura Strutturale," 299.

75. Most critics, nonetheless, make precisely this identification (Blenkinsopp, *Isaiah 40–55*, 184, 185; Childs, *Isaiah*, 301; Baltzer, *Deutero-Isaiah: A Commentary on Isaiah 40–55*, 61; Elliger, *Deuterojesaja 1: Teilband*, 31, 35 are a representative sample). In contrast, Sean McEvenue, "Who Was Second Isaiah?" in *Studies in the Book of Isaiah: Festschrift Willem A. M. Beuken* (ed. J. Van Ruiten and M.Vervenne; Leuven: Peeters, 1997), 218–21, considers the herald to be the prophetess responsible for Deutero-Isaiah. As will become clear, my view is that the figure is ambiguous. Merendino, *Der Erste und der Letzte*, 65, notes the female role of celebrating victory in the Hebrew Bible.

76. These are also frequently regarded as appositional. There is little reason, however, to reject the objective genitive, and in practice it makes little difference. Cf. McEvenue, "Who Was Second Isaiah?," 219; Francis Landy, "Prophetic Intercourse," in *Sense and Sensitivity: Essays on Reading the Bible in Memory of Robert Carroll* (ed. Alistair G. Hunter and Philip R. Davies; JSOTSup 348; Sheffield: Sheffield Academic Press, 2002), 272–73.

77. If McEvenue is right, there is no dissimulation; the prophet is female. However, he would have to account for the masculine gender used for the protagonist elsewhere in Deutero-Isaiah.

78. There is an evident wordplay between עלות, "nursing," and עלות, "ascending." See also Ettore, "Is 40,1–11: Una Lettura Strutturale," 292).

79. For the verbal connection, see Blenkinsopp, *Isaiah 40–55*, 185, and Koole, *Isaiah: Part 3. Vol. 1: Isaiah 40–48*, 70.

municate the advent of God. The voice anticipates and announces the vision that all flesh will see in v. 5,[80] and articulates the word, which lasts for ever in v. 8, especially if that word is in some sense the return of Yhwh. מבשרת, the female herald, mediates between the prior and ultimate condition of all flesh. But it also marks the transformation of flesh into word. Humans speak, and thus become more than flesh. At the same time they speak for and in the flesh, with the full vocal apparatus, at maximum volume, and with an excitement that cannot contain the news, which soars above the mountain and spreads from Zion/Jerusalem to the cities of Judah. The voice is permeated, however, with the divine imminence. "Behold your God!" opens a space in the human voice for God to enter, for the supersession of the messenger by the content of the message, which is not a signifying discourse, but the subject of speech, that which the words signify.[81] "Behold your God!" recollects, as some have noted, "says your God," in v. 1.[82] The structure of the passage is circular; we return to our initial point, just as God returns to Jerusalem. However, whereas in v. 1 God speaks so as to displace the function of speaking and comforting onto unnamed others, while he himself remains enigmatically or ambivalently in the background, here God is no longer quoted in parentheses, no longer absents himself from the task of comforting, which is not a consequence of verbal communication, but of that which precedes and validates every communication, the presence of the speaker. Up to this point, God has been apprehended metonymically, through his word, spirit, way, and most of all through voices; now, he is divested of qualifying accoutrements.

The herald is hurrying towards Zion/Jerusalem, climbing up the high mountain, spurred on and imagined by the prophetic spectator, a figure of desire as well as of reunification. The herald will become the inhabitant of Zion, and anticipates its repopulation, as the one who awaits her divine lover.

---

80. Some critics think that there is a contradiction between v. 5 and vv. 9–11, and hence attribute the latter to a later redactional layer cf. Kratz, "Der Anfang des Zweiten Jesaja in Jes 40,1f und seine literarischen Horizonte," 404. Vermeylen, "L'Unité du Livre d'Isaïe," 38–39, 46, on the contrary, proposes that vv. 1–3, 5 were modeled on vv. 9–11. However, van Oorschot, *Von Babel zum Zion*, 119 note 88, argues that we should not presuppose a chronological sequence to the passage. See also Freedman, "The Structure of Isaiah 40:1–11," 255–57.

81. For Carr, "Isaiah 40:1–11 in the Context of the Macrostructure of Second Isaiah," 63, the prologue is divided into two parts: vv. 1–8, which is concerned with authorization, and vv. 9–11, which is the authorized message. However, the distinction is subverted by the identity of the message with the authorizing subject.

82. Freedman, "The Structure of Isaiah 40:1–11," 237; Fokkelman, "Stylistic Analysis of Isaiah 40:1–11," 83.

The entrance of God into Zion is the culmination of the process. All three events, however, are one and the same. Zion, for instance, takes on the role of the herald, just as the latter restores to it its task of imparting Torah.[83] The herald is absorbed in and becomes one with Zion, but also disappears, effaces herself, in her message; she is the vanishing intermediary, that which measures the distance between the entities whose loss and longing for each other has so far constituted the poem just before it collapses. But of course that collapse never happens.

It does not happen because two figures intervene: the warrior and the shepherd. The advent is deferred and elaborated through metaphors, which both intensify anticipation and take us to a different world or era. As several critics remark, v. 10 derives from the divine warrior tradition,[84] and hence from the context of Yhwh's paradigmatic victories over Canaan or chaos; the metaphor of the divine and royal shepherd likewise draws on ancient liturgical and narrative resources. We are returning to a poetic as well as ancestral home. Nostalgia risks disappointment, since home is not as it used to be. The figure of Zion/Jerusalem as lover, herald, and purveyor of Torah encounters that of the devastated city. As in v. 2, to which v. 9 corresponds, Jerusalem is addressed over and despite its desolation and death. The word, and even more the presence, of God, as in v. 8, is that which gives life to the dead. The abandoned city awaits its population, its dead children represented by the survivors or their successors, who see in it an image of the irrecoverable past. The return is imminent, but we do not know to what we will return.

---

83. Most critics assume that Zion is the subject of the address to the cities of Judah in the second half of the verse, and therefore identify it with the herald. It may be, as Paul Del Brassey, *Metaphor and the Incomparable God in Isaiah 40–55* (Bibal Dissertaion Series 9; North Richland Hills, Tex.: Bibal, 2001), 184, remarks, included among the cities of Judah. Jerusalem and the cities of Judah are obviously complementary (cf. 44:26), and one can easily imagine the function of the herald being transferred to Jerusalem. Knut Holter, "Zur Funktion der *Städte* Judas in Jesaja XL 9," *VT* 46 (1996): 120, suggests that the cities of Judah are introduced here to announce the reversal of their devastation predicted in Isaiah's commissioning scene in 6:11.

84. See especially Tryggve Mettinger, "In Search of the Hidden Structure: Yhwh as King in Isaiah 40–55," in *Writing and Reading the Scroll of Isaiah*, 150, who argues that it anticipates the acclamation of Yhwh as king in 52:7, and the discussion of Mettinger in Brettler, "Incompatible Metaphors for Yhwh," 106–8. Brettler points out that both warrior and shepherd are sub-metaphors of Yhwh as king, though for some reason he does not think the metaphor of the shepherd is so in this instance (ibid., 119). Goldingay, *Isaiah 40–55*, 89, suggests particular associations with the Exodus traditions, as well as with 28:2.

The images of vv. 10–11 detain us, and add their own problems of interpretation and resolution. The divine warrior returns, as, for instance, in Ps 24, but where has he been? If he is returning from Babylon, his victory, which may subsequently be decoded as that of Cyrus,[85] is the obverse of apparent defeat, the captivity of Zion and thus of God, and of the motif of impotence which recurs repeatedly in Deutero-Isaiah. He comes "in strength" from the scene of the disaster, for which he too is responsible.[86] Hence the parallelism between the "hand of YHWH" in v. 2 and his "arm" in v. 10. God then moves from the position of adversary to that of protagonist, or perhaps he destroys for the sake of restitution. The oscillation points not only to an ambivalence on the part of God, an ability to change sides, to the other meaning of נחם as "changing one's mind," but to the background of imperial domination against which the ideology of divine conquest is reasserted. Divine authorization of Cyrus, to give the most proximate instance, will perpetuate Jerusalem's servitude, and is the antithesis of the rhetoric of Israel's independence and possession of the Promised Land.

He comes with his "reward" and the "recompense" for his labor, corresponding to the penalty Israel pays in v. 2.[87] The reward and recompense are perhaps Israel; the detail that his פעלה, "labor," is before him foreshadows the image of the flock in the next verse. If so, God has earned something, his people, among the foreign powers, and has experienced a servitude approximating theirs. Divine identification with and participation in Israel's suffering, for instance in accounts of his parturition, accompanies the insistence on his power.

In the last verse the metaphor of the victorious hero returning home is replaced by the pastoral one of the shepherd. The hero appears indirectly or implicitly, preceded by his attribute of strength (בחזק יבוא) and his governing arm (זרעו משלה לו); virile aggrandizement is intensified in preparation for the arrival, with its intimations of sexual union. Here the metaphor is displaced as a simile—כרעה, "like a shepherd"—so as to preempt premature identification. As with the simile of the "flower of the field" in v. 6, it suggests a dialectic of identity and non-identity, it insists on its difference, perhaps as a prelude to the advent of God as creator in v. 12.

---

85. Berges, *Jesaja 40–48*, 112, indeed, thinks that there is direct reference to Cyrus, reversing 28:2, where the "strong one" is Assyria.

86. There is a minor problem in the pointing of בחזק, which need not detain us here.

87. Stoebe, "Überlegungen zu Jesaja 40,1–11," 108–9, suggests that the reward may be Israel's (see Blenkinsopp, *Isaiah 40–55*, 186). But the metaphor of the shepherd in the next verse makes it more probable that YHWH is the recipient.

Matters are complicated by the relationship of the figures of the warrior and the shepherd. They may form a composite metaphor; warrior and shepherd are both metaphors for divine sovereignty, and hence presage the declaration that Yhwh reigns in the parallel passage in 52:7.[88] They may, however, be successive: Yhwh is *first* imagined as a warrior and *then* as a shepherd, so as to substitute a peaceful, utopian paradigm for the immediate political context. The alternatives are not exclusive: the reader may or should integrate the metaphors in one comprehensive image, and perceive them as separate impressions or revisions.

The shepherd presides over a flock of nursing ewes and lambs, a proliferating maternal economy. He himself, with his capacious bosom, has a maternal function. The fecundity of Zion has been transferred to the children and to God himself. Various critics have perceived in these verses a recollection of Jacob's return from Laban.[89] Not only has the crooked been made straight; God identifies with the transformation and escape of Jacob. Jacob and God, and hence Zion and God, are united. Jacob's miraculous multiplication of sheep, accomplished through the mounting (עלות) of the rams (Gen 31:10), is transformed into their nursing (Gen 33:3) on the ascent to Zion.

God leads (ינהל) the ewes; the verb נהל is associated, in particular, with pasture and with water.[90] In Exod 15:13, the guidance is precisely to the divine pasture of Zion. If, in Isa 51:18, mother Jerusalem has no one to guide (מנהל) her among all the children, now it is precisely her children, replications of her maternity, who are led. The ascent may suggest a pilgrimage, a journey to a cosmic mountain; it may be metaphorical as well as literal. But the guidance, like the carrying of the lambs in God's bosom, takes us back to the way of Yhwh in v. 3. The way replaces Zion as the site of communion. The peaceful idyll on the way is imagined from the perspective of Zion, the prophet and perhaps God, and is their meeting point. The journey may be interminably

---

88. Brettler, "Incompatible Metaphors for Yhwh," 118–19. Kiesow, *Exodustexte im Jesajabuch*, 33–34, finds the tension between vv. 10 and 11 sufficiently acute to attribute them to different redactional strata.

89. Elliger, *Deuterojesaja 1: Teilband*, 37–38; Baltzer, *Deutero-Isaiah: A Commentary on Isaiah 40–55*, 62; Zapff, *Jesaja 40–55*, 231–32, are, representative examples. Polliack, "Deutero-Isaiah's Typological Use of Jacob," 108–10, suggests the hidden presence of Rachel in these verses. However, she overlooks the possible connection between Rachel's name and the metaphor of the ewes, and strangely identifies Rachel with Zion. Though he does not note this connection, Sommer, *A Prophet Reads Scripture*, 68–70, notes several correlations with Jer 31:16, in which Rachel weeps over her children.

90. For the etymology of נהל, see Koole, *Isaiah: Part 3. Vol. 1: Isaiah 40–48*, 79; Elliger, *Deuterojesaja 1: Teilband*, 38, and KBL.

protracted, indefinitely forestalling the destination. Or the journey, on which God cares for his flock, is a moving Zion, Zion returning to itself.

The verse begins with a remarkable alliterative sequence: כרעה עדרו ירעה בזרעו, "As a shepherd grazes his flock, with his arm." The sequence may suggest an identification between shepherd and flock, and, more important, a sense of enclosure, since the word for "flock" is encircled by those for "shepherd" and "shepherding."[91] The maternal care elaborated in the rest of the verse is implicated in its inception. But the containment is expansive; the arm comes forth to gather in more lambs, a reach that is presumably uncircumscribed.[92] The word זרוע, "arm," is recollected from the previous verse, where it is a conventional figure for God's domination. God's power, exercised over the nations, is preliminary to, or is exhausted in, his care for Israel. The sideslip between vv. 10 and 11, and between the two usages of "arm," couples them together, and ensures that the simile of v. 11, the pastoral interlude whose illustrative range perhaps covers the whole sequence from v. 1 on, is potentially disarming, and has unlimited consequences.

There is always the possibility of subversion, especially in the wider context. The word עדר, "flock," recurs, with the opposite meaning, in v. 26: איש לא נעדר, "none is lacking." There the subject is the host of heaven, who may be associated with the nations and their gods. Israel, as God's flock, is an exemplification of God's universal care and dominion, just as in vv. 6–7, its transitoriness as a "people" represents the plight of "all flesh."

---

91. Fokkelman, "Stylistic Analysis of Isaiah 40:1–11," 84. The alliterative sequence is also noted by Yehoshua Gitay, "Why Metaphors: A Study in the Texture of Isaiah," in *Writing and Reading the Scroll of Isaiah: Studies of an Interpretive Tradition* (ed. Craig C. Broyles and Craig A. Evans; VTSup 70.1; Leiden: Brill, 1997), 62–63.

92. Burkhard M. Zapff, "Jes 40 und die Frage nach dem Beginn des deuterojesajanischen Corpus," in *Gottes Wege Suchen* (ed. Franz Sedlmeier; Würzburg: Echter, 2003), 362.

The Spider-Poet: Signs and Symbols in Isaiah 41

Hyun Chul Paul Kim

1. Introduction

Recent Isaiah scholarship has contributed to examination of the texts both holistically and multidimensionally, searching for both unity and diversity.[1] Synchronic and diachronic readings have offered many interpretive insights. Intertextuality[2] has risen to the surface, possibly sharing the accolades with redaction and rhetorical criticisms,[3] with which seemingly unrelated or remote bits and pieces have become interconnected in the canonical form of

---

1. For a survey of recent scholarship, see Roy F. Melugin and Marvin A. Sweeney, eds., *New Visions of Isaiah* (JSOTSup 214; Sheffield: Sheffield Academic Press, 1996); repr., Atlanta: Society of Biblical Literature, 2006; Craig C. Broyles and Craig A. Evans, eds., *Writing and Reading the Scroll of Isaiah: Studies of an Interpretive Tradition* (VTSup 70.1; Leiden: Brill, 1997); Alan J. Hauser, ed., *Recent Research on the Major Prophets* (Sheffield: Sheffield Phoenix Press, 2008).

2. Among numerous works, especially on Isaiah, consider Shalom M. Paul, "Literary and Ideological Echoes of Jeremiah in Deutero-Isaiah," in *Proceedings of the Fifth World Congress of Jewish Studies* (vol. 1; ed. P. Peli; Jerusalem: World Union of Jewish Studies, 1969), 109–21; Michael Fishbane, *Biblical Interpretation in Ancient Israel* (Oxford: Clarendon, 1985); Benjamin D. Sommer, *A Prophet Reads Scripture: Allusion in Isaiah 40–66* (Stanford: Stanford University Press, 1998); Patricia Tull Willey, *Remember the Former Things: The Recollection of Previous Texts in Second Isaiah* (SBLDS 161; Atlanta: Scholars Press, 1997); idem, "Intertextuality and the Hebrew Scriptures," *CR:BS* 8 (2000): 59–90.

3. James Muilenburg, "Form Criticism and Beyond," *JBL* 88 (1969): 1–18; Phyllis Trible, *Rhetorical Criticism: Context, Methods, and the Book of Jonah* (Minneapolis: Fortress, 1994); Patricia K. Tull, "Rhetorical Criticism and Intertextuality," in *To Each Its Own Meaning: An Introduction to Biblical Criticisms and their Applications* (ed. S. L. McKenzie and S. R. Haynes; Louisville, Ky.: Westminster John Knox, 1999), 156–80.

the texts. Particular words and motifs occur in distinct and hidden places, functioning as linking signs and symbols that form subtle connections almost like a spider's web.[4] Finding these features can help readers not only identify implied meanings within those interconnected texts but also appreciate the implications for a symbolic world created by such signs and symbols.[5] The present study, therefore, is intended to utilize these approaches to examine how interconnected signs and symbols function with respect to the editorial implications for the audiences and readers.

To do so, the present study will focus on one segment of the holistically connected book, Isa 41. In Isa 41, readers can find numerous words and motifs that echo and recur in other parts of Isa 40–55 and throughout the entire scroll of Isaiah. In an attempt to identify and analyze the signs and symbols, the present study will examine the way in which key words and motifs are linked together—both in the particular texts in which they appear (Immediate links) and in the larger perspective of the scroll (Interval Links and Overarching Links). In doing so, we will be able to find the poetic forces by which the same terms allude to unique or contrasting ideas and yet together present correlated themes. This analysis will suggest the thesis: that key correlated terms signify an intentional contrast between the nullification of the idols and the affirmation of Yhwh's restoration; that the key motif "to strengthen" (חזק) picks up the model of trust of King Hezekiah; and that this depiction transitions into another anointed deliverer King Cyrus, while accentuating the weaknesses of both these kings over against the true strengths of Yhwh. Here we see that the prophetic proclamations envision a symbolic world in which the people of Israel, identified as the servant(s) of Yhwh and the offspring of Daughter Zion, as well as the nations and coastlands, will truly see, hear, and know—and live with that indomitable faith

---

4. This metaphor of the "spider's web" is adopted here for the intentional pun with the modern-day internet "world wide web" connections. On another level, the metaphor of "a skillfully arranged piece of fabric" might be equally appropriate for describing the scribal and literary interconnectedness in Isaiah. For the latter metaphor, I am indebted to Annemarieke van der Woude in her response (SBL annual meeting, Atlanta, Ga., 2003).

5. Roy F. Melugin, "Figurative Speech and the Reading of Isaiah 1 as Scripture," in Melugin and Sweeney, *New Visions of Isaiah*, 295: "We encounter a figurative picture instead—more accurately, a 'mosaic' of portraits of Israel's past, present and future. And it is these carefully arranged *pictures*, rather than the 'real' history which supposedly lies behind the text, which the redactors preserved for us. It is this sequence of figurative representations of history which is 'scriptural' and which is the material from which a faith community can construct a symbolic world in which to live and to hear itself addressed by God."

amid ongoing hardships—the dawning age of hope and justice brought about by YHWH (41:20).

II. Immediate Links: Isaiah 40:31; 41:1 and 41:29; 42:1

Word links in biblical texts have long been identified by numerous scholars. As midrashic commentaries connect various words from multiple sources, biblical texts themselves have certain words that seem to be purposely connected. Modern interpreters have called these features concatenated "catch words,"[6] "links,"[7] "wortwörtlicher" influences,[8] "signposts," or "markers."[9] Others may call them wordplays or puns, but obviously these word links function as chains, nuts and bolts, clips, or flashbacks that may have served to knit diverse pieces together. Let us start with the links that are immediately put next to each other.[10]

Most notably, the beginning and ending verses of ch. 41 share certain distinct words with their neighboring chapters. Thus, 41:1, at the beginning of ch. 41, repeat an identical phrase from 40:31:

---

6. R. Norman Whybray, *Reading the Psalms as a Book* (JSOTSup 222; Sheffield: Sheffield Academic Press, 1996); Hans W. Wolff, *Joel and Amos* (Hermeneia; Philadelphia: Fortress, 1977), 7–8; James D. Nogalski, "Intertextuality and the Twelve," in *Forming Prophetic Literature: Essays on Isaiah and the Twelve in Honor of John D. W. Watts* (ed. J. W. Watts and P. R. House; JSOTSup 235; Sheffield: Sheffield Academic Press, 1996), 112–16.

7. Hugh G. M. Williamson, "Relocating Isaiah 1:2–9," in Broyles and Evans, *Writing and Reading the Scroll of Isaiah*, 266–67 and 269.

8. Odil Hannes Steck, *Studien zu Tritojesaja* (BZAW 203; Berlin: de Gruyter, 1991), 98–100.

9. Ronald E. Clements, "A Light to the Nations: A Central Theme of the Book of Isaiah," in Watts and House, *Forming Prophetic Literature*, 62; Ehud Ben Zvi, *Micah* (FOTL 21B; Grand Rapids: Eerdmans, 2000), 6.

10. This feature occurs in other places of Isaiah and other portions of the Hebrew Bible. But to find and go over all of them would be beyond the scope of this paper. For a few examples, scholars have pointed out the word link between Gen 2:25 and 3:1 by the same word yet with different connotations (Susan Niditch, *Oral World and Written Word* [Louisville, Ky.: Westminster John Knox, 1996], 31):
Gen 2:25, The man and his wife were both *naked* (ערומים) but were not ashamed;
Gen 3:1, The serpent was more *shrewd* (ערום) than any other wild animal.
The second example can be the well-known connection between 2 Chr 36:22–23 and Ezra 1:1–3, although the canonical order may put the two in a reversed sequence. For the third example, in Isaiah, it is noticeable that the name "Cyrus" occurs only in 44:28 and 45:1 and thus linking the two subunits together, although it can be argued that 44:28–45:7 comprises a unit.

40:31, Those who wait for Yʜᴡʜ shall *renew their strength* (יחליפו כח);

41:1, Listen to me in silence, coastlands; let the peoples *renew their strength* (יחליפו כח).

At first glance, the nuances and context of each text are quite dissimilar. But the phrase "renew their strength" is a verbatim duplicate. By using the same phrase, these two verses glue the two chapters—or, at least, the adjacent subunits—together.[11] What symbolic meanings can we retrieve from the use of this same phrase? In 40:31, following the message of renewed hope (40:1–8) and theological challenges (40:12–26), the rhetorical statements culminate in 40:27–31 where the prophet reasserts God's unparalleled greatness and the urgent need for Israel to "wait for Yʜᴡʜ." The issue of "strength" must have been an important theological topic for those who were confronted with their own weaknesses and the ineffectiveness of their faith traditions in exile. Here, to the people in utter despair, Yʜᴡʜ challenges, "Why do you say, Jacob, and speak, Israel, 'My way is hidden from Yʜᴡʜ....'?" (40:27), and assures that it is Yʜᴡʜ who gives "strength (כח) to the faint" (40:29). The prophet-poet emphatically proclaims that true strength lies only in God. Instead of relying on their own strength or idols, Israel—and all humanity—ought to "wait upon Yʜᴡʜ" utterly and resolutely (see Isa 8:17; 26:8; 33:2; 49:23; 51:5; 60:9).

Thus, this true Source of strength declared in 40:31 demands that the coastlands and peoples to renew their strength in 41:1. The literal sense indicates that the peoples as witnesses are to brace themselves for a legal disputation in court: "together let us draw near for lawsuit."[12] They are

---

11. Admitting that the chaptering system was a late phenomenon, dating all the way down to the rabbinical period, it still seems likely that 40:27–31 and 41:1–5 stood independently at one point, let alone the more apparent division between 41:21–29 and 42:1–10. For instance, the rhetorical interrogative questions of "Who ... ?" within ch. 41, together with the verb "to call, proclaim" (קרא) in 41:2, 4 and then in 41:25 (cf. v. 9 also), build a rough inclusio, occurring in 41:2, 4 and then in 41:26:

41:2, 4, Who has stirred up a righteous one from the east, and called (יקראהו) him at his feet? ... Who has worked and done it, calling (קרא) the generations from the beginning?;

41:25, 26, I stirred up one from the north so that he came, and from the rising of the sun he shall call (יקרא) by my name.

The linguistic and thematic connections of these beginning and ending portions of the same chapter build a well-constructed inclusio, making Isa 41 a delimited unit.

12. Roy F. Melugin, *The Formation of Isaiah 40–55* (BZAW 141; Berlin: de Gruyter, 1976), 93: "The trial speech in v. 1–7 has the basic elements typical of Deutero-Isaiah's trial speeches between the nations or their gods."

summoned both as witnesses and as defendants who should confess their ignorance of the risings and fallings of history (see 40:13–14). At the same time, the phrase also conveys its metaphorical sense in that the coastlands, peoples, and nations are challenged to renew their strengths—that is, if they can (see 40:15, 17, 23). Read in connection with 40:31 and the preceding subunits of 40:12–26, the answer to such a contest becomes evident—they cannot renew their strength by themselves at all, not even the vigorous youths (40:30).[13] The readers will instantly recall 40:31 and be reminded of the ironic contrast between those who wait for Yhwh and those who try to renew their strength by idols. This latter group, who attempt to renew their strength by themselves or by idols will find themselves powerless.

Likewise, the rhetorical question continues with a more specific hint of Yhwh's raising a "righteous one from the East," who is said to trample the nations and kings "like dust" (41:2; cf. 40:12). Both "coastlands" and "peoples" that are summoned to "draw near" (41:1) to see the incomparability of Yhwh fear and tremble, as they—"coastlands" and "ends of the earth"—"draw near" and come (41:5; cf. 40:28). These witnesses are already reminded of their finitude as "nations" and are declared to be a mere drop in the bucket while "coastlands" will be like dust (40:15). Therefore, coastlands, peoples, and nations are declared to be ineffective and insignificant. It is Yhwh who has the ultimate power to interrupt and redirect the course of history.

The ending of ch. 41, 41:29, contains at least two words that reappear immediately in 42:1:

> 41:29, *Look* (הן), all of them are naught; their works are nothing; their images are empty *wind* (רוח);
> 42:1, *Look* (הן), my servant whom I uphold, my chosen in whom my soul delights; I have given my *spirit* (רוחי) unto him, he shall bring forth justice to the nations.

At first glance, these words do not seem peculiar, except for the fact that they occur in both verses, thereby linking the two dissimilar subunits. However, the connection seems to be a deliberate authorial intention set out to convey certain messages. Just as the ignorance of the peoples was implied in 41:1, so here the naïveté of the peoples is reasserted in 41:25–29. Here Yhwh challenges the peoples, including the idol worshippers, to declare what had

---

13. Melugin, *The Formation of Isaiah 40–55*, 97: "We know in advance that this potentially hopeful word to the nations will come to naught. They will be unable to renew their strength."

been planned long ago and what is to occur. And their answer? When Yhwh looked, there was no one and no return of speech (דבר) in 41:28, as if this motif wraps up the initial challenge for the peoples to approach and speak (ידברו) in 41:1. Thus, in 41:29, all of the accused parties have disappeared; and the idols have become void.

Here, it is further noticeable that the word רוח makes a thematic pun in these two texts. In 41:29, this word denotes "wind" or "breath" that comprises a hendiadys with the following word "formlessness" (רוח ותהו). Accordingly, this combination of two words echoes the similar syntactical phrase תהו ובהו in Gen 1:2. It is as though readers are to recall "empty void" in Gen 1:2 when hearing the phrase "empty wind" in Isa 41:29:

> Gen 1:2, The earth was a formless void (תהו ובהו) and darkness was on the face of the deep; and the spirit (רוח) of God was hovering over the face of the waters.

Note that the word "spirit" or "wind" (רוח) is also extant in Gen 1:2. By using the similar figurative language, the prophet-poet of Isa 41:29 reminds the readers that these daunting nations (41:1, 5, 11–12), their human-made idols (41:6–7, 24), and their counselors (41:28; cf. 40:13) are merely chaotic tempests. In contrast, it is God's spirit that stands trustworthily, even over the chaotic forces depicted in Gen 1:2. Moreover, this phrase "empty wind" (Isa 41:29) together with the word "my spirit" (42:1) echoes Isa 40:7, as a reminder that all mortals are mere flesh and that just like flower and grass, every human being—whether noble or lowly—will wither and fade away "when the spirit (רוח) of Yhwh blows upon it." By echoing the notion of how human beings are ephemeral (40:6–8), the concept of God's outpouring the divine spirit (42:1; cf. 40:13; 42:5) intensifies the fact that God alone is the Creator, the Source of strength and life.[14]

On the contrary, in 42:1, the same words occur with a positive promise of hope. Whereas justice and deliverance seem impossible in mortals, Yhwh chooses a particular human being to be Yhwh's servant to carry out the divine salvific tasks. In this commissioning of one of the so-called servant songs, Yhwh promises to confer Yhwh's "spirit" upon this servant (42:1). Its outcome signals the servant's establishing "justice" (42:3). This "justice" (משפט) refers to Israel's earlier lament: "My justice disappears from my God"

---

14. Melugin, *The Formation of Isaiah 40–55*, 100: "41,21–29 and 42,1–9 share the contention that [Yhwh] alone can declare the future and make it come to pass (41,26–28; 42,9).... The gods are 'chosen' by [humans] (41,24), whereas [Yhwh] chooses the servant (42,1)."

(40:27; cf. 59:9, 14–15), which is now rebutted by the divine plan to bring forth justice (42:1, 3–4; cf. 40:14; 61:8).[15] In fact, this justice will reach the "nations" (42:1) and the "coastlands" (42:4), who have come trembling after they have witnessed Yhwh's majestic plan (41:1–5).

Therefore, the same terms in 41:29 and 42:1 together set out a bold contrast between the idols and the servant, between the downfall of the nations and the uplifting of the servant. The servant will not only receive Yhwh's spirit but will also, through divine commissioning, establish justice throughout the nations. Here, readers soon learn that it is Cyrus, the Persian king, who is to be the positive instrument within Yhwh's plan (41:2, 25; 45:13), in much the same way that an anonymous Assyrian king was earlier regarded as a negative instrument (10:5). Thus, Cyrus may mirror or even replace a Davidic king, already pronounced and anticipated in the preceding texts (9:5 [Eng 9:6]; 11:1, 10; 32:1). Nevertheless, Cyrus is never described as the servant of Yhwh.[16] In fact, the same text specifies that Cyrus' instrumentality is for the sake of Yhwh's "servant" Jacob and Israel (45:4). Moreover, in the present form of the text, the servant of Yhwh is consistently identified as none other than the people named Jacob-Israel (41:8; 44:1–2, 21; 45:4; 48:20; 49:3; cf. 63:11).[17] Later, another commissioned agent claims to have been given Yhwh's spirit and Yhwh's anointing (61:1) but yet remains anonymous. This anonymity thus symbolizes a significant suggestion that those more explicitly implied human candidates eventually disappear, for example, be they Hezekiah or Cyrus. Therefore, ch. 41 plays a significant role in that the future of the servant Jacob-Israel (41:8, 14) is intricately related to both King Hezekiah (chs. 36–39) and King Cyrus (chs. 44–45). By keeping the servant anonymous in 42:1, at the same time, readers would then be reminded not only of the achievements of these two kings—one Davidic and the other foreign—but also of their limitations, which increasingly highlight the creator God as divine King (41:10, 21).

To sum up, by reusing the same words or phrases, Isa 41:1 builds a linguistic connection with 40:31 and likewise 41:29 with 42:1. In addition to the obvious function of scribal correlation as if linking with the threads, these connections demonstrate how those seemingly disconnected parts become interconnected and together convey implicit but significantly heightened

---

15. Later, it will be reiterated in another lament with a vow of confidence: "Surely my justice is with Yhwh" (49:4).

16. Cyrus is called Yhwh's "shepherd" (44:24) and "anointed" (45:1).

17. Consider also that from ch. 54 on, the term is consistently pluralized—or democratized—as the "servants" of Yhwh (54:17; 56:6; 63:17; 65:9, 13–15; 66:14).

ideas, such as the concept of waiting for Yhwh as the true source of strength (40:31), in contrast to the peoples and nations who cannot even renew their own strength (41:1), as well as the notion of the incompetence or nothingness of the peoples and idols (41:29) as opposed to the powerful God who faithfully promises to grant the living spirit to God's chosen servant (42:1).

III. Interval Links: Isaiah 34–35, 36–39, and (40–)41

In addition to the Immediate links, Isa 41 has many words and motifs that function to connect with other texts in its vicinity. These links may not be connected to adjoining passages; but they certainly build symbolic correlations, much like skilled artisans who can weave together complex webs within a tapestry. They help readers to see an overall pattern or design. They help readers to hear the key refrains that echo over and over again. One of the most unique and intriguing links may be found in the relationship of chs. (40–)41 to chs. 36–39.

The distinctive word linking the two sections is the verbal root "to strengthen" (חזק). This term occurs five times in ch. 41—vv. 6, 7 (two times), 9, and 13.[18] In 41:6–7, this word occurs three times, denoting how the idol-makers try to encourage (literally, "strengthen") one another and fasten their product to no avail. In a sharp contrast with such futile human effort to "strengthen" themselves and their idols, in 41:9 and 41:13 this term recurs in the promise of Yhwh who will truly "strengthen" Israel and hold its right hand. Read together, the two subunits of 41:6–7 and 41:8–13 echo each other with the correlated word "to strengthen"; this contrasts sharply the powerlessness of the idols and idol-makers/worshippers with the trustworthy power of Yhwh and the servant Israel whom Yhwh promises to help, uphold, and strengthen (41:10).

When considering Isa 36–39, it is noteworthy to remember that the name of the Judean king Hezekiah has the same word חזק as its verbal root, with its literal meaning, "Yhwh has strengthened him" (or "Yhwh is my strength" or "strength of Yhwh"). Except for Isa 1:1 where Hezekiah is spelled a bit differently with the imperfect verbal form (יחזקיהו), in Isa 36–39 his name occurs in the perfect verbal form (חזקיהו). In chs. 36–39 the name Hezekiah occurs thirty-two times, by far the most concentrated occurrences of the root חזק

---

18. This verbal root occurs rather infrequently throughout the book of Isaiah. Outside chs. 36–39—which is a narrative section dealing with King Hezekiah (cf. 1:1), it occurs elsewhere in 4:1; 8:11; 22:21; 27:1, 5; 28:2, 22; 33:23; 35:3–4; 40:10; 42:6; 45:1; 51:18; 54:2; 56:2, 4, 6; 64:7.

in the entire book of Isaiah.[19] In this narrative, the readers learn of a devout king whose actions of repentance and trust demonstrate an ideal type of defiant faith and courage. At the end of this powerful narrative, Hezekiah is said to have "been sick and been healed [literally, 'had become strengthened']" (39:1).

It is fascinating to detect the literary pun as its symbolism becomes evident when read in connection with ch. 41. The metal worker is cynically depicted as one who will encourage (literally, 'strengthen' ויחזק) the goldsmith and together fasten (literally, 'strengthen' ויחזקהו) the anvil with nails (41:6–7).[20] The Hebrew word ויחזקהו without the vowel pointings in 41:7 resembles very closely the name Hezekiah חזקיהו (or יחזקיהו) in Isa 36–39.[21] Whereas the humble Hezekiah was healed of his disease (39:1), the haughty oppressors would be ruined and become nothing (41:11–12) just as the idol fabricators would lose their strength and security (41:6–7; cf. 40:19–20). Just as Hezekiah and his people prayed to God and were miraculously rescued, so the servant Jacob-Israel is not to fear but to be assured of rescue. In both texts, readers are firmly reminded that it is Yhwh who grants healing, help, and hope to those who wait upon Yhwh (40:31), be they Hezekiah, the survivors of Judah, or the servant Israel.

---

19. Another root that occurs frequently in this narrative is Isaiah (ישעיהו, literally, "Yhwh has saved him" or "Yhwh is salvation"). Inasmuch as the name Hezekiah so frequently occurs in Isa 36–39, so does the name Isaiah occur many times. In the symbolic world created by this key word-figure Isaiah, the issue of how we can be *saved* and who will save (ישע) us is cogently depicted in the confrontation between Sennacherib's enticement and Hezekiah's petition:

[Sennacherib's enticement:] Do not let Hezekiah misguide you by saying, Yhwh will deliver us. Has any of the gods of the nations delivered their land out of the hand of the king of Assyria? (36:18);

[Hezekiah's petition:] And now, Yhwh our God, *save* us from his hand, so that all the kingdoms of the earth may know that you alone are Yhwh;

[Yhwh's answer:] I will protect this city to *save* it, for my own sake and for the sake of David my servant;

[Hezekiah's petition:] Yhwh will *save* me, and we will play stringed instruments all the days of our lives in the house of Yhwh. (37:20, 35; 38:20)

20. In the similar way that the root word of the name Hezekiah occurs just prior to and right after Isa 36–39, it also occurs both at the start and at the end of the section led by woe-oracles, Isa 28–33 (28:2; 33:23).

21. In this case, it becomes noticeable that Hezekiah's name and speech conclude 39:8 whereas the word "to strengthen" will occur in the subsequent texts (e.g., 40:10; 41:6–7, 9, 13; 42:6; 45:1; 51:18), just as it did in the preceding texts (e.g., 33:23; 35:3–4).

There are further linguistic and thematic correlations between Isa 39 and 40–41.[22] Besides the unique correlation between the name Hezekiah (e.g., 39:1, 8) and the verb "to strengthen" (40:10; 41:6–7, 9, 13), the notion of "the word of Yhwh" can be found in both 39:8 and 40:2, 5, 8. Although the direct correlation can be made only by 39:8 (דבר־יהוה) and 40:8 (דבר־אלהינו), it can be argued that the very word of Yhwh to "comfort, comfort" of 40:1 may be considered as a renewed continuation of the word of Yhwh in 39:8.[23] Additionally, in this correlation, the motif of identifying something as "good" (טוב) can make a further interval link between 39:8 and 41:7. In 39:8, Hezekiah says that "*the word of Yhwh* that you [Isaiah] have spoken is good." In 41:7, ironically, the idol-makers describe their fabrication, "it is good" (הוא טוב).[24] Explicitly, this interval link can imply a thematic contrast between the faithful Hezekiah and the faithless idol-makers. Implicitly, however, this can also allude to an ironic correlation in which Hezekiah too may be seen as a mere creature because only Yhwh's utterance, not Hezekiah's, should ultimately be considered good.[25] Even as Hezekiah thought to make sure of "secured peace" from the word of God (39:8), the subsequent chapters declare that only God's word will stand forever (40:1–8).

Now that we have looked at key word connections between Isa 36–39 and (40–)41, let us examine similar connections between Isa 34–35 and 40–41.

---

22. For significant works on the relationship between Isa 39 and 40, see Melugin, *The Formation of Isaiah 40–55*, 177–78; Christopher R. Seitz, "The Divine Council: Temporal Transition and New Prophecy in the Book of Isaiah," *JBL* 109 (1990): 229–47; Peter R. Ackroyd, *Studies in the Religious Tradition of the Old Testament* (London: SCM, 1987), 105–20.

23. Edgar W. Conrad, *Reading Isaiah* (OBT; Minneapolis: Fortress, 1991), 99: "To hear the Lord's word is tantamount to the immediate fulfillment of that word. The coming to fulfillment of the Lord's word is like the creation by divine fiat in Genesis 1: 'And God said.... And it was so.' In 39:6–7 God said, and in 40:1 it was so!"

24. Note how it also echoes Gen 1:10, 31, where God says that "it is good" and "very good" after completing each component of creation, culminating with the making of human beings (and then Sabbath).

25. Consider also the unmistakably similar phrases in Yhwh's rhetorical questions to Hezekiah (Isa 37) and to the exilic people (Isa 40):
   Whom have you reviled and blasphemed?
   Against whom have you raised voice and haughtily lifted up your eyes? ...
   Have you not heard that I have made it long ago? (37:23, 26);
   Have you not known? Have you not heard? Has it not been told to you from the
      beginning? ... To whom will you liken me? ...
   Have you not known? Have you not heard? (40:21, 25, 28)
See Joseph Blenkinsopp, *Isaiah 1–39* (AB 19; New York: Doubleday, 2000), 477.

Scholars have convincingly observed that Isa 34–35 function to both recap the preceding chapters and to align Isa 36–39.[26] Various scholars have persuasively argued that Isa 34–35 function to connect chs. 1–33, 36–39, and 40–66.[27] Numerous Deutero-Isaianic phrases and overtones of Isa 34–35 make them stand apart from the preceding chapters so that Isa 34–35 have been considered an expansion (*Fortschreibung*) of the preceding chapters, much the same way that Isa 36–39 would then be a further expansion. To add to this observation, we now consider Isa 40–41 as another strand that is tied to Isa 36–39. All together, Isa 40–41 and 34–35 enclose the internal core section, Isa 36–39.

First, the phrase "for the mouth of Yhwh has spoken" occurs in both texts (34:16; 40:5).[28] Considering that this phrase occurs elsewhere only three times in the book of Isaiah (1:20; 58:14; 62:2), the usage of this phrase in these two texts is noteworthy. This phrase in ch. 34 summarizes the sure promise that Yhwh will punish the proud oppressing nations, especially turning Edom into utter desolation. The phrase in ch. 40 introduces the same promise that Yhwh will bring about restoration to the suffering Jerusalem. The divine

---

26. Ibid., 450: "Chapters 34 and 35 belong together.... Together they form a diptych in which the final annihilation of Edom is contrasted with the ultimate well-being of Zion"; Brevard S. Childs, *Isaiah* (OTL; Louisville, Ky.: Westminster John Knox, 2001), 255: "I judge that a convincing case can be made that chapters 34 and 35 together form a bridge between chapters 1–33 and 40–66."

27. Commentators have long noted that Isa 34–35 displays the editorial hands comparable to the redactor(s) of Isa 40–55 and/or Isa 56–66. In fact, some claim that Isa 34–35 may have originally belonged to the texts of Second Isaiah, which then became set apart by Isa 36–39. See Charles C. Torrey, *The Second Isaiah: A New Interpretation* (Edinburgh: Scribner's, 1928); Marvin H. Pope, "Isaiah 34 in Relation to Isaiah 35, 40–66," *JBL* 71 (1952): 235–43; Odil Hannes Steck, *Bereitete Heimkehr: Jesaja 35 als redaktionelle Brücke zwischen dem Ersten und dem Zweiten Jesaja* (SBS 121; Stuttgart: Katholisches Bibelwerk, 1985); Sommer, *A Prophet Reads Scripture*, 187–95. For a meticulous analysis on the correlated phrases, e.g., between Isa 13 and 34 as well as between Isa 35 and 40, see Ulrich Berges, *Das Buch Jesaja: Komposition und Endgestalt* (Herders Biblische Studien 16; Freiburg: Herder, 1998), 249–65.

28. According to John D. W. Watts, the place of Isa 36–39 should be taken as an intended follow-up of Isa 34:16, "Seek from the book of Yhwh and proclaim": "There is a pattern in these chapters. The bleak description of the destruction of the city and the land around it (34:9–15) and the bright picture of the restoration of the land and the city, which makes it ready for the pilgrims (34:17–35:10), are joined by the call for finding and reading the scroll of Yhwh (34:16). That is, reference to Scripture (chaps. 36–39, excerpted from 2 Kings) is used to explain what is going on" (*Isaiah 34–66* [rev. ed.; WBC 25; Waco, Tex.: Word, 2005], 543).

utterance is declared to come true both in the destruction of the enemy forces (Isa 34) and in the consolation of the exiled Judeans (Isa 40).

Second, the call to the nations (גוים) and peoples (לאמים) in 34:1 coincides with the similar summons to the coastlands (איים) and peoples (לאמים) in 41:1. In both accounts, just as the nobles of Edom are declared to become "nothing" (34:12), so all the idols and oppressors of Israel are ridiculed and condemned to become "nothing" (41:12, 29; cf. 40:17, 23; 41:11). Contrary to the imagery of the country of Edom being turned into thorns and thistles in a parched desert (34:9–15), Judah is depicted being transformed from wilderness into an oasis with luscious harvests (41:17–19; cf. 35:1–2, 6–10).

Third, the language and motif that the people shall "see" the "glory of Yhwh" in a new era can also be found uniquely in both texts (35:2; 40:5; cf. 58:8; 66:18):

> They shall *see the glory of Yhwh*, the majesty of our God (35:2; cf. 60:13);
> *The glory of Yhwh* shall be revealed, and all flesh shall *see* it together, for the mouth of Yhwh has spoken. (40:5)

In both texts, this phrase occurs in the motifs of the wilderness being turned into an oasis and a passage for the exilic people's homecoming in the second exodus: "The desert and the dry land shall rejoice" (35:1); "Every valley shall be lifted high, and every mountain and hill be brought down" (40:4).[29] In fact, the word "highway" occurs in both texts with the uniquely pertinent metaphors: "A *highway* shall be there" (35:8); "Make straight in the desert a *highway* for our God" (40:3). This word recurs in a few other texts in Isaiah (7:3; 11:16; 19:23; 36:2; 62:10), yet the conglomeration of the usage of this identical phrase and motif along with other correlated words between chs. 35 and 40 looks quite significant.

Last but not least, the insinuation that Yhwh is coming with "recompense" or "retaliation" to rescue the down-trodden people, and so they should "fear not," appears in both texts:

> Say to those dismayed in heart, "*Strengthen yourselves, fear not!*
> *Here is your God* (חזקו אל־תיראו הנה אלהיכם).
> He comes with vengeance, with divine retaliation,
> He is coming to save you" (35:4);
>
> Go up to a high mountain, O Zion, herald of good news,

---

29. Note that the same word combination of "desert" (מדבר) and "wilderness" (ערבה) can be found in both 35:1 and 40:3.

lift up your voice with might, O Jerusalem, herald of good news,
lift it up, *fear not* (אל־תיראי), say to the cities of Judah,
"*Here is your God!*" (הנה אלהיכם)
See, Adonay Yhwh comes with *strength* (בחזק), and his arm rules for him,
his reward is with him, and his recompense before him. (40:9–10)

These two texts share not only strikingly similar phrases but also comparable themes. In 35:4, the people are exhorted to encourage the faint-hearted, announcing God's coming as a righteous judge to establish justice and save the feeble. In 40:9–10, Zion personified is exhorted to proclaim the glad tidings of God's coming as a mighty warrior and a gentle shepherd.

All together, in addition to the relevant words of the root חזק, the above examples of the linguistic and metaphorical interconnections make a strong case for the close affinity between Isa 34–35 and 40–41.[30] Just as Isa 34–35 leads the readers into Isa 36–39, so Isa 40–41 picks up Isa 36–39 with uniquely similar signs and symbols. The combination of these illustrations thus strengthens the likelihood that chs. 34–35 and 40–41 were placed together in the final compositional structure as they envelop chs. 36–39—in which the name Hezekiah occurs numerous times—and thereby enclosing chs. 36–39 as a core of the entire scroll of Isaiah:[31]

---

30. As an added correlation, the motif of Yhwh strengthening the weak and feeble occurs in both texts (35:3; 40:29). In 35:3, by the imperative verbal forms, the audience is admonished to join in Yhwh's majestic restoration (35:1–2) to "strengthen [חזקו] the feeble hands and make firm the stumbled knees." In 40:29, it is Yhwh alone who "gives power to the faint and increases power to those without strength." Note also here that the verb to "strengthen" in 35:3 is the same verbal root for the name Hezekiah. In other words, the word play on the name Hezekiah in 35:3–4 and 40:10; 41:6–7, 9, 13 may provide a further case for the interrelationship between chs. 34–35 and 40–41.

31. Admittedly, some of the unique words and motifs that correlate Isa 34–35 and 40–41 occur elsewhere throughout the book of Isaiah, and thus there are other interconnections from these chapters with many other chapters. However, whereas those other interconnections are sporadic, the aforementioned examples are concentrated enough to consider the connections unique and significant.

34:1, Draw near, *nations*, to hear; *peoples*, pay attention	41:1, Listen to me in silence, *coastlands*; let the *peoples* renew their strength
34:16, for *the mouth of* Y<small>HWH</small> has spoken	40:5b, for *the mouth of* Y<small>HWH</small> has spoken
35:1, The *desert* and the *valley* shall rejoice	40:3abα, In the *desert* prepare the way of Y<small>HWH</small>, make straight in the *valley*....
35:2, They shall *see the glory of* Y<small>HWH</small>, the majesty of our God	40:5a, The glory of Y<small>HWH</small> shall be revealed, and all flesh shall *see* it together,
35:4, Say to those dismayed in heart, "*Strengthen yourselves, fear not! Here is your God.* He comes with vengeance, with divine retaliation, He is coming to save you"	40:9–10, Go up to a high mountain, O Zion, herald of good news, lift up your voice with might, O Jerusalem, herald of good news, lift it up, *fear not*, say to the cities of Judah, "*Here is your God!*" See, Adonay Y<small>HWH</small> comes with *strength*, and his arm rules for him, his reward is with him, and his recompense before him
35:8, A *highway* shall be there....	40:3bβ, ...a *highway* for our God

As a result, the structural feature is quite similar to what Mary Douglas calls the "pedimental composition." She argues that Lev 19 is sandwiched between chs. 18 and 20, thereby constructed as an apex of the book of Leviticus.[32] Although it would be difficult to detect a perfect chiastic structure for the entire book of Isaiah, it is worth pondering that Isa 36–39 may be intended as the legitimate center of this lengthy book, framed by Isa 34–35 and by 40–41. This consideration may then present further implications for understanding the book of Isaiah in its given form. Sandwiched by chs. 34–35 and 40–41, Isa 36–39 stands as an intentional apex of the book of Isaiah—more than a mere appendix or a functional bridge—which has recently been proposed by Ulrich

---

32. Mary Douglas, "Justice as the Cornerstone: An Interpretation of Leviticus 18–20," *Int* 53 (1999): 341–50, especially, 344: "We start by taking chapters 18 and 20 together because they echo each other in obvious ways. Between their paralleled repetitions lies ch. 19, which must be considered to be central and of prime importance if only because of the way it is framed by them"; idem, *Leviticus as Literature* (Oxford: Oxford University Press, 1999), 195–251.

Berges.³³ Located in the middle of the book, these chapters display several of the fundamental concepts of the entire book and thereby establish a central place with its linguistic and thematic interconnections to the rest of the book. In this reading, what is a central message of the book of Isaiah, located in chs. 36–39? It calls for the people's resolute faith against insurmountable threat and doubt, figuratively exemplified in the actions of *Hezekiah* (חזק). It points to the source and promise of salvation for Zion, symbolically proclaimed in the oracles of *Isaiah* (ישע). It ultimately highlights *God* who is the sure provider of strength and salvation, in contrast with the idols and nations whose seeming strongholds will eventually come to an end.

To sum up, more words and motifs build correlations with continuous connections or shifted implications. The linkage of the word חזק can remind readers of the historical account of Hezekiah's model trust, inspiring a symbolic place for the exilic communities to rekindle their hope and faith in Yhwh. Put differently, dominating nations will lose their grip on power, contrary to the despairing conditions familiar to the down-trodden people. Idols will prove to be of no help. Additionally, the distinctive linguistic and thematic similarities between Isa 34–35 and 40–41 offer further support for the view that these two textual units envelop Isa 36–39. Hezekiah and Cyrus mirror each other in terms of their roles of deliverance, though both heroic figures remain mere flesh. The core symbols present in the text repeatedly exhort the people not to fear but to "strengthen" their faith in the ultimate manifestation of the glory of Yhwh.

IV. Overarching Links: Isaiah 6, 41, and the Entire Book of Isaiah

Certain words and motifs also function as links that connect not only the neighboring subunits or texts but also the entire book of Isaiah. These overarching links occur quite repeatedly throughout the whole book of Isaiah. Their ubiquitous presence in the literary bulk signifies the intentional thematic interrelationship with the author's or final redactor(s)'s poetic purposes. These holistic links thus help correlate the whole thread of this prophetic scroll so that we have a book as if it is put in a bound form, that is, by these numerous connecting signs and symbols. There are quite a few of these

---

33. Ulrich Berges, "Die Zionstheologie des Buches Jesaja," *Estudios Bíblicos* 58 (2000): 167: "The hitherto neglected chapters 36–39 do not have the function of an annex, but rather they are the centre of the entire composition"; idem, *Das Buch Jesaja*, especially 256–63.

markers in the book of Isaiah, and earlier scholars have addressed many of them, for example, the servant of Yhwh,[34] the personified Zion-Jerusalem in companionship with Jacob-Israel,[35] the Holy One of Israel,[36] the kingship of Yhwh,[37] the idol imagery,[38] justice and righteousness,[39] and so on.

Another overarching theme is the language and motif of "light" and "darkness."[40] This motif not only occurs throughout the entire book of Isaiah but also is often closely associated with the related motifs of "seeing" and "hearing," together with "knowing" and "understanding," rooted in the call narrative in the thematically fundamental passage of Isaiah, ch. 6.[41] This phraseological association can be made more evident when reading in the context of exilic and postexilic settings as the metaphor of light becomes the pivotal source for the captives and prisoners in darkness to see, hear, know

---

34. We can list countless studies and debates on the identification and interpretation of the servant of Yhwh from the New Testament era all the way to twenty-first century scholarship. Among the recent studies, see Willem A. M. Beuken, "The Main Theme of Trito-Isaiah: The 'Servants of Yhwh,'" *JSOT* 47 (1990): 67–87; Joseph Alobaidi, *The Messiah in Isaiah 53: The Commentaries of Saadia Gaon, Salmon ben Yeruham and Yefet ben Eli on Is 52:13–53:12* (Bern: Lang, 1998); Bernd Janowski and Peter Stuhlmacher, eds., *The Suffering Servant: Isaiah 53 in Jewish and Christian Sources* (trans. D. P. Bailey; Grand Rapids: Eerdmans, 2004).

35. John F. A. Sawyer, "Daughter Zion and Servant of the Lord in Isaiah: A Comparison," *JSOT* 44 (1989): 89–107; Christopher R. Seitz, *Zion's Final Destiny: The Development of the Book of Isaiah: A Reassessment of Isaiah 36–39* (Minneapolis: Fortress, 1991); Marvin A. Sweeney, *Isaiah 1–39 with an Introduction to Prophetic Literature* (FOTL 16; Grand Rapids: Eerdmans, 1996).

36. J. J. M. Roberts, "Isaiah in Old Testament Theology," *Int* 36 (1982): 130–43.

37. Tryggve N. D. Mettinger, "In Search of the Hidden Structure: Yhwh as King in Isaiah 40–55," in Broyles and Evans, *Writing and Reading the Scroll of Isaiah*, 143–54; Thomas Wagner, *Gottes Herrschaft: Eine Analyse der Denkschrift (Jes 6,1–9,6)* (VTSup 108; Leiden: Brill, 2006).

38. Knut Holter, *Second Isaiah's Idol-Fabrication Passages* (Frankfurt: Lang, 1995).

39. Thomas L. Leclerc, *Yahweh is Exalted in Justice: Solidarity and Conflict in Isaiah* (Minneapolis: Fortress, 2001).

40. Ronald E. Clements, "A Light to the Nations," 57–69; idem, "Patterns in the Prophetic Canon: Healing the Blind and the Lame," in *Canon, Theology, and Old Testament Interpretation: Essays in Honor of Brevard S. Childs* (ed. G. M. Tucker, D. L. Petersen, and R. R. Wilson; Philadelphia: Fortress, 1988), 189–200.

41. Rolf Rendtorff, "Isaiah 6 in the Framework of the Composition of the Book," in *Canon and Theology: Overtures to an Old Testament Theology* (trans. and ed. M. Kohl; OBT; Minneapolis: Fortress, 1993), 170–80; Craig. A. Evans, *To See and Not Perceive: Isaiah 6.9–10 in Early Jewish and Christian Interpretation* (JSOTSup 64; Sheffield: JSOT Press, 1989), 40–46; Robert P. Carroll, "Blindness and the Vision Thing: Blindness and Insight in the Book of Isaiah," in Broyles and Evans, *Writing and Reading the Scroll of Isaiah*, 79–93.

and understand. Thus, let us walk through some of the passages where this significant link occurs and see how this theme functions as a sign or symbol in light of Isa 41 as well as in its relation to the rest of the book of Isaiah.

In Isa 6, the prophet Isaiah describes the vision in which he *sees* Yhwh "sitting on a throne" (v. 1) and *hears* the divine beings proclaiming, "Holy, holy, holy is Yhwh of hosts; the whole earth is full of his glory" (v. 3).[42] Yet Isaiah confesses his own sinfulness: "Woe to me! For I am doomed; for I am a man of unclean lips and I dwell among a people of unclean lips; for my *eyes* have seen the King, Yhwh of hosts" (v. 5).[43] But one of the seraphs with a live coal touches Isaiah's mouth. Thus his sin is pardoned and Isaiah *hears* the voice of Yhwh in a similar rhetorical question that echoes Isa 40:12 and numerous other passages later: "Whom shall I send? Who will go for us?" (6:8)[44] Then, following Isaiah's obedient response to his prophetic call, the prophet hears one of the core messages of the entire book of Isaiah, like a thesis statement:

> Go and say to this people:
> "*Hear* firmly, but do not *understand*;
> *See* firmly, but do not *know*."
> Make the heart of this people dull,
> and stop their *ears* and shut their *eyes*,
> lest they may *see* with their *eyes*,
> and *hear* with their *ears*,
> and *understand* with their hearts,
> and turn and be healed. (6:9–10)

Admittedly, seeing and hearing are vital elements of writing and speaking activities. Hence, frequent usage of these motifs may be too common a feature to make any significant remarks on its uniqueness in reading Isaiah. However, what can be helpful for the present study is the way in which this thesis statement is picked up, shifted, and reaffirmed in other passages, alluding to

---

42. Contrary to the hard-hearted Israelites who will not be able fully to see or hear, the prophet Isaiah himself is subtly but implicitly depicted to be able to "see" (6:1) and "hear" (6:8) in this call narrative.

43. For the notion of the communal self-awareness in Isaiah's commissioning in ch. 6, see Rolf P. Knierim, "The Vocation of Isaiah," *VT* 18 (1968): 47–68.

44. For an extensive study of the parallelism between Isa 6 and 40, see Melugin, *Formation of Isaiah 40–55*, 83–84; idem, "The Servant, God's Call, and the Structure of Isaiah 40–48," *SBLSP* 30 (1991): 21–30; idem, "Poetic Imagination, Intertextuality, and Life in a Symbolic World," (see the opening chapter in this volume).

the same metaphors and conveying continuing or contrasting messages. So, where else do these metaphors occur in Isaiah, and how do they correlate with this thesis? Let us *look* and *read* to locate answers!

First, how do these words function in Isa 41? In 41:17–20, Yhwh declares to turn the wilderness into "springs of water" and put "the cedar, the acacia, the myrtle, and the olive" in the desert. In 41:20, the purpose of this redemptive work is announced: "so that they may *see* and *know*, they may consider and comprehend together, that the hand of Yhwh has done this, the Holy One of Israel has created it." The purpose for the people to see and understand who God is and what God's plan is assertively connects to the same motif of Isa 6:9–10 in that whereas the obdurate people could not see or hear then, now they will see and know because God will do these things.[45] Next, this metaphor continues in 41:21–24 where the idolaters are challenged to proclaim just as God has declared in the previous subunit: "Tell us the former things ... so that we may *understand* them, and that we may *know* what may come later; or make us *hear* what is to come. Tell us what is to come hereafter, so that we may *know* that you are gods" (41:22–23). Here God joins the faithful in that God wants to *hear* and *know* from what the idolaters may be able to proclaim, if anything at all. The unequivocal result is that they are nothing (41:24). Thus, this metaphor is further developed in the following subunit of 41:25–29 in which God confirms again that only God plans and executes these things "from the beginning so that we might *know*," though "there was no one who *heard*" their words before (41:26). Therefore, using these key metaphors of seeing, hearing, knowing, and understanding, the latter part of Isa 41 connects to the beginning verses of the same chapter, to the pertinent metaphors of the call narrative of Isa 6, and to the unfolding chapters on God's salvific plans through the servant (42:1–9) so that all flesh may "see" together the glory of Yhwh (40:5; cf. 11:9; 35:2; 45:6; 49:26; 52:10).

Second, how do these words function in Isa 1–39? In 1:3, Israel's hardheartedness is illustrated in contrast to the apparently less intelligent ox or donkey that *knows* its owner, whereas "Israel does not *know*, my people do not *understand*." So, in 1:15, God warns that "when you spread out your hands, I will hide my *eyes* from you; even though you multiply your prayers, I will not *hear*; your hands are full of blood." In 11:2, the stump of Jesse as the Davidic descendant is promised that Yhwh will bestow Yhwh's spirit upon him along with "the spirit of wisdom and *understanding* ... the spirit of *knowledge*."

---

45. As will be addressed below, though certain connections seem more like subtle allusions, many recurrences throughout the book of Isaiah can evidently be taken as explicit metaphorical allusions or even linguistic citations, e.g., 11:3; 29:18; 35:5; 42:18–20.

Because of God's anointing, this Davidic heir "will not judge by what his *eyes see* or decide by what his *ears hear*" (11:3). The similar metaphor continues to occur in other parts of Isa 1–39, including 26:10–11 ("O Yhwh, your hand is lifted up, but they do not see it"); 27:11; 29:9–12, 15–16, 18 ("On that day the deaf shall hear the words of a scroll, and out of their gloom and darkness the eyes of the blind shall see"); 30:9–10; 32:3; 33:15–20; 34:1; 35:2, 5 ("Then the eyes of the blind shall be opened, and the ears of the deaf unstopped"); 36:11, 13; 37:6–7, 17, 20, 26–29; 38:5; 39:1–5. These numerous instances indicate that this metaphor functions as an overarching link connecting many of the pertinent texts linguistically and thematically, that many of those passages may have been composed or redacted by the poetic genius utilizing these recurrent words and motifs, and that these signs and symbols remind the readers of other echoing passages and thereby reaffirm or surprise them with similar or unexpected thematic messages.

Third, how do these words function in Isa 40–66? In addition to 40:5 and Isa 41 already expounded above, in 40:21 (cf. 40:28), Yhwh retorts to the people, "Have you not *known*? Have you not *heard*? Has it not been told to you from the beginning? Have you not *understood* from the foundations of the earth?"[46] In 40:26, Yhwh further challenges them to "lift up your *eyes* and *see*" that "Yhwh is the everlasting God, the Creator of the ends of the earth" (40:28). Then, in 42:18–20, we learn the reason they cannot see, hear, or understand: they themselves are blind and deaf: "Who is *blind* except my servant or *deaf* like my messenger whom I send? ... He *sees* many things, but does not observe them; his *ears* are open, but he does not *hear*." Thus, the whole people Israel is blinded as the captives in exile so that they cannot see or hear, just as their obduracy kept them from being able to see or hear in Isa 6. The similar language and metaphor occur in other places as well, including 43:8; 44:18; 45:4–6, 20; 47:11; 48:6–8 ("You have never heard, you have never known; from long ago your ear has not been opened. For I knew you would deal really faithlessly, and that from birth you were called a rebel"); 49:23, 26; 50:4–5 ("Adonay Yhwh has opened my ear, and I was not rebellious, I did not turn backward"); 52:8–10, 15; 53:11 ("From suffering his soul shall see, and he shall be satisfied by his knowledge"); 55:2–3; 56:9–11; 58:3 ("Why do we [Israel] fast, but you [Yhwh] do not see? Why do we humble ourselves, but you do not know?"); 58:9; 59:1–2, 8–10, 12–15; 60:16; 63:17.[47]

---

46. It is interesting that reading 6:9 and 40:21 together, the audience will recognize a chiastic sequence: whereas the verb "to hear" precedes the verb "to know" in 6:9, in Yhwh's rhetorical challenge the verb "to know" precedes the verb "to hear" in 40:21 and 40:28.

47. For an extensive intertextual study on the use of Isa 6 in Isa 65–66, see Marvin A.

These instances, by no means exhaustive, further demonstrate how the same language and motif are used in the latter portions of the book of Isaiah; how they form linguistic and thematic links with the rest of Isaiah, especially with the call narrative of Isa 6; and how, by adapting these metaphors, they reconceptualize the same ideas for renewed messages.

V. Conclusion

The above study has attempted to illustrate how certain words function as signs and symbols of a prophetic or poetic text, working outward from one location, Isa 41, and to look within and around it for the concatenated interrelations throughout the entire book of Isaiah. Some words serve as signs bridging two or three immediately neighboring verses, especially between adjoining chapters. Other words and motifs function to correlate seemingly separate subunits that are located in certain interval distances. Their recurrences often serve as "signposts" or "chains" that link diverse literary subunits, as if they are wrapped like a web by wires or threads. Furthermore, some words and motifs occur throughout the entire book of Isaiah, as principal links that bind the entire book together and offer explicit and/or hidden guidelines for readers to follow. In addition to the words and motifs discussed above, more examples could have been considered as well.[48]

What then are we to make out of these observations? What conclusions can we gather from these exemplifications for Isaiah study and Bible reading? To put these questions a bit differently, what may have been going on in

---

Sweeney, "Prophetic Exegesis in Isaiah 65–66," in Broyles and Evans, *Writing and Reading the Scroll of Isaiah*, 455–76.

48. For example, the language and motif of "gold" and "silver" occur in countless references in the book of Isaiah, with clear linguistic and thematic connections, contrasts, and shifts (e.g., 2:7, 20; 39:2; 40:19; 46:6; 55:1–2; 60:9, 17). The motif of a "high mountain" especially with subtle echoes of Zion is another major link (e.g., 2:2; 40:4; 41:15). The syntactical pattern of "setting someone as something" may also be a unique link with shifted nuances and overtones: e.g., 41:2 ("He makes them as dust with his sword, like driven stubble with his bow"), 41:15 ("I will set you as a threshing sledge, sharp, new, and with teeth"); 42:6 (I have set you as a covenant of the people and a light of the nations"); cf. 60:19–20 ("Yhwh shall be your everlasting light"). In addition, interestingly, the word הוי occurs *exactly six times* both in Isaiah 5 (vv. 8, 11, 18, 20, 21, 22) and in the woe-oracles of Isaiah 28–33 (28:1; 29:1, 15; 30:1; 31:1; 33:1). Can we argue that this is a mere coincidence? Last but not least, the phrase "crushed reed" in 36:6 (משענת הקנה הרצוץ) anticipates 42:3 (קנה רצוץ). For an intertextual reading of these phrases, see Melugin, *Formation of Isaiah 40–55*, 99; Hyun Chul Paul Kim, "An Intertextual Reading of a 'Crushed Reed' and a 'Dim Wick' in Isa 42:3," *JSOT* 83 (1999): 113–24.

the text-making? Why is it that there are so many links, chains, and markers that echo one another and bind the text into a cohesive—though not always coherent—whole? To use an analogy from the recent blockbuster movie based on the comic book series, "The Spider-Man," just as the female protagonist finally asks the spider-man, we may also ask this hidden poet the same question, "Who are you?"

Scholars have focused on these issues, especially on how the text is put together, and have come up with many valuable insights during the last century. In light of those insights, we may further proceed not only to analyze why those connecting words and motifs occur again and again but also to appreciate how they operate and interpret the resultant implications they offer both to their readers and to today's readers. In an effort to undertake such a task, several implications may be considered. First, these concatenated words and motifs may display the ways *writers and scribes* operated in connecting subunits, units, and larger texts. They tend to follow the rules—or may we say "recipes" (?)—of chiasm and inclusio as illustrated in rhetorical studies and of constant innerbiblical citations, allusions, and imaginative echoes as discovered in intertextual studies. If there were no book-binding system, no pagination, no chaptering system, and no computer software to make a backup file, it would make good sense that the scribes would have loved to find those "word chains" or "signposts" to connect the dots of the scrolls, as if putting the pieces of a puzzle together. To the modern readers, the only problem is that the book does not come with its own puzzle-solving manual. Yet, this problem can be seen as a possibility through which various concatenations build a complex picture to behold and appreciate, set the stage for mutual dialogue or contradictory debate, and thereby create a symbolic world of hermeneutical ideals, discernment, and transformation.

Observations from this reading approach may offer further insights on thematic and theological interpretations. These concatenated signs and symbols may look like pieces of tapestry, that are tangled up in many directions and complicated patterns. However, there also seems to be evidence for a certain systematic interaction and intended movement, as in a chain-link fence which can be untangled by following the threads. These chain-links may help us understand the implications of those related texts and how they correlate and reinforce each other. Sometimes we may confront a wrong way and may have to turn back or detour. But many of these threads may shed further light on our reading of these awe-inspiring texts of Isaiah. At certain points, these threads may block us entirely, tempting us to give up. But perhaps such complexity within the biblical texts may indeed be what makes them rich, aesthetic, and humbling. We might not need to write any more articles or books if we can figure all of them out. Besides, even if we are confounded here and there, the Spirit in the form of the "Spider-Person" may come to rescue, guide, and teach us!

Consider the Source: A Reading of the Servant's Identity and Task in Isaiah 42:1–9

James M. Kennedy

On the Unity of the Book of Isaiah

The issue of the unity of the book of Isaiah lies at the center of this paper's interpretive framework. For some scholars, the issue of unity does not work as an interpretive category. David M. Carr, for example, sees attention to unity regarding the book of Isaiah as deriving from an interest that would be alien to the ancient Israelite reader.[1] He agrees with much of contemporary scholarship that Isa 1 and 65–66 share parallel thematic expressions. In Carr's opinion, this means that for modern scholars an array of interpretive possibilities opens up. He agrees that what he calls "the semiotic potential of the book" offers materials with which to work. Nevertheless, he does not perceive the presence of any markers in the book that can operate as components capable of moderating between the various interpretive possibilities. In his view, the more one reads the texts in Isaiah with regard to issues of unity, the fainter become the indications that the various complexes of texts ever exhibited unity.

It may be true that literary unity as a focus of theoretical reflection was an alien category for an ancient Near Eastern reader; we cannot know. The ancient Israelites did not bequeath to the world a systematic poetics. However, Carr does not alert his readers to why a contemporary reading of the book of Isaiah as a literary unity is a doubtful enterprise. He does not provide

---

1. David M. Carr, "Reading Isaiah from Beginning (Isaiah 1) to End (Isaiah 65–66): Multiple Modern Possibilities," in *New Visions of Isaiah* (ed. Roy F. Melugin and Marvin A. Sweeney; JSOTSup 214; Sheffield: Sheffield Academic Press, 1996), 188–218.

a theoretical basis for why an obviously anachronistic descriptive category cannot lead to the enrichment of interpretations of Isaiah.

Biblical scholars have not often bothered to think about what literary unity is. Carr does not; he assumes a commonly shared understanding and then proceeds to downplay it as a category of interpretation. That literary unity *as such* was not a concern for the prophetic voices that speak through the book of Isaiah or of its Persian era compiler is finally irrelevant.

This paper grants the composite nature of the book of Isaiah and that its contents derive from the time of the prophet himself in the eighth century B.C.E. to the early Persian era, approximately 520–515 B.C.E. However, recognition of the book's composite nature does not require a diachronic program of reading. That the composite nature of a text necessitates a diachronic explanation is an argument based on insufficient data. That the book of Isaiah grew incrementally is a valid hypothesis but not logically necessary. It would be logically necessary if, and only if, the book of Isaiah could not exist apart from being the result of a complex process of development.

That one writer compiled the book from a number of sources during one life time is as feasible a hypothesis as any that assume that the book is the result of incremental development over decades.[2] Therefore, the description of Yhwh's servant, this paper advocates, does not derive from an approach that limits the significance of the servant to the late Babylonian period or to Isa 40–55 as a distinct text. It assumes the informative value of the entire book for comprehending the servant's identity and task. In part, it seeks to show how the book's presentation of Yhwh's servant presupposes the interactive variety of literary associations that occur throughout it.

Text as Linguistic System

Isaiah 42 is essentially lyric poetry, even mystical in character. Its lyrical quality rises from the playful juxtaposition of its components. Poetry is essentially symbolic. Meaning in poetry emerges from the reader's perception of the possibilities of equivalence the poem offers. The poetic work is itself a symbolic linguistic system into which the external language flows but in which

---

[2]. The scholarly voices advocating this view may not be many but they are significant. See Peter D. Miscall, *Isaiah* (Readings: A New Biblical Commentary; Sheffield: JSOT Press, 1993), 11; Robert H. O'Connell, *Concentricity and Continuity: The Literary Structure of Isaiah* (JSOTSup 188; Sheffield: Sheffield Academic Press, 1994), 236, 237; Zoltán Kustár, *"Durch seine Wunden sind wir geheilt": Eine Untersuchung zur Metaphorik von Israels Krankheit und Heilung im Jesajabuch* (BWANT; Stuttgart: Kohlhammer, 2002), 11.

the poetic text channels the external language in ways peculiar to the poem itself. The reader of a poem expects to encounter highly stylized language that does not necessarily depend on the denotation of the external lexicon but on the possibilities of meaning within the system of the poem itself. Roman Jakobson reasoned that the capacity of poetic language to exhibit a wide array of semantic variables and semiotic potentials derives from the superimposition of similarity on to contiguity.[3] In Jakobson's frame of reference, this is what imparts to poetry its symbolic, polysemantic essence. Ambiguity is thus a component of the focusing power of poetry. Denotatively clear words may, in poetic play, suggest a wide variety of meaning. For example, morphologically similar words may be distinct in the external lexicon, but in the poetic work, their juxtaposition allows identity of meaning. Ambiguity also works as a kind of verbal metonymy in which an elliptic phrase, typical of poetry, alludes to larger complexes of association and meaning. Christopher Collins configures Jakobson's embrace of poetics as an extension of linguistics to imply the significance of the reader's expectations and capacities.[4] Although Jakobson configures his comments with the confidence of a structural empiricist, Collins proposes that the final arbiter of meaning in Jakobson's poetics can only be the reader.

It is not simply words themselves that provide the raw stuff for assembling meaning but every element of the poem. The structural components of the poem, from the individual phoneme to complex grammatical arrangements, relate to each other in truly *significant* ways. Yuri Lotman observes:

> The equivalence of semantic units in an artistic text ... is based on the juxtaposition of lexical (and other semantic) units which on the level of the primary (linguistic) structure may be recognized as non-equivalent. Thereupon a secondary (artistic) structure is constructed in which these units are made parallel to each other, and this in turn is a signal that in the given system we should view the units as equivalent.[5]

Like Jacobson, Lotman approaches interpretation as an empirical structuralist. He is nevertheless aware that interpretation essentially depends on the linguistic quality of the reader's own experience and on the reader's willing-

---

3. Roman Jakobson, "Linguistics and Poetics," in *Language in Literature* (ed. Krystyna Pomorska and Stephen Rudy; Cambridge, Mass.: Belknap, 1987), 62–94.
4. Christopher Collins, *The Poetics of the Mind's Eye: Literature and the Psychology of Imagination* (Philadelphia: University of Pennsylvania Press, 1991), 50.
5. Yuri Lotman, *The Structure of the Artistic Text* (trans. Gail Lenhoff and Ronald Vroon; Ann Arbor: University of Michigan Press, 1977), 29.

ness to allow the poetic world to become his or her own. It is up to the reader to adjudicate the nature of the poetic system the poem entails.[6] To read a poem like this is to adopt the linguist's interest in the structures of a given language as an analogy for how meaning develops with regard to the poem itself.

The Semantics of עבד in the Book of Isaiah

Building on Jakobson and Lotman's perspective of the literary work as a system that establishes meaning on the basis of its own internal operations of language, this section examines the meaning of the root, עבד as a function of BI's semantics. In BI, the word עבד occurs most frequently to imply the hierarchical relationship between a king and his subjects. Its semantic field encloses the field of binary oppositions of lordship in which אדון and מלך occur. The term אדון applies to someone who exercises authority over the category of persons known as עבד. The phrase כעבד כאדניו in Isa 24:2 for instance, operates on the basis of this binary opposition. The word עבד applies to all subjects of a monarch but particularly to operatives in direct vocational service to the king, such as diplomats, ministers of state, mercenaries, and officers.[7] M. Goulder has proposed rendering עבד as "minister" as opposed to "servant."[8] Apart from 24:2, in the book of Isaiah the use of the word עבד presupposes a subordinate relationship to a king. Isaiah 36:11 offers an example of עבד as diplomatic deference when the envoys of Hezekiah address the Rabshekah. When, for instance, the Rabshekah refers to the king of Assyria as אדני (v. 12), "my lord," he positions himself as the king's עבד. In 36:9, the Rabshekah refers to his fellow servants as אחד עבדי אדני הקטנים, "one of the least of the servants of my master." Here the word אדני alludes to the Assyrian king. Similarly, when Isaiah sends Hezekiah's envoys back to Hezekiah with instructions prefaced with כה תאמרו אל אדנכם, "thus you shall say to your master," in 37:5, he implies that the envoys are עבדי חזקיהו, "servants of Hezekiah." The book of Isaiah thus associates עבד with אדון to the extent that the two words can be taken as relating a king and an official who waits on the king. In Isa 20:3; 22:20; 37:5; 41:8; 42:1, 19; 44:1; 48:20; 49:3; 49:6; 50:2; 52:13; 65:8, 9, 13, 14, 15; and 66:14 the word עבד occurs in a vari-

---

6. Yuri Lotman, *Analysis of the Poetic Text* (trans. D. Barton Johnson; Ann Arbor: Ardis, 1976), 69.

7. Dexter E. Callender, Jr., "Servants of God(s) and Servants of Kings in Israel and the Ancient Near East," *Semeia* 83/84 (1998): 67–82.

8. Michael Goulder, "Behold My Servant Jehoiachin," *VT* 52 (2001): 175–90.

ety of grammatical permutations that imply a configuration of its significance in terms of the relation between a monarch and subject. It seems reasonable for the reader to assume that references to the servant of Yhwh imply that the servant is loyal to Yhwh in the deity's specific status as מלך even when מלך is not part of the local context.

Isa 20:3; 41:21; 42:1; 43:15; 44:6 and 52:7 may serve as illustrations of the pragmatics of this inner systematization. In Isa 20:3, Yhwh's reference to Isaiah as עבדי builds on the prophet's having referred to Yhwh in Isa 6:1 as אדני and as המלך in 6:5. Isaiah 41:21 refers to Yhwh as מלך יעקב, thus implying that Jacob/Israel is Yhwh's עבד. Isaiah 43:15 conveys Yhwh's declaration אני יהוה קדושכם בורא ישראל מלככם, "I am Yhwh your Holy One, creator of Israel, your King." The reader understands that the addressee is Yhwh's עבד. Isaiah 44:6 contains an oracle beginning with כה־אמר יהוה מלך־ישראל, "thus says Yhwh, King of Israel." The reader may thereby identify Israel as Yhwh's עבד. Isaiah 52:7 portrays a messenger on the mountains announcing to Zion מלך אלהיך, "your God reigns." The reader may assume that עבד would appropriately describe the new Zion.[9] The book of Isaiah therefore constructs an implied paradigmatic focus on kingship and servant, whereby the reader may assume the informative value of Yhwh's kingship in those instances where the text exhibits the actions of the servant of Yhwh. When Yhwh states הן עבדי, "Here is my servant," in 42:1, the reader appropriately conceives of Yhwh speaking specifically as מלך and אדון.

The Cult Statue

The cult statue is a prominent object of the book of Isaiah's polemical force. Isaiah 41 describes Yhwh as convening an assembly of the nations for the purpose of putting their cult statues to the test. Yhwh challenges the cult statues to impart knowledge and, at least from the prophetic persona's perspective, the cult statues fail. In so far as the cult statue is such a prominent feature in Isa 41 a brief description of its significance in the ancient Middle East seems warranted.

In Egypt every stage of the manufacture of the sacred image was ritually celebrated. By way of the Ceremony of the Opening of the Mouth, the appropriate priestly personnel animated the statue with the *ka* of the god

---

9. Leland Edward Wilshire argues at length for interpreting the servant as Jerusalem-Zion. See his "The Servant-City: A New Interpretation of the 'Servant of the Lord' in the Servant Songs in Deutero-Isaiah," *JBL* 94 (1975): 356–67.

it represented.¹⁰ The god's *ka* entered the statue so that the statue's essence became divine. As any other living entity the cult statue needed housing, clothing, and feeding. It was the daily obligation of appointed priests to render such services to the image. On certain holy occasions the benefactors of the statue bore it aloft in procession during which times it could be consulted for divination.¹¹

A similar situation prevailed in ancient Mesopotamia where the appropriate personnel crafted the sacred image in the *bit mummi*, the "House of the Craftsmen." The cult image went through a series of liturgical enactments called *mīs pî*, "washing of the mouth" and at various times known as *pīt pî*, "opening of the mouth."¹² An integral component of the ritual complex was a liturgical separation of the statue from human manufacture to the world of the divine. Upon the completion of the *mīs pî*, the cult statue was considered to have been "born in heaven." Part of the ceremony included oaths from the artisans that they did not make the statue. The goal of the *mīs pî* ceremony was to achieve the transformation of the statue from a simple material object into a manifestation of the deity.¹³ Thorkild Jacobsen describes the cult statue as a theophany whereby the deity resides among humankind.¹⁴ For the Egyptians and Mesopotamians, the negative biblical prophetic assessment of the cult image as being the work of human hands would have rung hollow. Nevertheless, the prophetic persona's implied reader would not have been either Mesopotamian or Egyptian, but Israelite.

The use of cult statues was widespread throughout the ancient Middle East. There is evidence of a Hurrian variation of the washing of the mouth that occurs with a Hittite colophon from the Middle Hittite period.¹⁵ From

---

10. David Lorton, "The Theology of Cult Statues in Ancient Egypt," in *Born in Heaven, Made on Earth: The Making of the Cult Image in the Ancient Near East* (ed. Michael Dick; Winona Lake, Ind.: Eisenbrauns, 1999), 123–210.

11. Erik Hornung, *Conceptions of God in Ancient Egypt: The One and the Many* (trans. John Baines; Ithaca, N.Y.: Cornell University Press, 1982).

12. Christopher Walker and Michael B. Dick, "The Induction of the Cult Image in Ancient Mesopotamia: The Mesopotamian *mīs pî* Ritual," in Dick, *Born in Heaven, Made on Earth*, 55–121. See also Peggy Jean Boden, "The Mesopotamian Washing of the Mouth (*mīs pî*) Ritual: An Examination of Some of the Social and Communication Strategies which Guided the Development and Performance of the Ritual which Transferred the Essence of the Deity into Its Temple Statue" (Ph.D. diss., The Johns Hopkins University, 1998).

13. Boden, "The Mesopotamian Washing of the Mouth (*mīs pî*) Ritual," 170.

14. Thorkild Jacobsen, "The Graven Image," in *Ancient Israelite Religion: Essays in Honor of Frank Moore Cross* (ed. Patrick D. Miller et al.; Philadelphia: Fortress, 1987), 15–32.

15. Christopher Walker and Michael Dick, *The Induction of the Cult Image in Ancient*

ancient Israel there is evidence that Yhwh could be represented by a cult statue (Judg 17:3). The prophet Habakkuk dismisses the cult statue as a source of instruction and utters a woe against any who address the statue in what seems to have been some kind of ceremonial arousal of it (Hab 2:18–20), perhaps an Israelite variation of the mouth-washing or mouth-opening ceremony. Hosea 4:12 portrays the people consulting an object that appears to be a wooden cult statue.[16] Elsewhere I have argued that פתחון פה in Ezek 16:63 and 29:21 possibly refers to an Israelite version of the ceremony of the consecration of a cult statue.[17]

The cult statue was the focus of social elitist authority. By it the priestly powers could control not only large amounts of material productivity by way of daily sacrifice but the dissemination of knowledge from the divine realm. In political economic terms, the cult statue was a way to accumulate wealth; in political social terms, the cult statue was a way to control information. Knowledge about the world of the divine translates into knowledge about what policy should be. To call into question the validity of the cult statue is to call into question the significance of huge bureaucracies of authority and power over which the king reigns as the god's supreme representative.

The book of Isaiah associates the cult image with divination. Isaiah 2:6–7 refers to cult statues as אלילים, "worthless" and associates them with ענגים, "diviners." Isa 19:3 puts the אלילים in company with האטים, "necromancers," האבות, "ghosts," and הידענים, "soothsayers." Isa 30:21–22 configures the eschatological teacher as taking the place of פסילי כסף, "gold-plated carved images," and מסכת זהב, "silver-plated statues." It is the very capacity of the cult statue to serve as a device of communication between the gods and human beings that the trial in Isa 41 is all about.

The Local Textual Environs of Isaiah 42:1–9

Jerome Walsh describes Isa 41–42 as presenting "a legal action" aimed toward ascertaining "who is responsible for Israel's hope."[18] Indeed, Isa 41 describes Yhwh as calling for an assembly but not only for a legal decision. The pur-

---

Mesopotamia: The Mesopotamian Mīs Pî Ritual (SAALT 1; Helsinki: University of Helsinki, 2001), 22.

16. Francis I. Andersen and David Noel Freedman, *Hosea* (AB 24; Garden City, N.Y.: Doubleday, 1980), 366.

17. James M. Kennedy, "Hebrew *pithôn peh* in the Book of Ezekiel," *VT* 41 (1991): 233–35.

18. Jerome T. Walsh, "Isaiah XLV 1–20," *VT* 53 (1993): 351–71.

pose of the assembly is to challenge the validity and power of the cult statue; it is no more only a legal act than was the contest between Yhwh and Baal on Mount Carmel in 2 Kgs 18. There will be no debating at the assembly, only a revelation of the power of Israel's God to speak and to speak with effect.

There is an air of whimsy in the call for assembly as Yhwh demands that the far-flung islands "carve out" their cases beforehand. The imperative החרישו אלי in 41:1 may just as well bear the nuance of carving out a plot (cf. 1 Sam 23:9) as much as indicating being quiet. It is a sign of the skillful crafting of language that permeates Isaiah. After all, the crafter (חרש) of cult images (40:19; 41:7) is among those whom the Lord summons. The preposition אל in 41:1 may suggest that of direction and movement.[19] The form אלי may bear the sense of "concerning me" as well as "toward me." Besides, why would the Lord summon the iconodules by telling them to be quiet? The iconodules must present their cult statues to the assembly so that they can demonstrate the cult statues' capacity to speak and to make an impact on the course of events. Isaiah 42:2-4 portray Yhwh beginning to craft a case by referring to and taking credit for the meteoric rise of Cyrus. Isaiah 42:5 suggests that the far-flung islands and people took note of Yhwh's challenge and reacted with fear. What the far-flung isles saw that frightened them is not clear. Working retrospectively in the light of the context of vv. 10, 13, and 14, where Yhwh reassures the servant with אל תירא, the reader might find a hint concerning the object of fear by considering what it is that the context implies the servant may fear. Isaiah 41:8-11 suggest that the servant may fear the dangers of the desert terrain as well as political forces that might keep the servant captive with violence and oppression. The fear of traveling through desert and wilderness and of confronting what seem to be the overwhelming military forces of the servant's enemies are more than enough to give pause to the most ambitious plans for travel. In v. 5, regardless of the danger, the distant peoples draw near; they arrive, קרבו ויאתיון.

A scholarly consensus seems to understand 42:6-7 as depicting the manufacture of sacred statues.[20] That may be the case for Isa 40:18-20 but here

---

19. Ibid.
20. Claus Westermann, *Isaiah 40–66* (OTL; trans. David G. M. Stalker; Philadelphia: Westminster, 1969), 66; R. N. Whybray, *Isaiah 40–66* (NCBC; Grand Rapids: Eerdmans, 1975), 62; Peter D. Miscall, *Isaiah* (Readings: A New Biblical Commentary; Sheffield: JSOT Press, 1993), 102; Walsh, "Isaiah XLV 1–20"; Jan L. Koole, *Isaiah: Part 3. Vol. 1: Isaiah 40–48* (trans. Anthony P. Runia; HCOT; Kampen: Kok Pharos, 1997), 146; John N. Oswalt, *The Book of Isaiah: Chapters 40–66* (NICOT; Grand Rapids: Eerdmans, 1998), 85, 86; Klaus Baltzer, *Deutero-Isaiah* (trans. Margaret Kohl; Hermeneia; Minneapolis: Fortress, 2001), 91; Brevard S. Childs, *Isaiah* (OTL; Louisville: Westminster John Knox, 2001), 318; Joseph

the picture is not one of manufacturing but of preparing the cult statue for its arduous journey to the divine assembly. The iconodules fasten the statue's base to a pedestal, which is then loaded on the back of a beast for transport. In a similar way, the cult statue will later be borne into captivity (Isa 46:1, 2). Interpreters may envision a scene reminiscent of the famous procession of the gods in the carving at Maltaya in northern Iraq.[21]

Isaiah 41:8–13 convey Yhwh's assurance of divine sustenance and protection for the journey of the servant whom v. 8 clearly identifies as Israel. The identification of the servant as זרע אברהם אהבי, "the seed of Abraham, my friend," reminds the servant that the great ancestor was also a traveler and that the divine protection Abraham enjoyed will be the servant's as well. The relative pronoun that begins v. 9 indicates that what follows it continues the series of vocatives that began in v. 8: "But you are Israel (v. 8) ... whom I strengthened from the ends of the earth" (v. 9). Isaiah 41:14–16 express in hyperbolic, figurative language the effect the servant's testimony will have in the meeting of the council. Isaiah 41:17–20 describe Yhwh's provision for the servant as the latter makes the difficult journey through the desert to the place of assembly. At v. 21, the reader may imagine the council in action with the cult statues standing in place but, upon being challenged, they are mute. In v. 24 the divine king of the assembly accuses the cult statues of being מאין, "from nothing." Isaiah 41:25–27 then present Yhwh's testimony, which summarizes the essence of the case the divine judge began to prepare in vv. 2–4. Still, as vv. 28 and 29 indicate, the cult statues are quiet. The deictic particle הן at the beginning of v. 29 evokes a sense of solemnity as Yhwh issues the decision (cf. משפט from 41:1) that the cult statues are iniquitous and can claim no work whatever.

Isaiah 42:1–9

Without explanation, Klaus Baltzer configures the particle הן in 42:1 as initiating a new scene.[22] This is not a necessary conclusion. The shift is not scenic, but relates to variation involving a contrast between two entities in the same scene. Yhwh is contrasting his servant with the iconodules and their cult statues.[23] In 42:1, the word הן works, in part, as a contrastive balance to what

---

Blenkinsopp, *Isaiah 40–55* (AB 19A; New York: Doubleday, 2002), 192.
21. *ANEP* /537/.
22. Baltzer, *Deutero-Isaiah*, 124.
23. Oswalt, *The Book of Isaiah Chapters 40–66*, 109.

it introduces in 41:24 and 29. If 42:1 essentially carries forward the argument of Isa 41, then a sense of what Isa 41 conveys is therefore crucial to comprehending what Isa 42 depicts.

Apart from other texts in Isaiah that identify the servant as Israel,[24] Isa 41:8 lays to rest the question of the servant's identity. The only way to maintain that the servant is anything but collective Israel is to insist on interpreting 42:1–9 as a unit distinct from and not connected to Isa 41. In this way Baltzer interprets the servant as Moses. John D. W. Watts, J. Blenkinsopp, and M. Goulder take him as Cyrus.[25] Gerhard von Rad configures the servant as a prophet "like Moses."[26] Von Rad explains the servant as deriving from Deutero-Isaiah's theological reflections on his own experiences, the nature of prophecy, and the defining Moses played as a paradigm for prophecy.[27] Reflecting the prevailing critical mode of reference in his own era, von Rad interprets the servant in terms that relate them to a series of songs. He therefore does not think about them in relation to Isa 41:8 and 44:1, 2. These texts fall outside the delimited servant songs. It is the question of the socio-political analogy that forms the conceptual context of the servant's identity that is, in my view, the salient issue. Christopher Seitz has proposed that the servant represents a royal figure, a king.[28] In his view the phrase הן עבדי derives from a setting where a king is formally presented before an audience.[29]

Reading the book of Isaiah as a unified whole raises at least two problems for taking the servant as a royal figure. First, it gives short shrift to the book of Isaiah's testimony to the uniqueness of Yhwh's position *as king*. The book of Isaiah early resolves the issue of who Yhwh is relative to all other entities in the cosmos. In 6:5 Isaiah's fear of imminent dissolution stems from his having seen המלך, "*the* king." There the prophet shapes the emphasis of his testimony by putting the direct object at the beginning of the sentence, even subordinating the deity's name to the title of king. Furthermore, in 41:21 the prophetic persona refers to Yhwh as מלך יעקב, "the king of Jacob." In 43:15 Yhwh declares, אני יהוה קדושכם בורא ישראל מלככם, "I am Yhwh, your

---

24. For a thorough treatment of these texts see Sheldon Blank, *Prophetic Faith in Isaiah* (Detroit: Wayne State University Press, 1967), 74–116.
25. Watts, *Isaiah 34–66*, 119; Joseph Blenkinsopp, *Isaiah 40–55*, 210; Goulder, "Behold My Servant Jehoiachin," 175–90.
26. Gerhard von Rad, *Old Testament Theology: The Theology of Israel's Prophetic Traditions* (trans. D. M. G. Stalker; 2 vols.; New York: Harper and Row, 1965), 2:261.
27. Ibid., 2:276–77.
28. Christopher R. Seitz, "Isaiah 40–66" (*NIB* 6; Nashville: Abingdon, 2001), 361.
29. Ibid., 362.

holy one, creator of Israel, your king." Monarchy, like divinity, is an honor Yhwh will share with no one else. This is the realization that dawns on the prophet in his visionary experience narrated in ch. 6. Isaiah 42 does not portray Yhwh as presenting the servant with reference to the social analogy of any kind of installation service or ceremony. The servant is simply there among those convened to the council.

In Isa 20:3 Yhwh refers to Isaiah as עבדי. By analogy, therefore, it seems feasible that the servant is a prophetic figure. To configure the servant as a prophet seems simple enough but even the task of a prophet derives from socio-political analogies that can be varied and distinctive. Although it does not bear the specificity of analogy that one might desire, to speak of the servant as Yhwh's *courtier* seems more helpful than the more general term prophet. Indeed, in the canonical traditions the prophet is someone who has stood before the Lord in the assembly. Jeremiah accuses the rival prophets of not having stood בסוד יהוה, "in the council of Yhwh" (Jer 23:18, 22; cf. 1 Kgs 22:19, 21 and 2 Kgs 3:14). A prophet in this tradition is one of Yhwh's courtiers who announces the assembly's decisions.

Second, Yhwh is speaking in Isa 42:1-4 as king and is still addressing the assembled iconodules. The phrases in 42:1a that qualify Yhwh's relationship to the servant focus the iconodules' thoughts—as well as the reader's—not only on the servant but as well on Yhwh's capacity to uphold the servant in contrast to the cult statues that need to be upheld. The iconodules expend great energy fixing the cult statue to a base so that it will not topple during the journey to the assembly (41:7). In contrast, that Yhwh delegates divine spirit to the servant (42:1bα) and sets the servant in a position of authority that the iconodules and the cult statues cannot claim. The closest any kind of רוח comes to them is the windy chaos of the primeval abyss (41:29bβ).

This assessment of the presentation of the servant in the context of a challenge from Yhwh to the iconodules and their cult statues suggests the feasibility of the interpretation that משפט in 42:1 and 4 effectively refers to the results of the assembly, namely, a verdict.[30] The servant's task is to publish or to proclaim that the cult statues failed the challenge that Yhwh set before them. It is not, as many scholars have stated,[31] to establish or to realize

---

30. Watts, *Isaiah 34-66*, 111, 119; J. Alec Motyer, *The Prophecy of Isaiah: An Introduction and Commentary* (Downers Grove, Ill.: InterVarsity, 1993), 319. Cf. Blank's (*Prophetic Faith in Isaiah*, 82) rendering of משפט לגוים יוציא as "He will publish the truth among the nations."

31. See for example Willem A. M. Beuken, "Mišpaṭ: The First Servant Song and Its Context," *VT* 22 (1972): 1–30; Marvin A. Sweeney, "The Book of Isaiah as Prophetic Torah,"

socially the conditions of justice. In the book of Isaiah, such a reconfiguration of social conditions is uniquely Yhwh's task as cosmic monarch. The phrase, משפט לגוים יוציא, is more likely therefore to indicate the immediate commission of the servant to announce the cult statue's failure and to assert the success of Yhwh than to describe social transformation.

If we may take the servant in Isa 42 as a contrast with the cult statues of the nations, it seems reasonable that Isa 42:2, 3 may allude in some way to components of the conceptual structure of the use of cult statues in the religions of the ancient Near East. Incantation Tablet 6/8 is one of the final incantations of the *mīs pî* series according to the Babylonian ritual.[32] It contains an incantation that is spoken as the cult statue is taken in a ritual procession from ceremonies at the river to its permanent dwelling in the temple. The incantation describes Marduk walking about through town and witnessing the accidental pollution of an incantation priest. He seeks advice from his father Enki. Enki instructs Marduk to prepare a holy-water basin, as in the *mīs pî* ceremony, and to scatter the water from it through the streets so as to purify the town. Enki tells Marduk to shout, although what he is to shout is not clear. Apparently, from the lines that follow the command to shout, Marduk is to proclaim thereby that the city is bright, pure, and clean. That the servant will not cry out and make noise in the street may allude to the ceremonial forms involved in the transporting of a cult statue from one place to another. Assuming that Marduk's shout corresponds to a liturgical shouting in the context of transporting a cult statue, it seems reasonable that the statement that the servant will not make his voice heard in the street may allude to the lack of necessity for such a shout. Furthermore, what it is that the servant will not lift up (נשא) is a cult statue. In Isa. 46:1 the root נשא occurs twice in relation to describing the cult statue as a burden weary animals bear; first as a participle (נשאתיכם) then as a noun (משא). The servant will not be so burdened; indeed, it is Yhwh who bears the servant (46:4; cf. 41:8–10).

The famous crux about the broken reed and dimly burning wick may allude to the prominent role of reeds in the *mīs pî* ceremony. Tablet A of the Nineveh Ritual Tablet instructs the officiants in the consecration of the cult statue to make reed huts for Ea, Shamash, and Asalluḫi (Marduk) within a sacred enclosure which is itself constructed of bundles of reeds known as *urigallu*. The officiant is then to address the reed huts with two incantations

---

in Melugin and Sweeney, *New Visions of Isaiah*, 50–67; Oswalt, *The Book of Isaiah: Chapters 40–66*, 109, 110.

32. Walker and Dick, "The Induction of the Cult Image in Ancient Mesopotamia," 55–121; see also idem, *The Induction of the Cult Image in Ancient Mesopotamia*, 210.

referred to as "Pure reed, long reed, pure node of a reed" and "Marduk saw your pure clay in the *apsu*." A few lines later we find directions for the officiant to address what appears to be one of the reed huts with an incantation titled, "Reed grown from the Apsû."[33] On the second day of the consecration ceremonies, a morning repast is set out before the cult statue, part of which is "sweet reed and its pulp" [*qanâ ṭab ša in libbi*], which has been freshly cut.[34] Section A of Incantation Tablet 1/2 is completely dedicated to describing the significance and role of reeds in the induction ceremony of the cult statue.[35]

The obscure פשתה כהה is more difficult to account for. One wonders if the object this phrase designates might not be a lamp that parallels the torch (*gizillû*, literally, a lifted burning reed) used with a censor in the consecration ceremonies surrounding the cult statue. In essence, Isa 42:2–3 presents the poet's elliptically phrased claim that the task of Yhwh's servant has nothing to do with the liturgical moments that normally occur in the ceremonies consecrating a statue to serve as a vehicle for the earthly manifestation of the god it represents.

Verse 3b reprises v. 1bβ. לאמת is a unique construction in the Hebrew Bible. Jepsen makes the case for rendering לאמת יוציא משפט as "that (reliable) truth will be (known), he (my servant) will make known the sentence of judgment."[36] One might offer the rendering, "For the sake of the truth, he will take forth the verdict." לאמת is paradigmatically parallel to לגוים from v. 4b. Some scholars have therefore suggested reading it as לאמת "to the peoples," and thus providing a semantic parallel to לגוים. In a text without vowels לאמת could be either. The Masoretes opted for לאמת but without vowels the construction is ambiguous and finds its solution not in the decision between the two noted meanings but in maintaining the meaning of both simultaneously. In Jakobson's terms, similarity superimposed on contiguity yields poetic meaning.

After the two-fold משפט as the object of יוציא in vv. 1 and 3 the shift from יוציא to ישים in v. 4aβ will give readers pause. Conceivably, the phraseology יוציא משפט is not saying the same thing as עד ישים משפט. This may suggest a shift of nuance for משפט as well. In keeping with the notice that Yhwh is addressing the iconodules and their failed cult statues, it is worth keeping in mind that the journey to the assembly was heavy with various dangers. Why should there not be any dangers for the servant to face as he

---

33. Walker and Dick, *The Induction of the Cult Image in Ancient Mesopotamia*, 53, 54.
34. Ibid., 61.
35. Ibid., 91–96.
36. A. Jepson, "אֱמֶת; אָמַן; אֱמוּנָה; אָמֵן," *TDOT* 1: 292–323.

goes out to announce the outcome of the assembly? Thus, one may take v. 4a as indicating that the servant will not weaken or be crushed until he sets the verdict in place. Isaiah 42:4 concludes with Yhwh's statement that the distant islands await the servant's תורה, that is, the lands are waiting for concrete instruction about what to do in the light of the failure of the cult statues.

Isa 42:5 signals a shift in speaker from Yhwh to the servant. The servant continues through v. 9. The definite article on האל in v. 5 suggests a point of emphasis as to who Yhwh is. Yhwh is *the* god. The participial phrases that follow in v. 5 identify Yhwh's unique status more precisely. It seems to me that in vv. 5–7 we have the content of what it is that the servant will say to the nations. If the icondules assert that the cult statue was made in heaven, Yhwh claims the heavens themselves as his creation. Yhwh gives breath to the people. The lifeless cult statue receives no benefit from the true divine source of life. As if to reinforce the implication that v. 5bα alludes to the cult statue, the use of הלכים in v. 5bβ suggests the incapacity of the cult statue to move about on its own. Yhwh's life-giving power exercises itself on behalf of living creatures, a theme for which the word וצאצאיה prepares the reader in v. 5aγ. Instead of וצאצאיה in v. 5aγ, the reader might have expected something like וישבי בה (cf. Ps 24:1). Yet it is emergence and movement, indicating life and vitality, that the word וצאצאיה allows the poet to emphasize.

In v. 6 the servant transmits what Yhwh said to him and testifies that Yhwh summoned him בצדק, that is, "with regard to צדק." Martin Buber renders צדק as the "objectively accurate expression of judgment," that is, the "verdict" [*der Wahrspruch*].[37] Thus the servant asserts that it was for the purpose of announcing the verdict that Yhwh called him. The clause ואחזק בידך may allude to ceremonial moments in the statue's procession from the *bīt mummi*, "the House of the Craftsman," to the temple in which it will dwell. The text of the liturgical procession in the Babylonian Ritual Tablet (BM 45749) tells the priest four times "you shall take hold of the hand of the god," *qāt ili taṣbbatma*. The servant states that Yhwh promises to take him by the hand. The prophetic writer reverses the image of protection and support. The Babylonian priest seems obliged to take the hand of the god offering support or protection for the idol; in contrast, Yhwh initiates support and comfort for the servant.

The word ואצרך exhibits an ambiguity that moves the reader between two possible meanings, "I form you" or "I guard you." To read the word in

---

37. Martin Buber, "On Word Choice in Translating the Bible: In Memoriam Franz Rosenzweig," in *Scripture and Translation* (trans. Franz Rosenzweig and Lawrence Rosenwald; Bloomington, Ind.: Indiana University Press, 1994), 73–89.

terms of the possiblity of only one meaning is to read as if poetry were concerned with denotation. The two-fold appearance of the preposition in v. 6bβ suggests a nuance similar to how it modifies אמת in v. 3. Yhwh confers on the servant the responsibility of mediating a covenant between the deity and humankind.[38] The phrase לאור גוים describes the results of the covenant with the peoples. The book of Isaiah employs light as a metaphor for freedom from the influence of the cult statue and other forms of divination.[39]

The infinitive phrase, לפקח עינים עורות, not only carries forward the book of Isaiah's theme of Israel's blindness and healing but introduces the specific purpose for which Yhwh will grant insight. Isaiah 42:7b depicts the result of the opening of the blind eyes of unfair judges, namely, the emptying of prisons. Yet, the nature of the poetic text allows for an allusion to the exposing of the fraudulent cult statue. The cult statue is exposed as a mere prisoner in a dark place, an inhabitant of the dark cella where it was concealed from light and from the sight of all but an elite few. The superimposing of two different senses on the same sentence reminds the reader of the verbal strategy of identifying the woven pall with the cult statue in Isa 25:7.[40]

In verse 8, lest the reader wander from the conceptual framework of an anti-cult statue polemic, the prophetic persona portrays Yhwh as disallowing any association of his glory and praise with cult statues. This verse therefore represents a summary rejection of the ideological framework that allows a god's worshippers to envision the god as bestowing the divine qualities of power and radiance on the cult statue (לפסילים).

A text from the time of Esarhaddon (early-seventh century B.C.E.) describes the precious stones that will eventually bedeck the cult statue as bearing a "splendor" (*melammu*) that Ea generously bestowed on them.[41] Lines 49–52 of Incantation Tablet 3 of the Mesopotamian *mīs pî* ritual as Christopher Walker and Michael Dick have reconstructed it reads as follows:

49   Incantation: When the god was fashioned, the pure statue completed,
50   The god appeared in all the lands,

---

38. Jan L. Koole, *Isaiah: Part 3. Vol. 1: Isaiah 40–48*, 232.
39. See Isa 8:16–9:1 (Hebrew). In Isa 25:7 the prophetic poet manages to convey the sense that the cult statue is like a dark veil or covering by employing terms that evoke both the senses of "woven thing" and "molten image." In the clause, והמסכה הנסוכה על-כל-הגוים the phonemic contiguity between המסכה as "woven thing" or "covering" and מסכה, "cult statue" suggests the speaker's assessment of the cult statue by using a term that also means dark "covering."
40. See note 31 above.
41. Walker and Dick, *The Induction of the Cult Image in Ancient Mesopotamia*, 26.

> 51 bearing an awe-inspiring halo, he is adorned with lordliness; lordly, he is all pride;
> 52 Surrounded with splendor, endowed with an awesome appearance.[42]

Yhwh makes no such bestowal or concession.

As a system of meaning, the book of Isaiah configures the human community of Israel, as the agent through which divine teaching flows. Israel must not depend on the cult statue as a testimony to the power of the creator to make the divine will known but adopt a communal attitude that exhibits an awareness of being God's servant and, therefore, as standing and waiting to do the divine will.

---

42. Ibid., 149, 150.

"They All Gather, They Come to You":
History, Utopia, and the Reading of
Isaiah 49:18–26 and 60:4–16

Roy D. Wells

This essay is a modest footnote to a major conference at Kampen in 1994 on the implications of the work of Ferdinand de Saussure for biblical studies.[1] In the last years before his premature death in 1913, Saussure taught the course in "general linguistics" at the University of Geneva. In these lectures, which must be reconstructed from student notes (alas!), he advocated the privileging of "synchronic" linguistics over "diachronic" linguistics. This was, in other terms, a preference for the reading of texts, networks of words, as a single, "synchronic" expression of current usage—of current cultural constraints on expression. The relative clarity of the synchronic world was a respite from the messy, "accidental and particular" world of diachronic linguistics.[2] Two other

---

1. An earlier version of this study, now offered in memory of Professor Roy Melugin, was presented to the Formation of the Book of Isaiah Group, Society of Biblical Literature 2007. His sustained awareness of the role of the interpreter in the reading of polyvalent texts is a subtext here—see, e.g., Roy F. Melugin, "Recent Form Criticism Revisited in an Age of Reader Response," in *The Changing Face of Form Criticism for the Twenty-First Century* (ed. Marvin A. Sweeney and Ehud Ben Zvi; Grand Rapids: Eerdmans, 2003), 46–64.

2. Ferdinand de Saussure, *Course in General Linguistics* (ed. Charles Balley, Albert Sechehaye, and Albert Riedinger; trans. Wade Baskin; New York: McGraw-Hill, 1966), 93. Note in passing that current analysis of some twenty-four cartons of Saussure's papers has produced a revisionist reading. The radical privileging of synchronic reading described in the Balley/Sechehaye edition of Saussure's lectures does not hold up. Frank Lentriccia delineates a more dialectical approach to the two methods: Frank Lentricchia, *After the New Criticism* (Chicago: University of Chicago Press, 1980), 116–17. See Eisuke Komatsu's

–much broader—distinctions made by Saussure have been important for the Geneva/Paris trajectory of his work. His distinction between the "signifier" and the "signified" (signifiant/signifié) undermines the naïve connection between language and the reality to which language refers. The relationship between the words within the text and the things signified by the text is arbitrary—cultural—rather than essential. By extension, this study of texts as a network of cultural "signs" is a radical alternative to the study of texts in the service of reconstructing the precise reality that lies behind the text. His distinction between "language" and "speech" (langue/parole) places primary emphasis on the culture that regulates the speech, rather than on the individual act of speaking that produced the text.

Though the specific Geneva/Paris trajectory of Saussure's work had no immediate influence on biblical studies, the terms "diachronic" and "synchronic"—variously understood—have begun to reappear in the guild's quest for a sense of wholeness in texts that challenges our fascination with the stages in the formation of texts, and for a focus on narrative that challenges our fascination with historical hypothesis.[3] James Barr's analysis of this issue at the Kampen conference, and particularly his analysis of the interrelations between the "synchronic" reading of ancient texts and historical criticism, illuminates the issues addressed here.[4]

This essay on the problematic of "diachronic" and "synchronic" reading is an effort to understand the interrelationships between two quite distinct feminine singular apostrophes addressed to a woman who is a personification of Zion (Isa 49) and to the city of Zion (Isa 60). The texts are interrelated by an intricate pattern of verbal cross-connections, ranging from echoes of words and sounds to replication of specific and unusual phrases.[5] The analysis will concentrate on material enclosed by distinctive opening and closing phrases in both texts. Isaiah 60:4a is identical to Isa 49:18a, and 60:4b has significant verbal and phonetic links with 49:22b, 23a:

---

extensive newer edition of notes on Saussure's lectures from 1907–1911 (Oxford: Pergamon Press, 1993–1997).

3. See the programmatic statements in Brevard S. Childs, *Isaiah* (Louisville, Ky.: Westminster John Knox, 2001), passim.

4. James Barr, "The Synchronic, the Diachronic and the Historical: A Triangular Relationship?" in *Synchronic or Diachronic? A Debate on Method in Old Testament Exegesis* (ed. Johannes C. de Moor; OTS 34; Leiden: Brill, 1995), 1–14.

5. See the presentation of these connections in Alfred Zillessen, "'Tritojesaja' und Deuterojesaja. Eine literarkritische Untersuchung zu Jes. 56–66," *ZAW* 26 (1906): 231–76.

49:18 Lift up your eyes all around and see (שאי־סביב עיניך וראי); they all gather, they come to you (כלם נקבצו באו־לך).	60:4 Lift up your eyes all around and see (שאי־סביב עיניך וראי);[6] they all gather, they come to you (כלם נקבצו באו־לך).
22 Thus says the Lord God: I will soon lift up (אשא) my hand to the nations, and raise my signal to the peoples; and they shall bring (והביאו) your sons (בניך) in their bosom, and your daughters (ובנתיך) shall be carried on their shoulders (על־כתף תנשאנה).	your sons shall come from far away (בניך מרחוק יבאו), and your daughters shall be supported at their side (ובנתיך על־צד תאמנה).

Isaiah 60:16b, except for a change of subject echoing 49:23b (note that 60:16a is a peculiar echo of 49:23a.), is identical with 49:26b:

49:23 Kings shall be your foster fathers (אמניך), and their queens your nursing mothers (מיניקתיך).	60:16 You shall suck the milk of nations (וינקת חלב גוים), you shall suck the breasts of kings (ושד מלכים תינקי);
With their faces to the ground they shall bow down to you, and lick the dust of your feet. Then you will know that I am the Lord (וידעת כי־אני יהוה); those who wait for me shall not be put to shame.	
49:26 I will make your oppressors eat their own flesh (והאכלתי את־מוניך את־בשרם), and they shall be drunk with their own blood as with wine.	

---

6. *Mutatis mutandis*, the translation used in this paper is the NRSV.

Then all flesh shall know that I am the Lord (וידעו כל־בשר כי אני יהוה) your Savior, and your Redeemer, the Mighty One of Jacob (מושיעך וגאלך אביר יעקב).	and you shall know that I am the LORD (וידעת כי אני יהוה), your Savior and your Redeemer, the Mighty One of Jacob (מושיעך וגאלך אביר יעקב).

The comparison of the material enclosed by these specific phrases allows a description of the distinctive character of these addresses, and provides a modest basis for speaking of the intellectual perspective of the texts.

With malice toward none, and encouraged by Saussure's assumption that all interpretation begins with a reading of the text, this particular study—as stated at the outset—concentrates on the textual details of the connections between Isa 49 and Isa 60.[7] Other significant textual or intertextual connections have not been pursued. Though both of these texts are addressed to Zion, this study does not engage the cross connections with the theme "Zion, the city chosen by the Lord," in the first part of the book of Isaiah—the major subject of Roy Melugin's last paper for this group.[8] Though Isa 49 stands on the boundary between the poems about the Servant and the poems about Zion, this issue has not been addressed.[9] This is also an extremely limited analysis of the intertextual network that converges in these chapters. The work of Patricia Willey on ch. 49[10] and the work of Ronald Clements on ch.

---

7. Hayden White, "The Historical Text as Literary Artifact," in *The Writing of History: Literary Form and Historical Understanding* (ed. Robert H. Canary and Henry Kozicki; Madison: University of Wisconsin Press, 1978), 41–62, raises the issue adversarially. Walther Zimmerli's analysis, "Zur Sprache Tritojesajas," in *Gottes Offenbarung. Gesammelte Aufsätze* (TB 19; München: Chr. Kaiser, 1963), 217, is an homage to Ludwig Köhler: "Weil der Mensch nicht als der zeitlos in einer Idee Wesende, sondern nur als das je seiner geschichtlichen Stunde verhaftete Geschöpf ganz Mensch ist, wird sich in eines Menschen Sprache auch seine Zeit, seine Geschichte abschatten."

8. Roy F. Melugin, ("Zion in a Synchronic Reading of Isaiah," [paper presented at the annual meeting of the SBL, San Diego, Calif., Nov. 2007]), examines these two chapters in dialogue with 1:2–31. Gerhard von Rad, "Die Stadt auf dem Berge," in *Gesammelte Studien zum Alten Testament* (TB 8; München: Chr. Kaiser, 1961), 214.

9. Patricia Tull Willey, "The Servant of Yhwh and Daughter Zion," *SBLSP* 34 (1995): 267–303, discusses the literature.

10. Ibid., 280–84, and idem, *Remember the Former Things: The Recollection of Previous Texts in Isaiah* (SBLDS 161; Atlanta: Scholars Press, 1997), especially 175–208. Ulrich Berges, "The Growth of the Book of Isaiah: Continuation or Combination?" (paper presented at the annual meeting of the SBL. Boston, 2008), opens a broad network of connections with the temple liturgy.

60[11] underline the incompleteness of this study. This is a manageable, partial, analysis of the echoes of remembered texts in a world in which memory is a powerful force in discourse, keeping the world of texts alive and transforming it in the light of the present. Our painstaking and to some degree pitiful efforts to track these links with concordances only scratch the surface of intertextuality and rereading in the world of the book of Isaiah—though these efforts have the virtue of clarifying a small piece of this intertextual network.[12] Though the underlying methodology is redaction analysis (diachronic?), the analysis should provide the basis for a comparison of two poems on related themes (synchronic?).[13] Suspending the quest for the underlying history and the quest for conventional forms of expression (the trajectories through Duhm and Gunkel), the most productive way of clarifying the transformation and reinterpretation of Isa 49 in Isa 60 is to analyze the reading and rereading of metaphors and their function in the discourse.[14] Isaiah 49 is dominated by

---

11. Ronald E. Clements, "'Arise, Shine; For Your Light Has Come': A Basic Theme of the Isaianic Tradition," in *Writing and Reading the Scroll of Isaiah: Studies of an Interpretive Tradition* (ed. Craig C. Broyles and Craig A. Evans; VTSup 70.1; Leiden: Brill, 1997), 441–54. Hugo Odeberg, *Trito-Isaiah (Isaiah 56–66): A Literary and Linguistic Analysis* (UUA 1; Uppsala: A.-B. Lundequistska Bokhandeln, 1931), indicates the work that remains to be done.

12. In passing, there is a considerable debt to the meticulous research of H. G. M. Williamson, *The Book Called Isaiah: Deutero-Isaiah's Role in Composition and Redaction* (Oxford: Clarendon, 1994), who pays consistent attention, not only to the importance of textual echoes in the book of Isaiah, but also to the subtlety of these echoes, often involving commonplace words and scattered patterns of words. See his earlier essay, "Synchronic and Diachronic in Isaian Perspective," in *Synchronic or Diachronic? A Debate on Method in Old Testament Exegesis* (ed. Johannes C. de Moor; OTS 34; Leiden: Brill, 1995), 211–26.

13. James, Barr, "The Synchronic, the Diachronic and the Historical: A Triangular Relationship?," 10, finds no value in "canonizing one of these contrary approaches."

14. Peter D. Miscall, "An Adventure in Reading the Scroll of Isaiah" (paper presented at the annual meeting of the SBL, Denver, Colo., Nov. 2001), 1, speaks of "readings with imagery as the guiding thread and main focus." See idem, *Isaiah* (Readings: A New Biblical Commentary; Sheffield: JSOT Press, 1993). Reprinted with a new preface, *Isaiah* (2nd ed.; Sheffield: Sheffield Phoenix Press, 2006). See the treatment of the women in Isa 49 and Isa 60 by Katheryn Pfisterer Darr, *Isaiah's Vision and the Family of God* (Literary Currents in Biblical Interpretation; Louisville, Ky.: Westminster John Knox, 1994), 169–76, and her discussion of metaphor, 36–41. Our understanding of the theory and practice of reading metaphors has been advanced substantially by Francis Landy. See idem, *Beauty and the Enigma and Other Essays on the Hebrew Bible* (JSOTSup 312; Sheffield: Sheffield Academic Press, 2001), especially the introduction, 13–33. Note also the tracking of specific metaphors through the Book of Isaiah in Ronald E. Clements, "Beyond Tradition-History: Deutero-Isaianic Development of First Isaiah's Themes," *JSOT* 31 (1985): 95–113, cited from Ronald

the metaphors of a forsaken wife and a bereft mother, and by the assurance that their circumstances are being reversed.

The reading of Isa 60 in this essay focuses narrowly on the citations and echoes of Isa 49 in Isa 60—a small part of the "mosaic" of texts described by Lack.[15] As stated earlier, these echoes are described in terms of a redaction analysis, without the intention of "canonizing" diachronic reading. Ronald Clements' description of ch. 60 as a hermeneutic of ch. 49 cannot be improved: 1) "The allusions appear to be very consciously and deliberately contrived" and 2) there is "considerable literary license" in the use of ch. 49 in ch. 60.[16] Long ago, Zimmerli stated this connection from a theological perspective: the author of Isa 60 "seeks to speak in new times in such a way that that the validity of older proclamation is audible."[17]

Isaiah 60:1–3

In ch. 60, the summons to "look all around and see" is set within the metaphor of a brilliant dawn. The summons brought forward from ch. 49 is anticipated by a preliminary summons to respond to this new light, "rise, shine" (קומי אורי 60:1).[18] This is a substantial reconception of the metaphorical structure of ch. 49. Here, the lamenting woman survives only in a subtle trace—the preliminary feminine singular imperative "rise" (קומי). But this allusion is enwrapped in the metaphor of the dawn, and the woman is not the controlling metaphor in ch. 60.[19] Ch. 49 is both taken up and transformed in this

---

E. Clements, *Old Testament Prophecy: From Oracles to Canon* (Louisville, Ky.: Westminster John Knox, 1996), 78–92; idem, "Patterns in the Prophetic Canon," 189–200.

15. Rémi Lack, *La Symbolique du livre d'Isaïe*, 198.

16. Clements, "Arise, Shine; For Your Light Has Come," 451, 453. These comments about 49:23–26 have been expanded. Willem A. M. Beuken, *Jesaja. Deel IIIA* (POut; Nijkerk: G. F. Callenbach, 1989), 165, states the overwhelming tendency to allow the reading of ch. 49 to control the reading of ch. 60: "Het citaat is een aanwijzing dat we deze passage in het licht van de eerst moeten lezen." This is an effort to see the transformations that distinguish Isa 60 from Isa 49.

17. Walther Zimmerli, "Sprache Tritojesajas," 233, see especially 222–23, 230–32. See the discussion of the role of foreigners in Isa 60 in Michael Fishbane, *Biblical Interpretation in Ancient Israel* (Oxford: Clarendon, 1985, 1988), 118–19, 142, and his general comments about "mantological exegesis" of Isa 40–55 in 56–66.

18. Note that the Septuagint "shine, shine, Jerusalem" (cf. 51:17; 52:2), reads the chapter as an address to a personified city, without even this trace of the response to the lament of a forsaken wife.

19. *Pace* Beuken, *Jesaja. Deel IIIA*, 164–65 and Miscall, *Isaiah*, 136–37 (*Isaiah*, 2nd ed.,

allusion. The consoling response to the lament of the abandoned wife (49:14–18) has vanished entirely, along with the wedding regalia she is summoned to look at and see. This also applies to the word "forsaken" (עזובה) at 60:15, which has been read as an echo of the woman's complaint (עזבני) at 49:14. Koole has shown the consistency of this apostrophe to a city, reading 60:14 as an address to a ruinous city.[20] The images of the city Zion/Jerusalem, which are enfolded into the metaphor of the wife in ch. 49, are dominant in ch. 60.

The simple metaphor of the dawn is developed in numinous terms. There are echoes of cosmic significance of this darkness that "covers the earth" (60:2)—Fohrer sees an echo of the opening of the story of creation, suggesting an underlying metaphysical significance.[21] The association of "the glory of the Lord" (60:1, 2) with the temple links this with a sacral significance, anticipating the coming gifts to the temple. The divine light, the sacral radiance of the "glory" of God, is reflected off this particular place—this city (v. 3, "your light," "your dawn").

The nations and the kings come without a pejorative subtext. Neither the ruins nor the ruiners of the city are brought forward from ch. 49. The nations and kings, like everything else in this chapter, are drawn out of the darkness, attracted by the splendor of the radiance reflected by this particular city. There is a trace of the nemesis that dominates ch. 49 in 60:14, 16 (see the discussion there), but even there, the images of the nemesis upon the destroyers of Jerusalem are taken up and transformed in ch. 60.

Isaiah 60:4ab // 49:18a, 22b, 23a

At 60:4, the summons to "look and see" develops the summons to "rise and shine" (60:1):

> Lift up your eyes all around and see;
> they all gather, they come to you. (60:4)

In the light of the dawn, "all of them" (כלם) refers initially to this great convergence of nations and kings. Ultimately, "they all gather, they come to you" is now a summation of all that is drawn to this light—to Zion—in this poem.

165–66), who develop this echo into a full-blown replication of this metaphor.
  20. Jan L. Koole, *Isaiah: Part 3. Vol. 3: Isaiah 56–66* (trans. Anthony P. Runia; HCOT; Kampen: Kok Pharos, 1997), 247–48.
  21. Georg Fohrer, *Das Buch Jesaja. Vol. III: Kapitel 40–66* (ZBK; Zürich: Zwingli, 1964), 227.

49:22 they shall bring (והביאו) your sons (בניך) in their bosom,
and your daughters (ובנתיך) shall be carried on their shoulders (על־כתף תנשאנה).
23 Kings shall be your foster fathers (אמניך),
and their queens your nursing mothers.

60:4 your sons (בניך) shall come (יבאו) from far away,
and your daughters (ובנתיך)
shall be supported at their side (על־צד תאמנה).

This convergence is first elaborated in an allusion to the sons and daughters of 49:22–23, who now come with the kings, drawn out of the darkness. The parallel between the coming of the nations and the coming of the children, and particularly the parallel between the coming of the sons and the coming of the daughters is overlooked in most standard translations and commentaries. The tendency to bring forward the subjugated bearers of the children from 49:22–23[22] is most dramatic in the NRSV: "and your daughters shall be carried on [their nurses'] arms" (60:4). This is the ultimate triumph of ch. 49 over ch. 60. This obscure text may be read: "Your sons (בניך) shall come (יבאו) from far away, and your daughters (ובנתיך) shall be supported at their side (על־צד תאמנה)."[23] Here, the children come on their own, drawn to the light along with the nations and kings and the wealth of nations. In the only other reference to the children (60:9), they are included in the cargo of wealth brought by ships. The patriation of an expanded gola is a subtext, but there is no need to replicate the scene that dominates ch. 49.[24] The bereft mother

---

22. Odil Hannes Steck, "Heimkehr auf der Schulter oder/und auf der Hüfte Jes 49,22b/60,4b," in *Studien zu Tritojesaja* (BZAW 203: Berlin: de Gruyter, 1991), 97–100, reads this verse as a continuation of 49:22 and as a transformation of the abusive metaphor at Ezek 34:21.

23. See John F. Sawyer, *Isaiah* (vol. 2; The Daily Study Bible; Philadelphia: Westminster, 1986), 181, "your daughters shall be beside them and supported by them" and R. N. Whybray, *Isaiah 40–66* (NCB; Grand Rapids: Eerdmans, 1975), 232. See the discussion in Koole, *Isaiah: Part 3. Vol. 3: Isaiah 56–66*, 227, particularly the reading of the verb as "walk forward" (√אמם) = BHS, REB (see DCH).

24. This common opinion appears in Steck's Grundtext, 60:1–3, 4, 5–9, 13, which emphasizes the restoration of the children to Jerusalem, reducing this contrast between chs. 49 and 60. See the summary in "Der Grundtext in Jes 60 und sein Aufbau," in *Studien zu Tritojesaja*, 72–73. Lack, *La Symbolique du Livre d'Isaïe*, 201, finds two inclusions that emphasize the return of the children, first of Zion (60:4, 9), and then of foreigners (60:10, 14).

of ch. 49 now lies enfolded in this description of the convergence of nations, kings, and all manner of things toward the radiant city of Zion.²⁵

Isaiah 60:5ab; cf. 60:8a // 49:21

As Beuken and Koole have shown, the language of the description of what will be "seen" (ראה 60:5aα, cf. 60:4aα), as well as of the response to it, is dark and ambivalent, filled with textual problems that attest to its obscurity.²⁶ Here,²⁷ and again at 60:8 (the only other reference to the "children"),²⁸ there is a faint echo of the mother's dawning awareness of the arrival of new children at 49:21. Here, this is the city's response of awe at an overwhelming, numinous transformation of reality. This transformation is effected by what "turns to" (הפך על *nipʿal* 60:5b) the city: the "wealth of nations." In fact, this is a summation of the scenes that follow:

> The wealth of nations shall come to you.

This summation also applies to v. 8, which is a response to the mysterious sight of a cloud of sails on the horizon. The children are included in the cargo of bullion brought to make the city and its temple a place of splendor. The return of the children of a bereft mother, which dominates ch. 49, is enfolded in the description of the convergence of wealth that will make the temple and the city splendid.

Despite irregularities in the details of this description, there is substantial agreement on the division of the chapter into individual scenes.²⁹ These scenes typically conclude with intertextually rich, aphoristic statements of the

---

25. It is not necessary to go as far as Jacques Vermeylen, *Du prophète Isaïe à l'apocalyptique. Isaïe, I–XXXV, miroir d'un demi-millénaire d'expérience religieuse en Israël. Tome II* (EBib; Paris: J. Gabalda, 1978), 471–74, who sees the "end of the diaspora" in 4b, 9aβ as an addition, alien to the context of universalism. In ch. 60, the nations come to acknowledge that the כבוד has returned to the "centre cultuel de l'univers."

26. See Beuken, *Jesaja. Deel IIIA*, 166; Koole, *Isaiah: Part 3. Vol. 3: Isaiah 56–66*, 228–30. See ibid. and Blenkinsopp, *Isaiah 56–66*, 206 for details of the textual problems.

27. "your heart" = 49:21 לבבך.

28. "Who are these?" מי אלה: cf. 49:21, "Who has begotten me these?" מי ילד־לי אלה. Note the repetition of אלה in 49:21.

29. P.-E. Bonnard, *Le Second Isaïe: Son Disciple et Leurs Éditeurs. Isaïe 40–66* (EBib; Paris: Gabalda, 1972), 397–99, 402: 60:4–5, 6–7, 8–9, 10–11[+12], 13–14, 15–16. Bonnard's discussion of these sections of the poem (405–12) emphasized the echoes of Deutero-Isaianic words—now in the setting of the proclamation of the coming splendor of the temple cultus.

basis for or the purpose of the action described in the individual scenes. The cumulative effect of these statements underlines the cumulative effect of the scenes. Isaiah 60 is dominated by the irresistible and unconditional attraction of the God whose light dawns over Zion. The wealth of the world, along with the nations, their rulers and the children of Zion, is drawn in homage to this God, whose sanctuary is in Zion—whose city is Zion. This image overwhelms and absorbs the traces of the subjugated and humiliated destroyers and devourers that bring tribute—new children—to the vindicated mother Zion in Isa 49.[30]

In fact, the images of power and contravening power are not brought forward into this text. In his reading of this new vision in Isa 60, Leszek Ruszkowski draws on the concept of Judah as a "kingdom of priests" serving a community in which foreigners play the roles of traditional agricultural villagers (Isa 61:5–6).[31] Gary Stansell draws on the concept of the restoration of honor, which necessarily involves the restoration of means.[32] However it is described, this vision is driven by acknowledgment of Yhwh, and not by the prospect of dominion.

However it is understood, the center of Isa 60 is occupied by the details of rich gifts and service to the holy place where God is manifest. This universal homage will transform the holy place into a place suitable for the offering of sacrifices to the creator of the universe, the Holy One of Israel. The glori-

---

30. See the discussion of these aphoristic statements—60:6bβ, 7b, 9b, 10b(?), 13b—in Klaus Koenen, *Ethik und Eschatologie im Tritojesajabuch: Eine literarkritische und redaktionsgeschichtliche Studie* (WMANT 62; Neukirchen-Vluyn: Neukirchener Verlag, 1990), 137–57, 247–49, especially 151–53. Though Koenen treats these statements as reinterpretations from a later redactor, he accurately describes their cumulative effect.

31. *Pace* Paul Volz, *Jesaia II* (KAT 9; Leipzig: Deichert, 1931), 239 and Harry Meyer Orlinsky, "The So-Called 'Servant of the Lord' and 'Suffering Servant' in Second Isaiah," in *Studies on the Second Part of the Book of Isaiah* (VTSup 14; Leiden: Brill, 1967), 107. Leszek Ruszkowski, *Volk und Gemeinde im Wandel: Eine Untersuchung zu Jesaja 56–66* (FRLANT 191; Göttingen: Vandenhoeck & Ruprecht, 2000), 24–25, identifies a subtext of "Umkehrung der Rollen von Herrschenden und Beherrschten" in this vision of a "kingdom of priests" (cf. 62:12; 61:5–6; Exod 19:6), in which the temple is central, the wealth of nations is used for the cultus, and in which foreigners play the role of farmers and vintners.

32. In a number of studies from the point of view of "economic anthropology," Stansell has set these scenes in the context of a society in which economic activity is ethical, controlled by social convention. See especially Gary Stansell, "The 'Wealth of Nations': Tribute and Pilgrimage to Zion in Isaiah 60–61" (paper presented at the annual meeting of the SBL, Philadelphia, Pa., Nov. 2005); idem, "The Political Economy of the 'New Jerusalem' in Trito-Isaiah, Haggai and Zechariah" (paper presented at the annual meeting of the Society of Biblical Literature, Washington, D.C., November 2006).

fication of Zion is ultimately the glorification of the temple and the sacred precinct that surrounds it.

Isaiah 60:6–7

The first thing that is seen converging on the city is a horde of livestock, without specified attendants.[33] In the first of these two scenes, a massive caravan of camels "covers" (כסה *pi'el*) the city, followed by a flock of sheep and rams that "gather themselves" (קבץ *nip'al*). Like the nations and children, they come, presumably drawn by the light of the city. The widespread emphasis on the nations that bring gifts or even tribute is appropriate to ch. 49, but this is an overemphasis of a subtext in ch. 60.

The emphasis on the temple and its rites is immediately apparent. The first specification of the wealth of nations, "gold and frankincense" (זהב ולבונה), as well as the "praises" (תהלת v. 6b) have, among others, liturgical connotations. This is particularly true of v. 7b:

> All the flocks of Kedar will gather themselves to you,
> The rams of Nebaioth will be your ministers.
> They will ascend upon my acceptable altar. (60:7)[34]

Here, the sheep and goats "serve as ministers" and "ascend" (עלה *qal*) the altar.[35] This folkloristic, numinous scene, involving singing camels and self-sacrificing sheep and goats sets the tone for the descriptions that follow. The numinous character of this scene is underlined by the summation of this as a divine act, beautifying (פאר) the temple. Though it has been proved impossible to define the empirical status of the temple or the fortified city in this text, the temple and the city that surrounds and protects it like a sacred precinct are at the center of this narrative.

---

33. Note the tendency to emend toward Isa 56:7, where the emphasis is on those who make the sacrifices: Koole, *Isaiah: Part 3. Vol. 3: Isaiah 56–66*, 231–34, and citations there, and Beuken, *Jesaja. Deel IIIA*, 168.

34. Charles Cutler Torrey, *The Second Isaiah: A New Interpretation* (Edinburgh: T&T Clark, 1928), 448. Richard Challoner, ed., *The Holy Bible. Douay Rheims Version* (1609 ; repr. Rockford, Ill.: Tan Books, 1989) "upon my acceptable altar" = Vulgate, "super placabili altari meo," a literal translation of MT.

35. For details, see Koole, *Isaiah: Part 3. Vol. 3: Isaiah 56–66*, 232–33; Blenkinsopp, *Isaiah 56–66*, 206.

Isaiah 60:8ab, 9b // 49:12, 21

The metaphor of the descent of a flock of doves upon a cote is consistent with the previous metaphors that grant a degree of autonomy and perspicacity to the fauna of a civilized society. The enigmatic "these" (אלה 60:8) are elaborated in a phrase, "For the coastlands shall wait for me" (כי־לי איים יקוו 60:9aα—cf. 51:5; 49:23?), that is widely emended or reread.[36] As discussed earlier, "their(?) silver and gold" enwraps the children, who are at the center of the imagery in ch. 49, in the flood of wealth that is a central motif in ch. 60. The clearest thing about this mysterious, perplexing scene is its purpose. On behalf of the "name" of God, "the Holy One of Israel," this flotilla is an act of God, making Zion a "splendid place" (פארך).

Isaiah 60:10ab, 11ab // 49:8, 10; 49:9; [54:7]

At this point, in the metonyms of walls and gates, the apostrophe offers explicit images of the city that is the center of this mysterious gathering (60:10, 11). This contrasts with the minimal, allusive delineation of the ruined city in ch. 49 (vv. 16, 19). The foreign kings who "minister" (ישרתונך), in addition to raising substantial religio-historical problems (universalism, particularism; inclusivity, exclusivity et al.), echo the equally puzzling v. 7, where sacrificial rams "minister" (ישרתונך). Correspondingly, the characterization of (nations and) kings in ch. 49 is transformed in ch. 60. In this apostrophe to the city, the "foreigners" (here בני נכר) who are described in ch. 49 as overthrowers, devastators, devourers, and oppressors (49:17, 19, 26) now appear as servers and offerands and as the "builders" promised at 49:17.[37] They "build" either as patrons (Cyrus, "will build the city" יבנה עיר 45:1, 13[?]), or as laborers

---

36. Two emendations proposed by BHS exemplify reservations about this image of remote peoples driven by the hope that is central to this text. 1) For "To me" כִּי־לִי read "The ships of" כְּלֵי and 2) for "wait for" קוה I pi'el יְקַוּוּ read "gather" קוה II nip'al יִקָּוּוּ. Torrey, Second Isaiah, 448–49, defends the text, though he reads קוה pi'el as "gather."

37. At 49:17, the Tiberian Massoretes read the ambivalent consonantal text בניך as "your children" (בָּנָיִךְ), anticipating the restoration of the children later in the chapter. This confuses the image of the restoration of the status of the lamenting bride = the arrival of her "builders" (בֹּנָיִךְ), who will undo what was done by the "ruiners" (√הרס) and "devastators" (√חרב) of the city. See Goldingay, Isaiah 40–55, 188 and Blenkinsopp, Isaiah 40–55, 308–9, following the versions. Details for this and all text-critical discussion may be found in these commentaries, in Baltzer, Deutero-Isaiah: A Commentary on Isaiah 40–55, 3, and in Jan L. Koole, Isaiah: Part 3. Vol. 3: Isaiah 56–66 (HCOT; Leuven: Peeters, 2001).

(61:5—at 61:4, "those who mourn in Zion" אבלי ציון will restore the city)—the parallel of liturgical service (שרת) with building (בנה) suits the context of offerings brought to the city. The appearance of foreigners as instruments of restoration continues the numinous undertone of the whole text of ch. 60.[38] This undertone is a key element of the transformation of ch. 49 in ch. 60.

A gnomic statement, echoing 49:8 and particularly 54:7–8, expresses the theological basis for this scene. All restoration of this city is ultimately the work of God, and a sign of the beginning of a new future. The favor (רצון) and compassion (רחם) of God (60:10bβ), like the actions that express homage to God, underlie the scenes that follow.

The metonym of the gates (60:11), overturning the fundamental function of walls and gates, continues the apostrophe to the city. The gates, which are made necessary by the threat of foreigners, are perpetually open.[39] In these new circumstances, those who made them necessary are now oblation bearers who appear in such numbers that they break the routine of administering the city. The purpose of keeping the gates open is a summation of the scenes that have preceded, and that will follow this interlude:

> For bringing in the wealth of nations to you. (60:11)[40]

As in the preceding and following scenes, there is no specification of the ones who open the gates, or those by whose hands the wealth floods into the city or by whom the kings are led. It is not impossible that the builders of the walls from v. 10a are tacitly assumed, but the NRSV "so that the nations shall bring you their wealth" is clearly an over translation. This is another key element of the transformation of ch. 49 in this chapter. The emphasis here is upon the splendor of the city rather than upon the nemesis that has overtaken its destroyers. If "their kings led" (מלכיהם נהוגים) is read in the light of 49:10, "he who has compassion on them will lead them" (מרחמם ינהגם), the implications are substantially different.[41] In this mysterious scene, the foreigners do not play the same role as the foreigners in ch. 49. As Jon Levenson has pointed out, the mythos of the sanctuary at the center of the cosmos,

---

38. On this verse, see Beuken, *Jesaja. Deel IIIA*, 171.
39. On the question of the stem of פתח, see the discussion of the text in Watts, *Isaiah 34–66*, 293. Torrey, *Second Isaiah*, 450, 375.
40. Vv. 5, 6, 9, 11, 13—cf. the children in vv. 4, 9.
41. Duhm's popular emendation to "kings leading" נוהגים, *Das Buch Jesaia. Übersetzt und erklärt* (HKAT 3.1; Göttingen: Vandenhoeck & Ruprecht, 1892), 421 makes them menial laborers, as at 61:5.

the locus of the original creation and of the new creation, would account for the numinous character of these scenes, individually and collectively. In this world of discourse, the walls mark the boundary of the sacred precinct, and the sanctuary marks its center.[42]

Isaiah 60:12 // Jeremiah 27:8

In the place of the theological basis for this procession of nations and kings (כי v. 12), there is a malediction stating a principle of nemesis and retribution that would be more at home in ch. 49:

> For the nation and kingdom that will not serve you shall perish;
> those nations shall be utterly laid waste. (60:12)

Steck has argued persuasively that this verse is a transformation of the MT tradition of Jer 27:8, 10.[43]

Duhm is almost universally followed in rejecting this malediction upon nations that do not "serve" Zion (60:12), reading עבד, the acceptance of vassalage to Jerusalem's suzerainty, as a "late" gloss.[44] Paradoxically, the shadow of the excised text has influenced the reading of 60:10-11, bringing forward the dominant note of retaliation in 49:14-26 (49:22 // 60:4; 49:23).[45]

Isaiah 60:13ab [cf. 41:19, 1 Kings 5/ET4-5]

The brief emergence of the city in vv. 10-11 is an interlude in the account of the wealth that comes to Zion. The next scene (60:13) is an account of a gathering of trees. Though some of the trees echo materials assembled for the building of Solomon's temple,[46] all of them echo the list of trees that will flour-

---

42. Jon D. Levenson, "The Temple and the World," *JR* 64 (1984): 275-98, brings the insights of his Chicago colleague Mircea Eliade into the discussion of this text. Mircea Eliade, *The Sacred and the Profane* (New York: Harper & Row, 1961), especially 20-24.

43. Steck, locates this beyond the last stage of the Fortschreibung of Isaiah 60: "Der Grundtext in Jesaja 60 und sein Aufbau," *ZTK* 83 (1986): 262; *Studien zu Tritojesaja*, 50.

44. Duhm, *Das Buch Jesaia*, 421. Note that he identifies a cultic expression of this vassalage at Zech 14:16-19, which condemns the defeated nations that do not observe the Sukkoth rites in Jerusalem (השתוו not עבד).

45. Duhm, *Das Buch Jesaia*, 421: "Haben die Barbaren die Mauern zerstört, so müssen sie sie jetzt zur Frohn wieder aufbauen" (60:10).

46. See, e.g., "cedar from Lebanon" ארז אשר בלבנון 1 Kgs 5:13/ET 4:23 and "cedar

ish when the geography of the desert is miraculously transformed by floods and made hospitable to travelers (41:19; cf. 44:3–5; 49:9–12). Zimmerli treats the transfer of the locus of God's eschatological action from the wilderness to the temple as a fundamental motif in this rereading of Deutero-Isaiah—note that Steck transfers the flourishing of these trees to the temple courts.[47] This scene, in which trees "come" (בוא *qal*) into the city along with the camels, young camels, sheep, and rams has the same numinous undertone as the earlier gatherings to the new light that is dawning over Zion. Again, the goal of this numinous scene characterizes it as a divine action. The scenes described in this chapter provide the beauty appropriate to the sanctuary of the God of Israel: "to beautify (לפאר) the place of my sanctuary; and I will glorify (אכבד) where my feet rest" (60:13b; cf. 60:7, 9 [21]).

Isaiah 60:14ab // 49:23b, 26a; [49:7]

The human figures come to the surface again (60:14; cf. vv. 10–11), bringing other "children" (בנים), into the account (60:4, 9 בניך—note the colloquialism "foreigners" בני נכר at 60:10):

> They shall come bending low (שחוח) to you,
> the children of those who humiliated you (מעניך),
> and they shall bow down (והשתחוו) at the soles of your feet
> (על־כפות רגליך)
> all who despised you. (60:14a)

Echoes of 49:23 and 26[48] bring the shadow of the subjugation of formerly hostile nations over the text of ch. 60, beginning with the designation "humiliators" and "despisers." There are more specific links with ch. 49. "Those who humiliated you" (מעניך √ענה) echoes the sound of "your oppressors" (מוניך √ינה) whose cruel fate is the climax of their humiliation at 49:26. But the tone of retribution and subjugation is not the dominant tone in this text. "Bow down (והשתחוו) at the soles of your feet" (על־כפות רגליך 60:14) is a euphemistic echo of the ceremonial humiliation of the nurturing kings and queens

---

trees and cypress trees" בעצי ארזים ובעצי ברושים 5:22, 24/ET 5:8, 10; Clements, "Arise, Shine; For Your Light Has Come," 432.

47. Zimmerli, "Sprache Tritojesajas," 231–32. Odil Hannes Steck, "Jes 60,13: Bauholz oder Tempelgarten?" *BN* 30 (1985): 29–34 = idem, *Studien zu Tritojesaja*, 101–5, reads these as exotic trees that will flourish in the courts of the new temple.

48. Note the linking of 49:23 and 26 at 60:16b.

in ch. 49, "they shall bow down to you (יִשְׁתַּחֲווּ לָךְ), and lick the dust of your feet (וַעֲפַר רַגְלַיִךְ יְלַחֵכוּ 49:23)."[49]

In ch. 49, those who left the mother bereft of children bring new children to her. In ch. 49, those who destroyed the city come in subjugation to the devastated city of Zion. In ch. 60, the flood of wealth that comes for the splendor of the temple-city includes foreigners—includes the children of those who humiliated the city. At the end, the posture of these children is read as an act of homage to the city where Yhwh dwells—Zion, the locus of Isaiah's "Holy One of Israel."[50] The numinous quality of the narrative is manifest in the extension of the hallowing of the sanctuary into an acknowledgement that Zion and Yhwh, the Holy One of Israel are inseparably connected. This elaborates the homage to the temple (vv. 6b, 7b, 13) into an homage to its sacred precinct, the city that contains it. The wealth assembled and the homage paid to honor the city is homage to the Holy One of Israel. This is implicit in the apostrophe—in the voice of God—to the city. It is explicit in the homage to the "city of Yhwh," the "Zion of the Holy One of Israel" expressed in the voice of these abject supplicants. This universal homage to God and the temple in Zion continues Second Isaiah's understanding of God as the creator of the cosmos.

Isaiah 60:15; [49:14?]

When the apostrophe resumes, as discussed earlier (60:15a; cf. 60:5), the faint echo of the lamenting wife of 49:14a (עֲזָבָנִי) is enwrapped in an address (possibly hyperbolic) to an abandoned (עֲזוּבָה), deserted city (וְאֵין עוֹבֵר).[51] This suits the announcement of the transformation of the circumstances of the city, in terminology common in Isaiah:

> I will make you majestic forever, a joy from age to age. (60:15b)

---

49. Karl Elliger, "Der Prophet Tritojesaja," *ZAW* 49 (1931): 112–41, calls this a "(schwächere!) Abbild" of the Vorbild 49:23, 26. Note in passing that 60:14a LXX preserves a text or a hermeneutic that omits "all shall bow down at the soles of your feet (וְהִשְׁתַּחֲווּ עַל־כַּפּוֹת רַגְלַיִךְ)."

50. Note 49:7: "Kings shall see and stand up (וְקָמוּ), princes, and they shall prostrate themselves, (וְיִשְׁתַּחֲווּ) because of the Lord, who is faithful, the Holy One of Israel, (קְדֹשׁ יִשְׂרָאֵל) who has chosen you."

51. Note that the LXX ὁ βοηθῶν, reads "no helper" (עוֹזֵר) for "no one passing by" (עוֹבֵר), strengthening the metaphor of a woman.

This serves as a summation of the lengthy description of the assembling of gifts that transform Zion into a fabulous city.

Isaiah 60:16ab // 49:23a, 26ab

This faint echo of the metaphor of a lamenting wife, hidden to the vanishing point, gives way to a vivid somatic metaphor of Zion as an infant nurtured by the full breasts of nations and kings. In this striking image, which often embarrasses commentators,[52] the "wealth of nations" (חיל גוים) is transformed into the "milk of nations" (חלב גוים):

> You shall suck the milk of nations,
> you shall suck the breasts of kings; (60:16a)

This section opened at 60:4, with its cross links that brought 49:18 and 49:22 into the same perspective. It closes with 60:16, which again brings 49:18 and 49:22 into the same perspective. At 60:14, the description of the homage of the nations brought forward and transformed the image from 49:23b. Now, 60:16 has a number of cross links that bring 49:23a, c and 49:26 into the same perspective, reading:

> Kings shall be your wet-nurses,
> and their queens your nursing mothers. (49:23a)

This is a transformation—or elaboration—of the metaphor of God as a nursing mother who will never forget her child in the word of comfort at 49:15. But more important, it is a peculiar reading of אמן√ as "nurse" at 49:23: "Kings will be the ones who nurse you" (ינק // אמניך).[53]

This image, in which the feeding of a nursling evokes the acknowledgment of God, is a softened echo of 49:26, where a feeding frenzy ("eat their own flesh בשר ... drink their own blood" 49:26) evokes the acknowledgment of God by Zion's "oppressors" (מוניך). The violence that evokes acknowledg-

---

52. See Robert Alter's discussion of the somatic metaphors in 49:18–23, *The Art of Biblical Poetry* (New York: Basic Books, 1985), 158–61; see his more general discussion on pp. 139–47. The bowdlerization of the text in the LXX: "You shall eat the wealth of kings" καὶ πλοῦτον βασιλέων φάγεσαι (= ואכלת חיל מלכים) anticipates this embarrassment. This eating may be a transformation of the metaphor of eating at 49:26: "your oppressors shall eat their own flesh" (והאכלתי את־מוניך את־בשרם).

53. Berges, *Das Buch Jesaja*, 442: "intensiviert Tritojesaja seine Vorlage von 49:23, die von der Ammenfunktion der Könige ... gesprochen hatte."

ment of God from "all flesh" (בשר 49:26b, a grisly echo of this feeding frenzy, v. 26a) is subsumed and transformed. Here, this nurturing and enrichment, the wealth and homage that has been brought into the city, evokes Zion's acknowledgment of Yнwн, in contrast to 49:23, where Zion's acknowledgment of Yнwн is brought about by the subjugation and ceremonial humiliation of Zion's devastators and destroyers. Here Zion's acknowledgment of Yнwн is not a response to the subjugation of the nations (49:23b), but to the support and nourishment of Zion by the kings and queens who accompany her children:

> and you shall know that I am the Lord
> your Savior and your Redeemer,
> the Mighty One of Jacob. (60:16; 49:23)

The world that was brought to acknowledge the Lord in ch. 49 is now included in Zion's acknowledgment of the Lord.

Whether Isa 60 is read diachronically as a substantial redaction of Isa 49 or synchronically as quite a different poem that may be laid beside Isa 49, there are significant differences between the role of the nations and the role of the children in the two texts. There is also a striking difference in tenor between the two texts. The tendency to subordinate the reading of Isa 60 to the reading of Isa 49, and particularly the tendency to allow the metaphors of Isa 49 to control the reading of the echoes in Isa 60, obscures the radical differences between these texts. The shadow of Duhm's concept of the epigone, the lesser imitator of a master, still tends to obscure our reading of Isa 60 as an independent and audacious reading.

In this new proclamation, whatever "Judean nationalism" may be found in ch. 49 does not survive,[54] even in the form of "religious nationalism."[55] Though it is clear that the motifs of subjugation and punishment have been transformed, the nations—like the children of the diaspora—are not at the center of Isa 60. The homage to the temple, and to the city that contains it, overshadows the image of the pilgrimage of the nations.[56] Jon Levenson's gen-

---

54. Orlinsky, "The So-called 'Servant of the Lord,'" 107, cited above.
55. Volz, *Jesaia II*, 239: "Das Nationale ist stärker als das Religiöse." Note also the lists of tribute from "étrangers soumis" cited in Pierre Grelot, "Un parallèle Babylonien d'Isaïe LX et du Psaume LXXII," *VT* 7 (1957): 321.
56. See Gerhard von Rad, "Die Stadt auf dem Berge," 220–21, and particularly Antonin Causse, *La vision de la nouvelle Jérusalem [Esaïe LX] et la signification sociologique des assemblées de fête et des pèlerinages dans l'orient sémitique. Mélanges syriens ouferts à monsieur René Dussaud* (Bibliothèque archéologique et historique; Haut-commissariat de la République française

eral observation that "Third Isaiah sees the world as a sanctuary" is critical for understanding the controlling motif in the new proclamation in Isa 60.[57]

In the world of this text, the nations offer these rich gifts unconditionally. At the same time no conditions are imposed on the nations or the children that come to the splendor of this dawning light—except a desire to enhance the sanctuary that houses the source of this light.[58] The world of this text is inconsistent with the overwhelming emphasis on a virtuous subcommunity in Isa 56–66.[59] A number of "synchronic" readings require that the reading of Isa 60 must be controlled by this immediate or general setting in the book of Isaiah. O'Connell's summation is drawn entirely from the setting of Isa 60: "Yhwh will admit into future Zion only the faithful and just."[60] In fact, Isa 60 is driven by the irresistible attraction of Zion—the sacred precinct of the temple. The entire cosmos—the wealth, the people, the flora and fauna of the world—is drawn toward its true center. This controlling motif is lost in such a narrowly defined synchronic reading. In contrast to this style of "synchronic" reading, a "diachronic" reading allows the reading of Isa 60 without this loss of its distinctive voice. Ruszkowski's analysis of the audacious vision in Isa 60 as the starting point of a "chain reaction" that produced Isa 56–66 has the virtue of allowing a reading of Isa 60 that is not controlled by the reading of

---

en Syrie et au Liban, Service des antiquités 30; vol. 2; Paris: P. Geutner, 1939), 741.

57. Levenson, "The Temple and the World," 275–98. Shawn Zelig Aster, "Jerusalem Replaces Babylon: The Neo-Babylonian Background to Isaiah 60" (paper presented at the annual meeting of the SBL, San Diego, Calif., 2007), emphasized parallels with the cosmic undergirding of the temple in Babylonian texts.

58. Elliger, "Der Prophet Tritojesaja," 122, states this theologically: Isa 60 speaks of "Heil ohne irgendeine Bedingungen."

59. Marvin Sweeney offers a perceptive analysis of the centrality of the temple in these chapters, administered by the Zadokite clients of the Persian rulers. Marvin A. Sweeney, "The Priesthood and the Proto-Apocalyptic Reading of Prophetic and Pentateuchal Texts," in Sweeney, *Form and Intertextuality*, 245–47; idem, "The Book of Isaiah as a Prophetic Torah," in ibid., 13–27; idem, "Prophetic Exegesis in Isaiah 65–66," in Broyles and Evans, *Writing and Reading the Scroll of Isaiah*, 455–74. See the statement of the issue in Marvin A. Sweeney, "Zechariah's Debate with Isaiah," in *The Changing Face of Form Criticism for the Twenty-First Century* (ed. Marvin A. Sweeney and Ehud Ben Zvi; Grand Rapids: Eerdmans, 2003), 335–50. It is not certain, however, that the ethical teaching of the Zadokite priests, documented in his studies of Isa 56:1–8 and 66, must control the interpretation of this chapter.

60. Robert H. O'Connell, *Concentricity and Continuity: The Literary Structure of Isaiah* (JSOTSup 188; Sheffield: Sheffield Academic Press, 1994). See also Childs, *Isaiah*, 390–91; Koole, *Isaiah: Part 3. Vol. 3: Isaiah 56–66*, 222–23; Beuken, *Jesaja. Deel IIIA*, 164.

the rest of Isa 56–66.⁶¹ Whatever the future of what Gary Stansell has called an "uneasy partnership" between "diachronic" and "synchronic" reading strategies, the present state of diachronic (viz. redactional) reading does more justice to this numinous utopian vision.⁶²

Something radically new is here. If utopian narrative is understood as a vision of an impossible future, challenging the limitations of present reality and affirming possibilities beyond the comprehension of present reality, then this can be read as utopian narrative.⁶³ The folkloristic quality of the descriptions underlines the strange image of foreign rulers who make unconditional grants and the equally strange image of foreign worshippers who enter sacred space without condition. These two images are the starting point for understanding the concrete limitations of present reality. The numinous awe of Zion's temple, where what was begun with the creation will be brought to its conclusion is the starting point for understanding the concrete possibilities that lie beyond the comprehension of present reality.⁶⁴ Ernst Bloch speaks of the utopian affirmations implicit in the construction of a sanctuary:

> We … summon what is not, build into the blue, and build ourselves into the blue, and there seek the true, the real, where the merely factual disappears—*incipit vita nova*.⁶⁵

---

61. Ruszkowski, *Volk und Gemeinde im Wandel*, 22 et passim.

62. Gary Stansell, "Isaiah 60–62 as the 'Kernel' of Isaiah 56–66 in Light of Synchronic and Diachronic Perspectives" (paper presented at the annual meeting of the Society of Biblical Literature, San Diego, Calif., 2007), describes this eloquently: "these chapters, when specially singled out within the larger whole and invested with a particular thematic and compositional priority, may become problematic for a reading that stresses unity and the final form of the book."

63. See Ehud Ben Zvi, ed., *Utopia and Dystopia in Prophetic Literature* (Publications of the Finnish Exegetical Society 92; Helsinki: Finnish Exegetical Society, 2006), especially the introductory essay, Steven James Schweitzer, "Utopia and Literary Theory: Some Preliminary Observations," 13–26.

64. Levenson, "The Temple and the World," 275–98, links of the creation of the world with the building of the temple—and links the temple with the power of the creator to transform all things.

65. Ernst Bloch, *The Spirit of Utopia* (trans. Anthony A. Nassar; Stanford: Stanford University Press, 2000), 3.

From Desolation to Delight: The Transformative Vision of Isaiah 60–62

Carol J. Dempsey

Introduction

Isaiah 60–62 presents a glorious vision of transformation and defines the mission of the prophet who, as the one called by God, will proclaim the vision and will work to bring it to fruition. This vision of transformation does not begin in Isa 60–62; rather, it is a golden thread that runs throughout the book of Isaiah as a whole. This essay will try to do three things. First, from a literary and theological perspective, it will explore the vision and role of the prophet as presented in Isa 60–62. Second, it will offer a comment on how Isa 60–62, though linked to Isa 40–55, is distinct from Second Isaiah and contains echoes from Isa 1–39. And third, the essay will offer a comment on the links between redemption and restoration of the natural world, and the role that Jerusalem as a city and a people, plays in the unfolding vision of the new heavens and the new earth (Isa 65:17ff.). One sees this vision set forth earlier in Isa 2:2–4 and again in Isa 60–62.

Isaiah 60–62: A Defining Vision, A Liberating Mission

Recent events in the history of our planet have shown us the absolute agony and heartbreak of thousands and thousands of people who have lost their loved ones, their homes, their treasured possessions, their cities, their homelands, their sense of place, and even their sense of identity. Tragedies have come for people in Thailand, in Sri Lanka, in New Orleans, in Pakistan, in China, in Afghanistan, and in Iraq. Entire regions of our world have been devastated by a Tsunami, a hurricane, an earthquake, or the horrors of war. People who have experienced these tragedies have three things in common, namely, dashed hopes and dreams, a profound sense of displacement, and the struggle and challenge to re-establish their lives as they resettle in the land they once called "home."

People who are faced with reconstruction out of ruins can understand what the ancient Jewish people felt. After the Babylonian conquest, Jewish survivors were faced with the same challenges in their homeland: resettlement, reconstruction, and debilitating despair that often accompanies the aftermath of tragedy and loss. Their loss affected them in a host of ways, physically, especially, and emotionally, spiritually, psychologically, and economically. Heard in the context of the period of Jewish resettlement in the land after the Babylonian conquest, Isa 60–62 assures an ancient community that indeed God's transformative power is at work in their midst, saving, redeeming, liberating, renewing, and making all things new. What the poet Isaiah proclaimed to his people so many years ago has the potential of finding a place in the hearts of people today as we continue to listen for that word of hope, that vision of grace that makes age-old Isaiah ever new.[1]

Turning now to the text itself, Isa 60–62 is a vision of hope and promise that can be outlined as follows:

60:1–7	Address to Jerusalem
60:8–22	List of Promises
vv. 8–16	Concerning Jerusalem and the Nations
vv. 17–18	Concerning Jerusalem
vv. 19–22	Concerning God's Relationship with Jerusalem and the People's Transformation
61:1–4	Confession: The Prophet's Vocation and Mission
61:5–9	Divine Promises to Jerusalem and the Nations
61:10–11	Jerusalem's Response
62:1–5	Prophet's Proclamation on Behalf of Jerusalem
62:6a–b	Divine Address to Jerusalem
62:6c–9	Prophet's Address to the Watchmen
62:10–12	Prophet's Address to Jerusalem

---

1. John N. Oswalt (*The Book of Isaiah: Chapters 40–66* [NICOT; Grand Rapids: Eerdmans, 1998], 534) has argued persuasively that chs. 60–62 form the centerpiece of Isa 56–66. These chapters "show Israel's final destiny as the restored people of God in whom the reality of God's salvation is displayed to all the earth."

The speakers in all three chapters are either the prophet, God, or the prophet quoting God as in Isa 62:8b–9. The focus of Isa 60 is Jerusalem; in Isa 61 the focus is on the poet himself and the people of Zion; and in Isa 62, the focus shifts back to Jerusalem until Isa 62:12, the final verse in the Isa 60–62 segment. This final verse brings the entire segment to a crescendo. Jerusalem and its people, in process of being fully glorified and transformed by God, are becoming a reflection of each other, and the two are, in essence, becoming one. Unifying themes among the three chapters include light, salvation, glory, redemption, restoration, righteousness, mercy, and transformation. Let us turn now to Isa 60, our first segment.

Isaiah 60:1–22

With gusto and great enthusiasm, the poet opens the first part of the poem, Isa 60:1–7, with a double imperative, "arise," "shine" in Isa. 60:1, which begins the first subunit—Isa 60:1–3—of the poem's first unit—Isa 60:1–7. The use of the second person pronoun "you" and "your" used in Isa 60:1 and throughout the chapter adds a personal tone to the poem, but to whom or to what do these pronouns refer? The antecedent is not clear. It seems likely that the one being addressed is Jerusalem/Zion, judging from Isa 60:11–18 especially, but might not it also be a subtle embedded suggestive reference to the people of Zion as well, eclipsed here, and brought into full view in Isa 61 and Isa 62? This first verse whets our appetite and captures our imagination:

> Arise, shine; for your light has come
> and the glory of the Lord has risen upon you. (Isa 60:1)

Through the use of past perfect tenses, "has come" and "has risen," otherwise known as tenses of vision or the prophetic perfect, the poet assures the one addressed—Jerusalem—that what he is proclaiming will surely come to pass. In Isa 60:2 the poet sets up a contrast. Darkness will cover the earth and a thick cloud the peoples. The phrase, "but on you," signals a shift, and once again, the poet proclaims a wondrous message to Jerusalem:

> but on you, the Lord will dawn
> and his glory will be seen upon you.

Characteristic of theophanies, God's כבד, "glory," presents itself as an overwhelming majestic reality (Exod 24:17; 33:22; Num 14:10; 1 Kgs 8:11; Ezek 1:28; Isa 4:5; Hab 2:14). Only God is "glorious" (Isa 24:33; 40:5; 42:8, 12; 48:11;

58:8; 59:19), for "glory" belongs to God alone (Isa 2:10), which God will share with God's people (Isa 11:10; 43:7) but not with idols (Isa 42:8; 48:11). The backdrop of darkness covering the earth and a heavy cloud that enwraps the people make the brightness of Jerusalem ever more brilliant. Significant here is the fact that Jerusalem will be glorious because of God's glory. As God's glory rises upon Jerusalem, so Jerusalem arises glorious. Thus, Jerusalem becomes the embodiment of God's glory.[2] Such beauty, the poet declares, will have profound consequences:

> And nations will walk to your light
> and kings to the brightness of your dawning. (Isa 60:3)

Jerusalem, as the embodiment of God's glory, will be an alluring presence, a leader of nations and rulers. In Isa 60:3 we hear the familiar strains of Isa 9:2b:

> The people who walked in darkness
> have seen a great light;
> those who lived in a land of deep darkness—
> on them light has shined.

Together Isa 9:2b and Isa 60:1–3 present variations on a theme that now opens up the possibility that in Isa 60:1–3 Jerusalem is becoming universally messianic (cf. Isa 2:1–4 and Mic 4:1–5). Thus, I suggest that Isa 60:1–3 is not about deliverance from Babylon, sin, or guilt. Rather, these verses are about Jerusalem's transformation by and into God's glory. Jerusalem is becoming the transparent glory of God and, in so doing, is becoming a beacon, banner, and signal of hope for all peoples.

Like the first part of Isa 60:1–7, the second part, Isa 60:4–7, also opens up with a double imperative, "lift up," and "look all around." Here the poet advances his polyvalent themes introduced in Isa 60:1–3. Because of Jerusalem's alluring presence and beauty, she will be attractive not only to other peoples but also to her own who will gather together and come to her—her sons and her daughters. Verse 4a is identical to Isa 49:18a, and heard in the context of Isa 49:14–23, Isa 60:4 picks up the theme of gathering first heard in Isa 49:14–23. Thus, Jerusalem has a world-wide, universal role in the lives of all peoples (cf. Isa 25:6–7). Isaiah 60:5 is consequential. Only when Jerusalem's "own" return to her will she see and be radiant. Only then will her heart

---

2. For further discussion on the imagery of light and the glory of God, see Joseph Blenkinsopp, *Isaiah 56–66* (AB 19B; New York: Doubleday, 2003), 211.

thrill and rejoice. For Jerusalem, her transformed self is not the source of her exhilaration; rather, the return of those whom she loves deeply—her exiled sons and daughters—is what will make her heart swell (cf. Isa 43:6–7), along with the abundance and wealth that will be given to her by other nations (Isa 60:5–7). Gifts will include choice animals and precious treasures—gold and frankincense (Isa 60:6). The reference to Sheba recalls 1 Kgs 10:10, which describes the queen of Sheba bringing exotic tribute to enhance King Solomon's splendor (1 Kgs 10:1–13).

The reference to "gold" and "frankincense" points forward to Matt 2:11, which describes the wise people from the Gentile world bringing these sorts of gifts to the Christ child, thereby acknowledging him as Messiah. As Walter Brueggemann has pointed out, "For as long as anyone can remember, Israel had paid imperial tribute to others—the Assyrians, the Babylonians, the Persians—all money going out. Now the process is reversed."[3] Heard in the context of 1 Kgs 10:1–13 and Matt 2:11, Isa 60:5–7 has both royal and messianic overtones.

The allusions to Midian and Midian's firstborn, Ephah, recalls Gen 25 where both are described as descendants of Abraham through Keturah. Midian, also a former dreaded spoiler of the Israelites (Judg 6:1), has become the source of gifts, and here we begin to see the transforming effects that transformed Jerusalem has on other peoples. Two other references in Isa 60:7, namely, "Kedar" and "Nebaioth" also appear in Gen 25 where they are identified as the children of Ishmael. Midian and Sheba shall proclaim the praise of God (Isa 60:6), and with the acceptable offerings of Kedar and Nebaioth, God will glorify God's house. Thus, the preeminence of God is inextricably linked to the vitality of Jerusalem, and vice versa. Jerusalem, then, becomes the central place of gathering and homecoming for all God's people. Finally, John Oswalt makes an astute observation about the word "house" in Isa 60:7: "The reference to house here is already moving toward the figurative, as is made plain in Mal 2:11. God will glorify [God's] people (Isa 60:9) by imparting [God's] righteousness to them (Isa 60:21). They are [God's] temple; in their beauty, [God's] beauty will be seen."[4] Thus, the understanding of Jerusalem as both place and people, together with God's temple as both place and people, begins to unfold as the poet's vision of transformation and its effects take on ever more subtle and deeper nuances.

---

3. See Walter Brueggemann, *Isaiah 40–66* (Westminster Bible Companion; Louisville, Ky.: Westminster John Knox, 1998), 205.

4. See Oswalt, *The Book of Isaiah: Chapters 40–66*, 542.

The second part of Isa 60, Isa 60:8–22, is a list of divine promises. Isaiah 60:8–16 concerns divine promises directed toward Jerusalem and the nations. In these verses, we hear God speaking through the poet. The poet opens this next section with a double simile couched in a double rhetorical question:

> Who are these that fly like a cloud?
> and like doves to their cotes? (Isa 60:8)

Here the poet's attention turns to a fleet of ships as he continues to describe in greater detail the gathering and homecoming event (Isa 60:8–9) foreshadowed in Isa 60:3–4. The procession toward Jerusalem is ready to begin, with the ships of Tarshish in the lead, bringing Jerusalem's children. Thus, the nations and Jerusalem's "own" will journey together to Jerusalem, a vision hinted at in Isa 2:1–4 and Mic 4:1–5. The journey, however, will not commence at the nations' or the exiles' initiative. It will begin at God's initiative, for the sake of God's name, and for the sake of God *because* God has glorified Jerusalem (Isa 60:9). Thus, the poet informs Jerusalem that she—in her glorified state—will be a means by which God will draw all peoples to God's self; Jerusalem will be the living testimony to God's transformative and transforming power, a banner of restoration and redemption, an invitation to salvation, and a sign of hope for all. In coming to Jerusalem, all will encounter not only God's work and ways but also God (Isa 60:13). The phrase "the glory of Lebanon" that will come to Jerusalem already hints at God's transformative work among the nations (cf. Isa 29:17; 32:15; 33:9; and 35:2).

The theme of divine promise continues in Isa 60:10–16. Here the poet outlines how the nations will contribute to the restoration of Jerusalem. They will build up her walls, and their kings will minister to her (Isa 60:10). The nations will also bring to Jerusalem their wealth (Isa 60:11), inclusive of Lebanon bringing its choice lumber (Isa 60:13) to beautify the place of God's sanctuary, the place where God's feet rest, the place that will also be glorified (cf. Ezek 43:7; Zech 14:4). Thus, the poet promises Jerusalem that not only will her walls be rebuilt but also her sanctuary, a reference that presumes the rebuilding of Jerusalem's temple. In 1 Kgs 5:1, Hiram of Lebanon was the primary builder of Solomon's temple. Now, goods from Lebanon will contribute to the enhancement of the sanctuary of the rebuilt temple.

In Isa 60:14, the poet envisions a time of reconciliation and healing for Jerusalem and the nations. These events will take place at the initiative of the nations' descendants. The descendants of those who once oppressed and despised Jerusalem (see, e.g., Isa 34:1–17; 36; Jer 4:11–18; 34:1–7; 39:1–10) will perform acts of respect and deference: they will bend low and bow down at Jerusalem's feet (Isa 60:14a–b; cf. Gen 19:2; 2 Sam 9:8).[5] Such acts also reverse the homage paid to idols on the part of both Israel and the nations (see, e.g., Isa 2:6–8; 44:17). The nations' descendants will also call Jerusalem "the City of Yhwh—Zion of the Holy One of Israel." The appellation that the nations' descendants will ascribe to Jerusalem indicates the bondedness that exists between Jerusalem and God, and the descendants' recognition and acknowledgement of Israel's God in whose image and likeness Jerusalem has become. Jerusalem, then, will become a transparent reality of who God is and God's work. By affirming Jerusalem, the nations indirectly affirm Israel's God. Such affirmation and acknowledgement would fulfill God's hope expressed in Isa 45:20–25.

God's divine promises to Jerusalem reach their climax in Isa 60:15–16. Here the poet uses contrasting images to covey to Jerusalem that the old order is past with respect to her life. God's restorative and transformative work will be enduring, and Jerusalem will be "majestic forever" and a "joy from age to age" (Isa 60:15; cf. Isa 33:20–22). Of note, this is quite a different image of Jerusalem who once experienced itself to be full of corruption and depravity (Isa 1:21–31), and who, as the biblical writer of Isaiah imagines, has been chastised by God (Isa 1:24–26; 3:1–26; 60:10). In v. 16, the poet assures Jerusalem of choice care that will be offered by the nations and their leaders. The poet's imagery is suggestive of reconciliation between Jerusalem and the rest of the peoples and powers of the world. In Isa 60:16b, the poet drives home God's central purpose and message to Jerusalem:

> and you shall know that I, the Lord, am your Savior
> and your Redeemer, the Mighty one of Jacob.

Jerusalem will come to know God as Savior and Redeemer, a gift that Jerusalem will receive, meant to be a catalyst for the transformation of the world.

The poet continues his focus on Jerusalem in Isa 60:17–18. Whereas the nations will bring their treasures to Jerusalem (Isa 60:6 and 13), now God pledges to bring treasures to Jerusalem as well (Isa 60:17a–b). Added to this promise is another divine promise:

---

5. Some scholars, e.g., J. Alec Motyer (*The Prophecy of Isaiah* [Downers Grove, Ill.: InterVarsity, 1993], 497) and Brueggemann (*Isaiah 40–66*, 208) argue that the gestures of bending low and bowing down at the feet are signs of humiliation, submissiveness, and subordination. While this may be true in some contexts, I would argue here that in the context of Isa 60, these gestures indicate respect, especially in light of Jerusalem being glorified by God.

> I will appoint Peace as your overseer
> and Righteousness as your taskmaster. (Isa 60:17c)

The power that is envisioned to reign over Jerusalem will be virtuous and not oppressive as in the days of Egypt. Such imagery suggests the presence of the reign of God (cf. Isa 32:16–20), an image developed further in Isa 60:18 that speaks of the enduring absence of violence, devastation, and destruction.[6]

The final verses of Isa 60 speak of a relationship that Jerusalem and all the peoples will enjoy with God. These verses are filled with promise and hope. No longer will Jerusalem need the light of the great luminaries. God's light will be Jerusalem's "everlasting light," a message that the poet repeats twice (Isa 60:19, 20) and one that echoes Isa 60:1–3. God will be Jerusalem's "glory" (Isa 60:19bc), and Jerusalem's people "shall be righteous" and "shall possess the land forever" (Isa 60:21a–b). The use of the second person pronouns to describe "your God" and "your people" indicate relationship, bondedness, and intimacy. The reference to the people being the "shoot" that God planted recalls Isa 11:1. The shoot that came out of the stump of Jesse, that was planted by God, has now become God's righteous ones—the work of God's own hands—the ones whom God will continue to transform (Isa 60:22) and through whom God will be glorified (Isa 60:21). This final verse in Isa 60 shifts the focus from Jerusalem to the nations—to all peoples, with Jerusalem included as part of the whole. Having transformed the city, God will now transform all of Jerusalem's people, and they will be empowered beyond their size. The verse speaks of the fullness of the messianic age. This new creation that God is bringing into existence will be entirely God's work.

In sum, with literary skill and deep theological understanding, the poet of Isa 60 holds out a marvelous vision for Jerusalem and for the nations. The poet makes these points:

1. the God of Israel is the same God as the God of the nations.
2. the divine work of transformation with its fruits of redemption, salvation, and restoration is meant not only for Jerusalem, and by extension, the Jewish people, but also for nations and peoples far and wide. Isaiah's divine vision is a universal one.
3. God's transformative work is meant to be a sign of God's enduring fidelity and presence to all.
4. God's final efforts in creation and human history are for recreation and not destruction, for peace and not violence.

---

6. This imagery is also found in Isa 32:17.

5. Jerusalem, home to exiles and foreigners alike, is a symbol of hope. God can change apostate, idolatrous, unjust, forsaken, and woeful Jerusalem into an image of grace and glory and beauty. God can, therefore, in God's time do the same to the rest of the world as well.
6. Israel's prophets and their prophetic messages are meant not only for their own people but also for all peoples throughout the world. The prophetic word, however, is spoken first to one's own and then to everyone else.

To Jerusalem and to the nations far and wide, the poet becomes a sign of hope and the standard bearer of good news, both of which are expressions of the prophetic vocation and mission at its best. For listeners today, the poet reminds us that despite our failings and feeble attempts to change our ways, and in the midst of global upheaval and chaos, God's transformative spirit and mercy remain ever constant and ever active.[7]

Isaiah 61:1-11

In Isa 61, the poet continues the theme of hope and envisions a restored and transformed people, a vision introduced at the end of Isa 60:21-22. The chapter can be divided into four units: Isa 61:1-4, Isa 61:5-9, 10, and Isa 61:11.

In Isa 61:1-4 the poet is the speaker. He confesses to his own relationship with the Holy One of Israel. This relationship is the foundation of his vocation, his mission as a prophet, and the message he bears (Isa 61:1-4). With gusto, the poet declares that the Spirit of the Lord God is upon him because the Lord has anointed him. The poet's description recalls 1 Sam 16:1-13, David's anointing. Immediately after Samuel anointed David, the Spirit of God rushed upon him (1 Sam 16:13; cf. 1 Kgs 19:16; Isa 45:1). The presence of the Spirit upon the poet recalls Isa 42:1-4 that speaks of God putting God's spirit upon the servant. Empowered by God's Spirit, the poet unveils his mission that comes to life through a list of infinitive phrases:

- to bring good news to the oppressed (cf. Isa 40:9; 41:27; 52:7; 60:6)
- to bind up the brokenhearted
- to proclaim liberty to the captives (cf. Isa 58:6) and release to the captives

---

7. For further study on Isa 60, see Gregory J. Polan, O.S.B., "Zion, The Glory of the Holy One of Israel: A Literary Analysis of Isaiah 60," in *Imagery and Imagination in Biblical Literature* (ed. Lawrence Boadt and Mark Smith; CBQMS 32; Washington, D.C.: The Catholic Biblical Association of America, 2001), 50-71.

- to proclaim the year of the Lord's favor and a day of vengeance of our God
- to comfort all who mourn
- to provide for those who mourn in Zion—
- to give them a garland instead of ashes.... (Isa 61:1c–3a)

This list of infinitive phrases describes the transformative actions that the poet, with God's Spirit, will initiate.

Scholars have argued that the ministry and mission will be to "the weak, the powerless, and the marginalized to restore them to full function in a community of well-being and joy."[8] While this may be true, I would argue further that in the context of Isa 60–62, the verses also pertain to the nations—the peoples—who have oppressed Israel because of their own sinful attitudes and ways, and who themselves are held captive and imprisoned by their own wickedness for which they have received their "just deserts" from Israel's God (see, e.g., Isa 14–23). They too have experienced broken heartedness, mourning, and lamentation, though their voices are not heard in this regard in the biblical text. "The year of the Lord's favor" in Isa 61:2 refers to the jubilee year,[9] a time of forgiveness of debt (Lev 25). Here the jubilee year is contrasted with a day of vengeance of God. Though the latter reference may seem troubling, and it is, I suggest that heard in the context of the jubilee year, the connotation is more positive. The "day of vengeance of the Lord" will be a time of restoration, of returning to people what is rightfully theirs but was lost to another through circumstances beyond one's control (also see Isa 34:8). The God of justice will indeed restore to another what is rightfully his—salvation and redemption from sin, from death, with restoration to life being the final act and gift.

The triple use of "instead" helps to create a further series of contrasts in Isa 61:3 and signals the radical transformation that will take place among the people. A garland, the oil of gladness, and the mantle of praise will replace ashes, mourning, and a faint spirit (Isa 61:3). In Isa 61:3b-4, the poet's fourfold repetitious use of the word "they," followed by various positive descriptions, depicts the strength and vigor of the transformed people who will aid in bringing Israel and all its inhabitants back to life. The shoot that God once planted in Isa 60:21 will become oaks of righteousness, the planting of the

---

8. See, e.g., Brueggemann, *Isaiah 40–66*, 213.

9. For additional study on the jubilee year, see Richard Lowery, *Sabbath and Jubilee* (Understanding Biblical Themes; St. Louis: Chalice, 2000); Oswalt, *The Book of Isaiah: Chapters 40–66*, 561–68; and Brueggemann, *Isaiah 40–66*, 212–15.

Lord to display God's glory (see Isa 60:21; 61:3b). Those who are restored will, in turn, become restorers and repairers (cf. Isa 57:12).

Isaiah 61:5–7 are a series of divine promises that God addresses to both the people of Israel, and specifically the Judahites (Isa 61:5–6) and to the nations (Isa 61:7). In Isa 60:5–7, 9, 13, the poet describes the nations bringing all sorts of gifts and treasures to Jerusalem. Now for the first time, the people will "enjoy the wealth of the nations" and "glory in their riches" (Isa 61:6). A people transformed, they will now be holy to God, leaders in positions of service as priests and ministers (Isa 61:6). Furthermore, the people will receive a double portion of what God has promised them because they have already received a double dose of divine chastisement for their transgressions (Isa 40:2).

In Isa 61:8–9, the poet provides a glimpse into who God is and who God's people will be. Israel's God is a God of justice, fidelity, mercy, and covenant loyalty (Isa 61:8). God's transformative work will be continuous, signaled by the reference to Israel's descendants and offspring who themselves will be a people whom the Lord has blessed (Isa 61:9).

In Isa 61:10, the poet, as a representative of his community, expresses the people's sentiments evoked by God's goodness. He/they are a joyous people, reveling in God because God has done great things on his/their behalf: God has clothed the people in salvation and righteousness. The marital similes in Isa 61:10c hint at covenant relationship and union that will exist between God and the people. The concluding Isa 61:11 offers a word of hope and certainty. Just as the natural world brings forth its blossoms, so God will cause righteousness and praise—Jerusalem—the people—to spring up before the nations. Jerusalem's and the people's fate are divinely sealed.

In sum, Isa 61 develops themes that were introduced earlier in Isa 60. Additionally, in this chapter, the poet who has been acting prophetically in Isa 60 now discloses the power behind his person, mission, and ministry, and lays claims to his vocation which, ironically, is also Jerusalem's and the people's vocation—to be and bring a ray of hope to all.

Isaiah 62:1–12

Isaiah 62 continues the thought present in Isa 60 and 61, and develops several themes introduced earlier, including those of light, glory, and transformation. The first unit, Isa 62:1–5, is the poet's proclamation on behalf of Jerusalem. He expresses his proclamation with a sense of determination and urgency (Isa 62:1). What God will do for Zion will capture the attention and imagination of the world community (see also Isa 49:7; 52:15; 60:3, 10–11, 16). As in Isa 60 and 61, the poet offers Jerusalem a vision, a message of hope: Jerusalem will be glorified, will receive a new name (Isa 62:2), will be a crown of beauty and a royal diadem in the hand of God (Isa 62:3), and will no longer be called "Forsaken," and "Desolate" (Isa 62:4). Jerusalem will be called "My delight" by her God who delights in her (Isa 62:4). Finally, Jerusalem and all its land will be married to God who will rejoice over Jerusalem just as a bridegroom rejoices over the bride. What has been eclipsed in Isa 60:8, with its reference to an everlasting covenant, now comes into full view in Isa 62:5. Transformation by God leads not only to complete union with God but also to fertility. In Isa 54:1 "desolate" meant to be without children. Now Jerusalem will be God's "delight" (Isa 62:4), beautiful and fertile.

In Isa 62:6a–b, the passage's second unit, God informs Jerusalem that she will be protected day and night by sentinels who will never be silent. The lack of silence on the sentinels' part and their watchfulness recalls Isa 62:1 where the poet pledges not to be silent and to take no rest until Jerusalem's vindication shines out like the dawn and her salvation like a burning torch. Isaiah 62:6c–9 is an address made by the poet to the sentinels. The reference to "rest" harks back to Isa 62:1, and now the sentinels are to allow God no rest either until Jerusalem is made known throughout the earth (Isa 62:7). In Isa 62:8 the poet recalls for Jerusalem God's oath made on her behalf, namely, that Jerusalem's grain would not become food for her enemies, and that foreigners will not drink the wine for which she has labored. Those who harvest will eat it and give praise to God, and those who gather will drink it in God's holy courts (Isa 62:8–9). This image of Jerusalem enjoying her own produce and the fruit of her own labor describes what life will be like in the new heavens and the new earth (Isa 65:17–25). Thus, Isa 62 points forward to Isa 65:17–25, to the fullness of life, joy, shalom, and the reign of God. The notion of "Delight" heard in Isa 62:4 surfaces again in Isa 65:18 where it is used in reference to Jerusalem's people who will be a "delight" and in whom God will "delight" (Isa 62:18–19).

The last unit, Isa 62:10–12, expresses a sense of urgency and offers a collection of allusions to Second Isaiah (see Isa 40:3, 10; 49:16; cf. Isa 57:14). This sense of urgency is created by the poet's use of a series of imperatives: "go through," "prepare," "build up," "clear," "lift up," "say," and "see" (Isa 62:10–11). The urgency is further heightened by two of the imperatives used twice to form a set of double imperatives: "go through," "go through," "build up," "build up" (Isa 62:10). Those who have helped to build up the walls of Jerusalem (Isa 60:10) and beautify God's sanctuary (Isa 60:13), along with those who have been building up the ancient ruins, raising up the former devastations, and repairing the ruins of many generations (Isa 61:4), are now called upon to go through the gates, prepare the way for the people, build up the highway (Isa 62; 35:8; 40:3), clear the stones, and lift up an ensign over the peoples. The work of Jerusalem has been completed; the city has been transformed; and now the nations and Jerusalem's exiles will come to her (cf. Isa 60:1–7). More importantly, now God—Jerusalem's salvation—its light and its glory—comes (Isa 60:16; 62:11). When God comes, then the people will be called "The Holy People" (Isa 62:12) after "the Holy One of Israel" (Isa 60:9, 15), "The Redeemed of the Lord" (Isa 62:12) after the Redeemer, the Mighty One of Jacob (Isa 60:16; cf. Isa 59:20). When God comes, then Jerusalem will be called "Sought out" (Isa 62:12) and "A City Not Forsaken" (Isa 62:12; cf. Isa 49:14).

In sum, the poet bears glad tidings, once again, to Jerusalem and to the people. Both Jerusalem and the people are transformed. Both mirror each other, and both are the recipients of God's grace and God's indwelling. Through the poet, the word of hope that speaks of radical transformation is proclaimed, anticipated, and assured.

Isaiah 60–62 in Context

Isa 60–62 presents us with a wondrous vision of transformation, unity, and union. Jerusalem, God's Holy City, once depraved and in ruins, is transformed by God into the embodiment of God to become the transparent glory of God through whom God is glorified and made known. Likewise, peoples exiled and peoples at odds with one another will be gathered together from all corners of the earth; they will stream toward Jerusalem. Transformed by God, they will work together to repair Jerusalem, and Jerusalem will be a place of welcome for all nations, all peoples. Together, these three chapters show that God's work of transformation involves the human community whose participation in this divine activity is essential. Finally, the work of transformation precedes but leads up to full union with God which is realized, to some degree, now but which remains eschatological. Just as Isa 60 moves toward Isa 61, and Isa 61 toward Isa 62,[10] the work of transformation is a process forever evolving as our union with God becomes ever deeper within the context of ongoing transformation by God.

---

10. The vision of the New Jerusalem presented in Isa 62 anticipates the glorious vision presented in Isa 63:17ff that speaks of Jerusalem being created as a joy, its people as a delight. God will rejoice in Jerusalem and will delight in the people (Isa 65:18–19).

Thus, the poet has given the people of his day a hope and a vision that continues to unfold today. To be completely transformed into "The Holy People" is to embody the fullness of what it means to be like Jerusalem and like the poet—"prophetic." God's "Holy People are called to be those who point the way to God and those through whom God is glorified. Finally, the past tenses used throughout Isa 60–62 assure us that, indeed, God will accomplish the vision held out by the poet, and the use of future tenses, especially at the end of Isa 62:12, remind us that God's vision is eschatological even though it is unfolding in our midst. Thus, we live in hope and move forward with hope until we find ourselves in the midst of the new heavens and the new earth wherein God dwells in all fullness and all dwell fully in God.

Isaiah 60–62 in Relation to Isaiah 40–55 and Isaiah 1–39: A Comment

Isaiah 60–62 shares many themes with Isa 40–55. Some common points include: a message of comfort to God's people (Isa 40:1–2; 49:13; 60:1–22); a word of hope to Jerusalem (Isa 40:9; 52:1–6; 62:6–7); God as Israel's redeemer (Isa 43:14; 44:23–24; 49:7; 54:5, 7–8; 62:12); the promise of blessings and everlasting salvation and deliverance (Isa 43:3–5; 44:1–8; 51:4–6; 53:10; 54:7–8; 60:18; 61:10; 62:11); and the suggestion of an eternal covenant of peace, and one extended to all (Isa 54:10; 55:3; 61:8). Strains of a same melody are also heard between Isa 40–55 and Isa 60–62:

> Lift up your eyes all around and see;
> They all gather, they come to you. (Isa 49:18; 60:4)

Although Isa 40–55 and Isa 60–62 share similarities, Isa 60–62 is fundamentally different from Isa 40–55 in one important way. Isaiah 40–55 maintains that God's salvation and redemption will occur not only through God but also through a servant—a messiah (Isa 42:1–9; 52:13–53:12) who will be light to the nations so that God's salvation may reach to the end of the earth (Isa 49:6; cf. 42:6). Isaiah 60–62 sees God's salvation and redemption occurring not only through God but also through Jerusalem, through God's people (Isa 60:1–3), and through one like the servant in Isa 42 and 49 (cf. Isa 61:1–3a).

With respect to links between Isa 1–39 and Isa 60–62, one can hear echoes of Isa 1–39 in Isa 60–62. Streaming nations come to the mountain of the Lord's house (Isa 2:2), to Jerusalem (Isa 60:1–7). A people who walked in darkness have seen a great light (Isa 9:2b; cf. Isa 60:1–3). The spirit of the Lord shall rest upon one like the servant of Isa 42:1–4 (cf. Isa 11:2–3 and Isa 61:1–3). One day there will be peace for, "they will not hurt or destroy on all [God's] holy mountain" (Isa 11:9a), and violence "shall no more be heard in [the] land" (Isa 60:18). Isaiah 11:10 presents an eschatological vision:

> On that day the root of Jesse
> shall stand as a signal to the peoples;
> the nations shall inquire of him,
> and his dwelling shall be glorious.

Isaiah 60:7, 11 speaks of God glorifying his glorious house. Isaiah 60:11 features God proclaiming to the end of the earth that salvation comes—God, the Holy One of Israel will come to Jerusalem, to the people. Isaiah 12:5-6 is anticipatory as well:

> Shout aloud and sing for joy,
> O royal Zion,
> For great in your midst is the
> Holy One of Israel. (Isa 12:6)

Together, Isa 1–39 and 60–62 speak of the coming of God, peace, and the fullness of life associated with God's reign, the transformation of Jerusalem. Isaiah 1–39, Isa 40–55, and Isa 60–62 all speak of a servant-type person who is intricately part of the transforming process. Unlike Isa 1–39 and Isa 40–55, Isa 60–62 does not focus on wickedness, sin, injustice or unrest. Isaiah 60–62 presents an exclusively positive picture, one that is part of the fabric of First and Second Isaiah, but not the fabric itself. With Isa 60–62, one draws closer to the reign of God and the transformation of all life.

Redemption, Restoration, and Jerusalem: A Comment

Throughout Isa 1–39 and 40–55, one sees that as the people are redeemed from their sins, so the land is restored to life, and the people restored to the land (Isa 35:1–10; 41:17–20; 44:23). Hints of this connection can be heard in Isa 61:11. Perhaps of all the images presented in the Isaiah scroll, the one most striking is in Isa 60–62, namely, Jerusalem—a city transformed into God's glory and radiating that glory. Jerusalem, as a city and as a people, offers a vision of hope for the world. By the time we arrive at Isa 62:12, Jerusalem and the Holy People are envisioned as becoming "one." Jerusalem—God's Holy People—is a sign and symbol of God's vision for all people, for all creation.

Conclusion

The central theme of transformation heard in Isa 60–62 and later echoed in Isa 65:17ff. finds a home in the book of Revelation as well (see Rev 21:1–3 and Rev 21:22–26). Would that we who ponder these ancient texts might come to realize that we are God's Holy People, being transformed from light into

Light. We are "a City Not Forgotten"—Jerusalem—wherein dwells God. We are a temple, called to be a "house of prayer for all peoples" (Isa 56:7) where all are welcome at the table. When we become, in God's grace, who we are meant to be as a human race, maybe then we too will be called "Sought Out," for we too will have gone from desolation to delight, dwelling fully in God and God dwelling fully in us.

The Nations' Journey to Zion: Pilgrimage and Tribute as Metaphor in the Book of Isaiah

Gary Stansell

Introduction

Ancient Israel, like other surrounding tribal groups and nations, made annual pilgrimages to its sacred places. Israelite tribes visited Shiloh (Judg 21) in an early period. Later, with the establishment of the state cult in Jerusalem, Israelite pilgrims made Zion their goal, as the "pilgrimage song" in Ps 122 attests. In the book of Isaiah, Israel's historical pilgrimages, three main annual festivals,[1] have been poetically reshaped into a dramatic, colorful metaphor that is found throughout the book's three main divisions (Proto-Isaiah, chs. 1–39 [PI]; Deutero-Isaiah, chs. 40–55 [DI]; Trito-Isaiah, chs. 56–66 [TI]). Indeed, a certain prominence to the pilgrimage metaphor is given by its occurrence toward the beginning (Isa 2:2–4) and end of the book (Isa 60; 66:18–21), where we find visions of a pilgrimage to Jerusalem. Remarkably, it is the Gentiles, the "nations/peoples," and their kings, who "stream" (Isa 2:2; cf. 66:12) to the Holy City. Moreover, often combined with this imagery of pilgrimage is a second metaphor that imaginatively and colorfully extends the pilgrimage of the nations and kings; they come to Zion, not with empty hands but bearing gifts or tribute, signified by the metaphor "wealth of nations."

It is particularly in TI that these two metaphors for *pilgrimage* and *tribute* converge and have their most potent, imaginative representation. In Isa 60:3–7, for example, the poet presents the metaphors, expanded by dramatic

---

1. 1 Kgs 9:25; Hans-Joachim Kraus, *Worship in Israel* (trans. Geoffrey Buswell; Oxford: Basil Blackwell, 1966), 208.

images of camels carrying precious commodities, followed by rams and flocks from exotic lands. The grand theme is sounded in verses 3–5:

> *Nations [and kings] shall come* [to Zion]....
> They all gather together,
> they come to you....
> the abundance of the sea shall be turned to you,
> the *wealth of nations* shall come to you.

The metaphor "wealth of nations"—a phrase perhaps known best from the famous work by Adam Smith[2]—occurs no less than four times (60:5, 11; 61:6; 66:12) within so-called Trito-Isaiah. But these texts pick up from earlier parts of the book instances of this thematic. Working backwards, the theme of nations who make pilgrimage to Zion with tribute or gifts has precursors in Isa 55:5; 49:22–23; 45:14; 35:2; 23:18; 18:7; and 2:2–4. It is these two metaphors, pilgrimage and tribute, in the book of Isaiah, singly and together, that are the object of this study. Several general questions will inform the essay: What is the function and significance of the metaphors in their varying contexts? What intertextual or literary connections are made by the metaphors? What is their contribution to "the richness of the poetic vision of the book" of Isaiah?[3]

The ancient Israelite prophets were poets, and they were masters of metaphorical language. That was the argument made by Bishop Robert Lowth, Professor of Poetry at Oxford (1741–1750), in his famous series of public lectures on Hebrew poetry.[4] To him, prophets as poets speak in metered and parallel sentences replete with sublime, figurative language. But for Lowth it is the book of Isaiah that ranks above all other prophets and Psalms in imaginative power:

---

2. Adam Smith, *An Inquiry into the Nature and Causes of the Wealth of Nations* (Indianapolis: Liberty Classics, 1981).

3. Roy F. Melugin, to whose memory this essay is dedicated, helped contemporary Isaian scholarship to appreciate the interpretive significance of figurative language in the book of Isaiah. The quotation is from his essay, "Poetic Imagination, Intertextuality, and Life in a Symbolic World" (paper presented at the annual meeting of the Society of Biblical Literature, Toronto, Canada, November 2002), 1, reprinted in this volume, p. 7; also Melugin, "Figurative Speech and the Reading of Isaiah 1 as Scripture," in *New Visions of Isaiah* (ed. Roy F. Melugin and Marvin A. Sweeney; JSOTSup 214; Sheffield: Sheffield Academic Press, 1996), 282–305.

4. The lectures (in Latin) were later published in English as Robert Lowth, *Lectures on the Sacred Poetry of the Hebrews* (trans. G. Gregory; 3rd ed.; London: Chadwick, 1847).

> Isaiah, the first of the prophets, both in order and dignity, abound [sic!] in such excellences, that he may be said properly to afford the most perfect model of prophetic poetry .... In his sentiments there is uncommon elevation and majesty; in his imagery, the utmost propriety, elegance, diversity ....[5]

More recently, after decades of critical preoccupation with form-, tradition-, and redaction-criticism, scholars have again taken up a wide-ranging interest in the poetic elements in prophecy, not the least in the book of Isaiah. In his commentary on Isaiah 1–39 (3 vols.), Hans Wildberger, emphasizing that "Isaiah's manner of speech is distinguished by a wide variety of images," classifies these images or metaphors according to the "arenas of life" from which they are drawn.[6] Providing copious examples, he stops short of further analysis of function, meaning, larger context, significance, or conceptual worlds created by Isaiah's metaphorical speech. In the meantime, other scholars have narrowed the focus and probed deeper into the metaphorical language in Isaiah. In his study of Isa 60, Ronald Clements reminds us of the exegetical gains that result from attention to the metaphorical language in Isaiah, noting the sometimes futile or uncertain attempts to anchor poetic, elusive (and allusive) prophetic texts in some original historical event or context. For example, he thinks the message of Isa 60:1–6 expresses "pure poetry, replete with metaphorical imagery," which suggests an "almost timeless ... range of promise for later readers and hearers of prophetic proclamation."[7]

Before proceeding to a study of our theme in appropriate texts in Isaiah, a more precise definition of the terms metaphor, imagery, figurative language, etc. will prove helpful. Philosophers and literary theorists—from Aristotle to J. Derrida—present complex discussions of metaphorical language.[8] Many

---

5. Ibid., 233. Lowth more fully applied his poetics to the book of Isaiah in his now all-but-forgotten *Isaiah: A New Translation; with a Preliminary Dissertation, and Notes, Critical, Philological, and Explanatory* (2 vols. 1778; 15th ed.; London: Tegg, 1857); on this work, see Gary Stansell, "The Poet's Prophet: Bishop Robert Lowth's Eighteenth-Century Commentary on Isaiah," in *"As Those Who Are Taught": The Interpretation of Isaiah from the LXX to the SBL* (ed. Claire Mathews McGinnis and Patricia K. Tull; SBLSymS 27; Atlanta: Society of Biblical Literature, 2006), 223–42.

6. Hans Wildberger, *Isaiah 28–39* (trans. Thomas H. Trapp; Continental; Minneapolis: Fortress, 2002), 675–79.

7. Ronald E. Clements, "'Arise, Shine; For Your Light Has Come': A Basic Theme of the Isaianic Tradition," in *Writing and Reading the Scroll of Isaiah: Studies of an Interpretive Tradition* (ed. Craig C. Broyles and Craig A. Evans; VTSup 70.1; Leiden: Brill, 1997), 444–45.

8. It is beyond the scope of this essay to discuss the "new theory of metaphor," in which

scholars, but not all, speak of metonymy, synecdoche, and personification as subcategories of metaphor. In general, I shall use the term "metaphor" as a broad category, following the accepted axiom that figures or metaphors are "words or expressions that denote one kind of thing [that is] applied to a distinctly different kind of thing, without asserting a comparison."[9] Metaphor, figure of speech, image or imagery and the like will embrace poetic usage in which either 1) one term is substituted for another (metonymy; e.g., "crown" used to signify "king"); or 2) a figure or trope in which a "word or phrase is shifted to a new domain" ("He is a fox").[10] Thus, the phrase "wealth of nations comes to you" (Isa 60:5) could be a metaphor for tribute or gifts that one foreign power presents to another; both the noun and the verb are metaphors. Israel represented as priests who "eat the wealth of nations" (Isa 61:6) is a double metaphor for 1) the nations' material support available to a particular class of individuals (priests); and for 2) the consumption or use of the wealth by the graphic image of "eating." Further, it may be helpful to note I. A. Richards's analytic distinctions concerning metaphor.[11] Richards distinguishes between the metaphor as "vehicle" (e.g., wealth of nations comes) and its "tenor" (e.g., foreign nations bring and present tribute), the tenor thus being the "subject to which the metaphorical word is applied."[12]

I. The Wealth of Nations and the Pilgrimage to Zion in Trito-Isaiah (Isa 60 and 61; 66)

Within Isa 56–66, scholars find a particular unity and coherence in 60–62, which form a "core" of material exhibiting a close connection to Isa 40–45.[13] But Isa 60–61 are particularly linked by thematic connections. In both

---

objections are posed to understanding metaphor merely as non-literal speech. A major issue, according to Eberhard Jüngel, is whether metaphor is a "peripheral phenomenon [or] rather a process fundamental to language" ("Metaphorical Truth: Reflections on the Theological Relevance of Metaphor as a Contribution to the Hermeneutics of Narrative Theology," in his *Theological Essays* [trans. John Webster; Edinburgh: T&T Clark, 1989], 22–23).

9. Meyer H. Abrams, *A Glossary of Literary Terms* (Boston: Wadsworth, 2005), 101.

10. Gilbert D. Chaitin, "Metonymy/metaphor," in *Encyclopedia of Literary Critics and Criticism* (ed. Chris Murray; London: Dearborn, 1999), 2:589–90.

11. I. A. Richards, *The Philosophy of Rhetoric* (Oxford: Oxford University Press, 1965), 89–112.

12. Abrams, *A Glossary of Literary Terms*, 163.

13. Many scholars find a metrical, stylistic, and thematic unity in Isa 60–62; e.g., Paul D. Hanson, *Isaiah 40–55* (IBC; Louisville, Ky.: John Knox, 1995), 46; Seizo Sekine, *Die*

chapters, Zion is the object of good news (cf. 60:1 and 61:2–3); in both, righteousness will shape the new reality for Zion (60:17; 61:11); both expect that foreigners will serve the interests of the Holy City (e.g., 60:10; 61:5). A further literary connection is established by the metaphor, "wealth of nations," which occurs twice in Isa 60 (vv. 5, 11) and once in 61 (v. 6). Let us give particular attention to this phrase and its corollaries, as well as to its connection with the motif, "the nations' pilgrimage to Jerusalem."

A. Isaiah 60

Isa 60 contains a "collage of quotations, revisions, and allusions" to a variety of older texts on the significance of Zion.[14] The vision's center of gravity is surely the future salvation of Zion, which is emphasized at the outset by the symbols of light and Yhwh's glory (60:1). Kraus's comment may be taken as representative of scholarly consensus: "Das ganze Kapitel ist gekennzeichnet durch visionäre Kraft und eindringliche Preisung des Heils der Endzeit."[15] Two significant aspects, or rather, metaphors, for eschatological salvation in Isa 60 are (a) the coming of the nations and (b) the wealth that accompanies them.

1. The Nations Come to Zion
The extensive speech to Zion in Isa 60 thematizes the *coming* of the nations to Zion.[16] Indeed, the catchword בוא occurs no less than eleven times in the chapter: the "theophanic" appearance (בא) of the light and glory of Yhwh (v. 1) at the beginning of the chapter signals a substantive, earthly "coming": the exiles (v. 4b); wealth and goods (vv. 5–7, 9, 11); Lebanon's glory (wealth and

---

Tritojesajanische Sammlung (Jes 56–66) redaktionsgeschichtlich untersucht (BZAW 175; Berlin: de Gruyter, 1989), 10; Wolfgang Lau, *Schriftgelehrte Prophetie in Jes 56–66: Eine Untersuchung zu den literarischen Bezügen in den letzten elf Kapiteln des Jesajabuches* (BZAW 225; Berlin: de Gruyter, 1994), 22. Joseph Blenkinsopp, *Isaiah 56–66* (AB 19B; New York: Doubleday, 2003), 209–10, with reserve, argues for a "unifying intent" of "an assemblage of different types of material."

14. Clements, "Arise, Shine; For Your Light Has Come," 450.
15. Hans-Joachim Kraus, *Das Evangelium des Unbekannten Propheten: Jesaja 40–66* (Kleine Biblische Bibliothek; Neukirchen-Vluyen: Neukirchener, 1990), 206.
16. Klaus Koenen, *Ethik und Eschatologie im Tritojesajabuch: Eine literarkritische und redaktionsgeschichtliche Studie* (WMANT 62; Neukirchen-Vluyn: Neukirchener, 1990), 137, 139.

produce, v. 13).[17] The logic is that of cause and effect. The כבוד Yhwh (vv. 1–2) does not come empty handed, as it were, but brings (causes) material wealth with it. But it is especially the nations and their kings who journey to Zion: they "walk" (הלכו v. 3), "come" (באו v. 4a) ; kings are "led (to Zion) in procession" (נהוגים v. 11). The mention of nations/kings in vv. 11–12 presupposes the arrival of foreign royalty, as also v. 14 (children of enemy nations), and v. 16 (again, nations/kings).

The motif "nations come to Jerusalem" is often understood in relation to the "Zion tradition," of which the book of Isaiah knows several aspects.[18] On the one hand, scholars speak of an onslaught or aggressive attack of the foreign nations (*Völkersturm*) upon Zion, as represented in PI (e.g., 8:8–9; 17:12–14) and the Zion Psalms. A very different purpose and meaning of the "nations' coming" may be designated a "*Völkerwallfahrt*," "the nations' pilgrimage," when foreign peoples come to Jerusalem without compulsion to pay homage to Israel and/or acknowledge her God, or to hear Torah (e.g., Isa 2:2–4). Concerning Isa 60, critics disagree whether the metaphor, "nations come to Zion," is best represented as a kind of *pilgrimage* (*Völkerwallfahrt*),[19] or rather as a *journey* (*Völkerzug*), a neutral term, without reference to a cultic purpose.[20] While this distinction may bear significance for tradition- and redaction-critical purposes, in what follows, we understand the two types of "travel to Zion" as two variants of one metaphor, "the nations go to Zion." In I. A. Richards's terms, the vehicle can have various tenors (e.g., cultic or confessional acts, submission/homage and tribute, bringing home the exiles), depending on context and associated imagery. In Isa 60 and 61 the nations' coming to Zion

---

17. The switch between *qal* (vv. 1, 4–[twice], 5, 6, 13, 20) and *hip'il* (vv. 9, 11, 17 [twice]) approaches a word-play with the term: people and things "come," but they are also "brought" (= caused to come).

18. Hans Wildberger, "Die Völkerwallfahrt zum Zion: Jes II 1–5," *VT* 7 (1957): 62–81.

19. The word "pilgrimage" connotes travel to a holy place by the faithful for the purpose of worship and then a *return* to one's own place. For further definitions and social scientific perspectives on pilgrimage, see Luigi Tomasi, "Homo Vitator: From Pilgrimage to Religious Tourism via the Journey," in *From Medieval Pilgrimage to Religious Tourism: The Social and Cultural Economics of Piety* (ed. William H. Swatos, Jr. and Luigi Tomasi; Westport, Conn.: Praeger, 2002), 3–4.

20. Thus Claus Westermann, *Isaiah 40–66: A Commentary* (trans. David M. G. Stalker; OTL; Philadelphia: Westminster, 1969); Odil Hannes Steck, "Der Grundtext in Jes 60 und sein Aufbau," in *Studien zu Tritojesaja* (BZAW 203; Berlin: de Gruyter, 1991), 71–72, note 93; Koenen, *Ethik und Eschatologie im Tritojesajabuch*, 139, note 485: not "*Völkerwallfahrt*" but "*Völkerzug*" or "*Völkerstrom*," a "streaming," or traveling. A contrary position is represented, among others, by W. Lau, *Schriftgelehrte Prophetie in Jes 56–66*, 33, who defends a cultic purpose in the coming of the nations.

is ultimately about their submission and service to the people of Zion. Isaiah 60:11 states that "kings are led (נהוגים MT) in" as prisoners.[21] They come under duress; hence the Targum correctly understands the sense of the text when it adds "in chains."[22] Isaiah 60:14 reinforces the note of submission, for the oppressors' children must bend low and bow down. They do not come to be near sacred space and then to return home spiritually refreshed (pilgrimage). Rather, Jerusalem is their new home, where their work is to build walls, while their kings must "minister" to Zion's inhabitants (vv. 10, 12; cf. 61:4–5).

As a whole, Isa 60 envisions as reversal of wealth (and of course status)—Zion, formerly despoiled and oppressed, will gain back her wealth, while the prideful oppressors will assume the position of the servant class. Indeed, it is an enduring process, as 60:11 suggests ("your gates shall always be open"), for the nations will journey continuously to Zion. Isaiah 60 is then misread if the nationalistic tone is overlooked. The metaphor "nations/kings come to Zion" in Isa 60 is part of a larger vision in which all the world (including the animal world, vv. 6–7) and its wealth trek to the Holy City, where they are to remain.

2. The Wealth of Nations

The nations who come to Zion at the dawning of salvation must bring their wealth. The metaphor "wealth of nations," a key phrase in Isa 60, occurs not once but twice:

> Then you shall see and be radiant ...
>   because the abundance of the sea shall be brought to you,
>   *the wealth of nations* (חיל גוים) shall come to you. (60:5)
> Your gates shall be open ...
>   so that *nations shall bring you their wealth* (חיל גוים),
>   with their kings led in procession. (60:11)

---

21. The term נהג here refers to the taking away of prisoners; cf. 1 Sam 30:2; Isa 20:4; Lam 3:2. The passive part. נהוגים (MT) should not be changed (Westermann, *Isaiah 40–66*; Koenen, *Ethik und Eschatologie im Tritojesajabuch*, 139, note 485) to an active part. נוהגים (thus BHS, et al.); cf. Blenkinsopp's (*Isaiah 56–66*) caution in taking the act. participle to imply, fitting the context, that "the kings are reduced to leading the pack animals." Koenen (139, note 485) rightly remarks that the gloss in v. 12 did not cause a change in the MT (from an original active part. to passive part.), but the other way round: the glossator understood the passive verb to (rightly) mean that the kings are brought against their will and may possibly rebel: "nation and kingdom that will not serve you will perish ..." (v. 12).

22. Koenen, *Ethik und Eschatologie im Tritojesajabuch*, 139, note 485.

Further, v. 13, which picks up and continues vv. 10–11, slightly reshapes the metaphor:

> The glory (כבוד) of Lebanon shall come to you. (60:13)[23]

The "כבוד of Lebanon," that is, it's (natural) wealth, will come, too, thus making the "wealth of nations" more geographically specific (as in 60:6–7: Midian, Ephah, Sheba, etc.).[24] The key words for "wealth, riches" are חיל (vv. 5, 11; parallel to המון abundance, v. 5) and כבוד (v. 13). In 61:6, חיל and כבוד stand parallel, while in 66:12 כבוד replaces חיל in the phrase "wealth of nations."[25] The chapter is surprisingly replete with details of the riches and prosperity that make their way to Jerusalem and how they get there. The poet does not tire of enumerating: silver, gold, frankincense, flocks of sheep, rams, cypress, and pine (vv. 6–7, 9, 13). Such wealth not only "comes"; it is "brought" by camels of Midian and ships of Tarshish. Commentators have not overlooked the fact that the riches and goods come from three directions, west (the sea), east (desert, Midian, Ephah, etc.), and the north (Lebanon). Is the south missing?[26] The arrival of foreigners with their wealth is well-nigh universalized by the poet.

The "wealth of nations" metaphor is picked up and reshaped again in Isa 60 with what some commentators call an "absurd" metaphor:

> You shall suck the milk of nations (חלב גוים);
> You shall suck the breasts of kings. (60:16)[27]

---

23. Westermann, *Isaiah 40–66*.

24. The כבוד of Lebanon not only picks up the חיל of the nations but the כבוד YHWH (v. 2) and concretizes them, for a spiritual presence must become tangible under the agency of the deity (v. 13b אכבד "I will glorify"). See note 35 below.

25. In addition to 60:5, 11; 61:6, the metaphor occurs in Zech 14:14, which envisions that, at the final war and victory for Jerusalem, "the wealth of all the surrounding nations shall be collected." Cf. Isa 10:14, where the "wealth of peoples" (חיל העמים) refers to the plunder gathered by the king of Assyria.

26. Pierre Grelot, "Un parallèle babylonien d'Isaïe LX et du Psaume LXXII," *VT* 7 (1957): 319–21, finds in Isa 60 reference to the four points of the compass and compares the Akkadian conception of the four ends of the earth. Koenen, *Ethik und Eschatologie im Tritojesajabuch* (140, note 488), however, argues that Kedar and Nabioth (v. 7) are not to be understand as lying to the south but to the east. Koenen: "Vom Süden in Jes. 60 ist keine Rede."

27. See, e.g., Blenkinsopp, *Isaiah 56–66*; Walter Zimmerli, "Zur Sprache Tritojesajas," in *Gottes Offenbarung: Gesammelte Aufsätze* (TB 19; 2nd ed.; Munich: Kaiser, 1963), 222: "uneigentlich[e] Bildrede."

The milk and breast of the גוים, their "wealth," will replenish all the lost riches of Zion's past plunderings and humiliation (in Isa 10:13–14 the king of Assyria boasts that he has plundered the "wealth of the peoples"). Blenkinsopp thinks that the intent of the metaphor "is to convey the idea of a rich and satisfying prosperity," possibly with a mythic overtone not unlike a poem from Ugarit ("you shall draw the milk of Asherah/suck the breasts of the maiden Anath," *ANET*, 146).[28] In any case, v. 16 restates the expectation that the prosperity of the nations will become Zion's, thus emphasizing by repetition the essential thought of 60:5, 11. In v. 16, the "milk of nations" pointedly refers back to vv. 5, 11 (wealth of nations), and "kings" picks up vv. 10, 11 (kings shall wait on you; the kings in procession). The "milk-metaphor" poetically elucidates the joy and life-giving power of the riches implied by the thrice-occurring phrases "wealth of nations," "wealth of Lebanon" of vv. 5, 11, and 13. The "wealth of nations" and the "service" given to Zion (note the repeated "to you" in v. 4, 5, 7, 10, 11, 13, 14), as well as the servant status of the kings/nations, should be taken as strong qualifiers of v. 3 (nations/kings walk by your light), indicating for what purpose the nations and kings come to Zion. This observation lends further support to the interpretation above—that the nations "journey" to Zion is everything but a freely undertaken pilgrimage (*Völkerwallfahrt*).

But not only the arrival of nations and their kings (vv. 5, 11, 13, 16), of camel caravans from the desert and ships from Tarshish (vv. 6–7, 9), bring magnificent wealth. Even God himself becomes an agent in the bringing of wealth to Zion:

> Instead of bronze I will bring (Heb. "cause to come") gold,
> instead of iron I will bring silver,
> instead of wood, bronze,
> instead of stones, iron. (60:17)

According to Muilenburg, "the repetition emphasizes the reversal of conditions" from poverty and humility to wealth and glory.[29] He also finds in the entire poem that the writer "seems to be playing on the coming of various gifts and treasures to Jerusalem, and Yhwh's 'causing them to come.'" The poet appears to speak from the perspective of economically depressed times; indeed, the change from inferior to superior materials suggests not only an alteration in material fortunes, but a change from shame to honor.[30]

---

28. Blenkinsopp, *Isaiah 56–66*.
29. James Muilenburg, *The Book of Isaiah Chapters 40–66* (ed. George A. Buttrick; IB 5; Nashville: Abingdon, 1956).
30. Westermann, *Isaiah 40–66*.

Isaiah 60 goes to some length, therefore, to present and emphasize, in various rhetorical ways (announcement of salvation; eschatological description; first-person Yhwh speech), the eschatological reversal of Zion's economic status. The nations come to Jerusalem, along with the returning exiles (vv. 4, 9), bringing all forms of wealth and prosperity. It seems best to understand this returning wealth as "tribute," exacted from the nations as (re)payment (cf. 61:7) that now restores national honor. Whereas pilgrims bring *gifts*[31] to a shrine to signify worship and adoration, subdued nations must present tribute, as foreign nations did especially under Solomon.[32] Thus Isa 60 speaks not of pilgrim gifts freely offered as homage to Israel's God, but of the tribute brought by subdued nations to personified Zion (vv. 10–12, 14).[33] Isa 60 expects no return of the glory days of the Davidic dynasty, but its former wealth and honor will come to Zion when the Kingdom of Yhwh appears in all its glory (60:1–3). Paul Volz was surely correct in claiming that "the poet [Isa 60] is more concerned with *economics* than with politics," and that an extensively material, this-worldly conception of the age of salvation is determinative for the "new Jerusalem."[34] Indeed, as we have seen, the elucidation of wealth (glory/honor) in Isa 60 bulks large and is hardly a subsidiary theme.[35]

---

31. On gift giving in ancient Israel, see Gary Stansell, "The Gift in Ancient Israel," *Semeia* 87 (1999): 65–90.

32. 1 Kings 5:1 [Eng. 4:21], "They brought Solomon tribute (מנחה) and were subject to him all his life." Tribute in ancient Israel is to be distinguished from other kinds of "gifts." Tribute is neither largesse (superior to inferior), nor a sacred contribution, tax, or offering, but an enforced or exacted "gift" from inferior to superior. In Hebrew the all-purpose word for gift is מנחה, which can mean gift, tribute, or offering, depending on the context.

33. Marvin A. Sweeney, "Prophetic Exegesis in Isaiah 65–66," in Broyles and Evans, *Writing and Reading the Scroll of Isaiah*, 459, understands the wealth from the nations as tribute paid to Yhwh who, in Isa 60–62 and similar Isaian texts, "is acknowledged as king by the nations in a manner consistent with the tribute paid by subject nations to the Persian monarch from the time of Cyrus on."

34. Paul Volz, *Jesaja II* (KAT; Leipzig: Deichert, 1932), cited in Kraus, *Das Evangelium des unbekannten Propheten*, 210.

35. The catchword כדוב, its root occurring no less than four times at critical junctures in the chapter (vv. 1, 2, 13 [twice]), חיל synonymous with כדוב in its sense of economic strength and riches, as well as the thrice occurrence of the term פאר (vv. 7, 13), all connote the material riches, power, and honor of economic prosperity.

B. Isaiah 61

Isaiah 61 is closely related to ch. 60, with general similarities found in theme, mood, and outlook, as well as similar motifs (salvation, praise, joy, etc.).[36] According to Blenkinsopp, the close connection of 60 and 61 is seen by the continuation of 60:10–16 in 61:3c-7. For our purposes, it is the verbal link between 61:6 and 60:5, 11 that is significant:

> You shall eat the wealth of nations (חיל גוים),
> and in their riches (כבוד) you shall glory. (61:6b)

The word כבוד picks up 60:13 (כבוד of Lebanon), while the phrase "wealth of nations" forms a precise verbal link with vv. 5, 11. Isaiah 61:6b also points forward to ch. 66, where in v. 16 the phrase "wealth of nations" (כבוד instead of חיל) occurs for the fourth and final time in Isa 56–66.

Isaiah 61:6 is often taken as a subunit with v. 5.[37] Then vv. 5 and 6 would provide an important juxtaposition between the foreigners who work at menial tasks (v. 5) and the Yahwists who serve as priests in v. 6. This service is possible precisely because they can feed off of (אכל eat) the Gentiles' productive work (tending flocks, plowing, vine trimming), that is, the "wealth of the nations."

The line of thought here obviously goes back to Isa 60; however, the theme "journey of the nations to Zion" in ch. 61:4–6 is not explicit but presupposed.[38] Again, it becomes clear that chs. 60–61 is not about a "pilgrimage" to Zion to worship God but a journey toward the nations' servitude (v. 5).[39] Pilgrims go to a sacred place to be in touch with the deity and then return home refreshed; not so the nations in 60 and 61. But a change in literary form (from a prophecy in 60, to a "description of conditions" of the new Zion in 61:5–6)[40] signals several differences between 61:6 and 60:5, 11, 16.

In Isa 60, the tenor of the metaphor "wealth of nations" is that the Gentiles contribute to the new, increasing power, economic well-being, and prestige of the city; their contribution brings glory to the people and to their

---

36. Cf. Muilenburg, *The Book of Isaiah Chapters 40–66*, et al.
37. Westermann, *Isaiah 40–66*, 466, who takes vv. 5–6, cautiously, as a later insertion; Bernhard Duhm, *Das Buch Jesaia. Übersetzt und erklärt* (5th ed.; HKAT 3.1; Göttingen: Vandenhoeck & Ruprecht, 1968), adds v. 4b to the subunit; Muilenburg makes a strophe division between v. 5 and 6, thus the subunit is vv. 6–7.
38. Westermann, *Isaiah 40–66*; Kraus, *Das Evangelium des unbekannten Propheten*.
39. Kraus, ibid., speaks of "Frondienst der Völker."
40. Westermann, *Isaiah 40–66*.

God. Grammatically, "wealth" is a subject in ch. 60; it "comes" or is caused to come. Here in 61:6, it is an object: "wealth" is "eaten" (אכל) by priests, who can now serve spiritual functions and no longer do menial labor.[41] Hence, the wealth of nations in ch. 60 refers to the economic glory of Zion, while here (61:6) it supports the "priests" so that they may minister to the heathen world, or at least to those who now serve (support) them. The socio-political-economic reversal is clear in 61:5-7. Oppressors become the servants (v. 5); the oppressed become priests (v. 6), with financial support; the status of shame is replaced by the status of honor, in double measure (v. 7, "therefore they shall possess a double portion"; cf. 40:2). Isaiah 61:6 thus continues the metaphor in ch. 60, but with a shift in emphasis. According to Blenkinsopp,[42] the servitude (their wealth, the produce of their labor) of the Gentiles, enabling the Judeans to be priests, is a "more vivid restatement of the 'despoiling of the Egyptians' theme" in 60:5-7, 16. Hence, the motif of "wealth" narrows in focus in ch. 61 and is nuanced in the direction of priests rather than a general "riches for Zion." But the servitude of the Gentiles in 61 (strangers/foreigners shall feed your flocks ... till your land, etc., v. 5) retains its close link with 60:10 (foreigners shall build your walls, v. 10). Finally, we note that the context of the "wealth" metaphor in 61 is no longer about the glory of Zion and the joy of its inhabitant (60:5, 7, 9, 15); rather, these motifs have been replaced by the recompense theme (vv. 2, 7, 8), which means that, compared to Isa 60, Isa 61:5 represents a different function of the metaphor, "wealth of nations."

C. Isaiah 66

Isaiah 65-66 belong together,[43] despite certain dissonances between the two chapters. Carr's[44] recent study concludes that Isa 65-66, like Isa 1:2-31, is a "strategic, selective construal of central themes from the Isaiah tradition."[45] Isa 66 may be divided into four subunits, vv. 1-6, 7-14, 15-21, 22-24.[46] Accord-

---

41. Duhm, *Das Buch Jesaia*, 5th ed.
42. Blenkinsopp, *Isaiah 56-66*, 226.
43. Steck, "Beobachtungen zur Anlage von Jes 65-66," in *Studien zu Tritojesaja*, 217-28, esp. 225-27.
44. David M. Carr, "Reading Isaiah from Beginning (Isaiah 1) to End (Isaiah 65-66): Multiple Modern Possibilities," in Melugin and Sweeney, *New Visions of Isaiah*, 188-218.
45. Ibid., 212-14.
46. Blenkinsopp, *Isaiah 56-66*, reviews a range of proposals for subdivisions within the chapter.

ing to Beuken, 66:7–14 present an "epilogue" to TI.[47] Within vv. 7–14, the metaphor "wealth of nations" (v. 12) occurs for the fourth and final instance, closely linking Isa 66 to the "core" chs. 60–62 (61:5, 6, 11):

> For thus says Yhwh,
> I will extend prosperity (נטה שלום) to her like a stream (כנהר),
> and the wealth of nations (כבוד גוים)
> like an overflowing torrent. (66:12)

Here the metaphor "wealth of nations" reads כבוד גוים instead of חיל גוים, but the meaning is equivalent. The construct chain expressing "wealth of. . . ." thus occurs no fewer than five times in Trito-Isaiah (60: 5, 11, 13; 61:6; 66:12). In Isa 60, the nations/kings journey to Zion and bring their wealth with them. By contrast, in 66:12 it is Yhwh who brings the riches; that is, he "extends" the wealth of nations to Zion. The divine agency is now explicit, with the graciousness of the act implied by the verb "extend" (נטה) (66:12).[48] It is not surprising then, that in the immediately surrounding context of 66:12, neither nations nor kings play any role. In v. 12 שלום ("prosperity") stands parallel with כבוד. This is hardly insignificant, for it suggests a shift in the metaphor's function. Indeed, it is Yhwh's shalom, combined with the wealth of nations, that is graciously extended to Zion. Hence, now the wealth motif of Isa 60–61, which brought rejoicing and glory to Zion and support for the "priests," is joined directly to the saving comfort brought by Yhwh, as the motifs of "consoling" in 66:11 and "motherly comfort" (66:13) indicate. This is a shift in nuance, representing a reinterpretation and application of the metaphor of "wealth of nations."

The nursing metaphor in 66:11, 13 encloses the prophecy that Yhwh will bring the wealth of nations (v. 12). Thus the metaphor of wealth/prosperity is closely associated in vv. 11–13 with images of warm consolation. In 60:16, however, the image is not a mother's comforting milk (a salvation image), but the "royal milk" of empires whose power, wealth, prestige will be transferred to Zion, such that her previous forsakenness in the world's political hierarchy

---

47. Willem A. M. Beuken, "Isaiah Chapters LXV–LXVI: Trito-Isaiah and the Closure of the Book of Isaiah," in *Congess Volume: Leuven* (ed. J. Emerton; VTSup 43; Leiden: Brill, 1991), 204–21, thinks that 66:7–24 presents a series of epilogues: vv. 7–14 to TI; vv. 15–21 to TI and DI; vv. 22–24 to the entire book. Steck, "Zu jüngsten Untersuchungen von Jes 56,1–8; 63,7–66, 24," in *Studien zu Tritojesaja*, 263–64, is critical of this interpretation, while Blenkinsopp (*Isaiah 56–66*) mostly agrees.

48. In Gen 39:21 Yhwh "extends kindness" to Joseph—an act of grace and favor; cf. Westermann, *Isaiah 40–66*.

will be reversed; she had been forsaken (shamed) but now will be majestic (honored). The context within Isa 60 makes clear that this "majesty" (v. 15) is about political power and wealth. It is therefore a salvation message of a different order than in Isa 66. Indeed, here (66:12) the metaphor "wealth of nations" takes on a function subordinate to a message of consolation, losing its thrust of material blessing, as Isa 60–61 presents it.

The metaphor of the "journey" in Isa 60 (not only kings and the nations' wealth, but camels, ships, various kinds of merchandise "come") is replaced by the image of wealth coming like an "overflowing stream" (RSV 66:12; JPS "a wadi in flood"; Blenkinsopp, "a torrent in full spate"). But such forward, hurrying movement, a powerful force behind it, is also suggested by 60:5–11. So the metaphor in 66:12 is apt and does not depart from this sense in Isa 60. Sailing ships and flowing rivers appear to belong to the same stock of images.[49] Isaiah 66:12 provides the motivation for the call to "rejoice" in verse 10: rejoice with Jerusalem, *because* YHWH brings shalom/wealth. This connection echoes the close relationship of rejoicing and wealth in 60:5: Zion will be thrilled and rejoice because (כי-clause) the wealth of nations "comes to you."

In Isa 66, the metaphor "journey of the nations," is not immediately connected to the wealth motif as in Isa 60. In the literary unit 66:18–21, the nations do indeed travel to Zion, but here it is YHWH himself who "gathers" them: "I am coming to gather all nations" (v. 18). In contrast to Isa 60, where the nations are compelled, as a subdued and humiliated people now made servants (vv. 11, 12, 14, 16; 61:5), there is no hint of second-class status for the nations in 66:18–21. Here then is not a "journey" (*Völkerzug* as in 60), but a "pilgrimage" (*Völkerwallfahrt*). In Isa 66 the nations make *pilgrimage* to Zion. The purpose is clear: like genuine pilgrims, they are to declare the glory of YHWH (v. 19).[50] One notes especially that they do not come with the wealth presented as gift and homage, as required of pilgrims to a shrine. Rather, they bring with them Zion's children from the Diaspora, as an offering to the YHWH (v. 20). Thus Isa 66 picks up from Isa 60 the journey of nations, a journey in which the scattered children of Zion are brought home (60:4, 9), but the

---

49. The "flowing wealth" (66:12 כנהר שלום) recalls 48:18 (כנהר שלום), a text that also speaks of prosperity unrelated to the nations' tribute. Indeed, in 48:18 such wealth/prosperity is lacking because the commandments are disregarded. Is there perhaps a play on נהר in 60:5 ("you will glow" JPS), even if the verb in 60:5 is נהר II, as Blenkinsopp (*Isaiah 56–66*) argues ("be radiant")? The Vulgate translates *adflues*, "flow."

50. In Isa 60, the nations come to Zion to see *her* glory: vv. 3 ("your light"; "your brightness"); v. 7 (Zion's house is glorious); v. 9 (the Holy One of Israel has glorified *you*); cf. v. 15.

nation's wealth as such is no longer a part of the metaphor. While the interpretation of vv. 18–21 remains puzzling in many regards, not least because there is a lack of unity and connection between the verses,[51] it is nevertheless clear that the status of the nations is rehabilitated in vv. 18–21. Unlike 60 and 61, nations no longer belong to the menial, servant class. Their goal is to witness the glory of Yhwh and to help bring home the Diaspora Israelites as an offering, and thus an act of worship.[52]

The wealth of nations metaphor in Isa 60–61 points forward to 66; or, 66 picks up, echoes and refurbishes the motif from 60–61. But the metaphor fades in Isa 66; it is no longer connected to the metaphor of the nations' journey to Zion; the economic status (and thus glory) of Zion in Isa 60–61 has become subordinated to the message of comfort and consolation of the "mother" (66:10–14). In 66:18–21 the nations no longer lose their dignity, as in Isa 60–61; indeed, now the nations come as "pilgrims" bringing "gifts" (v. 20); it is not tribute (wealth) as such but the exiles ("all your brethren") that they "present."

2. The Wealth of Nations and the Pilgrimage to Zion in Deutero-Isaiah (55:5; 49:22–23; 45:14)

In Trito-Isaiah, we have analyzed two metaphors, the "pilgrimage/journey of the nations," and the "wealth of nations." But these metaphors reach back to preceding texts, to which they have verbal and thematic links. Let us now briefly examine similar texts in Isa 40–55 and pursue the chosen metaphors a step further.

A. Isaiah 55:5

The journey of the nations in 60:4–14 recalls 55:5, where the prophet announces, "Nation[s] (singular in Hebrew, with a plural verb form) that do not know you shall run to you (גוי ירוצו), because of Yhwh your God, the Holy One of Israel, for he has glorified you." Zimmerli has called particular attention to the connection of 60:9b with 55:5.[53] In 55:5 the nations "run" because they have been "summoned"; קרא can mean "to summon to a feast" (Exod 34:15; Judg 14:15; 1 Sam 16:3; BBD, 895). The agent is apparently

---

51. Thus Westermann, *Isaiah 40–66*.
52. Blenkinsopp, *Isaiah 56–66*.
53. W. Zimmerli, "Zur Sprache Tritojesajas," 223, thinks 60:9b "cites" 55:5.

Israel ("you" 55:2–3); the invitation, however, is everything but compulsion (unlike Isa 60). According to B. Duhm, Israel's summons to the nations is like the summons of a lord to a servant (he refers to 49:7); he thus rejects the interpretation that the nations "run" in order to become worshipers of Israel's God and therefore incorporated into the community.[54] By contrast, Baltzer interprets 55:5 in light of the *Völkerwallfahrt* theme (pilgrimage and feast), finding its nearest analogue in Isa 2:2–4[55] (see below on this passage). If this is accepted, then 55:5 is to be distinguished from the "journey" of the nations in 60 and 61; nor is there any hint of gifts or tribute being brought to Israel. Westermann finds in 55:5 no reference to subjugation of the nations as enemies; rather, the foreign peoples come to join with Israel in worship and thus become a blessing of increase in Israel's numbers.[56] The close analogue in 56:6–7, where Yhwh brings (בוא *hiphil*) "foreigners" to his holy mountain to worship, would lend support to the view that 55:5 presents the image of a pilgrimage. Finally, the purpose of the nations' coming to Israel in 55:5 remains somewhat unclear.[57]

B. Isaiah 49:22–23

In the "salvation oracle" in Isa 49:22–26, a forsaken Zion "lifts up her eyes" to see that "they gather, they come to you" (v. 18). Indeed, responding to Yhwh's "signal," it is the nations who come. But they come neither to assault Zion (5:26; 13:3–5; 18:3), nor to bring their wealth (60:5, 11; 61:6), nor to see the glory of Zion (60:2–3, 9) or of Yhwh (66:18–21). Rather, the nations come in order to help repatriate the sons and daughters of Zion (49:22b). Kings and queens are assigned a special function:

> Kings shall be your foster fathers
> and their queens your nursing mothers.
> With their faces to the ground they
> and lick the dust of your feet. (49:23a)

---

54. Duhm, *Das Buch Jesaia*, 5th ed.
55. Klaus Baltzer, *Deutero-Isaiah: A Commentary on Isaiah 40–55* (trans. Margaret Kohl; Hermeneia; Minneapolis: Fortress, 2001).
56. Westermann, *Isaiah 40–66*.
57. Blenkinsopp (*Isaiah 40–55*) thinks the matter is inconclusive, for the purpose of the nations' coming is unclear: Do they "converge on Jerusalem" to seek instruction (Isa 2:2–4; 19:24–25; 56:1–8) or do they come as slaves or menials (60:4–7, 10–14; 61:5–7)?

In Isa 49:22–23 the nations/peoples come to Zion, assuming the status of helper and servant (queens as nursing mothers, v. 23a). The nursing metaphor, likely meant as an image of support and physical sustenance, is transformed in 60:16, where, consonant with the "wealth of nations" motif, Zion hungrily "sucks" at the royal teat, thirstily drinking down (cf. the metaphor of "eating" wealth in 61:6) the "milk" (wealth) of nations and kings (60:16).[58] This "female royalty serving as wet nurse" in 49:23a "turns into a metaphor for 'milking' the resources of the Gentiles and their rulers" in 60:16.[59] Such "child-friendly" succor of kings/queens/nations brings, however, not prestige and reward but a deep humiliation (v. 23b; cf. 60:10–11; 14; 61:5–6). That they "bow down" (v. 23) seems hardly to signify worship, whereby the passage would qualify as a pilgrimage text.[60]

Although Isa 49:22–23 is similar to 60:4–16 on several points (nations come and bring the exiles; the nations are humbled and provide service), several contrasts must be noted: (1) in 60:4–16, the transfer of wealth is a key reason for the nation's journey to Zion; (2) in 49:22–23, not wealth but children of the exile are transported home by the nations. Moreover, (3) whereas the motif "the nations lead home Zion's children" is central for 49:14–26, this motif is subordinate in ch. 60, where the wealth of nations stands in the foreground.[61] On the other hand, 49:22 points forward to 66:18–20, where, similarly, a gathering of the nations to Zion includes the transport of her children. But the elements of worship and thus pilgrimage found in 66:18–21 are missing in 49:22–23. Accordingly, the metaphor of the nations' journey in 49:22–23 is hardly to be understood as a pilgrimage (*Völkerwallfahrt*). Israel's God is not worshiped; rather, the nations and royalty come to provide

---

58. W. Zimmerli ("Zur Sprache Tritojesajas," 222), again, thinks in terms of a citation of Deutero-Isaiah by Trito-Isaiah.

59. Blenkinsopp, *Isaiah 40–55*.

60. In 49:23 it is Zion, not the nations, "that will know that I am the Lord." Klaus Baltzer, *Deutero-Isaiah: A Commentary on Isaiah 40–55*, on the other hand, interprets the passage in terms of *proskynesis*, paying homage to Jerusalem, and thus a pilgrimage of the nations. That kings and queens should "bow down and lick the dust," is, according to J. Muilenburg (*The Book of Isaiah Chapters 40–66*, following Skinner), an extravagant oriental metaphor; in this light, we have not a metaphor for worship but courtly humility and good manners. Similar terms occur in 60:14 (bending low, bowing down); but within the context of unwilling service and status reversal (60:10–14; 61:5), 60:14 must be taken as much harsher than 49:23. The loss of the nations' wealth in 60; 61; 66 (v. 12) indicates a more negative view of the kings and nations than in 55:5 and 49:22–23.

61. Odil Hannes Steck, "Lumen gentium: Exegetische Bemerkungen zum Grundsinn von Jes 60,1–3," in *Studien zu Tritojesaja*, 87–88.

child-care service; nor is it a high-status job, for they must grovel (v. 23b) and display humility (v. 23b).

C. Isaiah 45:14

The above two passages (55:5; 49:22–23) are useful for our purposes because, while establishing the absence of any specific wealth of nations motif, as in Isa 60 and 66, they underscore the contrast between variants of the metaphor, the nations' journey to Zion to serve her (49:22–23) and the "nations' pilgrimage" (*Völkerwallfahrt*), with its purpose to offer worship (55:5). In a passage framed as a prophetic speech (thus says Yhwh), 45:14–17 envisions a coming time of prosperity, at the expense of foreign nations and their political submission. According to v. 14:

> The wealth of Egypt and the merchandise of Ethiopia,
> And the Sabeans, tall of stature,
> Shall come over to you and be yours,
> Pass over and shall follow you in chains,
> bow down to you;
> They shall pay homage to you....[62]

A major issue in understanding this passage is the addressee; is it Israel in general, or Zion,[63] or Cyrus? Klaus Baltzer[64] recently has taken up Ibn Ezra's proposal that the original addressee is Cyrus, whom Baltzer identifies as a main character "in the whole act from 44:24 onward." In any case, the similarities with Isa 60, 61 are quite apparent. Indeed, the close connection of 45:14 and Isa 60 is often remarked.[65] The parallel terms "wealth/merchandise" (יגיע/סחר) in 45:14 are equivalent to the word pairs in Isa 60:5 (המון/חיל) and 61:6 (חיל/כבוד) and 66:12 (שלום/כבוד). The words "wealth/merchandise"

---

62. Thus Westermann's (*Isaiah 40–66*) translation.
63. Roy F. Melugin, *The Formation of Isaiah 40–55* (BZAW 141; Berlin: de Gruyter, 1976), 127; Kraus, *Das Evangelium des unbekannten Propheten*.
64. See Baltzer's (*Deutero-Isaiah: A Commentary on Isaiah 40–55*) discussion of changing the fem. suffix ("your") to masc.
65. Westermann, *Isaiah 40–66*; Kraus, *Das Evangelium des unbekannten Propheten*; Baltzer, *Deutero-Isaiah: A Commentary on Isaiah 40–55*. Westermann thinks the similarity between 45:14 and 60 so great, and 45:14 so out of place in Deutero-Isaiah, that 45:14 is a displaced fragment. Baltzer's reading, in which the nations and their wealth come to Cyrus, not Zion, wants to interpret the text as it stands, synchronically.

form a construct-chain with place-names (Egypt, etc.), as in 60:13 ("wealth of Lebanon"). In 45:14 the nations come as prisoners—thus unwillingly, as in ch. 60:11, 14. Further, they come bearing gifts. K. Baltzer's interpretation allows the question: voluntary gifts of a worshiping people, or tribute required of a subjugated people? He appeals to the iconography of prisoner nations coming to offer tribute to the victor as a parallel, admitting that the answer to the question depends on point of view (conqueror or conquered). Blenkinsopp, on the other hand, connects 45:14 closely with Isa 60 and understands the "you" (2nd pers. fem. sing.) to be Zion, who receives the "tribute of subject peoples." If the "confession of faith" in v. 14b be construed as an act of worship,[66] then the nations are pictured pilgrims who in some sense join with Israel as worshipers of YHWH.[67] But "worshipers in chains" appears to the modern reader as a difficult concept.[68]

III. The Wealth of Nations and the Pilgrimage to Zion in Proto-Isaiah (35:1–2; 23:1–18; 2:2–4)

A. Isaiah 35:1–2

The metaphor "wealth of nations" occurs in Isa 35:2 in a variant formulation, "כבוד (wealth) of Lebanon," which links 35:2 directly with 60:13 (כבוד הלבנון; the phrase occurs only in these two instances), but it also points further to 66:12 (כבוד גוים). These lexical and thematic linkages, along with many others, connect Isa 35 to Isa 60–62.[69] Isaiah 35, an "oracle of salvation," concerns a restored Judah, a dry land, which will bloom and blossom (v. 1). The poet paints a verbal picture of the land's future beauty:

---

66. The following confessional statement in v. 15, addressed to Israel's God, is likely not to be attributed to the Gentiles, according to Blenkinsopp, *Isaiah 40–55*.

67. Note, however, Blenkinsopp's caution in reading religious universalism into 45:14.

68. Some commentators find an analogue in Isa 18:7 (Ethiopians bring tribute to Zion); Blenkinsopp is skeptical of a significant comparison.

69. Odil Hannes Steck, *Bereitete Heimkehr: Jesaja 35 als redaktionelle Brücke zwischen dem Ersten und dem Zweiten Jesaja* (SBS 121; Stuttgart: Katholisches Bibelwerk, 1985), 76–79; Marvin A. Sweeney, *Isaiah 1–39 with an Introduction to Prophetic Literature* (FOTL 16; Grand Rapids: Eerdmans, 1996), 450–54, summarizes the "bridge" function of Isa 35 between 1–33 and 40–66; further, see Christopher R. Seitz, *Isaiah 1–39* (IBC; Louisville, Ky.: John Knox, 1993), 239–42.

> The glory of Lebanon shall be given to it,
> The majesty of Carmel and Sharon.
> They shall see the glory of Yhwh,
> The majesty of our God. (35:2)

In 35:2 the prophecy of a transformed land (desert to fertile soil) includes the receiving of the "כבוד of Lebanon." However, verse 2, unlike its successor in 60:13 (the כבוד of Lebanon "comes" to you) is not part of a larger image of the nations' journey (e.g., "wealth of Egypt/the Sabeans ... come over to you," 45:14; 60:5, 11, 13). The transfer of כבוד from Lebanon, etc., to Judah is expressed merely by the passive verb "will be given." In 35:2 the metaphor "Lebanon's wealth/glory," its beauty and majesty, is now closely connected to the realm of the natural world as a symbol for Israel's eschatological salvation, but this is a long way from the picture language of Isa 60, with its political and economic overtones. What is significant regarding 35:2 is that the metaphor of enrichment and fertility for Israel's land comes from outside Israel, in the region of the Phoenicians. When Isa 35 is read in the context of Isa 34, where the nations are punished, the loss of the כבוד of Lebanon, which glorifies Israel, constitutes a part of that punishment (34:2); indeed, it is a year of recompense for the cause of Zion (34:8). Loss of the nations' wealth and glory means gain for Zion and her land.

B. Isaiah 23

Isa 23:1–14 presents a summons to lament a past event, "an ironic injunction to others to lament,"[70] the misfortune of Phoenicia. A connection is made between 60:9 and 23, especially by the phrase, "ships of Tarshish" (23:1, 14; elsewhere, 1 Kgs 10:22; Ezek 27:25; Ps 48:8). These ships are merchandise-bearing vessels capable of hauling grain and other goods (23:3). In Isa 60:9 ships of Tarshish help transport the wealth of nations to Zion. Just as the nations' wealth comes to Zion in Isa 60, 61, and 66, so the city of Tyre will, after her own punishment is passed, "dedicate her merchandise and her wages to Yhwh" and to "those who dwell before Yhwh" (23:18). The word "dedicate" (קדש) refers to sacred gifts or offerings for the deity, for the support of cultic personnel.[71] The close connection with 61:6 is clear, where foreign riches will also support the work of "priests." Indeed, the "eating of wealth"

---

70. Blenkinsopp, *Isaiah 1–39*.
71. Wildberger, *Jesaja 13–27*.

in 61:6 is reminiscent of "the abundant food" for the priest (those who dwell before Yhwh") in 23:18. The wealth ("trade and commerce") of kingdoms (23:18), imaged as a "revitalized trade activity" (Blenkinsopp), anticipates the "wealth of nations" that provides for Zion's economic well-being in Isa 60, 61, and 66.

C. Isaiah 2:2-4

The close connections of Isa 60 with 2:2-4 have long been noted. The classic study by Gerhard von Rad, "The City on the Hill,"[72] compares and contrasts Isa 60 and 2:2-4 (along with Hag 2:6-9). Von Rad thinks that, when reduced to their simplest terms, these two texts correspond in their general "outline" of thought, with Isa 60 having the much wider scope.[73] Both Isa 60 and 2:2-4 envision a journey of the nations to Zion; but in 2:2-4 the purpose of the nations' coming to "the mountain of the house of Yhwh" is to be instructed (ירנו) by the divine word, the תורה.[74] The nations as *pilgrims* seek contact with the sacred mountain; like Israel, they "go up" (עלה) to Jerusaelm, a *terminus technicus* for pilgrimage (Ps 122:4).[75] According to Steck,[76] Isa 2:2-4 belongs to those texts, different from Isa 60 (also 45:14; 49:23), in which the nations come respectfully to a holy space for help or counsel, the motif of pilgrimage (*Völkerwallfahrt*; Zech 8:20-22; Mic 7:11-12; Ps 102:16-17, 23 [Eng. vv. 15-16, 22]). Furthermore, in 2:2-4 the nations come, not to give (tribute/their wealth), but to receive (torah). Finally, while Isa 60 focuses almost exclusively on the city and the wealth brought by the nations, 2:2-4 "concentrates on the heathen nations and the significance a transfigured Jerusalem has for them."[77] In the end, the two texts take their readers to different goals,

---

72. Gerhard von Rad, "The City on the Hill," in *From Genesis to Chronicles: Explorations in Old Testament Theology* (ed. K. C. Hanson; Minneapolis: Fortress, 2005), 115-22.

73. von Rad, "The City on the Hill," 119.

74. The significance of "Torah" in Isaiah has received much attention; e.g., Joseph Jensen, *The Use of tôrah by Isaiah: His Debate with the Wisdom Tradition* (CBQMS 3; Washington, D.C.: The Catholic Biblical Association of America, 1973); Sweeney, "The Book of Isaiah as Prophetic Torah," in Melugin and Sweeney, *New Visions of Isaiah*, 50-67.

75. Wildberger, *Isaiah 1-12*. Further, in 2:2-3, the nations "flow" or "stream" (נהר), they "go" (הלך) to Zion; the verb נהר I seldom occurs in the Hebrew Bible; besides the parallel in Mic 4:1-3, see Jer 51:44 ("nations will not stream to Bel of Babylon"); the root possibly occurs in Jer 31:12 (RSV translates as נהר II "be radiant").

76. Steck, "Lumen gentium," *Studien zu Tritojesaja*, 95.

77. von Rad, "The City on the Hill," 119-20.

employing the metaphor of the nation's coming in very different ways. After hearing "torah" and learning about peace, the pilgrim nations must return home to practice it (2:2–4). How different from the "symbolic world" created by Isa 60, 61, where the nations bring their wealth, come in submission to glorify *Zion*, work as her builders and shepherds and serve her "priests." The metaphor of the nation's journey functions in entirely different ways in 2:2–4 and 60–61, the former a pilgrimage of the nations (*Völkerwallfahrt*), the latter a journey of the nations (*Völkerzug*). On the other hand, the epilogue to the book, 66:18–21, does employ the pilgrimage metaphor. Indeed, it points back to Isa 2:2–4, returning the reader to the beginning, thus making the pilgrimage metaphor a kind of frame or envelope around the book. The nations who come to Zion for instruction (Isa 2:2–4) finally, like Moses, must make pilgrimage to see God's glory (66:18).[78] In the chapters between these two visions, however, "the wealth of nations," and therefore economic power and political prestige, must be transferred to Zion, from which place the kingdom of God will finally rule.

Conclusion

We have worked our way backward from Trito-Isaiah, with focus on two metaphors, "the nations come to Zion" and the "wealth of nations." But readers, let us assume, read from beginning from to end. The "nations" are introduced to the reader almost at the outset, with a contrast between the "sinful nation" in 1:4 and the "nations" who make pilgrimage to Zion (2:2–4). These pilgrims come without gifts, but they also come without weapons, in peace, to hear Torah. But menacing "nations" (Assyria) do come later (10:5–6), against a "godless nation" (Israel), to rob them of their wealth (spoil and booty), steal their treasures (10:13), and otherwise gather in the "wealth of peoples" (10:14). But wealth is not only taken; nations who are subjugated or humbled are compelled to "offer" tribute/gifts to their sovereign (18:7). Wealth in the form of tribute thus begins to return to Zion. As with Ethiopia (18:7), so with Tyre and Sidon: ships of Tarshish, momentarily stymied in their sea routes, will bring their merchandise in abundance to the priests in Zion (23:7). Other nations, such as Phoenicia (Lebanon), send their prized goods, their valuable produce (the כבוד of Lebanon) and get to partake of the כבוד Yhwh (35:2).

---

78. Isaiah 2:2–4 is further linked to 66 by the metaphor of "stream/steaming"; the nations' streaming to Zion points forward to Zion's future prosperity which, "like a stream" (כנהר), will be given to her (66:12).

Further, Egypt, Ethiopia, and Saba journey to Jerusalem (45:14); here for the first time "nations" specifically journey to Zion in order to bring their wealth and pay homage, not to Yhwh but to Zion. The nations gain momentum, and, upon a signal, travel to Zion to pay homage, again, to Zion, carrying not gifts but the sons and daughters of the Diaspora (49:22–23). Even nations that do not know Zion's people will "run" to her, apparently drawn by the magnetic "glory" conferred upon her by Yhwh (55:5). Indeed, nations from (almost) all directions converge on Zion, with wealth coming by ships of Tarshish and camel caravans (60:4–16). While the wealth of the nations is enormous, the status of those who bring it diminishes; they come now as a servant class, not willingly, but rather in a dramatic reversal of roles. They come to build, farm, and provide food for a priestly nation (60:10–14; 61:5–6). The wealth, which flows like a stream, is however more than riches, for, finally, it comforts and consoles (66:12–13). At the end, the treasury of the nations being exhausted, their journeys to Zion are no longer accompanied by their wealth. But they come not empty handed, for their gifts of homage are the formerly scattered sons and daughters of Zion (66:18–20). Thus the metaphors of "pilgrimage" (the journey of the nations) and of "tribute" (the "wealth of nations") lace themselves throughout the book of Isaiah, with key texts placed both at the beginning and the end (Isa 2:2–4; 66:18–21). The dramatic imagery functions not only to help establish a certain literary unity to the book, but more importantly, to create a "symbolic world" that constitutes the "richness of the poetic vision in the book"[79] in which, whatever the many tensions, Israel and the Gentile world finally come together before Yhwh (66:18–21).

---

79. Roy F. Melugin, see note 3 above.

Contributors

Willem A. M. Beuken is Professor Emeritus of Old Testament at the Katholieke Universiteit Leuven, Leuven, Belgium.

Carol J. Dempsey is Professor of Theology (Biblical Studies) at the University of Portland, Portland, Oregon.

A. Joseph Everson is Professor of Religion at California Lutheran University, Thousand Oaks, California.

Chris A. Franke is Professor of Old Testament/Hebrew Bible at the College of St. Catherine, St. Paul, Minnesota.

James M. Kennedy is Associate Professor of Religion, Baylor University, Waco, Texas.

Hyun Chul Paul Kim is Associate Professor of Hebrew Bible in the Williams Chair of Biblical Studies at Methodist Theological School in Ohio, Delaware, Ohio.

Francis Landy is Professor of Religious Studies at the University of Alberta, Edmonton, Canada.

Gary Stansell is Professor of Religion at St. Olaf College, Northfield, Minnesota.

Marvin A. Sweeney is Professor of Hebrew Bible at Claremont School of Theology and Professor of Religion at Claremont Graduate University, Claremont, California.

Patricia K. Tull is Arnold Black Rhodes Professor of Hebrew Scriptures at Louisville Presbyterian Theological Seminary, Louisville, Kentucky.

Roy D. Wells is Professor Emeritus of Religion at Birmingham-Southern College, Birmingham, Alabama.

Hugh G. M. Williamson is Regius Professor of Hebrew at the University of Oxford, a Student of Christ Church, and a Fellow of the British Academy, Oxford, United Kingdom.

Bibliography

Abma, R. *Bonds of Love: Methodic Studies of Prophetic Texts with Marriage Imagery (Isaiah 50:1–3 and 54:1–10, Hosea 1–3, and Jeremiah 2–3*. SSN. Assen: Van Gorcum, 1999.
Abrams, Meyer. H. *A Glossary of Literary Terms*. Boston: Wadsworth, 2005.
Ackroyd, Peter R. *Studies in the Religious Tradition of the Old Testament*. London: SCM, 1987.
Ainger, Katherine. "The New Peasant Revolt." *The New Internationalist*, January/February 2003. (http://www.thirdworldtraveler.com/Food/New_Peasants_Revolt.html).
Albertz, Rainer. "Darius in Place of Cyrus: The First Edition of Deutero-Isaiah (Isaiah 40.1–52.12) in 521 B.C.E." *JSOT* 27 (2003): 371–83.
Alexander, Joseph A. *Commentary on the Prophecies of Isaiah*. 2 vols. New York: Scribner, 1874. Repr., Grand Rapids: Zondervan, 1976.
Alobaidi, Joseph. *The Messiah in Isaiah 53: The Commentaries of Saadia Gaon, Salmon ben Yeruham and Yefet ben Eli on Is 52:13–53:12*. Bern: Lang, 1998.
Alonso Schökel, Luis. *A Manual of Hebrew Poetics*. SubBi 11. Rome: Pontifical Biblical Institute, 1988.
Alter, Robert. *The Art of Biblical Poetry*. New York: Basic Books, 1985.
———. *The Pleasures of Reading in an Ideological Age*. New York: Simon and Schuster, 1989.
Andersen, Francis I. and David Noel Freedman. *Hosea*. AB 24. Garden City, N.Y.: Doubleday, 1980.
Asen, Bernhard A. "The Garlands of Ephraim: Isaiah 28:1–6 and the *Marzeah*." *JSOT* 71 (1996): 73–87.
Aster, Shawn Zelig. "Jerusalem Replaces Babylon: The Neo-Babylonian Background to Isaiah 60." Paper presented at the annual meeting of the SBL. San Diego, Calif., 2007.
Baltzer, Klaus. *Deutero-Isaiah: A Commentary on Isaiah 40–55*. Translated by Margaret Kohl. Hermeneia. Minneapolis: Fortress, 2001.
———. *Deutero-Jesaja*. KAT 10.2. Gütersloh: Gütersloher, 1999.
Barker, Debi. "Globalization and Industrial Agriculture." Pages 313–19 in *Fatal Harvest: The Tragedy of Industrial Agriculture*. Edited by Andrew Kimbrell. Washington: Island Press, 2002.
Barr, James. "The Synchronic, the Diachronic and the Historical: A Triangular Relationship?" Pages 1–14 in *Synchronic or Diachronic?: A Debate on Method in Old Testament Exegesis*. Edited by Johannes C. de Moor. OTS 34. Leiden: Brill, 1995.
Barstad, Hans. "Isa 40,1–11: Another Reading." Pages 225–40 in *Congress Volume Basel 2001*. Edited by A. Lemaire. VTSup 92. Leiden: Brill, 2002.

Barthes, Roland. *The Pleasure of the Text*. Translated by Richard Miller. New York: Hill and Wang, 1975.
Baumann, Gerlinde. *Love and Violence: Marriage as Metaphor for the Relationship between YHWH and Israel in the Prophetic Books*. Collegeville, Minn.: Liturgical, 2003.
Ben Zvi, Ehud. "Introduction: Writing, Speeches, and the Prophetic Books – Setting an Agenda." Pages 1–29 in *Writings and Speech in Israelite and Ancient Near Eastern Prophecy*. Edited by Ehud Ben Zvi and Michael H. Floyd. Atlanta: Society of Biblical Literature, 2000.
———. *Hosea*. FOTL 21A; Grand Rapids: Eerdmans, 2005.
———. *Micah*. FOTL 21B. Grand Rapids: Eerdmans, 2000.
———, ed. *Utopia and Dystopia in Prophetic Literature*. Publications of the Finnish Exegetical Society 92. Helsinki: Finnish Exegetical Society, 2006.
Berges, Ulrich. *Das Buch Jesaja: Komposition und Endgestalt*. Herders Biblische Studien 16. Freiburg: Herder, 1998.
———. "The Growth of the Book of Isaiah: Continuation or Combination?" Paper presented at the annual meeting of the SBL. Boston, Mass., 2008.
———. *Jesaja 40–48*. HTKAT. Freiburg: Herder, 2008.
———. "Personifications and Prophetic Voices of Zion in Isaiah and Beyond." Pages 54–82 in *The Elusive Prophet*. Edited by Johannes C. de Moor. Leiden: Brill, 2001.
———. "Die Zionstheologie des Buches Jesaja," *EstBib* 58 (2000): 167–98.
Beuken, Willem A. M. *Jesaja 1–12*. HTKAT. Freiburg: Herder, 2003.
———. "Jesaja 33 als Spiegeltext im Jesajabuch." *ETL* 67 (1991): 5–35.
———. *Jesaja 13–27*. HTKAT. Freiburg: Herder, 2007.
———. "Isaiah Chapters LXV–LXVI: Trito-Isaiah and the Closure of the Book of Isaiah." Pages 204–21 in *Congress Volume: Leuven*. Edited by J. A. Emerton. VTSup 43. Leiden: Brill, 1991.
———. *Jesaja. Deel IIIA*. POut. Nijkerk: G. F. Callenbach, 1989.
———. *Jesaja. Deel IIIB*. POut. Nijkerk: G. F. Callenbach, 1989.
———. "The Main Theme of Trito-Isaiah: The 'Servants of Yhwh.'" *JSOT* 47 (1990): 67–87.
———. "Mišpaṭ: The First Servant Song and Its Context." *VT* 22 (1972): 1–30.
———. "Woe to Powers in Israel that Vie to Replace Yhwh's Rule on Mt. Zion! Isaiah Chs. 28–31 from the Perspective of Isaiah Chs. 24–27" in FS A. van der Kooij. Leiden: Brill, forthcoming.
Black, Fiona C. *The Artifice of Love: Grotesque Bodies and the Song of Songs*. Edinburgh: T&T Clark, 2009.
Blank, Sheldon. *Prophetic Faith in Isaiah*. Detroit: Wayne State University Press, 1967.
Blenkinsopp, Joseph. *A History of Prophecy in Israel*. Louisville, Ky.: Westminster John Knox, 1996.
———. *Isaiah 1–39*. AB 19. New York: Doubleday, 2000.
———. *Isaiah 40–55*. AB 19A. New York: Doubleday, 2002.
———. *Isaiah 56–66*. AB 19B. New York: Doubleday, 2003.
Bloch, Ernst. *The Spirit of Utopia*. Translated by Anthony A. Nassar. Stanford: Stanford University Press, 2000.
Blum, Erhard. *Die Komposition des Vätergeschichte*. WMANT 57. Neukirchen-Vluyn: Neukirchener, 1984.
Boden, Peggy Jean. "The Mesopotamian Washing of the Mouth (*mīs pî*) Ritual: An Examination of Some of the Social and Communication Strategies which Guided the

Development and Performance of the Ritual which Transferred the Essence of the Deity into Its Temple Statue." (Ph.D. diss., The Johns Hopkins University, 1998).

Bonnard, P.-E. *Le Second Isaïe: Son Disciple et Leurs Éditeurs. Isaïe 40-66*. EBib. Paris: Gebalda, 1972.

Borowski, Oded. *Agriculture in Iron Age Israel*. Boston: American Schools of Oriental Research, 2002.

Brassey, Paul Del. *Metaphor and the Incomparable God in Isaiah 40-55*. Bibal Dissertaion Series 9. North Richland Hills, Tex.: Bibal, 2001.

Brettler, Marc Zvi. "Incompatible Metaphors for Yhwh in Isaiah 40-66." *JSOT* 78 (1998): 97-120.

Broyles, Craig C. and Craig A. Evans, eds. *Writing and Reading the Scroll of Isaiah: Studies of an Interpretive Tradition*. 2 vols. VTSup 70. Leiden: Brill, 1997.

Brueggemann, Walter. *Isaiah 40-66*. WBC. Louisville, Ky.: Westminster John Knox, 1998.

———. "Unity and Dynamic in the Isaiah Tradition." *JSOT* 29 (1984): 89-107.

Buber, Martin. "On Word Choice in Translating the Bible: In Memoriam Franz Rosenzweig." Pages 73-89 in *Scripture and Translation*. Bloomington, Ind.: Indiana University Press, 1994.

Budde, Karl. *Jesaja's Erleben: Eine Gemeinverständliche Auslegung der Denkschrift des Propheten (Kap. 6,1-9,6)*. Gotha: Leopold Klotz, 1928.

Callender, Jr., Dexter E. "Servants of God(s) and Servants of Kings in Israel and the Ancient Near East." *Semeia* 83/84 (1998): 67-82.

Campbell, Antony F. and Mark A. O'Brien. *Sources of the Pentateuch: Texts Introductions, Annotations*. Minneapolis: Fortress, 1993.

Carr, David M. "Isaiah 40:1-11 in the Context of the Macrostructure of Second Isaiah." Pages 51-73 in *Discourse Analysis of Biblical Literature: What It Is and What It Offers*. Edited by R.Walter Bodine. Atlanta: Scholars Press, 1995.

———. "Reaching for Unity in Isaiah." *JSOT* 57 (1993): 61-80.

———. "Reading Isaiah from Beginning (Isaiah 1) to End (Isaiah 65-66)." Pages 188-218 in *New Visions of Isaiah*. Edited by Roy F. Melugin and Marvin A. Sweeney. JSOTSup 214. Sheffield: Sheffield Academic Press, 1996. Repr., Atlanta: Society of Biblical Literature, 2006.

Carrerio, Margaret S. "Helping Louisville Become Ecologically Sustainable." Mending the Earth Teach-In, September 4-5, 2007, Louisville Presbyterian Seminary.

Carroll, Robert P. "Blindsight and the Vision Thing: Blindness and Insight in the Book of Isaiah." Pages 79-93 in *Writing and Reading the Scroll of Isaiah: Studies of an Interpretive Tradition*. Edited by Craig C. Broyles and Craig A. Evans. VTSup 70.1. Leiden: Brill, 1997.

Causse, Antonin. *La vision de la nouvelle Jérusalem [Esaïe LX] et la signification sociologique des assemblées de fête et des pèlerinages dans l'orient sémitique. Mélanges syriens ouffert à monsieur René Dussaud*. Bibliothèque archéologique et historique. Haut-commisariat de la République française en Syrie et au Liban. Service des antiquités 30. vol. 2. Paris: P. Geutner, 1939.

Celan, Paul. *Collected Prose*. Translated by Rosemary Waldrop. Manchester: Carcanet, 1999.

Chaitin, Gilbert D. "Metonymy/metaphor." Pages 589-91 in *Encyclopedia of Literary Critics and Criticism*. Edited by Chris Murray. 2 vols. London: Dearborn, 1999.

Challoner, Richard, ed. *The Holy Bible. Douay Rheims Version*. Rockford, Ill.: Tan Books, 1609, 1989.

Chapman, Cynthia R. *Gendered Language of Warfare in the Israelite-Assyrian Encounter*. HSM 62. Winona Lake, Ind.: Eisenbrauns, 2004.

Childs, Brevard S. *Introduction to the Old Testament as Scripture*. Philadelphia: Fortress, 1979.

———. *Isaiah*. OTL. Louisville, Ky.: Westminster John Knox, 2001.

Cixous, Hélène. *Three Steps on the Ladder of Writing*. Translated by Sarah Cornell and Susan Sellers. New York: Columbia University Press, 1993.

Clements, Ronald E. "'Arise, Shine; For Your Light Has Come': A Basic Theme in the Isaianic Tradition." Pages 441–54 in *Writing and Reading the Scroll of Isaiah: Studies of an Interpretive Tradition*. Edited by Craig C. Broyles and Craig A. Evans. VTSup 70.1. Leiden: Brill, 1997.

———. "Beyond Tradition-History: Deutero-Isaianic Development of First Isaiah's Themes." *JSOT* 31 (1985): 95–113.

———. *Isaiah 1–39*. NCB. Grand Rapids: Eerdmans, 1980.

———. "A Light to the Nations: A Central Theme of the Book of Isaiah." Pages 57–69 in *Forming Prophetic Literature: Essays on Isaiah and the Twelve in Honor of John D. W. Watts*. Edited by J. W. Watts and P. R. House. JSOTSup 235. Sheffield: Sheffield Academic Press, 1996.

———. *Old Testament Prophecy: From Oracles to Canon*. Louisville, Ky.: Westminster John Knox, 1996.

———. "Patterns in the Prophetic Canon: Healing the Blind and the Lame." Pages 189–200 in *Canon, Theology, and Old Testament Interpretation: Essays in Honor of Brevard S. Childs*. Edited by G. M. Tucker, D. L. Petersen, and R. R. Wilson. Philadelphia: Fortress, 1988.

Clifford, Richard J. *Fair Spoken and Persuading: An Interpretation of Second Isaiah*. New York: Paulist, 1984.

———. "The Unity of the Book of Isaiah and its Cosmogonic Language." *CBQ* 55 (1993): 1–17.

Clines, David J. A. "The Parallelism of Greater Precision," Pages 77–100 in *Directions in Biblical Hebrew Poetry*. Edited by Elaine R. Follis. JSOTSup 40. Sheffield: JSOT Press, 1987.

Cody, Aelred. "A Palindrome in Isaiah 40.4b." *CBQ* 66 (2004): 551–60.

Collins, Christopher. *The Poetics of the Mind's Eye: Literature and the Psychology of Imagination*. Philadelphia: University of Pennsylvania Press, 1991.

Conrad, Edgar W. *Reading Isaiah*. OBT. Minneapolis: Fortress, 1991.

Cross, Frank M. "The Council of YHWH in Second Isaiah." *JNES* 12 (1953): 274–77.

Dalman, Gustaf. *Der Ackerbau*. vol. 2 of *Arbeit und Sitte in Palästina*. Gütersloh: Bertelsmann, 1932.

Darr, Katheryn Pfisterer. *Isaiah's Vision and the Family of God*. Literary Currents in Biblical Interpretation. Louisville, Ky.: Westminster John Knox, 1994.

———. "Two Unifying Female Images in the Book of Isaiah." Pages 17–30 in *Uncovering Ancient Stones: Essays in Memory of H. Neil Richardson*. Edited by Lewis M. Hopfe. Winona Lake, Ind.: Eisenbrauns, 1994.

Davis, Ellen F. "Becoming Human: Biblical Interpretation and Ecological Responsibility." https://www.vts.edu/ftpimages/95/misc/misc_53462.pdf.

———. *Scripture, Culture, and Agriculture: An Agrarian Reading of the Bible.* Cambridge: Cambridge University Press, 2009.
Delitzsch, Franz. *Commentar über das Buch Jesaia.* Biblischer Commentar über das Alte Testament. 3 vols. Leipzig: Dörffling & Franke, 1889.
Derrida, Jacques. "Shibboleth." Page 311 in *Midrash and Literature.* Edited by Geoffrey Hartman and Sanford Budick. New Haven: Yale University Press, 1986.
Detienne, Marcel. *The Gardens of Adonis: Spices in Greek Mythology.* Translated by J. Lloyd. Princeton: Princeton University Press, 1994.
Dick, Michael B. "Prophetic Parodies of Making the Cult Image." Pages 1–53 in *Born in Heaven, Made on Earth: The Making of the Cult Image in the Ancient Near East.* Edited by Michael B. Dick. Winona Lake, Ind.: Eisenbrauns, 1999.
Dijkstra, Meindert. "YHWH as Israel's Go'el." *ZABR* 5 (1999): 236–57.
Dille, Sarah J. *Mixing Metaphors: God as Mother and Father in Deutero-Isaiah.* JSOTSup 398. Gender, Culture, Theory 13. London: T&T Clark, 2004.
Douglas, Mary. "Justice as the Cornerstone: An Interpretation of Leviticus 18–20." *Int* 53 (1999): 341–50.
———. *Leviticus as Literature.* Oxford: Oxford University Press, 1999.
Downie, Andrew. "The Amazon Gets Less and Less Green." *Time* (Jan 25, 2008; http://www.time.com/time/health/article/0,8599,1707121,00.html).
Duhm, Bernhard. *Das Buch Jesaia. Übersetzt und erklärt.* HKAT 3.1. Göttingen: Vandenhoeck & Ruprecht, 1892.
———. *Das Buch Jesaia. Übersetzt und erklärt.* 4th ed. HKAT 3.1. Göttingen: Vandenhoeck & Ruprecht, 1922.
———. *Das Buch Jesaia. Übersetzt und erklärt.* 5th ed. HKAT 3.1. Göttingen: Vandenhoeck & Ruprecht, 1968.
Eagleton, Terry. *How to Read a Poem.* Malden, Mass.: Blackwell, 2007.
Ehring, Christina. *Die Rückkehr JHWHs: Traditions- und religionsgeschichtliche Untersuchungen zu Jesaja 40,1–11, Jesaja 52,7–10 und verwandten Texten.* WMANT 116. Neukirchen-Vluyn: Neukirchener, 2007.
Eliade, Mircea. *The Sacred and the Profane.* New York: Harper & Row, 1961.
Elliger, Karl. *Deuterojesaja 1: Teilband. Jesaja 40,1–45,7.* BKAT 11.1. Neukirchen-Vluyn: Neukirchener, 1989.
———. "Der Prophet Tritojesaja." *ZAW* 49 (1931): 112–41.
Ettore, Franco. "Is 40,1–11: Una Lettura Strutturale." *RevistB* 28 (1980): 285–304.
Evans, Craig. A. *To See and Not Perceive: Isaiah 6.9–10 in Early Jewish and Christian Interpretation.* JSOTSup 64. Sheffield: JSOT Press, 1989.
Evans, Desiree. "Bearing the Fruits of Their Labors." *Facing South*, Dec. 5, 2008 (http://www.southernstudies.org/2008/12/bearing-the-fruits-of-their-labor.html).
Everson, A. Joseph. "Isaiah." Pages 648–52 in *Eerdmans Dictionary of the Bible.* Grand Rapids: Erdmann, 2000.
Feldmann, Franz. *Das Buch Isaias.* EHAT 14. 2 vols. Münster: Aschendorff, 1925–1926.
Fish, Stanley. *Is There a Text in this Class? The Authority of Interpretive Communities.* Cambridge: Harvard University Press, 1980.
Fishbane, Michael. *Biblical Interpretation in Ancient Israel.* Oxford: Clarendon, 1985.
Fohrer, Georg. *Das Buch Jesaja.* 3 vols. ZBK. Zürich: Zwingli, 1964. Repr. Zurich: Theologischer Verlag, 1991.
Fokkelman, Jan P. "Stylistic Analysis of Isaiah 40:1–11." *OtSt* 21 (1981): 68–90.

Foster, Julie A. "The Motherhood of God: The Use of Ḥyl as God-Language in the Hebrew Scriptures." Pages 93–102 in *Uncovering Ancient Stones: Essays in Memory of H. Neil Richardson*. Edited by Lewis M. Hopfe. Winona Lake, Ind;: Eisenbruans, 1994.

Freedman, David Noel. "The Structure of Isaiah 40:1–11." Pages 232–57 in *Poetry and Orthography*. Vol. 2 of *Divine Commitment and Human Obligation. Selected Writings*. Edited by David Noel Freedman. Grand Rapids: Eerdmans, 1997).

Frymer-Kensky, Tikva Simone. "The Planting of Man: A Study in Biblical Imagery." Pages 129–36 in *Love and Death in the Ancient Near East: Essays in Honor of Marvin H. Pope*. Edited by John H. Marks and Robert M. Good. Guilford, Conn.: Four Quarters, 1987.

Galambush, Julie. *Jerusalem in the Book of Ezekiel: The City as YHWH's Wife*. SBLDS 130. Atlanta: Scholars Press, 1992.

Gardner, A. E. "The Nature of the New Heavens and New Earth in Isaiah 66:22." *ABR* 50 (2002): 10–27.

Garnett, Tara. "The World on a Plate: Food and Its Contribution to Climate Changing Emissions." (December 2007: http://www.climateactionprogramme.org/features/article/the_world_on_a_plate_food_and_its_contribution_to_climate_changing_emission/).

Gärtner, Judith. *Jesaja 66 und Sacharja 14 als Summe der Prophetie: Eine traditions- und redaktionsgeschichtliche Untersuchung zum Abschluss des Jesaja- und des Zwölfprophetenbuches*. WMANT 114. Neukirchen-Vluyn: Neukirchener, 2006.

Geller, Stephen A. "A Poetic Analysis of Isaiah 40:1–2." *HTR* 77 (1984): 413–24.

———. "Were the Prophets Poets?" *Prooftexts* 3 (1983): 211–21.

Gesenius, Wilhelm. *Philologisch-kritischer und historischer Commentar über den Jesaia*. 2 vols. Leipzig: Vogel, 1821.

Gibbs, Robert. *Why Ethics?* Princeton: Princeton University Press, 2002.

Gitay, Yehoshua. "Why Metaphors: Study in the Texture of Isaiah." Pages 57–65 in *Writing and Reading the Scroll of Isaiah: Studies of an Interpretive Tradition*. Edited by Craig C. Broyles and Craig A. Evans. VTSup 70. Leiden: Brill, 1997.

Goldingay, John. *Isaiah*. NIBC. Peabody: Hendrikson, 2001.

———. "Isaiah 40–55 in the 1990s: Among Other Things Deconstructing, Mystifying, Intertextual, Socio-Critical, Hearer-Involving." *BibInt* 5 (1997): 225–46.

———. *The Message of Isaiah 40–55*. London: T&T Clark, 2005.

Goldingay, John and David Payne. *Isaiah 40–55*. Vol. 1. ICC. London: T&T Clark, 2006.

Gorenberg, Gershom. *The End of Days: Fundamentalism and the Struggle for the Temple Mount*. Oxford: Oxford University Press, 2000.

Görg, Manfred. "Revision von Schöpfung und Geschichte: Auf dem Wege zu ein Strukturbestimmung von Jes 40,1–8 (11)." Pages 135–56 in *Ich bewirke das Heil und erschaffe das Unheil (Jesaja 45,7): Studien zur Botschaft der Prophet. Festschrift Lothar Ruppert*. Edited by F. Diedrich and Bernd Willmes. Würzburg: Echter, 1998.

Gottwald, Norman K. "Social Class and Ideology in Isaiah 40–55: An Eagletonian Reading." *Semeia* 59 (1992): 43–57.

Goulder, Michael. "Behold My Servant Jehoiachin." *VT* 52 (2001): 175–90.

Gowan, Donald E. "Isaiah 6:1–8." *Int* 45 (1991): 172–76.

Gray, George B. *A Critical and Exegetical Commentary on the Book of Isaiah I–XXVII*. ICC. Edinburgh: T&T Clark, 1912.

Grelot, Pierre. "Un parallèle babylonien d'Isaïe LX et du Psaume LXXII." *VT* 7 (1957): 319–21.
Gruber, M. E. "The Motherhood of God in Second Isaiah." *RB* 90 (1983): 351–59.
Gurian-Sherman, Doug. "CAFOs Uncovered: The Untold Costs of Confined Animal Feeding Operations." (Union of Concerned Scientists, April 2008: http://www.ucsusa.org/assets/documents/food_and_agriculture/cafos-uncovered.pdf).
Habel, Norman. "The Form and Significance of the Call Narratives." *ZAW* 77 (1965): 297–323.
Hanson, Paul D. *Isaiah 40–55.* IBC. Louisville, Ky.: John Knox, 1995.
Haran, Menahem. "The Literary Structure and Chronological Framework of the Prophecies in Is. xl-xlviii." Pages 127–55 in *Congress Volume: Bonn 1962.* VTSup 9. Leiden: Brill, 1963.
Hauser, Alan J. ed. *Recent Research on the Major Prophets.* Sheffield: Sheffield Phoenix Press, 2008.
Hayes, John H. and Stuart A. Irvine. *Isaiah, the Eighth Century Prophet: His Times and His Preaching.* Nashville: Abingdon, 1987.
Hayes, Katherine M. *"The Earth Mourns": Prophetic Metaphor and Oral Aesthetic.* SBLAcBib 8. Atlanta: Society of Biblical Literature, 2002.
Hedges, Chris. *War is a Force That Gives Us Meaning.* New York: Random House, 2002.
Hillel, Daniel. *The Natural History of the Bible: An Environmental Exploration of the Hebrew Scriptures.* New York: Columbia University Press, 2006.
Holland, Norman. *The Brain of Robert Frost: A Cognitive Approach to Literature.* New York: Routledge, 1988.
Holter, Knut. *Second Isaiah's Idol-Fabrication Passages.* Frankfurt am Main: Lang, 1995.
———. "Zur Funktion der *Städte* Judas in Jesaja XL 9." *VT* 46 (1996): 119–21.
Hornung, Erik. *Conceptions of God in Ancient Egypt: The One and the Many.* Translated by John Baines. Ithaca, N.Y.: Cornell University Press, 1982.
Jacobsen, Thorkild. "The Graven Image." Pages 15–32 in *Ancient Israelite Religion: Essays in Honor of Frank Moore Cross.* Edited by Patrick D. Miller et al. Philadelphia: Fortress, 1987.
———. *The Harab Myth.* SANE 2.101. Malibu: Undena, 1984.
Jakobson, Roman. "Linguistics and Poetics." Pages 62–94 in *Language in Literature.* Edited by Krystyna Pomorska and Stephen Rudy. Cambridge, Mass.: Belknap, 1987.
Janowski, Bernd and Peter Stuhlmacher, eds. *The Suffering Servant: Isaiah 53 in Jewish and Christian Sources.* Translated by D. P. Bailey. Grand Rapids: Eerdmans, 2004.
Jensen, Joseph. *The Use of tôrah by Isaiah: His Dispute with the Wisdom Tradition.* CBQMS 3. Washington, D. C.: The Catholic Biblical Association of America, 1973.
Jepson, A. "אָמֵן; אָמַן; אֱמוּנָה; אֱמֶת." *TDOT* 1: 292–323.
Jones, Barry A. "Canon of the Old Testament." Pages 215–17 in *Eerdmans Dictionary of the Bible.* Grand Rapids: Eerdmans, 2000.
Josipovici, Gabriel. *The Book of God: A Response to the Bible.* New Haven: Yale University Press, 1989.
Jüngel, Eberhard. "Metaphorical Truth: Reflections on the Theological Relevance of Metaphor as a Contribution to the Hermeneutics of Narrative Theology." Pages 16–71 in *Theological Essays.* Translated by John Webster. Edinburgh: T&T Clark, 1989.
Kaminsky, Joel S. and A. Stuart. "God of All the World: Universalism and Developing Monotheism in Isaiah 40–66." *HTR* 99 (2006): 139–63.

Kennedy, James M. "Hebrew *piṯḥôn peh* in the Book of Ezekiel." *VT* 41 (1991): 233–35.
Kiesow, Klaus. *Exodustexte im Jesajabuch: Literarkritische und Motivgeschichtliche Analysen*. OBO 24. Göttingen: Vandenhoeck & Ruprecht, 1979.
Kilian, Rudolf. "'Beut eine Strasse für unseren Gott': Überlegungen zu Jes 40,3–5." Pages 173–82 in *Studien zu alttestamentlichen Texten und Situationen*. Edited by Wolfgang Werner and Juergen Werlitz. Stuttgart: Katholisches Bibelwerk, 1999.
Kim, Hyun Chul Paul. *Ambiguity, Tension, and Multiplicity in Deutero-Isaiah*. Studies in Biblical Literature 52. New York: Lang, 2003.
———. "An Intertextual Reading of a 'Crushed Reed' and a 'Dim Wick' in Isa 42:3." *JSOT* 83 (1999): 113–24.
Kissane, Edward J. *The Book of Isaiah, Translated from a Critically Revised Hebrew Text with Commentary*. 2 vols. Dublin: Browne & Nolan, 1941.
Knierim, Rolf P. "The Vocation of Isaiah." *VT* 18 (1968): 47–68.
Koenen, Klaus. *Ethik und Eschatologie im Tritojesajabuch: Eine literarkritische und redaktionsgeschichtliche Studie*. WMANT 62. Neukirchen-Vluyn: Neukirchener, 1990.
Koole, Jan L. *Isaiah: Part 3. Vol. 1: Isaiah 40–48*. Translated by Anthony P. Runia. HCOT. Kampen: Kok Pharos, 1997.
———. *Isaiah: Part 3. Vol. 3: Isaiah 56–66*. HCOT. Leuven: Peeters, 2001.
Korpel, Marjo C. A. and Johannes C. de Moor. *The Structure of Classical Hebrew Poetry: Isaiah 40–55*. OTS 61. Leiden: Brill, 1998.
Kratz, Reinhard G. "Der Anfang des Zweiten Jesaja in Jes 40,1f. und das Jeremiabuch," *ZAW* 106 (1994): 243–61.
———. "Der Anfang des Zweiten Jesaja in Jes 40,1f und seine literarischen Horizonte." *ZAW* 105 (1993): 400–419.
Kraus, Hans-Joachim. *Das Evangelium des unbekannten Propheten: Jesaja 40–66*. Kleine Biblische Bibliothek. Neukirchen-Vluyn: Neukirchener, 1990.
———. *Worship in Israel*. Translated by Geoffrey Buswell. Oxford: Basil Blackwell, 1966.
Krinetzki, Leo. "Zur Stilistik von Jesaja 40:1–8." *BZ* 16 (1972): 54–69.
Kristeva, Julia. *Revolution in Poetic Language*. Translated by Margaret Waller. New York: Columbia University Press, 1984.
Kustár, Zoltán. *"Durch seine Wunden sind wir geheilt": Eine Untersuchung zur Metaphorik von Israels Krankheit und Heilung im Jesajabuch*. BWANT. Stuttgart: Kohlhammer, 2002.
Kutscher, E. Yechezkel. *The Language and Linguistic Background of the Isaiah Scroll (1QIsa^a)*. STDJ 6. Leiden: Brill, 1974.
Laato, Antti. *"About Zion I Will Not Be Silent": The Book of Isaiah as an Ideological Unity*. Stockholm: Almqvist and Wiksell, 1998.
Labahn, Antje. *Wort Gottes und Schuld Israels: Untersuchungen zu Motiven deuteronomistischer Theologie im Deuterojesajabuch mit einem Ausblick auf das Verhältnis von Jes 40–55 zum Deuteronomismus*. Stuttgart: Kohlhammer, 1999.
Lack, Rémi. *La symbolique de livre d'Isaïe: Essaie sur l'image littéraire comme élément de structuration*. AnBib 59. Rome: Pontifical Biblical Institute, 1973.
Landy, Francis. *Beauty and the Enigma and Other Essays on the Hebrew Bible*. JSOTSup 312. Sheffield: Sheffield Academic Press, 2001.
———. "The Ghostly Prelude to Deutero-Isaiah." *BibInt* 14 (2006): 332–63.

———. "Prophetic Intercourse." Pages 261–79 in *Sense and Sensitivity: Essays on Reading the Bible in Memory of Robert Carroll.* Edited by Alistair G. Hunter and Philip R. Davies. JSOTSup 348. Sheffield: Sheffield Academic Press, 2002.

———. "Strategies of Concentration and Diffusion in Isaiah 6." *BibInt* 6 (1999): 58–86.

Lau, Wolfgang. *Schriftgelehrte Prophetie in Jes 56–66: Eine Untersuchung zu den literarischen Bezügen in den letzten elf Kapiteln des Jesajabuches.* BZAW 225. Berlin: de Gruyter, 1994.

Leclerc, Thomas L. *Yahweh Is Exalted in Justice: Solidarity and Conflict in Isaiah.* Minneapolis: Fortress, 2001.

Leene, Henk. "Isaiah 27:7–9 as a Bridge between Vineyard and City." Pages 199–225 in *Studies in Isaiah 24–27: The Isaiah Workshop – de Jesaja Werkplaats.* Edited by Hendrik J. Bosman et al. OTS 43. Leiden: Brill, 2000.

Leeuwen, K. van. "An Old Crux: הַמְסֻכָּן תְּרוּמָה in Isaiah 40,20." Pages 274–87 in *Studies in the Book of Isaiah: Festschrift Willem A.M. Beuken.* Edited by J. Van Ruiten and M. Vervenne. Leuven: Leuven University Press, 1997.

Lentricchia, Frank. *After the New Criticism.* Chicago: University of Chicago Press, 1980.

Lévinas, Emmanuel. *Otherwise than Being or Beyond Essence.* Translated by Alphonso Lingis. Pittsburgh: Pennsylvania University Press, 1998. [Original publication, *Autrement qu'être ou audelà de l'essence* (The Hague: Martinus Nijhoff, 1974)].

Levine, Etan. "The Land of Milk and Honey." *JSOT* 87 (2000): 43–57.

Levenson, Jon D. "The Temple and the World." *JR* 64 (1984): 275–98.

Lewis, Theodore J. *Cults of the Dead in Ancient Israel and Ugarit.* HSM 39. Atlanta: Scholars Press, 1989.

Lindars, Barnabas. *Judges 1–5: A New Translation and Commentary.* Edinburgh: T&T Clark, 1995.

Løland, Hanne. *Silent or Salient Gender?: The Interpretation of Gendered God-Language in the Hebrew Bible, Exemplified in Isaiah 42, 46 and 49.* Tübingen: Mohr Siebeck, 2008.

Lorton, David. "The Theology of Cult Statues in Ancient Egypt." Pages 123–210 in *Born in Heaven, Made on Earth: The Making of the Cult Image in the Ancient Near East.* Edited by Michael Dick. Winona Lake, Ind.: Eisenbrauns, 1999.

Lotman, Yuri. *Analysis of the Poetic Text.* Translated by D. Barton Johnson. Ann Arbor: Ardis, 1976.

———. *The Structure of the Artistic Text.* Translated by Gail Lenhoff and Ronald Vroon. Ann Arbor: University of Michigan Press, 1977.

Lowery, Richard. *Sabbath and Jubilee.* Understanding Biblical Themes. St. Louis: Chalice, 2000.

Lowth, Robert. *Isaiah: A New Translation; with a Preliminary Dissertation, and Notes, Critical, Philological, and Explanatory.* 2 vols. 1778; 15th ed. London: Tegg, 1957.

———. *Lectures on the Sacred Poetry of the Hebrews.* Translated by G. Gregory. 3rd ed. London: Chadwick, 1847.

Lund, Øystein. *Way Metaphors and Way Topics in Isaiah 40–55.* FAT 28. Tübingen: Mohr Siebeck, 2007.

Maier, Christl M. *Gender, Space, and the Sacred in Ancient Israel.* Minneapolis: Fortress, 2008.

March, W. Eugene. *God's Land on Loan: Israel, Palestine, and the World.* Louisville, Ky.: Westminster John Knox, 2007.

Marti, Karl. *Das Buch Jesaja*. KHAT 10. Tübingen: Mohr Siebeck, 1900.

McDonagh, Sean. "The Transition from Agriculture to Agribusiness" [cited Apr. 26, 2009]. Online: http://www.columban.com/stateofplanet2.htm#_edn20.

McEvenue, Sean. "Who Was Second Isaiah?" Pages 213–22 in *Studies in the Book of Isaiah: Festchrift Willem A. M. Beuken*. Edited by J. Van Ruiten and M. Vervenne. Leuven: Peeters, 1997.

McGinnis, Claire Mathews and Patricia K. Tull, eds., *"As Those Who Are Taught": The Interpretation of Isaiah from the LXX to the SBL*. SBLSymS 27. Atlanta: Society of Biblical Literature, 2006.

McKane, William. "The Interpretation of Isaiah vii 14–25." *VT* 17 (1967): 208–19.

McKibben, Bill. *Deep Economy: The Wealth of Communities and the Durable Future*. New York: Holt, 2007.

Mellon, Margaret and Jane Rissler. "Environmental Effects of Genetically Modified Food Crops—Recent Experiences." Paper presented at conference entitled Genetically Modified Foods—The American Experience, sponsored by the Royal Veterinary and Agricultural University. Copenhagen, Denmark, June 12–13, 2003 [cited Apr. 26, 2009]. Online: http://www.ucsusa.org/food_and_agriculture/science_and_impacts/impacts_genetic_engineering/environmental-effects-of.html.

Melugin, Roy F. "The Book of Isaiah and the Construction of Meaning." Pages 39–55 in *Writing and Reading the Scroll of Isaiah: Studies of an Interpretive Tradition*. Edited by Craig C. Broyles and Craig A. Evans. VTSup 70.1. Leiden: Brill, 1997.

———. "Figurative Speech and the Reading of Isaiah 1 as Scripture." Pages 282–305 in *New Visions of Isaiah*. Edited by Roy F. Melugin and Marvin A. Sweeney. JSOTSup 214. Sheffield: Sheffield Academic Press, 1996. Repr., Atlanta: Society of Biblical Literature, 2006.

———. *The Formation of Isaiah 40–55*. BZAW 141. Berlin: de Gruyter, 1976.

———. "Recent Form Criticism Revisited in an Age of Reader Response." Pages 46–64 in *The Changing Face of Form Criticism for the Twenty-First Century*. Edited by Marvin A. Sweeney and Ehud Ben Zvi. Grand Rapids: Eerdmans, 2003.

———. "Texts to Transform Life: Reading Isaiah as Christians." *WW* 19 (1999): 109–16.

———. "Zion in a Synchronic Reading of Isaiah." Paper presented at the annual meeting of the SBL, San Diego, Calif., Nov. 2007.

Melugin, Roy F. and Marvin A. Sweeney, eds. *New Visions of Isaiah*. JSOTSup 214. Sheffield: Sheffield Academic Press, 1996. Repr., Atlanta: Society of Biblical Literature, 2006.

Merendino, Rosario Pius. *Der Erste und der Letzte: Eine Untersuchung von Jes 40–48*. VTSup 31. Leiden: Brill, 1981.

Mettinger, Tryggve M. "In Search of the Hidden Structure: YHWH as King in Isaiah 40–55." Pages 143–54 in *Writing and Reading the Scroll of Isaiah: Studies of an Interpretive Tradition*. Edited by Craig C. Broyles and Craig A. Evans. Leiden: Brill, 1997.

Milbank, John. "'I Will Gasp and I Will Pant': Deutero-Isaiah and the Birth of the Suffering Subject. A Response to Norman Gottwald, 'Social Class and Ideology in Isaiah 40–55.'" *Semeia* 59 (1992): 59–72.

Miscall, Peter D. "An Adventure in Reading the Scroll of Isaiah." Paper presented at the annual meeting of the SBL, Denver, Colo., 2001.

———. *Isaiah*. Readings: A New Biblical Commentary. Sheffield: JSOT Press, 1993.

———. *Isaiah*. 2nd ed. Sheffield: Sheffield Phoenix Press, 2006.

Moor, Johannes C. de. "The Integrity of Isaiah 40." Pages 181–216 in *Mesopotamica, Ugaritica, Biblica*. Edited by M. Dietrich and O. Loretz. AOAT 232. Neukirchen-Vluyn: Neukirchener, 1993.
Moor, Johannes C. de, ed. *Synchronic or Diachronic? A Debate on Method in Old Testament Exegesis*. OTS 34. Leiden: Brill, 1995.
Moore, Stephen D. *Mark and Luke in Poststructuralist Perspectives*. New Haven: Yale University Press, 1992.
Morgenstern, Julian. "The Message of Deutero-Isaiah in Its Sequential Unfolding." *HUCA* 29 (1958): 1–67; *HUCA* 30 (1959): 1–102.
Morison, Carole. "Organizing for Justice: DelMarVa Poultry Justice Alliance." (Johns Hopkins Bloomberg School of Public Health, 2007: http://ocw.jhsph.edu/courses/nutritionalhealthfoodproductionandenvironment/PDFs/Lecture8.pdf).
Mosis, Rudolf. "Der verlässliche Grund der Verkündigung: Zu Jes 40,6–8." Pages 153–71 in *Gesammelte Aufsätze zum Alten Testament*. FB 93. Stuttgart: Echter, 1999. [Previously published, pages 113–22 in *Der Dienst für den Menschen in Theologie und Verkündigung; Festschrift für Alois Brems*. Edited by Reinhard M. Hübner, Bernhard Mayer and Ernst Reiter. Regensburg: F. Pustet, 1981)].
Motyer, J. Alec. *The Prophecy of Isaiah: An Introduction and Commentary*. Downers Grove, Ill.: InterVarsity, 1993.
Moughtin-Mumby, Sharon. *Sexual and Marital Metaphors in Hosea, Jeremiah, Isaiah, and Ezekiel*. Oxford: Oxford University Press, 2008.
Muilenburg, James. *The Book of Isaiah Chapters 40–66*. Edited by George A. Buttrick. *IB* 5. New York: Abingdon, 1956.
———. "Form Criticism and Beyond." *JBL* 88 (1969): 1–18.
Niditch, Susan. *Oral World and Written Word*. Louisville, Ky.: Westminster John Knox, 1996.
Nielsen, Kirsten. "'From Oracles to Canon'—and the Role of Metaphor." *SJOT* 17 (2003): 22–33.
———. "Metaphors and Biblical Theology." Pages 263–73 in *Metaphor in the Hebrew Bible*. Edited by Pierre van Hecke. Leuven: Peeters, 2005.
———. *There Is Hope for a Tree: The Tree as Metaphor in Isaiah*. JSOTSup 65. Sheffield: JSOT Press, 1989.
Nogalski, James D. "Intertextuality and the Twelve." Pages 102–24 in *Forming Prophetic Literature: Essays on Isaiah and the Twelve in Honor of John D. W. Watts*. Edited by J. W. Watts and P. R. House. Sheffield: Sheffield Academic Press, 1996.
O'Connell, Robert H. *Concentricity and Continuity: The Literary Structure of Isaiah*. JSOTSup 188. Sheffield: Sheffield Academic Press, 1994.
Odeberg, Hugo. *Trito-Isaiah (Isaiah 56–66): A Literary and Linguistic Analysis*. UUA 1. Uppsala: A.-B. Lundequistska Bokhandeln, 1931.
Oorschot, Jürgen van. *Von Babel zum Zion: Eine literarkritische und redaktionsgeschichtliche Untersuchung*. Berlin: de Gruyter, 1993.
Orlinsky, Harry M. *The So-Called 'Servant of the LORD' and 'Suffering Servant' in Second Isaiah*. VTSup 14. Leiden: Brill. 1967.
Orr, David W. "The Uses of Prophecy." Pages 171–87 in *The Essential Agrarian Reader*. Edited by Norman Wirzba. Washington, D.C.: Shoemaker & Hoard, 2003.
Oswalt, John N. *The Book of Isaiah: Chapters 1–39*. NICOT. Grand Rapids: Eerdmans, 1986.

———. *The Book of Isaiah: Chapters 40–66*. NICOT. Grand Rapids: Eerdmans, 1998.
Ottley, Richard R. *The Book of Isaiah according to the Septuagint (Codex Alexandrinus)*. 2 vols. Cambridge: Cambridge University Press, 1906.
Page, S. "A Stele of Adad Nirari III and Nergal-ereš from Tell al Rimnah." *Iraq* 30 (1968): 139–53.
Paul, Shalom M. "Literary and Ideological Echoes of Jeremiah in Deutero-Isaiah." Pages 109–21 in *Proceedings of the Fifth World Congress of Jewish Studies*. Vol. 1. Edited by P. Peli. Jerusalem: World Union of Jewish Studies, 1969.
Pimentel, David. "Environmental and Economic Costs of Pesticide Use." *Environment, Development and Sustainability* 7 (2005): 229–52.
———. "Environmental and Economic Costs of Soil Erosion and Conservation Benefits." *Science* 267 (1995): 1117–23.
Polan, Gregory J. "Zion, The Glory of the Holy One of Israel: A Literary Analysis of Isaiah 60." Pages 50–71 in *Imagery and Imagination in Biblical Literature*. Edited by Lawrence Boadt and Mark Smith. CBQMS 32. Washington, D.C.: The Catholic Biblical Association of America, 2001.
Polaski, Donald C. *Authorizing an End: The Isaiah Apocalypse and Intertextuality*. BibInt 50. Leiden: Brill, 2001.
Pollan, Michael. *The Botany of Desire: A Plant's Eye View of the World*. New York: Random House, 2002.
———. *The Omnivore's Dilemma: A History of Four Meals*. New York: Penguin, 2007.
Polliack, Meira. "Deutero-Isaiah's Typological Use of Jacob in the Portrayal of Israel's National Renewal." Pages 72–110 in *Creation in Jewish and Christian Tradition*. Edited by Henning Graf Reventlow and Yair Hoffman. JSOTSup 319. Sheffield: Sheffield Academic Press, 2002.
Pope, Marvin H. "Isaiah 34 in Relation to Isaiah 35, 40–66." *JBL* 71 (1952): 235–43.
Procksch, Otto. *Jesaia I*. KAT 9.1. Leipzig: Deichert, 1930.
Rad, Gerhard von. "The City on the Hill." Pages 115–24 in *From Genesis to Chronicles: Explorations in Old Testament Theology*. Translated by E. W. Trueman Dicken. Minneapolis: Fortress, 2005.
———. *Old Testament Theology: The Theology of Israel's Prophetic Traditions*. Translated by D. M. G. Stalker. 2 vols. New York: Harper and Row, 1965.
———. "Die Stadt auf dem Berge." Pages 214–24 in *Gesammelte Studien zum Alten Testament*. TB 8; München: Chr. Kaiser, 1961.
Rendtorff, Rolf. *Canon and Theology: Overtures to an Old Testament Theology*. Translated and edited by Margaret Kohl. Minneapolis: Fortress, 1993.
———. "The Composition of the Book of Isaiah." Pages 146–69 in *Canon and Theology: Overtures to an Old Testament Theology*. Minneapolis: Fortress, 1993.
———. "Isaiah 6 in the Framework of the Composition of the Book," Pages 170–79 in *Canon and Theology: Overtures to an Old Testament Theology*. Minneapolis: Fortress, 1993.
———. "Jesaja 6 im Rahmen der Komposition des Jesajabuches." Pages 83–82 in *The Book of Isaiah/Le Livre d'Isaïe*. Edited by Jacques Vermeylen. Leuven: Peeters, 1989.
———. *The Problem of the Process of Transmission in the Pentateuch*. JSOTSup 89. Sheffield: Sheffield Academic Press, 1990.
Richards, I. A. *The Philosophy of Rhetoric*. New York: Oxford University Press, 1965.
Ringgren, Helmer. "מִחְיָה ;חַי ;חַיִּים ;חָיָה ;חָיָה ." *TDOT* 4:324–44.

Roberts, J. J. M. "Isaiah in Old Testament Theology." *Int* 36 (1982): 130–43.
Robinson, H. Wheeler. "The Council of Yahweh." *JTS* 45 (1944): 151–57.
Rosset, Peter. "Small Is Bountiful." *Ecologist* 29 (1999): 452–56.
Ruszkowski, Leszek. *Volk und Gemeinde im Wandel: Eine Untersuchung zu Jesaja 56–66*. FRLANT 191. Göttingen: Vandenhoeck & Ruprecht, 2000.
Sanders, James A. *From Sacred Story to Sacred Text*. Philadelphia: Fortress, 1987.
Saussure, Ferdinand de. *Course in General Linguistics*. Edited by Charles Balley, Albert Sechehaye, and Albert Riedinger. Translated by Wade Baskin. New York: McGraw-Hill, 1966.
Sawyer, John F. A. "Daughter Zion and Servant of the Lord in Isaiah: A Comparison." *JSOT* 44 (1989): 89–107.
———. *Isaiah*. vol. 2. The Daily Study Bible. Philadelphia: Westminster, 1986.
Scherer, Andreas. "Hyperbolisch oder juridisch? Zu einigen Deutungen von כפלים in Jes 40,2 und zur Semantik der übrigen Belege der Würzel כפל im Alten Testament." *ZAW* 115 (2003): 231–40.
Schlosser, Eric. *Fast Food Nation: The Dark Side of the All-American Meal*. Boston: Houghton Mifflin Harcourt, 2001.
Schmid, Konrad. "Herrscherwartungen und -aussagen im Jesajabuch." Pages 37–74 in *Prophetische Heils- und Herrschererwartungen*. Edited by K. Schmid. SBS 194. Stuttgart: Katholisches Bibelwerk, 2005.
Schmitt, John J. "Motherhood of God and Zion as Mother." *RB* 92 (1985): 557–69.
Sefati, Yitzchak. *Love Songs in Sumerian Literature*. Bar Ilan Studies in Near Eastern Language and Culture. Ramat Gan: Bar Ilan University Press, 1998.
Seitz, Christopher R. "The Divine Council: Temporal Transition and New Prophecy in the Book of Isaiah." *JBL* 109 (1990): 229–47.
———. *Isaiah 1–39*. IBC. Louisville, Ky.: John Knox, 1993.
———. "Isaiah 40–66." Pages 307–552 in *NIB* 6. Nashville: Abingdon, 2001.
———. *Zion's Final Destiny: The Development of the Book of Isaiah: A Reassessment of Isaiah 36–39*. Minneapolis: Fortress, 1991.
Sekine, Seizo. *Die Tritojesajanische Sammlung (Jes 56–66) redactionsgeschichtlich untersucht*. BZAW 175. Berlin: de Gruyter, 1989.
Selms, Adrianus van. "Hunting." *ISBE* 2:782–84.
Severson, Lucky. "Kosher Ethics." *Religion and Ethics Newsweekly* (Oct. 3, 2008: http://www.pbs.org/wnet/religionandethics/week1205/cover.html).
Shiva, Vandana. "Force-Feeding GMOs to the Poor." (www.organicconsumers.org/ge/poor.cfm).
———. *Stolen Harvest: The Hijacking of the Global Food Supply*. Cambridge, Mass.: South End Press, 2000.
Simian-Yofre, Horacio. "Exodo en Deuteroisaias." *Bib* 61 (1980): 530–53.
———. "La teodicea del Deuterisaias." *Bib* 62 (1981): 55–72.
Smith, Adam. *An Inquiry into the Nature and Causes of the Wealth of Nations*. Indianapolis: Liberty Classic, 1981.
Smith, Jonathan Z. *Relating Religion: Essays in the Study of Religion*. Chicago: Chicago University Press, 2004.
Sommer, Benjamin D. "Allusions and Illusions: The Unity of the Book of Isaiah in Light of Deutero-Isaiah's Use of Prophetic Tradition." Pages 156–87 in *New Visions of Isaiah*.

Edited by Roy F. Melugin and Marvin A. Sweeney. JSOTSup 214. Sheffield: Sheffield Academic Press, 1996. Repr., Atlanta: Society of Biblical Literature, 2006.

———. *A Prophet Reads Scripture: Allusion in Isaiah 40–66*. Contraversions. Stanford: Stanford University Press, 1998.

Sonnet, Jean-Pierre. "Le Motif de l'endurcissement (Is 6,9–10) et la lecture d'Isaïe." *Bib* 73 (1992): 208–39.

Stansell, Gary. "The Gift in Ancient Israel." *Semeia* 87 (1999): 65–90.

———. "The Poet's Prophet: Bishop Robert Lowth's Eighteenth-Century Commentary on Isaiah." Pages 223–42 in *"As Those Who are Taught": The Interpretation of Isaiah from the LXX to the SBL*. Edited by Claire Mathews McGinnis and Patricia K. Tull. SBLSymS 27. Atlanta: Society of Biblical Literature, 2006.

———. "The Political Economy of the 'New Jerusalem' in Trito-Isaiah, Haggai and Zechariah." Paper presented at the annual meeting of the SBL. Washington, D.C., Nov. 2006.

———. "The 'Wealth of Nations': Tribute and Pilgrimage to Zion in Isaiah 60–61." Paper presented at the annual meeting of the SBL. Philadelphia, Pa., Nov. 2005.

Starmer, Elanor. "Power Buyers, Power Sellers: How Supermarkets Impact Farmers, Workers, and Consumers—And How We Can Build a Fairer Food System." *Leveling the Field—Issue Brief #3* (http://www.ncrlc.com/1-pfd-files/AAI_Issue%20Brief%203_color_low.pdf).

Stassen, S. L. "The Plot in Isaiah 40–55." *AcT* 17 (1997): 128–42.

Steck, Odil Hannes. "Beobachtungen zur Anlage von Jes 65–66." Pages 217–28 in *Studien zu Tritojesaja*. BZAW 203. Berlin: de Gruyter, 1991.

———. *Bereitete Heimkehr: Jesaja 35 als redaktionelle Brücke zwischen dem ersten und dem zweiten Jesaja*. SBS 121. Stuttgart: Katholisches Bibelwerk, 1985.

———. "Der Grundtext in Jes 60 und sein Aufbau." Pages 49–79 in *Studien zu Tritojesaja*.

———. "Der Grundtext in Jesaja 60 und sein Aufbau," *ZTK* 83 (1986): 261–96.

———. "Deuterojesaja als theologische Denker." Pages 204–20 in *Wahrnehmungen Gottes im Alten Testament: Gesammelte Studien*. Edited by Odil Hannes Steck. Munich: Kaiser, 1982.

———. "Lumen gentium: Exegetische Bemerkungen zum Grundsinn von Jes 60,1–3." Pages 80–96 in *Studien zu Tritojesaja*.

———. "Jesaja 60,13: Bauholz oder Tempelgarten?" Pages 101–5 in *Studien zu Tritojesaja*.

———. *Studien zu Tritojesaja*. BZAW 203. Berlin: de Gruyter, 1991.

———. "Zu jüngsten Untersuchungen von Jes 56,1–8; 63,7–66,24." Pages 229–65 in *Studien zu Tritojesaja*.

Stoebe, Hans-Joachim. "Überlegungen zu Jesaja 40,1–11: Zugleich der Versuch eines Beitrages zur Gottesknechtfrage." *TZ* 40 (1984): 104–13.

Stringfellow, William. *A Public and Private Faith*. Grand Rapids: Eerdmans, 1962.

Sweeney, Marvin A. *I and II Kings: A Commentary*. OTL; Louisville, Ky.: Westminster John Knox, 2007.

———. "The Book of Isaiah as Prophetic Torah." Pages 50–67 in *New Vision of Isaiah*.

———. "Ezekiel's Debate with Isaiah." *Congress Volume: Ljubljana 2007*. Edited by A. Lemaire. VTSup. Leiden: Brill, forthcoming.

———. *Form and Intertextuality in Prophetic and Apocalyptic Literature*. FAT 45. Tübingen: Mohr Siebeck, 2005.

———. "Form Criticism." Pages 58–89 in *To Each Its Own Meaning: An Introduction to*

Biblical Criticisms and their Applications. Edited by S. L. McKenzie and S. R. Haynes. Louisville, Ky.: Westminster John Knox, 1999.

———. *Isaiah 1–4 and the Post-Exilic Understanding of the Isaianic Tradition.* BZAW 171. Berlin: de Gruyter, 1988.

———. *Isaiah 1–39 with an Introduction to Prophetic Literature.* FOTL 16. Grand Rapids: Eerdmans, 1996.

———. *King Josiah of Judah: The Lost Messiah of Israel.* Oxford: Oxford University Press, 2001.

———. "Metaphor and Rhetorical Strategy in Zephaniah." Pages 120–30 in *Relating to the Text: Interdisciplinary and Form-Critical Insights on the Bible.* Edited by T. J. Sandoval and C. Mandolfo. JSOTSup 384. London: T&T Clark, 2003.

———. "Prophetic Exegesis in Isaiah 65–66." Pages 455–74 in *Writing and Reading the Scroll of Isaiah: Studies of an Interpretive Tradition.* Edited by Craig C. Broyles and Craig A. Evans. VTSup 70.1. Leiden: Brill, 1997.

———. *The Prophetic Literature.* IBT. Nashville: Abingdon, 2005.

———. "Puns, Politics, and Perushim in the Jacob Cycle: A Case Study in Teaching the English Hebrew Bible." *Shofar* 9 (1991): 103–18.

———. "The Royal Oracle in Ezekiel 37:15–28: Ezekiel's Reflection on Josiah's Reform." Pages 239–53 in *Israel's Prophets and Israel's Past: Essays on the Relationship of Prophetic Texts and Israelite History in Honor of John H. Hayes.* Edited by B. E. Kelle and M. B. Moor. LHBOTS 446. London: T&T Clark, 2006.

———. *The Twelve Prophets.* vol. 1. Berit Olam; Collegeville, Minn.: Liturgical, 2000.

———. "Zechariah's Debate with Isaiah." Pages 335–50 in *The Changing Face of Form Criticism for the Twenty-First Century.* Edited by Marvin A. Sweeney and Ehud Ben Zvi. Grand Rapids: Eerdmans, 2003.

———. *Zephaniah.* Hermeneia. Minneapolis: Fortress, 2003.

Thompson, Charles Dillard and Melinda Wiggins, *The Human Cost of Food: Farm Workers' Lives, Labor, and Advocacy.* Austin, Tex.: University of Texas Press, 2002.

Tomasi, Luigi. "Homo Viator: From Pilgrimage to Religious Tourism." Pages 1–24 in *From Medieval Pilgrimage to Religious Tourism: The Social and Cultural Economics of Piety.* Edited by William H. Swatos, Jr. and Luigi Tomasi. Westport, Conn.: Praeger, 2002.

Torrey, Charles C. *The Second Isaiah: A New Interpretation.* Edinburgh: Scribner's, 1928.

Trible, Phyllis. *Rhetorical Criticism: Context, Methods, and the Book of Jonah.* Minneapolis: Fortress, 1994.

Tucker, Gene M. "The Book of Isaiah 1–39." Pages 25–305 in *NIB* 6. Nashville: Abingdon, 2001.

Tudge, Colin. *The Tree: A Natural History of What Trees Are, How They Live, and Why They Matter.* New York: Crown, 2006.

Tull, Patricia K. "Intertextuality and the Hebrew Scriptures." *CR:BS* 8 (2000): 59–90.

———. *Remember the Former Things: The Recollection of Previous Texts in Second Isaiah.* SBLDS 161. Atlanta: Scholars Press, 1997.

———. "Rhetorical Criticism and Intertextuality." Pages 156–80 in *To Each Its Own Meaning* Rev. ed. Edited by S. L. McKenzie and S. R. Haynes. Louisville, Ky.: Westminster John Knox, 1999.

———. "The Servant of Yhwh and Daughter Zion." *SBLSP* 34 (1995): 267–303.

Vermeylen, Jacques. *Du prophète Isaïe à l'apocalyptique. Isaïe, I–XXXV, miroir d'un demi-millénaire d'expérience religeuse en Israël. Tome II. Ebib.* Paris: J. Gabalda, 1978.

———. "L'Unité du Livre d'Isaïe." Pages 11–53 in *The Book of Isaiah/Le Livre d'Isaïe*. Edited by Jacques Vermeylen. BETL 81. Leuven: Peeters, 1989.

Volz, Paul. *Jesaja II*. KAT. Leipzig: Deichert, 1931.

Wagner, Thomas. *Gottes Herrschaft: Eine Analyse der Denkschrift (Jes 6,1–9,6)*. VTSup 108. Leiden: Brill, 2006.

Walker, Christopher and Michael B. Dick. *The Induction of the Cult Image in Ancient Mesopotamia: The Mesopotamian Mīs Pî Ritual*. SAALT 1. Helsinki: University of Helsinki, 2001.

———. "The Induction of the Cult Image in Ancient Mesopotamia: The Mesopotamian *mīs pî* Ritual." Pages 55–121 in *Born in Heaven, Made on Earth: The Making of the Cult Image in the Ancient Near East*. Edited by Michael Dick. Winona Lake, Ind.: Eisenbrauns, 1999.

Walsh, Carey. *The Fruit of the Vine: Viticulture in Ancient Israel*. Winona Lake, Ind.: Eisenbrauns, 2000.

Walsh, Jerome T. "Isaiah XLV 1–20." *VT* 53 (1993): 351–71.

Watson, Wilfred G. E. *Classical Hebrew Poetry: A Guide to Its Techniques*. JSOTSup 26. Sheffield: JSOT Press, 1984.

Watts, John D. W. *Isaiah 1–33*. WBC 24. Waco, Tex.: Word, 1985.

———. *Isaiah 34–66*. WBC 25. Waco, Tex.: Word, 1987. Rev. ed. 2005.

Weber, Timothy P. *On the Road to Armageddon: How Evangelicals Became Israel's Best Friend*. Grand Rapids: Baker, 2004.

Werner, Wolfgang. *Eschatologische Texte in Jesaja 1–39: Messias, Heiliger Rest, Völker*. FB 46. Würzburg: Echter, 1982.

Westcott, C. *Plant Disease Handbook*. New York: Van Nostrand, 1950.

Westermann, Claus. *Isaiah 40–66*. Translated by David M. G. Stalker. OTL. Philadelphia, Westminster, 1969.

White, Hayden. "The Historical Text as Literary Artifact." Pages 41–62 in *The Writing of History: Literary Form and Historical Understanding*. Edited by Robert H. Canary and Henry Kozicki. Madison: University of Wisconsin Press, 1978.

Whybray, R. Norman. *Isaiah 40–66*. NCB. Grand Rapids: Eerdmans, 1975.

———. *Reading the Psalms as a Book*. JSOTSup 222. Sheffield: Sheffield Academic Press, 1996.

Wildberger, Hans. *Isaiah 1–12*. Translated by Thomas H. Trapp. CC. Minneapolis: Fortress, 1991.

———. *Isaiah 13–27*. Translated by Thomas H. Trapp. CC. Minneapolis: Fortress, 1997.

———. *Isaiah 28–39*. Translated by Thomas H. Trapp. CC. Minneapolis: Fortress, 2002),

———. *Jesaja 1–12*. Vol. 1 of *Jesaja*. 2nd ed. BKAT 10.1; Neukirchen-Vluyn: Neukirchener, 1980.

———. *Jesaja 28–39*. Vol. 3 of *Jesaja*. BKAT 10.3. Neukirchen-Vluyn: Neukircher, 1982.

———. "Die Völkerwallfahrt zum Zion: Jes II 1–5." *VT* 7 (1965): 62–81.

Willey, Patricia Tull. (see Tull, Patricia K.)

Williamson, Hugh G. M. *The Book Called Isaiah: Deutero-Isaiah's Role in Composition and Redaction*. Oxford: Clarendon, 1994.

———. *A Critical and Exegetical Commentary on Isaiah 1–27*. Vol. 1 of *Commentary on Isaiah*. ICC. London: T&T Clark, 2006.

———. "The Messianic Texts in Isaiah 1–39." Pages 238–70 in *King and Messiah in Israel and the Ancient Near East*. Edited by John Day. JSOTSup 270. Sheffield: Sheffield Academic Press, 1998.

———. "Relocating Isaiah 1:2–9." Pages 263–77 in *Writing and Reading the Scroll of Isaiah: Studies of an Interpretive Tradition*. Edited by Craig C. Broyles and Craig A. Evans. VTSup 70.1. Leiden: Brill, 1997.

———. "Synchronic and Diachronic in Isaian Perspective." Pages 211–26 in *Synchronic or Diachronic? A Debate on Method in Old Testament Exegesis*. Edited by Johannes C. de Moor. OTS 34. Leiden: Brill, 1995.

———. *Variations on a Theme: King, Messiah and Servant in the Book of Isaiah*. Carlisle: Paternoster, 1998.

Wilshire, Leland Edward. "The Servant-City: A New Interpretation of the 'Servant of the Lord' in the Servant Songs in Deutero-Isaiah." *JBL* 94 (1975): 356–67.

Wirzba, Norman. *The Paradise of God: Renewing Religion in an Ecological Age*. Oxford: Oxford University Press, 2003.

Wolff, Hans W. *Joel and Amos*. Hermeneia. Philadelphia: Fortress, 1977.

Yee, Gale A. *Poor Banished Children of Eve: Woman as Evil in the Hebrew Bible*. Minneapolis: Fortress, 2003.

Zalcman, L. "Ambiguity and Assonance at Zephaniah II 4." *VT* 36 (1986): 365–71.

Zapff, Burkhard M. "Jes 40 und die Frage nach dem Beginn des deuterojesajanischen Corpus." Pages 355–73 in *Gottes Wege Suchen*. Edited by Franz Sedlmeier. Würzburg: Echter, 2003.

———. *Jesaja 40–55*. Würzburg: Echter, 2001.

Zevit, Ziony. "Seeing God in All the Right Places." Paper presented at the annual meeting of the SBL. Boston, Mass., 2008.

Ziegler, Joseph. *Untersuchungen zur Septuaginta des Buches Isaias*. ATA 12.3. Münster: Aschendorff, 1934.

Zillessen, Alfred. "'Tritojesaja' und Deuterojesaja. Eine literarkritische Untersuchung zu Jes. 56–66." *ZAW* 26 (1906): 231–76.

Zimmerli, Walter. "Zur Sprache Tritojesajas." Pages. 217–33 in *Gottes Offenbarung: Gesammelte Aufsätze*. TB 19. 2nd ed. Munich: Kaiser, 1963.

Index of Scripture References

Hebrew Bible

Genesis

Ref	Page
1	21, 168
1:21	49, 151, 164
1:10	168
1:11	20
1:26	20
1:29	21
1:31	168
2:25	161
3	27, 33
3:1	161
6:6	136
6:7	136
12:16	84
13:1–6	84
19	40
19:2	223
20:14	84
21:10	80
24:35	84
25	221
25–35	111, 120
25:19–35:29	113
25:25	114
25:30	113, 114
27:3	80
27:11	114
29:32	114
29:33	114
29:34	114
30:6	114
30:8	114
30:11	114
30:12	114
30:16	114
30:18	114
30:20	114
30:21	114
30:23–24	114
30:43	84
31:10	157
31:47	113, 114
32:1–3	115
32:8–9	115
32:11	115
32:14–15	84
32:24	115
32:28	113
32:29	115
32:31–32	115
33:3	157
35:10	113
35:18	114
37–50	74
39:21	245
45:7–8	74
50:20	74
50:21	139

Exodus

Ref	Page
3–4	61

Exodus, *cont'd*

3:1–17	60	25	226
7:3	65, 74	26:3–5	84
7:14	65, 74	26:3–6	27
7:21	19	26:10	27
7:22	65, 74	26:41	140
8:15	65, 74	26:43	140
8:19	65, 74		
8:32	65, 74	**Numbers**	
9:7	65		
9:12	65, 74	14:10	219
9:34	65, 74	34	115
9:35	65, 74		
10:1	65, 74		
10:14	84	**Deuteronomy**	
10:20	65, 74		
10:27	65, 74	18:20–22	58
11:10	65, 74	28:1–14	84
14:4	65, 74	28:2–5	27
14:8	65, 74	28:11–12	27
14:17	65, 74	29:22	39
15:13	157	31:11	42
15:17	23		
16:20	19		
17:1–7	46	**Joshua**	
19:6	206		
24:1	104	9:15	85
24:11	104	11:17	114
24:16	104	13–23	115
24:17	219	19:15	82
33:22	219	21:35	82
34:15	247		
34:23–24	42		
		Judges	
		1:30	82
Leviticus		6:1	221
1:4	140	14:8	124
5:15	79	14:15	247
16	126	17:3	187
18	172	21	233
19	172		
20	172		

INDEX OF SCRIPTURE REFERENCES

1 Samuel

15:11	136
15:35	136
16:1–13	225
16:3	247
16:13	225
23:9	188
30:2	239

2 Samuel

9:8	223

1–2 Kings

1 Kings 16–2 Kings 14	115

1 Kings

4:21	242
4:23	210
5:1	222, 242
5:8	211
5:10	211
5:13	210
5:22	211
5:24	211
8:11	219
9:25	233
10:1–13	221
10:10	221
10:22	252
12:25	115
19:16	225
20:26–34	116
22:19	191
22:19–22	60
22:19–23	61
22:21	191

2 Kings

3:14	191
5	210
4–5	210
8:20–24	116
16:1–20	65
16:3	65
18	188
18:13–27	73

Isaiah

1	9, 10, 24, 38, 44, 50, 66, 67, 135, 139, 140, 142, 145, 181
1–2	102
1–12	58, 64, 91
1–33	169, 251
1–39	6, 101, 177, 217, 230, 231, 233, 235
1–66	12, 70
1:1	8, 38, 135, 166
1:2	107, 145
1:2–3	8, 67
1:2–31	38, 200, 244
1:3	141, 176
1:4	8, 12, 40, 71, 142, 254
1:4–9	8
1:5	8
1:7	8, 39, 54
1:7–9	38, 54
1:7–26	3, 35, 38, 51
1:7–27	37
1:8	38, 39, 43, 54
1:9	8, 39, 40, 50, 51, 54, 138, 153
1:10–15	40
1:10–17	9
1:10–20	41
1:11	9
1:11–25	42
1:12	41, 42
1:12–26	41
1:13	11

Isaiah, *cont'd*

Ref	Pages
1:14	41, 42, 54
1:15	42, 176
1:16–17	9, 64
1:17	68
1:18	9
1:19–20	9, 23
1:20	39, 42, 145, 169
1:21	9, 38, 42, 49
1:21–23	43
1:21–31	223
1:22	9
1:23	9
1:24	136
1:24–25	9
1:24–26	223
1:25	42
1:26	9, 38
1:26–27	43, 49
1:27	9
1:29–31	9
1:30	23
1:31	23
2	144
2–12	58, 66, 67
2:1	66, 67, 146
2:1–4	220, 222
2:1–5	64, 67
2:2	152, 178, 230, 233
2:2–3	99, 253
2:2–4	6, 14, 26, 217, 233, 234, 238, 248, 251, 253–55
2:4	3, 75
2:5	64, 107
2:6–7	187
2:6–8	223
2:6–22	68
2:7	178
2:10	220
2:14	99
2:20	106, 178
3:1–26	223
3:12	23, 47
3:13–15	68
3:14	22
3:14–15	68
4:1	166
4:2–6	64
4:3	87
4:5	104, 219
4:6	65
5	23, 68, 80, 82, 83, 178
5:1	80
5:1–7	3, 19, 68, 79, 81
5:4	58
5:4–5	68
5:5	81
5:5–6	25
5:6	79, 81–82
5:7	23
5:8	23, 178
5:10	23, 79
5:11	178
5:18	178
5:20	58, 178
5:21	178
5:22	178
5:24	24
5:26	82, 248
6	2, 3, 10–14, 26, 59–62, 66–71, 74, 75, 87, 88, 131, 132, 134, 135, 137, 141, 173–78, 191
6–11	66
6–39	151
6:1–8:18	88
6:1	71, 104, 175, 185
6:1–4	60
6:1–8	62
6:1–11	66
6:1–13	3, 57–60, 66, 67, 70, 74, 75
6:3	13, 104, 175
6:3–4	60
6:5	14, 61, 175, 185, 190
6:5–8	60, 61
6:7	12, 61, 73
6:8	11, 62, 70, 142, 175

INDEX OF SCRIPTURE REFERENCES

Reference	Pages	Reference	Pages
6:9	63, 72, 177	8:11	166
6:9–10	57, 63, 175, 176	8:11–14	67
6:9–13	60, 62, 63, 64	8:11–15	66
6:10	63	8:11–22	66
6:11	11, 73, 155	8:16–17	67
6:11–12	13, 70	8:16–18	137
6:12	87	8:16–9:1	195
6:12–13	66	8:17	162
6:13	12, 25, 26, 66	9	10
7	3, 65, 66, 83, 84, 87, 88	9:1–7	65
7–8	66	9:2	220, 230
7:1–9	66	9:5	165
7:1–17	87, 88	9:6	27, 88, 165
7:1–25	66	9:7	27
7:2	24, 84	9:8–12	73
7:3	170	9:10	24
7:3–4	65	9:17	25, 79
7:7	14	9:18	25
7:9	67	9:19	25
7:10–17	66	10:1–2	31
7:12	66	10:5	165
7:15	85, 86	10:5–6	254
7:17	77, 88	10:5–19	10, 68
7:18	77, 78, 82, 87	10:13	254
7:18–19	66, 81, 83, 84, 88	10:13–14	241
7:18–25	3, 77, 78, 87	10:14	240, 254
7:19	78, 84	10:16–19	25
7:20	66, 78, 83, 87	10:17	79
7:21	66, 78, 86	10:27–34	68
7:21–22	84, 88	10:33–34	25
7:21–25	88	11	10
7:22	78, 85–87	11:1	26, 165, 224
7:23	78	11:1–9	65
7:23–25	66, 79, 81	11:2	176
7:24	79–81	11:2–3	230
7:25	79–81	11:3	176, 177
8	66, 88	11:4	27
8:1–4	66	11:6	27
8:5–8	10, 66	11:9	176, 230
8:6	142	11:10	165, 220, 230
8:8–9	238	11:11	83
8:9–10	66	11:15–16	83
8:10	14	11:16	170

Isaiah, cont'd			
		23	6, 252
12:1	13, 101	23:1	252
12:1–6	65, 67	23:1–14	252
12:5–6	231	23:1–18	251
12:6	101, 153, 231	23:3	252
13	169	23:5	47, 48
13–23	69, 70, 91	23:7	254
13–35	58, 66, 69	23:14	252
13:1	69	23:18	234, 252, 253
13:3–5	248	24	94
13:6–8	47, 48	24–27	4, 70, 91, 92, 103, 107
13:19	39	24:1	95
14–23	226	24:1–13	97
14:8	28	24:2	184
14:13	99	24:4	28, 107
15–16	21	24:4–9	25
16:5	148	24:5	33
16:10	21	24:5–6	95
17:4–6	25	24:7	95
17:10–11	24	24:9	95
17:12–14	238	24:11	95
18:3	248	24:13	25, 102
18:4–6	25	24:14	97, 101
18:7	234, 251, 254	24:18	107
19:3	187	24:21	107
19:5–10	25	24:21–23	97
19:23	170	24:23	91, 95, 98–100, 103, 104, 106, 107
19:23–25	83	24:33	219
19:24–25	248	25	95
20	88	25:1	97
20:1–6	66	25:6	104
20:3	184, 185, 191	25:6–7	99, 220
20:4	239	25:7	102, 195
21:9	101	25:9	92, 99, 102
21:10	25, 101	25:10	99
22	69	26	103
22:1	146	26:1	95, 99
22:1–14	73	26:1–2	97
22:5	73	26:1–9	92
22:14	12, 73	26:5	107
22:15–19	69	26:8	162
22:20	184	26:8–9	106
22:21	166	26:10–11	177

INDEX OF SCRIPTURE REFERENCES

26:11	106	30:13	12		
26:13	97	30:15	66		
26:15	104	30:21–22	187		
26:17–18	47, 48	30:23–24	26		
26:21	92	30:30	73, 101		
27	19, 26	31:1	92, 178		
27:1	106, 166	32	10		
27:2	94	32:1	165		
27:3–4	19, 94	32:3	177		
27:4	79, 94, 106	32:5	27		
27:5	166	32:6	28		
27:6	26	32:9–13	25		
27:7	94	32:15	26, 222		
27:9–11	103	32:16–18	28		
27:10–11	25	32:16–20	224		
27:11	177	32:17	224		
27:12–13	103, 105	33	28, 92		
27:13	91–93, 99, 100, 103, 106, 107	33–35	104		
28	91, 146	33–39	99		
28–32	92, 99	33:1	178		
28–33	102, 107, 167, 178	33:2	101, 162		
28–35	98	33:5	104		
28–39	91, 92, 100	33:8	96		
28:1	14, 146, 178	33:9	28, 222		
28:1–4	24, 92	33:11–12	25		
28:1–5	146	33:15–20	177		
28:2	155, 156, 166, 167	33:20–22	223		
28:4	14	33:22	92, 99		
28:12	66	33:23	166, 167		
28:14	92	33:24	73		
28:16	92	34	92, 169, 170, 252		
28:22	166	34–35	5, 92, 166, 168, 169, 171–73		
28:23–29	25, 26, 34	34:1	170, 172, 177		
29	92	34:1–17	222		
29:1	178	34:2	106, 252		
29:9–12	177	34:5–6	106		
29:15	178	34:8	136, 226, 252		
29:15–16	177	34:9–15	25, 169, 170		
29:17	222	34:12	170		
29:18	3, 58, 69, 176, 177	34:16	169, 172		
30:1	92, 178	34:17–35:10	169		
30:9–10	74, 177	35	6, 27, 69, 92, 169, 170, 251, 252		
30:10	18	35:1	170, 172, 251		

Isaiah, cont'd

Reference	Pages
35:1–2	1, 170, 171, 251
35:1–7	26
35:1–10	231
35:2	101, 104, 170, 172, 176, 177, 222, 234, 251, 252, 254
35:3	171
35:3–4	166, 167, 171
35:4	99, 170–72
35:5	3, 58, 70, 176, 177
35:6	101
35:6–10	170
35:8	95, 172, 229
35:8–9	96
35:8–10	96
35:9	101
35:9–10	95, 96, 100
35:10	95, 96
36	222
36–37	92, 96, 98, 99, 107
36–39	5, 13, 88, 92, 104, 165–69, 171–73
36:1	13, 73
36:1–2	96
36:2	99, 170
36:4	98
36:6	178
36:9	184
36:11	177, 184
36:12	184
36:13	98, 177
36:13–20	97
36:14	98
36:16	98
36:18	102, 167
36:20	97, 98
36:21	99
37	168
37:1	98, 99, 104
37:3	97
37:4	97
37:5	99, 184
37:6	98
37:6–7	177
37:10	98, 99
37:10–13	97
37:11	98
37:12	102
37:13	100
37:14	104
37:16	100, 102, 107
37:16–20	97
37:17	177
37:20	96, 98–100, 102, 167, 177
37:22–35	96
37:23	168
37:23–24	97
37:23–25	97
37:24	98
37:24–25	98
37:26	168
37:26–27	25
37:26–29	177
37:29	96
37:31	26
37:31–32	105
37:33–35	96
37:35	98, 99, 167
37:36–38	13
37:37	96
37:38	106
38	92
38:5	177
38:6	99
38:9	99
38:20	104, 167
39	13, 92, 136, 168
39:1	99, 167, 168
39:1–5	177
39:2	178
39:3	99
39:5–8	13
39:6–7	168
39:7	99
39:8	167, 168
40	2, 5, 11, 13, 14, 70, 71, 94, 99, 100, 102, 131, 132, 135, 136, 140, 142,

INDEX OF SCRIPTURE REFERENCES

	146, 168–70, 175	40:12–26	162, 163
40–41	5, 166, 168, 169, 171–73	40:12–31	71, 102, 135
40–45	236	40:13	149, 164
40–48	4, 109, 110, 112, 113, 128	40:13–14	162
40–51	100	40:14	106, 165
40–55	3, 4, 6, 13, 49, 89, 102, 104, 107, 109, 110, 127, 128, 160, 169, 181, 202, 217, 230, 231, 233, 247	40:15	71, 102, 147, 163
		40:15–26	102
		40:16	141
40–66	44, 46, 58, 70–72, 138, 169, 177, 251	40:17	163, 170
		40:18–20	188
40:1	11, 13, 46, 100, 101, 138, 141, 145–47, 149–51, 154, 158, 168	40:19	178, 188
		40:19–20	167
40:1–2	5, 12, 13, 135, 141, 152, 230	40:21	72, 168, 177
40:1–3	154	40:21–26	102
40:1–5	71	40:23	163, 170
40:1–8	11–13, 152, 154, 162, 168	40:23–24	25
40:1–11	4, 58, 93, 100–102, 131, 134, 146, 149	40:24	149
		40:25	168
40:2	12, 70, 71, 136, 139, 141, 144, 148, 152, 155, 156, 168, 227, 244	40:26	71, 158, 177
		40:27	106, 136, 162, 164
40:3	4, 11, 139, 146, 149, 150, 152, 153, 157, 170, 172, 228, 229	40:27–28	112
		40:27–31	102, 162
40:3–4	139, 147	40:28	72, 163, 168, 177
40:3–5	5, 12, 13, 141, 143, 151	40:29	162, 171
40:4	143, 152, 170, 178	40:29–30	71
40:5	13, 42, 101, 104, 138, 148, 149, 154, 168–70, 172, 176, 177, 219	40:30	163
		40:31	161–163, 165–67
40:6	4, 11, 14, 47, 148, 150–52, 156	41	5, 14, 159, 160, 162, 163, 165–67, 173, 175–78, 185, 187, 190
40:6–7	46, 47, 158	41–42	187
40:6–8	5, 11, 12, 14, 141, 146, 147, 151, 152, 164	41–51	102
		41:1	161–166, 170, 172, 188, 189
40:7	25, 164	41:1–5	162, 165
40:8	14, 150, 154, 155, 168	41:1–7	162
40:9	101, 155, 225, 230	41:2	25, 99, 162, 163, 165, 178
40:9–10	141, 171, 172	41:2–4	189
40:9–11	5, 152–54	41:4	162
40:10	71, 93, 97, 99–101, 155–58, 166–68, 171, 228	41:5	71, 163, 164, 188
		41:5–20	112
40:10–11	107, 156	41:6	166
40:10–12	101	41:6–7	164, 166–68, 171
40:11	13, 157, 158	41:7	166–68, 188, 191
40:12	139, 144, 156, 163, 175	41:8	105, 165, 184, 189, 190
40:12–13	140		
40:12–14	102		

Isaiah, cont'd

Reference	Pages
41:8–9	112
41:8–10	192
41:8–11	188
41:8–13	166, 189
41:9	162, 166–68, 171, 189
41:10	165, 166, 188
41:11	170
41:11–12	164, 167
41:12	170
41:13	166–68, 171, 188
41:14	101, 165, 188
41:14–16	189
41:15	178
41:17–18	46
41:17–19	170
41:17–20	71, 176, 189, 231
41:19	210, 211
41:20	72, 161, 176
41:21	99, 100, 165, 185, 189, 190
41:21–24	176
41:21–29	162, 164
41:22	72
41:22–23	176
41:23	72
41:24	164, 176, 189, 190
41:25	162, 165
41:25–27	189
41:25–29	163, 176
41:26	72, 162, 176
41:26–28	164
41:27	100, 225
41:28	163, 164, 189
41:29	161, 163–66, 170, 189–91
42	182, 190–92, 230
42:1	161, 163–66, 184, 185, 189–91, 193
42:1–4	191, 225, 230
42:1–9	5, 14, 164, 176, 181, 187, 189, 190, 230
42:1–10	162
42:2	192
42:2–3	193
42:2–4	188
42:3	164, 178, 192, 193, 195
42:3–4	165
42:4	165, 191, 193, 194
42:5	164, 188, 194
42:5–7	194
42:6	166, 167, 178, 194, 195, 230
42:6–7	188
42:7	195
42:8	104, 195, 219, 220
42:9	72, 164, 194
42:12	219
42:13–14	49
42:14	149
42:16	72
42:18–19	27
42:18–20	176, 177
42:18–21	3, 71
42:18–25	58, 112
42:19	184
42:23–25	94
42:24	71
42:25	106
43	14
43:1	101, 105
43:1–8	112
43:3–5	230
43:6–7	221
43:7	104, 220
43:8	177
43:8–9	3, 72
43:8–13	58, 72
43:10	72
43:14	101, 230
43:15	100, 185, 190
43:18–19	72
43:19	72
43:20	46
43:22–28	112
43:24	140
44–45	165
44:1	73, 184, 190
44:1–2	165
44:1–8	112, 230

44:2	144, 190	46:13	100
44:3	105	47:1	96
44:3–4	27	47:1–5	112
44:3–5	211	47:4	101
44:5	105	47:5	96
44:6	100, 101, 185	47:9	140
44:9	72	47:11	177
44:15	106	48	14
44:17	106, 223	48:1	73, 105
44:18	177	48:1–22	112
44:21	165	48:6–8	177
44:21–22	112	48:11	104, 219, 220
44:22–23	73	48:12	73
44:22–24	101	48:14	101
44:23	28, 101, 231	48:17	101
44:23–24	230	48:18	246
44:24	165, 250	48:18–19	105
44:26	155	48:19	105, 113
44:28	71, 72, 104, 161	48:20	101, 165, 184
44:28–45:7	161	48:20–21	109
45	6, 14	48:20–22	113
45:1	71, 99, 161, 165–67, 208, 225	48:21	46
45:1–8	112	49	5, 6, 73, 137, 198, 200–212, 214, 230
45:3	72	49–55	4, 109, 110
45:3–4	105	49:1–6	147
45:4	72, 165	49:3	165, 184
45:4–6	177	49:4	150, 165
45:6	72, 176	49:6	184, 230
45:8	27, 72	49:7	99, 101, 211, 212, 228, 230, 248
45:13	71, 165, 208	49:8	209
45:14	234, 247, 250–53, 255	49:9–10	46
45:14–17	250	49:9–12	211
45:19	105	49:10	209
45:20	105, 177	49:12	208
45:20–25	223	49:13	101, 230
45:22	102	49:14	49, 100, 203, 212, 229
45:25	105	49:14–18	203
46:1	189, 192	49:14–23	220
46:2	189	49:14–26	249
46:3	49	49:15	55, 136, 137, 213
46:3–4	49, 112	49:16	208, 228
46:4	192	49:17	208
46:6	106, 178	49:18	198, 199, 203, 213, 220, 230, 248

Isaiah, cont'd		52:4	96
49:18–23	213	52:4–6	100
49:18–26	5, 197	52:5	97, 98
49:19	208	52:6	72, 97, 98
49:21	205, 208	52:7	95, 97–101, 153, 155, 157, 185, 225
49:22	198, 199, 203, 204, 213, 248, 249	52:7–8	96
49:22–23	138, 204, 234, 247–50, 255	52:7–9	101
49:22–26	248	52:7–10	92, 93, 98, 100, 103, 107
49:23	72, 99, 162, 177, 198, 199, 203, 204, 208, 211–14, 248–50, 253	52:8	73, 100, 101, 138
		52:8–9	101
49:23–26	202	52:8–10	96, 177
49:26	72, 101, 176, 177, 199, 208, 211–14	52:9	96, 100, 101
50:2	184	52:9–10	101
50:4–5	177	52:10	73, 96, 99, 101, 102, 176
51	94	52:11–12	93
51:3	27, 100, 101	52:13	184
51:4–6	230	52:13–53:12	230
51:5	101, 162	52:15	99, 177, 228
51:7	72	53	141
51:9	101	53:5	73
51:9–16	93	53:5–6	140
51:9–52:12	93	53:7	13
51:10	101	53:10	105, 230
51:10–11	96	53:11	177
51:11	100	54	165
51:12	13, 101	54:1	228
51:16	100	54:2	166
51:17	93, 94, 106	54:5	101, 230
51:17–23	93, 94	54:6	39
51:17–52:6	92, 93, 103, 107	54:7–8	209, 230
51:17–52:12	95	54:8	101, 137, 148
51:18	157, 166, 167	54:9	136
51:19	101, 140	54:10	148, 230
51:20	94, 106	54:17	165
51:22	94, 106	55	6, 13
51:22–23	94, 95	55:1	46
51:23	94	55:1–2	178
52	4, 91, 99, 100	55:2–3	177, 248
52:1	93, 95, 96	55:3	75, 148, 230
52:1–6	93, 95–97, 230	55:5	234, 247–50, 255
52:1–10	101	55:10–13	34
52:2	96	55:12–13	28
52:3	94, 96, 101	56–66	38, 103, 169, 202, 215, 216, 218,

INDEX OF SCRIPTURE REFERENCES

Reference	Pages
	233, 236, 243
56:1–8	102, 104, 107, 215, 248
56:1–7	103
56:2	166
56:3–5	105
56:4	166
56:6	103, 165, 166
56:6–7	248
56:7	207, 232
56:8	103
56:9–11	177
57:5	23
57:12	227
57:14	228
58	42
58:3	177
58:6	225
58:8	104, 170, 220
58:9	177
58:11	27
58:14	42, 169
59:1–2	177
59:8–10	177
59:9	164
59:12	72
59:12–15	177
59:14	145
59:14–15	164
59:19	13, 104, 220
59:20	229
59:21	105
60	5, 6, 104, 198, 200–212, 214, 215, 219, 222–25, 227–29, 233, 235–40, 242–54
60–61	236, 243, 245–47, 254
60–62	6, 217–19, 226, 229–31, 236, 242, 245, 251
60:1	202, 203, 219, 237, 238, 242
60:1–2	13, 104, 238
60:1–3	202, 204, 219, 220, 224, 230, 242
60:1–6	235
60:1–7	218–20, 229, 230
60:1–22	219, 230
60:2	203, 219, 240, 242
60:2–3	248
60:3	99, 203, 220, 228, 238, 241, 246
60:3–4	222
60:3–5	234
60:3–7	233
60:4	198, 199, 203–5, 209, 211, 213, 220, 230, 237, 238, 241, 242, 246
60:4–5	205
60:4–7	220, 248
60:4–14	247
60:4–16	5, 197, 249, 255
60:5	205, 209, 212, 220, 234, 236–41, 243–46, 248, 250, 252
60:5–7	221, 227, 237, 244
60:5–9	204
60:5–11	246
60:6	206, 207, 209, 212, 220, 221, 223, 225, 238
60:6–7	205, 207, 239–41
60:7	206–8, 211, 212, 221, 231, 240–42, 244, 246
60:8	205, 208, 222, 228
60:8–9	205, 222
60:8–16	218
60:8–22	218, 222
60:9	162, 178, 204–6, 208, 209, 211, 221, 222, 227, 229, 237, 238, 240–42, 244, 246–48, 252
60:10	204, 206, 208, 210, 222, 223, 228, 237, 239, 241, 244
60:10–11	99, 205, 210, 211, 228, 240, 249
60:10–12	242
60:10–14	248, 249, 255
60:10–16	222, 243
60:11	208, 209, 222, 231, 234, 237–41, 243, 245, 246, 248, 251, 252
60:11–12	238
60:11–18	219
60:12	100, 205, 210, 239, 246
60:13	170, 204, 206, 209–12, 222, 223, 227, 228, 238, 240–43, 245, 251, 252
60:13–14	205
60:14	203, 204, 211–13, 222, 223, 238, 239, 241, 242, 246, 249, 251

Isaiah, cont'd
60:15   39, 203, 212, 223, 229, 244, 246
60:15–16   205, 223
60:16   72, 99, 177, 199, 203, 211, 213, 214, 223, 228, 229, 238, 240, 241, 243–46, 249
60:17   178, 223, 224, 237, 238, 241
60:17–18   218, 223
60:18   224, 230
60:19   224
60:19–20   178
60:19–22   218
60:20   224, 238
60:21   211, 221, 224, 226, 227
60:21–22   225
60:22   224
60:23   252
61   6, 219, 225, 227–29, 236, 238, 243, 247–49, 252–54
61:1   165
61:1–3   226, 230
61:1–4   218, 225
61:1–11   225
61:2   226, 244
61:2–3   237
61:3   27, 226, 227
61:3–4   226
61:3–7   243
61:4   209, 229, 243
61:4–5   239
61:4–6   243
61:5   209, 237, 243–46, 249
61:5–6   206, 227, 243, 249, 255
61:5–7   227, 244, 248
61:5–9   218, 225
61:6   227, 234, 236, 237, 240, 243–45, 248–50, 252, 253
61:6–7   243
61:7   227, 242, 244
61:8   165, 227, 230, 244
61:8–9   227
61:9   105, 227
61:10   225, 227, 230, 244
61:10–11   218
61:11   225, 227, 231, 237, 245
62   219, 227–29
62:1   227, 228
62:1–5   218, 227
62:1–12   227
62:2   99, 169, 228
62:3   228
62:4   39, 228
62:5   228
62:6   138, 218, 228
62:6–7   230
62:6–9   218, 228
62:7   228
62:8–9   219, 228
62:9   104
62:10   170, 228
62:10–11   228
62:10–12   218, 228
62:11   229, 230
62:12   206, 219, 229–31
62:18–19   228
63:3   25, 106
63:5–6   106
63:6   25
63:11   165
63:17   74, 165, 177, 229
64:7   166
64:10   104
65   103
65–66   38, 103, 177, 181, 244
65:8   184
65:9   105, 165, 184
65:11   106
65:13   184
65:13–15   165
65:14   184
65:15   105, 184
65:17   107, 217, 231
65:17–25   228
65:18   228
65:18–19   229
65:21   27

INDEX OF SCRIPTURE REFERENCES

65:23	105	66:22	105–7
66	4, 43, 46, 48, 49, 91, 93, 102–4, 215, 236, 243–47, 249, 250, 252–54	66:22–23	107
		66:22–24	244, 245
66:1	103, 104, 107	66:23	44, 103, 106
66:1–2	104, 107	66:24	43, 44, 47, 106
66:1–6	244		
66:5	104, 105		
66:5–6	104	**JEREMIAH**	
66:7	44, 46, 54		
66:7–12	44	1:4–10	60
66:7–14	3, 35, 37, 43, 44, 46, 48–52, 54, 244, 245	1:10	61
		1:15	118
66:7–24	245	2	111, 118, 119
66:8	44, 46, 54	2–6	123
66:9	44, 54	2:1–4:2	122
66:10	54	2:18	123
66:10–11	45	2:36	83
66:10–14	247	3:6–13	123
66:11	45, 46, 54, 245	4:3–6:30	123
66:11–13	46	4:11–18	222
66:12	37, 45, 54, 233, 234, 240, 245, 246, 249–51, 254	4:28	28
		12:4	28
66:12–13	255	12:11	28
66:13	3, 13, 45, 46, 49, 51, 54, 245	13:4	82
66:14	27, 46, 47, 54, 165, 184	16:16	82
66:15	106	16:18	140
66:15–16	106	23:10	28
66:15–21	244, 245	23:18	191
66:15–24	93, 102, 105, 107	23:22	191
66:16	105, 106, 243	27:8	210
66:17	23, 105	27:10	210
66:18	13, 103, 105, 170, 246, 254	30–31	117, 119, 120, 122, 123
66:18–19	105	30:1–2	117
66:18–20	249, 255	30:3–4	117
66:18–21	233, 246–49, 254, 255	30:5–11	117
66:18–23	103	30:10	119
66:18–24	106	30:12–17	117
66:19	105, 246	30:17	118
66:20	104, 105, 246	30:18–31:1	117
66:20–21	105	30:24	119
66:20–23	93	31:1	118
66:21	105, 106	31:2–6	117
66:21–22	106	31:4	118

Jeremiah, cont'd		Hosea	
31:7–14	117		
31:8	119	1–3	111
31:9	119	1:2–2:3	122
31:10	119	2	118, 119
31:11	119	2:4–3:5	122
31:12	253	2:16	138
31:15	117, 120, 128	3:4–5	122
31:16	157	4:3	28
31:16–22	117, 119	4:12	187
31:23–26	117	9:3	83
31:26	118	11:5	83
31:27–30	117	11:11	83
31:31–34	117	13:14	136
31:35	120		
31:35–36	117		
31:37	117, 118	Joel	
31:38–40	117		
34:1–7	222	1	39
39:1–10	222	1:10	28
49:11	85	4:18	84
49:18	39		
50:40	39		
51:44	253	Amos	
		1:2	28
Ezekiel		4:11	39
		6:7	24
1–3	60	9:13–15	84
1:28	219		
3:27	61		
16	111, 125, 126	Micah	
16:7–8	126		
16:15	126	1:6–7	123
16:63	187	4:1–5	220, 222
18:27	85	4:1–3	253
27:25	252	4:4	42
29:21	187	7:11–12	253
37:15–28	125		
40–48	125		
43:7	222	Habakkuk	
		2:14	219

INDEX OF SCRIPTURE REFERENCES

2:18–20	187	**PSALMS**	
		6:5	101
ZEPHANIAH		24	156
		24:1	194
1:1	124	27:10	55
3:1–15	124	29	62
3:1–20	124	48:8	252
3:14–20	111, 124, 125	65	27
3:16–19	124	72	27
3:17	124, 125	80:8	23
3:18–19	125	80:9	23
3:19	125	90:2	144
3:20	124, 125	102:15–16	253
		102:16–17	253
		102:22	253
HAGGAI		102:23	253
		122	233
2:6–9	253	122:4	253
		131:2	55

ZECHARIAH		**JOB**	
1:3	101		
1:7–17	11	1:3	84
1:12	11	14:7–12	26
1:14	11	41:26–29	80
1:17	11	42:12	84
8:3	101		
8:20–22	253		
10:8	82	**PROVERBS**	
14:4	222		
14:14	240	8:24	144
14:16–19	210		

		RUTH	
MALACHI			
		2:13	139
2:11	221		

Song of Songs

8:11 — 79

Lamentations

3:2 — 239

Ezra

1:1–3 — 161
9:2 — 64

2 Chronicles

28:3 — 65
36:22–23 — 161

New Testament

Matthew

2:11 — 221
13:14–15 — 61

Mark

4 — 61

4:11–12 — 62
4:12 — 61

Luke

8:10 — 61

John

3:1–17 — 62
12:40 — 61

Acts

28:26–27 — 61, 62

Romans

8:12–17 — 62

Ephesians

3:14 — 55

Revelation

21:1–3 — 231
21:22–26 — 231

Index of Authors

Abma, R. 120
Abrams, Meyer H. 236
Ackroyd, Peter R. 168
Ainger, Katherine 31
Albertz, Rainer 137
Alexander, Joseph A. 94, 98
Alobaidi, Joseph 174
Alonso Schökel, Luis 36, 41
Alter, Robert 132, 213
Andersen, Francis I. 187
Aristotle 235
Asen, Bernhard A. 24
Aster, Shawn Zelig 215
Auerbach, Erich 36
Auerbach, Red 36, 53

Baltzer, Klaus 97, 98, 137, 140, 143, 144, 147, 148, 150, 153, 157, 188–90, 208, 248–51
Barker, Debi 30
Barr, James 198, 201
Barstad, Hans 137, 143
Barthel, Jörg 89
Barthes, Roland 132
Baumann, Gerlinde 120
Ben Zvi, Ehud 133, 161, 216
Berges, Ulrich 38, 99, 135, 138, 139, 141–47, 156, 169, 172, 173, 200, 213
Beuken, Willem A. M. 4, 85, 91, 101, 104, 106, 174, 191, 202, 205, 207, 209, 215, 245
Blank, Sheldon 190, 191
Blinkinsopp, Joseph 39, 40, 45, 46, 94, 109, 112, 136, 137, 140, 141, 143, 151, 153, 156, 168, 188, 190, 205, 207, 208, 220, 237, 239–41, 243–49, 251–53
Bloch, Ernst 216
Blum, Erhard 113
Boden, Peggy Jean 186
Bonnard, P.-E. 205
Borowski, Oded 19
Brassey, Paul Del 155
Brettler, Marc 137, 157
Broyles, Craig C. 59, 159
Brueggemann, Walter 135, 221, 223, 226
Buber, Martin 194
Budde, Karl 77

Callender, Dexter E. 184
Campbell, Antony F. 113
Carr, David M. 143, 152, 154, 181, 182, 244
Carreiro, Margaret S. 33, 34
Carroll, Robert P. 69, 134, 174
Causse, Antonin 214
Celan, Paul 132
Chaitin, Gilbert D. 236
Challoner, Richard 207
Chapman, Cynthia R. 36, 47–49, 52
Childs, Brevard S. 15, 57, 60, 64, 68, 112, 135, 143, 146, 153, 169, 188, 198, 215
Clements, Ronald E. 83, 161, 174, 200–202, 211, 235, 237
Clifford, Richard J. 143
Clines, David J. A. 143
Cody, Aelred 144

Collins, Christopher 183
Conrad, Edgar W. 135, 151, 168
Cross, Frank M. 137

Dalman, Gustaf 82
Darr, Katheryn Pfisterer 47, 201
Davis, Ellen F. 19, 21, 27, 33
Dempsey, Carol J. 6, 217
Derrida, Jacques 132, 235
Dick, Michael B. 186, 192, 193, 195
Dille, Sarah J. 47
Delitzsch, Franz 94
Detienne, Marcel 24
Dietrich, Walter 89
Dijkstra, Meindert 140
Douglas, Mary 172
Downie, Andrew 30
Duhm, Bernhard 83, 137, 201, 209, 210, 243, 244, 248

Eagleton, Terry 37, 53
Ehring, Christina 93, 100, 101
Eliade, Mircea 210
Elliger, Karl 136, 138–41, 143, 152, 153, 157, 212, 215
Ettore, Franco 142, 144, 151, 153
Evans, Craig A. 59, 159, 174
Evans, Desiree 31
Everson, A. Joseph 3, 6, 57, 69

Feldmann, Franz 87
Fish, Stanley 133
Fishbane, Michael 42, 159, 202
Fohrer, Georg 203
Fokkelman, Jan 136, 137, 143, 147, 150, 152, 154, 158
Foster, Julie A. 47
Franke, Chris A. 3, 35
Freedman, David Noel 138, 139, 146–48, 150, 152, 154, 187
Frei, Hans 15
Frymer-Kensky, Tikva S. 21

Galambush, Julie 125
Gardner, A. E. 105
Garnett, Tara 29
Gärtner, Judith 103
Geller, Stephen 138, 140, 147–49
Gesenius, Wilhelm 81
Gibbs, Robert 133
Gitay, Yehoshua 158
Goldingay, John 109, 112, 135, 138, 139, 143, 145, 146, 150, 151, 155, 208
Gorenberg, Gershom 32
Görg, Manfred 149, 150
Goulder, Michael 184, 190
Gowan, Donald E. 61
Gray, George B. 83, 86, 87
Grelot, Pierre 214, 240
Gressmann, Hugo 59
Gruber, M. E. 47
Gunkel, Hermann 59, 201
Gurian-Sherman, Doug 30

Habel, Norman 60
Hanson, Paul D. 236
Haran, Menahem 110
Hauser, Alan J. 159
Hausmann, Jutta 87
Hayes, John H. 39
Hayes, Katherine M. 28
Hedges, Chris 58
Hillel, Daniel 25
Holland, Norman 132
Holter, Knut 155, 174
Hornung, Erik 186
Huber, Friedrich 89

Ibn Ezra, Abraham ben Meir 82, 250
Irvine, Stuart A. 39, 89

Jacobsen, Thorkild 124, 186
Jakobson, Roman 183, 184, 193
Janowski, Bernd 174
Jensen, Joseph 253
Jepson, A. 193

Jones, Barry A. 58
Josipovici, Gabriel 132
Jüngel, Eberhard 236

Kaminsky, Joel S. 106
Kennedy, James M. 5, 181, 187
Kiesow, Klaus 112, 138, 141, 143, 157
Kilian, Rudolf 142
Kim, Hyun Chul Paul 5, 6, 142, 159, 178
Kissane, Edward J. 83
Knierim, Rolf P. 175
Koenen, Klaus 206, 237–40
Komatsu, Eisuke 197
Koole, Jan L. 139, 144, 153, 157, 188, 195, 203–5, 207, 208, 215
Korpel, Marjo C. A. 93
Kratz, Reinhard G. 135, 137, 139, 146, 152, 154
Kraus, Hans-Joachim 233, 237, 242, 243, 250
Krinetzki, Leo 136, 147, 150
Kristeva, Julia 132
Kustár, Zoltán 182
Kutscher, E. Yechezkel 82

Laato, Antti 135
Labahn, Antje 146, 148, 151
Lack, Rémi 36, 38, 202, 204
Landy, Francis 4, 37, 131, 153, 201
Lau, Wolfgang 237, 238
Leclerc, Thomas L. 23, 174
Leene, Henk 94
Lentricchia, Frank 197
Levenson, Jon D. 210, 215, 216
Lévinas, Emmanuel 133
Lewis, Theodore J. 24
Lindars, Barnabas 82
Lindbeck, George 15
Levine, Etan 86
Løland, Hanne 49, 137
Lorton, David 186
Lotman, Yuri 183, 184
Lowery, Richard 226

Lowth, Robert 234, 235
Lund, Øystein 96

Maier, Christl M. 46
March, W. Eugene 33
Marti, Karl 83, 87
McDonagh, Sean 30
McEvenue, Sean 153
McGinnis, Claire Mathews 2
McKane, William 85
McKibben, Bill 18
Mellon, Margaret 30
Melugin, Roy F. 1, 2, 6, 7, 17, 35–37, 40, 43, 50, 52, 53, 59, 78, 107, 112, 131–33, 135, 142, 147, 152, 159–64, 168, 175, 197, 200, 234, 250, 255
Merendino, Rosario Pius 110, 137–39, 141, 145, 150, 153
Mettinger, Tryggve N. D. 155, 174
Milbank, John 138, 143
Miscall, Peter D. 37, 182, 188, 201, 202
Moor, Johannes C. de 37, 93, 148
Moore, Stephen D. 151
Morgenstern, Julian 110
Morison, Carole 30
Mosis, Rudolf 150
Motyer, J. Alec 191, 223
Moughtin-Mumby, Sharon 137
Muilenburg, James 159, 241, 243, 249

Niditch, Susan 161
Nielsen, Kirsten 19, 20, 79
Nogalski, James D. 161

O'Brien, Mark A. 113
O'Connell, Robert H. 182, 215
Odeberg, Hugo 201
Oorschot, Jürgen van 138, 141, 143, 146, 154
Orlinsky, Harry M. 206, 214
Orr, David W. 18
Oswalt, John N. 51, 83, 188, 189, 192, 218, 221, 226

Ottley, Richard R. 86

Page, S. 121
Paul, Shalom M. 159
Payne, David 109, 112
Pimentel, David 30
Plato 24
Polan, Gregory J. 225
Polaski, Donald C. 79
Pollan, Michael 28, 31
Polliack, Meira 144, 157
Pope, Marvin H. 169
Procksch, Otto 77, 87
Rad, Gerhard von 190, 200, 214, 253
Rashi 82
Rendtorff, Rolf 70, 73, 113, 139, 142, 174
Richards, I. A. 236, 238
Ricoeur, P. 7, 10, 15
Ringgren, Helmer 85
Rissler, Jane 30
Roberts, J. J. M. 174
Robinson, H. Wheeler 60
Robinson, Theodore H. 58, 59
Rosset, Peter 32
Ruszkowski, Leszek 206, 215, 216

Sanders, James A. 58
Saussure, Ferdinand de 197, 198, 200
Sawyer, John F. A. 174, 204
Scherer, Andreas 140
Schlosser, Eric 30
Schmid, Konrad 99
Schmitt, J. J. 47
Schweitzer, Steven James 216
Sefati, Yitzchak 124
Seitz, Christopher R. 146, 168, 174, 190, 251
Sekine, Seizo 236
Selms, Adrianus van 80
Severson, Lucky 31
Shiva, Vandana 30
Simian-Yofre, Horacio 143
Smith, Adam 234

Smith, Jonathan Z. 134
Sommer, Benjamin D. 110, 112, 135, 140, 144, 146, 157, 159, 169
Sonnet, Jean-Pierre 131
Stansell, Gary 6, 45, 206, 216, 233, 235, 242
Starmer, Elanor 31
Stassen, S. L. 150
Steck, Odil Hannes 143, 161, 169, 204, 210, 211, 238, 244, 245, 249, 251, 253
Stoebe, Hans-Joachim 140, 141, 156
Stringfellow, William 65
Stuart, A. 106
Stuhlmacher, Peter 174
Sweeney, Marvin A. 1, 2, 4, 59, 65, 66, 87, 88, 109, 110, 112, 113, 115, 117, 120, 123–25, 129, 135, 159, 174, 177, 191, 215, 242, 251, 253

Thompson, Charles Dillard 31
Tomasi, Luigi 238
Torrey, Charles C. 97, 169, 207–9
Trible, Phyllis 159
Tucker, Gene M. 60
Tudge, Colin 20
Tull, Patricia K. 2, 17, 110, 112, 135, 152, 159, 200

Vermeylen, Jacques 89, 142, 154, 205
Volz, Paul 206, 214, 242

Wagner, Thomas 84, 174
Walker, Christopher 186, 192, 193, 195
Walsh, Carey 19
Walsh, Jerome T. 187, 188
Watson, Wilfred G. E. 144
Watts, John D. W. 41, 44, 136, 138, 139, 169, 190, 191, 209
Weber, Timothy P. 32
Wells, Roy D. 5, 197
Werner, Wolfgang 85, 87
Westcott, C. 19
Westermann, Claus 51, 112, 136, 148, 152, 188, 238–41, 243, 245, 247, 248, 250

White, Hayden 200
Whybray, R. Norman 161, 188, 204
Wiggins, Melinda 31
Wildberger, Hans 24, 79, 89, 104, 235, 238, 252, 253
Willey, Patricia Tull (see Tull, Patricia K.)
Williamson, Hugh G. M. 3, 28, 77, 82, 83, 88, 135, 146, 161, 201
Wilshire, Leland Edward 185
Wirzba, Norman 18, 21, 32
Wolff, Hans W. 161
Woude, Annemarieke van der 160

Yee, Gale 47

Zalcman, L. 39
Zapff, Burkhard M. 140, 141, 157, 158
Zevit, Ziony 41, 42
Ziegler, Joseph 86
Zillessen, Alfred 198
Zimmerli, Walther 200, 202, 211, 240, 247, 249

www.ingramcontent.com/pod-product-compliance
Lightning Source LLC
Chambersburg PA
CBHW021820300426
44114CB00009BA/248